Teaching Students with
Special Needs
A GUIDE FOR FUTURE EDUCATORS
Second Edition

Christopher O'Brien | John Beattie

The University of North Carolina at Charlotte

Kendall Hunt
publishing company

Cover image © Shutterstock, Inc.

Kendall Hunt
publishing company

www.kendallhunt.com
Send all inquiries to:
4050 Westmark Drive
Dubuque, IA 52004-1840

Copyright © 2015, 2017 by Kendall Hunt Publishing Company

ISBN 978-1-5249-1666-4

Printed in the United States of America

CONTENTS

CHAPTER 11:

CHAPTER 12:

CHAPTER 13:

Kelly R. Kelley

CHAPTER 14:

Jane Diane Smith

CHAPTER 15:

Tara Galloway, Melissa A. Miller, Chris O'Brien, and LuAnn Jordan

PREFACE

Our text, *Teaching Students with Special Needs: A Guide for Future Educators* is written for a specific audience and may appear a bit different than some other popular and excellent textbooks on special education. We have tailored the design, content, and writing style for an audience of aspiring educators who need a text to give them a solid foundation rather than an exhaustive summary. Further, the text has been written to convey important concepts in a manner that is more practical and accessible to future educators with an emerging understanding of the processes that occur to support learners experiencing difficulty in school. We would expect that there will be future special education teachers reading this book, but it is not intended for those individuals, specifically. In fact, the book is designed to highlight the fundamental issues relevant to ALL educators in American public schools. Because the first edition was used at the University of North Carolina at Charlotte by the authors in a survey course on special education, case examples and policy may reflect the experiences of educators in the southeastern United States.

The text highlights the "big ideas" and critical content of special education, as it currently exists in this area, answering the essential questions:

Who are the children in special education?
How did they become eligible for special education services?
What are my responsibilities for meeting the needs of children in special education?

This text has been designed with the intent of applying principles of *explicit instruction* to a textbook. Throughout the text, you will find graphic organizers, summaries of key points, support in developing background knowledge of key concepts and new terms, explanations of terminology in accessible language, and an ongoing emphasis of the "big ideas" of special education. We would hope that future educators reading this book would be able to develop appropriate background knowledge to understand the historical and contextual issues associated with special education and find the chapters on disability categories useful as primers on vast and complicated topics. Readers looking for more extensive information on special education may benefit from some of the more detailed texts designed for graduate students and special education majors, such as *Exceptional Children* by William Heward.

Our text can be viewed as having three general sections organized by themes. Chapters 1-4 are intended as introductory material addressing assumptions of the discipline, background knowledge, and contextual issues. The next chapters relate to individual disability topics. In each disability chapter you will find an overview of the characteristics of the population, areas of need, and a brief overview of methods for providing appropriate instruction. Finally, Chapter 15 summarizes movements in educational reform (RTI, UDL, PBIS) that seek to change (on a grand scale) how we address learner differences and prevent school failure for children who experience difficulty in school. Although discussions of effective instructional practices are explicitly included and infused throughout the text, we would expect that educators would continue to seek more detailed materials related to teaching students with special needs in their specific area of instruction (e.g., grade level, content area). We hope that this text will be a positive first step in your development as highly effective teachers for all students in your future classes.

ACKNOWLEDGMENTS

This text was intended to reflect the knowledge and talents of an array of our excellent peers. The authors would like to acknowledge the contributions of the faculty, teachers, and scholars who added considerably to the breadth of expertise offered in the revised printing of this text including the following individuals who contributed to the final product:

JaneDiane Smith, The University of North Carolina at Charlotte
Melissa A. Miller, The University of North Carolina at Chapel Hill
Lan Kolano, The University of North Carolina at Charlotte
Theresa Perez, The University of North Carolina at Charlotte
LuAnn Jordan, The University of North Carolina at Charlotte
Victoria Knight, Vanderbilt University
Julie L. Thompson, Michigan State University
Tara Galloway, Gaston County Schools
Kelly R. Kelley, Western Carolina University
Tammy Pereboom, North Carolina Assistive Technology Program
Alicia Brophy, The University of North Carolina at Charlotte
Shaqwana Freeman, Illinois State University
Jeremy Lopuch, University of North Carolina at Charlotte
Debra Holzberg, University of North Carolina at Charlotte
Karen Diegelmann, University of North Carolina at Charlotte
Melissa Hudson, East Carolina University

Additionally, Melissa Hudson and Shaqwana Freeman offered considerable editorial feedback on the first edition of the text. Their perspectives were extremely beneficial. Revisions and critical editing efforts for the second edition were coordinated by Adrienne Anderson of Western Carolina University.

Chris O'Brien
John Beattie

Christopher O'Brien | John Beattie

Teaching Students
with Special Needs
A Guide for Future Educators

CHAPTER 1

Introduction to Special Education: Children with Special Needs in U.S. Schools and Society

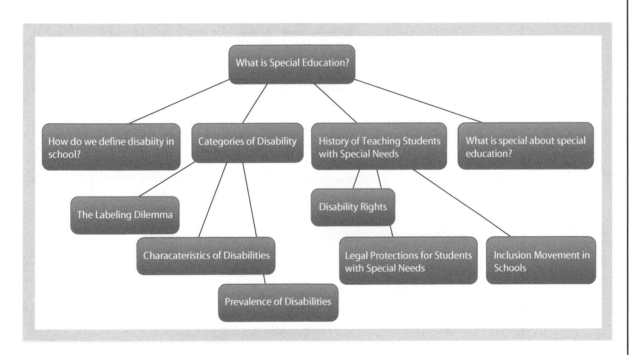

THE TOP TEN TERMS FOR CHAPTER 1:

The following key terms or big ideas are critical to your understanding of the content for chapter 1 and the in-class discussions to follow.

• Special Education	• LRE
• Disability	• Continuum of services
• Exceptionality	• Zero reject
• IDEA	• IEP
• FAPE	• Inclusion

WHO ARE CHILDREN WITH SPECIAL NEEDS?

To begin a discussion of teaching students with special needs and the idea of *special education* in schools, future teachers must contemplate what might be considered special needs both in school and society. The most common terms used related to special education include **disability**, as in *students with disabilities* or **exceptionality**, as in *exceptional children*. In essence, the connotation of the word, disability, relates to *inability* or the idea that a child is *not able* to do something, often the result of some *impairment*. Of course, we all have things we cannot do (or at least cannot do well) in school and in life, but the notion of disability implies that a student's characteristics or special needs exist significantly outside of the mainstream of the school population. For example, a child with a hearing impairment that prevents them from being able to hear conversational speech sounds will require additional supports to be successful in the mainstream school experience. In contrast, a child with physical limitations requiring him to walk with crutches at school might not be considered to have a disability, unless this physical limitation "adversely affects educational performance" (NICHY, 2009).

Although the intent of providing special supports for children categorized as having a disability is intended to be understanding of the considerable differences among children, the term can still have a rather negative perspective as it focuses on limitations that a child might have without examining what strengths that child might have (strengths that sometimes compensate for the other limitations). Generally speaking, the term *disability* is in wide use in school settings and refers to the difficulty that individuals might experience in performing tasks in school as a result of some impairment or limitation of ability. It is important to understand that special education categories and definitions of disability are specifically related to the school experience. In fact, many of the disabilities defined in school settings are only vaguely understood or discussed in general society (e.g. specific learning disability, behavior disorder, etc.).

Many professionals prefer the term *exceptionality*, which generally refers to atypical characteristics of children. As such, gifted children are also considered to be exceptional because they exhibit atypical (advanced) patterns of intellectual development, just as children with intellectual disabilities exhibit atypical (delayed) patterns of intellectual development. The term *exceptional children* might not have the same level of implied negativity. It is, however, a common terminology used for children who require specialized instruction or support in order to actualize their potential in school settings.

Another important term is **handicap**. The term *handicap* has become largely unpopular among parents, individuals with disabilities, and members of the advocacy community. Handicap is quickly leaving the professional vernacular, as it is considered an antiquated and pejorative term for children focusing on low expectations of an individual's ability to function in mainstream society. In fact, Smith (2004) explains that, although an individual whose disability is blindness will clearly experience challenges associated with the visual impairment, the individual is not necessarily *handicapped* by that disability. A handicap is likely to exist when society holds prejudices against an individual with a disability and potentially creates barriers for that individual to be successful in life.

> **Simplified Key Terms**
> (Based on abridged definitions developed by the World Health Organization)
>
> **Impairment:** deficit or loss of function; intrinsic to the individual
> **Disability:** the functional limitations caused by an impairment
> **Handicap:** social or societal limitations imposed on the basis of a disability

LABELING AND CATEGORIZATION OF HUMAN DIFFERENCES

There are a few key ideas that future educators should understand related to the language of special education. The most notable are the use of *labels*, or disability categories in order to serve the needs of students in special education, the use of *person-first language*, and the ongoing challenge to find categorical descriptions for children that are "politically correct" or non-offensive to the children and families served. Children with disabilities are supported by numerous passionate advocacy groups. These groups are often comprised largely of parents who want the best for their children as well as teachers and support personnel in schools and community agencies. A challenge arises, though, when so many people want to advocate for their children, but don't want their children unfairly lumped into categories or called names that seem to judge or stigmatize them.

Why do we label children in special education?

Labels in special education allow schools to group or categorize students receiving special education services in accordance with their main characteristics and needs in school. Of course, the most obvious school disability categories are based on characteristics of students that would create challenges to learning and experiencing success in daily life—physical disabilities, hearing impairments, visual impairments, etc. Notably, though, the vast majority of children who receive special education services in schools have labels based on phenomena defined by psychology professionals (i.e., The Diagnostic and Statistical Manual of Mental Disorders) and the characteristics of difference might be either subjective or difficult to directly observe.

Consider a category like *learning disability* (the most commonly identified disability in schools). For years there have been disputes about a valid definition or identification process for this label in schools. Some professionals argue that students identified as such, simply need more motivation or better instruction. Others respond with evidence from cognitive and language testing, and even neurological observation to defend the construct as an inherent trait that some students have throughout life. There is no clear agreement, because the answer cannot be easily observed or quantified. Also, it is not easy to differentiate between the child who has a learning disability in reading based on his neurological profile and a student who simply received poor instruction in reading. Most professionals agree that these are two separate cases, but that doesn't mean it will be obvious to the child's classroom teachers.

There is a range of opinions about how appropriate or necessary labels are for children in schools. Many professionals are quick to observe the potential for stigmatizing effects related to labeling a child's difficulty in school. Consider a parallel in your own experiences. How would you feel if your weaknesses were labeled as disorders or disabilities? For example, many talented students have struggled through math for years, perhaps just barely getting passing grades despite considerable effort. It would be very easy to call this difficulty a math disability or disorder, but we seldom do. Partly this is because we don't find it unusual to struggle with math, so it does not appear to be sufficiently atypical to qualify as a disability.

The Labeling Dilemma in Special Education

Table 1.1. Aspects of Labeling

Positive Aspects of Labeling	Negative Aspects of Labeling
Promotes awareness of the population and their needs to the general public	May stigmatize the child and hamper self esteem
Supports formation of advocacy groups that can lobby on behalf of the population	May lead others to view students with biased preconceived notions of what the student can accomplish
Supports research related to the needs of the population	Leads students to define themselves by one aspect of their identity—their shortcomings
Demystifies student's difficulties in school so they can better understand their own needs	May reinforce low expectations
Streamlines the process of funding for special education services based on categorization of disability	May reinforce segregation of children into special settings
	Labels are not infallible and represent inevitably heterogeneous populations

Calling attention to a child's disability and subsequently naming that disability is a controversial idea. A key point in the labeling argument is the question of whether telling a child that she has a disability will help her to advocate for her needs or if defining the problem will lead the child to assume she is not capable of what other children can do in life. Classification of students with labels like learning disability and Attention Deficit Hyperactivity Disorder (ADHD) are classic examples of this challenge. Many professionals and family members believe it is best to keep children "in the dark" related to their learning problems, so they can avoid the chance that the student might feel inadequate or hopeless. Levine, in his book written for children to understand learning problems, *Keeping a Head in School*, uses the word *demystification* to describe the process of informing a child about the nature of his learning problems. His perspective supports the complicated idea of labeling echoing the potentially damaging effects of a label on a child's identity and confidence, but runs contrary to the "sheltering" philosophy suggesting that children who are "left in the dark" might secretly feel that there is something wrong with them without knowing how to do better. They might feel helpless and alienated from fellow students. He proposes that the educational professional demystify learning problems for children by explaining the unique and specific nature of their needs while emphasizing a way forward utilizing good teaching and compensatory techniques, so that students are encouraged of their ability to actualize their vast potential. The excerpt below highlights the dilemma of labeling for children. In *Keeping a Head in School*, Levine (1990) describes the challenging perspective of children with learning problems in school:

> [Students] may even articulate the possibility that people are trying to protect or shield them from the truth with terms such as *learning disability, dyslexia*, or *attention deficit disorder*. Many youngsters interpret these labels as polite ways of describing a brain that is wholly inadequate.

> Some students vacillate between believing that they are retarded and feeling that there is absolutely nothing wrong with them. They further speculate that if there is nothing wrong with them, then they are certainly 'losers,' since someone who is 'normal' should be able to do well in school. Such a sense of being a loser can induce feelings of futility and needless guilt (p. xii).

Clearly, such an experience of describing a student's special needs requires a delicate and nuanced explanation focused on a student's ability to use self-knowledge to serve them as self-advocates. Students with learning disabilities, for example, must understand that they are "neither pervasively defective nor perfectly normal," (Levine, 1990, p. xii) but further that all individuals have both strengths and weaknesses. Sometimes, though, one child's weaknesses are more obvious given the expectations of a social situation like school. A struggling student who knows how and why they struggle in school is more likely to learn how they can use their strengths to overcome their weaknesses to be successful in school.

WHAT ARE THE CATEGORIES OF DISABILITY IN SPECIAL EDUCATION?

In this section we will provide an overview of the categories and the basic definitions of disabilities that exist in special education in American public schools. Some of these may be new or ambiguous concepts. The later chapters in this text will clearly describe the characteristics and special needs of the students in these disability categories.

Table 1.2.

Disability Categories used in Federal Definitions (in order of incidence)	Other Professional Language or Abbreviations used to describe children in this category
Autism	Students on the spectrum; Students with autism, ASD
Blindness and Visual Impairment	VI
Deaf-blindness	
Deafness and Hearing Impairments	Students with hearing impairments; hard of hearing
Developmental Delay**	
Emotional Disturbance*	Students with EBD, EH, BED, SED; behavior disorders, serious emotional disturbance, emotional/behavioral disorders
Intellectual Disability	Intellectual Disability, Cognitive Disability, Developmental Disability; formerly Students with Mental Retardation (MR)
Multiple Disabilities	
Orthopedic Impairments	Students with physical disabilities
Other Health Impairments	Students with OHI; Large number of students with ADHD
Specific Learning Disability	Students with LD, SLD; Students with a learning disability
Speech and Language Impairment	Students with speech disorders; language disorders
Traumatic Brain Injury	Students with TBI

Term used in federal legislation, but not typically at state or district level
**Term only applicable to children ages 3 to 9*

The following brief definitions are designed to build the reader's background knowledge for the discussion going forward. Definitions are paraphrased and excerpted from National Dissemination Center for Children with Disabilities (2009) and the Individuals with Disabilities Education Act (2004). All definitions are assumed to adversely affect the student's educational performance in order to qualify for special education services.

Simple Definitions of Disability Categories (NICHCY, 2009)

Autism – "developmental disability significantly affecting verbal and nonverbal communication and social interaction, generally evident before age three." Common characteristics of students on the autism spectrum include "engaging in repetitive activities and stereotyped movements, resistance to environmental change or change in daily routines, and unusual responses to sensory experiences."

Deaf-Blindness – severe communication and developmental disability characterized by both impairments of hearing and vision.

Deafness – severe hearing impairment characterized by impaired ability to effectively process "linguistic information through hearing, with or without amplification" (e.g., hearing aids).

Developmental Delay – a broad descriptor applied to younger children who have not yet been given a specific disability classification (e.g., developmental/intellectual disability), when a student experiences delay in development compared to typical milestones in the areas of physical, communication, social/emotional, cognitive/intellectual, and/or adaptive behavior development.

Emotional Disturbance – a broad term applied to children who experience difficulty with social/emotional development and/or maintaining appropriate behavior. Students must exhibit problematic patterns of emotional or behavioral difficulty "over a long period of time and to a marked degree." Students typically have difficulty with both peer and adult relationships and generally present "inappropriate types of behaviors or feelings under normal circumstances."

Gifted – term used to describe students with special talents associated with creative ability, advanced intellectual development, and unique needs in school. Children who are gifted are considered exceptional children, but they are not served by special education.

Hearing Impairment – a limitation in hearing; implies less impact on use of hearing to process linguistic information compared to Deafness.

Intellectual Disability – limitations in intellectual ability with a considerable range of severity "manifested during the developmental period." Classification must include assessment of "deficits in adaptive behavior." Few states use this term at present.

Multiple Disabilities – a broad description for children who have more than one disability/impairment that qualifies individually under special education law. The combined impact of multiple disabilities (e.g., intellectual disability and blindness) causes severe limitations for the student.

Orthopedic Impairment – term used to describe students whose orthopedic (bone/muscle) impairments have sufficient severity to impact the school experience. Typically relates to limitations in movement or physical development (e.g. cerebral palsy).

Other Health Impairment – term used to describe classroom limitations due to "chronic or acute health problems such as asthma, attention deficit disorder or attention deficit hyperactivity disorder, diabetes, epilepsy, a heart condition, hemophilia, lead poisoning, leukemia, nephritis, rheumatic fever, sickle cell anemia, and Tourette syndrome."

Specific Learning Disability – term used to describe a "disorder in one or more of the basic psychological processes involved in understanding or in using language, spoken or written, that may manifest itself in the imperfect ability to listen, think, speak, read, write, spell, or to do mathematical calculations." This term does not apply to students who experience learning problems due to other disabilities.

Speech or Language Impairment – a disorder of communication related to the ability to create speech sounds (e.g., stuttering, articulation problems, or voice disorders) or process linguistic information (both expressively and receptively).

Traumatic Brain Injury – "acquired injury to the brain caused by an external physical force, resulting in total or partial functional disability or psychosocial impairment." Children born with brain injuries or acquired due to birth trauma do not fit this description.

Visual Impairment Including Blindness – children with limited vision including children with partial impairment and blindness that impacts school experiences even when corrected.

Often professionals in special education specialize in working with certain populations, as there is a vast array of characteristics and special needs associated with the various populations served by special education. For example, the learning needs of students who are blind using Braille or students who are Deaf using American Sign Language, require highly trained and specialized professionals in support roles. Further, special education teachers often specialize in working with subgroups of students with what are considered *mild disabilities* (e.g., learning disability, ADHD, mild intellectual disability, speech and language impairment) who are most likely to receive the majority of their education in regular classrooms. These disability categories are also referred to as *high-incidence disabilities* because they comprise the majority of the special needs population in schools (see figure for prevalence of disabilities by category). The most common disabilities in schools are specific learning disabilities, speech and/or language impairments, intellectual disability, emotional disturbance, and health impairments. A considerable majority of the students identified in the category Other Health Impaired (OHI) are students with ADHD. The addition of ADHD to special education qualification in the 1990s, has resulted in huge increases in the prevalence of OHI. As these student populations make up such large proportions of the special needs population and share so many common characteristics (e.g., learning and reading problems, social/behavioral challenges, difficulty maintaining standard academic expectations without additional support), schools are often the most prepared to serve these students. The remaining disability categories have traditionally been referred to as *low-incidence disabilities* due to the lower numbers of students with these disabilities in schools, although it is increasingly difficult to view Autism as a low-incidence disability, as the prevalence has increased dramatically in recent years. Special education professionals tend to be more specialized in working with children in these categories: multiple disabilities, deafness/hearing impairments, orthopedic impairments, blindness/visual impairments, autism, deaf-blindness, and TBI.

Table 1.3. Students ages 6 through 21 served under IDEA, Part B, by disability category and state: Fall 2011 (U.S. states and outlying areas).

Disability Category	Approximate Numbers	Approximate Percentages
Specific Learning Disability*	2,356,483	40.7
Speech or Language Impairment	1,071,129	18.5
Other Health Impairments (including ADHD)	735,315	12.7
Intellectual Disability	4,284,514	7.4
Autism*	4,052,919	7.0
Emotional Disturbance	3,705,526	6.4
Multiple Disabilities	127,377	2.2
Developmental Delay	115,798	2.0
Hearing Impairments	69,479	1.2
Orthopedic Impairments	52,109	0.9
Blindness/Visual Impairments	23,160	0.4
Traumatic Brain Injury	23,160	0.4
Deaf-blindness	1,158	0.02
Total Number of Students Receiving Special Education Services	5,789,884	100

* Note that Specific Learning Disability decreased to its lowest point in decades down from approximately 50% in previous counts. Increases in ADHD recognition (OHI) may account for some of the reduction, as many students exhibit comorbid patterns of SLD and ADHD.
** Note that Autism has reached its highest percentage reflecting a steady yearly increase since the advent of the categorical label in IDEA. For the first time, Autism eclipses Emotional Disturbance in percentage of children with special needs in American public schools.

HISTORICAL AND PHILOSOPHICAL FOUNDATIONS OF THE EDUCATION AND TREATMENT OF INDIVIDUALS WITH DISABILITIES

A comprehensive review of the history and foundations of modern special education should include a reflection on the disheartening history of oppression experienced by individuals with disabilities throughout distant and even recent American history. Modern day special educators are often considered somewhat radical or impassioned by their school peers, and for many professionals these strong feelings are spurred by knowledge of very limited opportunities and the actual mistreatment of individuals with disabilities that is our legacy.

The Disability Rights Struggle: A Long Road from Institutions to Inclusion

Historically, most care for individuals with disabilities in American history derived from religious compassion, but rarely led to any educational expectations or civil rights for the individuals. The era of the eugenics and institutionalization is a particularly disturbing reflection of our society's desire to exclude and eliminate individuals with any disabilities significant enough to make them a "burden" on other productive citizens.

> Eugenics – Social movement that suggested that society could be improved by controlling the breeding practices of undesirable individuals. Most notably, in the U.S. certain individuals were deemed to be "feeble-minded" and thus unable to contribute positively to society. Eugenics proponents determined that the best course of action was to eradicate or separate these individuals via forced sterilization.

The term "feeble-minded" was used commonly to refer to individuals who appeared to have lower than average levels of intellect. The "feeble-minded" in American society became targets of both the eugenics and sterilization movements. Much of the rationale for eugenics and institutionalization stems from an ideological trend known as "social Darwinism," a peculiar application of the theory of natural selection or "survival of the fittest" to industrial society in the late 1800s and early to mid 1900s. The thought process was that the weakest members of society, including apparently unproductive citizens and those with disabilities that prevented their contribution to society, were ultimately a drain on society and should not be allowed to reproduce. Further, whenever possible, "feeble-minded" individuals should be excluded from mainstream society. Individuals with disabilities were seen as inherently flawed and incapable of meaningful improvement or contribution to society. Industrialization era beliefs about efficiency led to the systematic institutionalization of large numbers of individuals with disabilities (Smith, 2004).

> Institutionalization – a dominant process in American history wherein children and other individuals with disabilities were excluded from mainstream and housed in state-run institutions. Prevailing wisdom suggested that these individuals were largely incapable of benefitting from teaching or interaction with non-disabled children.

THE EUGENICS MOVEMENT IN NORTH CAROLINA:

Frank Boston/Shutterstock.com

http://againsttheirwill.journalnow.com/

Carl Crothers, executive editor of the special report *Against Their Will: North Carolina's Sterilization Program* presented by the Winston-Salem Journal, reports the profound impact that the eugenics movement had on citizens in North Carolina.

Many of the individuals sterilized were mental patients housed in state institutions. Most of them, though, were individuals deemed "unfit" to have children based on the fact that they were "poor and illiterate, hypersexual or homosexual, even lazy." Numerous criteria led to classification of individuals as "feebleminded." Ultimately, the North Carolina eugenics movement added racial bias to its discriminatory process by focusing forced sterilization on young African-American women, particularly during the 1950s and 1960s. The program came to an end in 1974.

Major sites of the eugenics movement in the U.S. were the states of North Carolina and Virginia in the early 20th century. Virginia's law allowed sterilization of anyone diagnosed as incompetent and likely to pass on inferior genes to their offspring. As individuals in poor communities were most likely to be deemed unable to contribute to society, the eugenics movement, in some cases, amounted to the sterilization of poor young girls who could not demonstrate intellectual prowess on intelligence tests. The approach, arguably, targeted generationally poor communities and racial minorities whose ways of life conflicted most significantly with the overseers of the implementation of the law (see Winston Salem case).

Hehir (2006) clarifies that the era of eugenics and institutionalization reflects a belief system that greatly contrasts with the contemporary emphasis on "early intervention" services and the prolific research on the effectiveness of special education to improve outcomes for children with disabilities. The dominant belief system of the time suggested that conditions like mental retardation (as it was known at the time) were purely determined by heredity. More importantly, though, professionals generally viewed limitations in intellect to be "fixed traits" that could be consistently and accurately evaluated using a standardized assessment of intelligence (i.e., I.Q. test). In fact, individuals were deemed unfit for life in general society and assigned to institutional settings on the basis of poor performance on intelligence tests.

Typically, contemporary professionals are aghast at the idea of segregating individuals with disabilities into institutional settings. Burton Blatt, in his critical work *Christmas in Purgatory*, exposed the state institutions for their abysmal treatment of individuals with disabilities, which included extensive neglect and even direct abuse. Exposure of the deplorable conditions in institutions also led to a greater recognition that the exclusion of individuals with disabilities from mainstream society and concentration of these individuals with other similarly challenged individuals, will almost certainly amplify the impact of their disabilities. In other words, children with delay in intellectual development benefit most from education and training, not placement in separate rooms with no resources or expectations.

After exposure of the poor treatment in institutions and tremendous advocacy by parents of children with disabilities, social attitudes began to shift toward a greater recognition of the need for education and training for individuals with disabilities (Hehir, 2006). Burton Blatt's (1970) quote below signifies a substantial shift in the philosophy of educators working with youth with disabilities:

> We are reinforced again and again in our conviction that intelligence, that all human development, is plastic and a function of practice and training, motivation and stimulation, as well as it is a function of neurology, chromosomes, and genes (p. 254).

> The prophecy of incompetency … is self-fulfilling. Equally self-fulfilling can be the prophecy of competency and achievement (p. 258).

The importance of these statements can hardly be overstated as fundamental beliefs of the special education discipline. Although there are substantial genetic influences on characteristics of children and the likelihood that children will have disabilities in schools, it is well established that children are also the products of their learning environment. Children who have extreme deficits in life skills or communication development are unlikely to improve these conditions by being shut away in institutional settings. The "plasticity" of human ability, the ability to show incremental improvement over time is a critical understanding of the special education teacher and support professional. Further, Blatt's statement of the "self-fulfilling… prophecy" is an excellent way of examining the impact of expectations on student performance. Teachers who demand excellence from their students consistently get a significant return on their investment. Given the exposure of the deplorable conditions in state institutions for children with disabilities and a gradual shift in belief systems regarding the ability to show improvements in outcomes for children with disabilities and youth in underprivileged learning environments, the stage was set for an era of change and access for children with disabilities.

SIGNIFICANT LEGAL CASES THAT LED TO THE CONTEMPORARY STATE OF SPECIAL EDUCATION IN AMERICAN PUBLIC SCHOOLS (YELL, 2005)

Brown v. Board of Education (1954)

A critical case in the civil rights movement, the outcome set the tone for civil rights protections and constitutional protection of minority children in schools. Served as an impetus for parental advocacy on behalf of children with disabilities who were similarly segregated and denied access to equal educational opportunities.

PARC v. the Commonwealth of Pennsylvania (1972)

The Pennsylvania Association for Retarded Children (PARC) sued the Commonwealth of Pennsylvania based on a claim that the state had failed to provide publicly funded education for students with mental retardation. The finding of the court established a precedent for later special education legislation, as the court resolved that children with mental retardation ages 6 to 21 have a right to a free public education. Included in the decision were conclusions that early services for students were beneficial for long-term outcomes, states could not deny access to children with mental retardation, and education programs for children with mental retardation should be similar to their peers without disabilities. The case served as a foundation for a contemporary educational principle referred to as "Free Appropriate Public Education" (FAPE), a guiding principle for special education policy.

Mills v. Board of Education

Another class-action suit was filed on behalf of students with disabilities in Washington, D.C. who were not receiving education in the local school district. Again parents of children with disabilities were the driving force, although these parents had children with an array of special needs beyond mental retardation. The court found in favor of the children's rights and ordered that the district provide due process procedural safeguards, which included the parents' rights to a hearing with the district, rights to appeal district decisions, written communication regarding steps taken regarding the education of their child, and rights of access to records. The case again affirmed the rights of children with disabilities to a free appropriate public education.

Legislative Trends Promoting Rights of Individuals with Disabilities (Yell, 2005)

Section 504 of the Rehabilitation Act of 1973

A reflection of federal legislation that guaranteed civil rights and prohibited discrimination on the basis of race (i.e., the Civil Rights Act of 1964), this legislative language included in the Rehabilitation Act served to protect the rights of individuals with disabilities. Specifically, any federally funded activity or agency must be in compliance with this legislation guaranteeing that individuals with disabilities cannot be excluded and that, when necessary, appropriate accommodations would be made in order to provide access to individuals with disabilities. As schools are publicly funded agencies, the legislation set the groundwork for accommodating children with disabilities in schools. Even after the advent of more formal special education policy, some children with disabilities continue to benefit from "504 Plans" which affirm their rights to accommodations in schools.

Americans with Disabilities Act (ADA)

Although the legislation is not specifically related to schools, the ADA serves to protect the rights of American individuals with disabilities and has the broadest impact on the lives of individuals with disabilities' ability to full participate in society. The legislation banned discrimination against individuals with disabilities including the lack of access to public buildings, transportation, and private businesses that may have been previously inaccessible due, for example, to physical limitations. The ADA has been controversial in some of its implementations, but is generally known for common sense improvements to the design of modern buildings and services (e.g., Universal Design in architecture).

[handwritten margin notes: beneficial. → more related to banning discrimination in society.]

The Individuals with Disabilities Education Act

Historical Development of Special Education in the United States

Relevant to an analysis of the current status of services for children with disabilities through a historical lens is consideration of the volatile period of civil rights reform in the United States during the 1950s and 60s (Hardman & Nagle, 2004). *Brown v. Board of Education* is generally considered to be the landmark court case, which dismantled the segregationist policy of "separate but equal" in the U.S. asserting that in contrast, separate is "inherently unequal" (Brown v. Board of Education of Topeka, Kansas, 1954). This case had far-reaching consequences when one considers the true nature of this finding—no children can be fairly excluded from public education. Clearly, the bold mandates of this case did not effect change in schools immediately, and certainly, those involved did not initially have the needs of children with disabilities in mind at the time (Smith, 2004). Further involvement at the federal level would ultimately be required to make the next steps toward equitably educating students with disabilities. Given the deep-rooted segregation practices employed during the institutionalization era, it should not be surprising that families with children with disabilities were commonly denied access to local public schools. In fact, some school districts were required to deny access to children with disabilities prior to the inaction of federal legislation, although most school districts simply did not believe they had the resources to provide educational opportunities for children with disabilities (Hehir, 2006).

The Elementary and Secondary Education Act of 1965 (ESEA) was the first major effort by the federal government to develop federal oversight in public education, an institution that previously was left up to state authority. This particular act was amended shortly after its initial passage to include federal funding to support students with disabilities. Following this action was a long period of emerging legislation and significant litigation rooted in parent concerns about the dramatically inequitable educational opportunities for children with significant disabilities (e.g. *Pennsylvania Association for Retarded Children v. Commonwealth of Pennsylvania*, and *Mills v. Board of Education of the District of Columbia*) which lead to the creation by congress of the **Bureau for the Education of the Handicapped**. Ultimately in 1975, the United States congress passed the legislation that would ultimately serve as the foundation for special education services in American public schools, Public Law 94-142, **the Education for All Handicapped Children Act** (Yell, Drasgow, Bradley, & Justesen, 2004). This legislation marked an important transition in the manner in which schools would be required to meet the needs of children with disabilities. Prior to P.L. 94-142, public schools came far short of meeting the needs of children with disabilities, with most children either receiving an inadequate, inappropriate level of support in their regular school or being forced into a segregated, often institutional educational setting (Katsiyannis, Yell, & Bradley, 2001). The Education for All Handicapped Children Act of 1975 was renamed the **Individuals with Disabilities Education Act (IDEA)** in 1990 and reauthorized most recently in 2004 at the **Individuals with Disabilities Education Improvement Act**. The law that supports special education implementation is most commonly referred to simply as IDEA.

Table 1.4.

Notable Impact of IDEA on School Policy (Yell, 2005)	
Zero Reject	State must guarantee that schools educate all children with disabilities regardless of severity from birth to age 21.
Free Appropriate Public Education	Guarantees special education and related services will be provided by the school district consistent with the needs outlined in the Individualized Education Program.
Least Restrictive Environment	Students with disabilities must be educated with children without disabilities to the maximum extent appropriate.
Identification and Evaluation Procedures	Schools must use non-discriminatory, multifactored methods of evaluation.
Procedural Safeguards	Parents' and children's rights are protected; parents are partners in educational decision making. Provides guidelines for "due process" or resolution of conflicts between parents and schools.

Trends in Philosophy and Legislation for Students with Disabilities

The **IDEA** has been periodically reviewed by the United States legislative bodies and subsequently reauthorized (amended) with sometimes subtle and sometimes dramatic changes related to the concerns of parents and advocacy groups, and changing political currents.

Parents and Advocates Responsible for Changes for Students with Disabilities

Parents of children with disabilities in the United States have long served as the primary advocates for the rights of their children to an equal quality education and improved quality of life in American society. Yell (2005) suggests parents were at the forefront of a disability rights movement focused on educational opportunity at a time when the nation was changing and attention turned to the humane treatment and education of children with disabilities. Numerous organizations such as the Council for Exceptional Children (CEC) and The Association for Persons with Severe Handicaps (TASH) took leadership roles in the advocacy movement and continue to do so today.

One consistent shift in the most recent reauthorizations of IDEA has been the ever-increasing emphasis on serving the needs of students with disabilities in the most inclusive environment (Gable & Hendrickson, 2000). A first step in this process was the **Regular Education Initiative** sponsored by the Department of Education in the mid to late 1980s (Olson & Platt, 2004).

IDEA 1990 affirmed the notion of the general education classroom as the **"least restrictive environment" (LRE)**. This clarification of the LRE language meant that schools were to consider on a case by case basis which setting was optimal for each student—with the trend toward placing students in the closest placement possible to a general education classroom. Previously, students with disabilities were likely to be served in residential settings, special schools, and special classes. Special educators consistently refer to the **continuum of services** when considering the many steps possible to bring each student closer to the ultimate goal of education in the general curriculum. This trend toward placement in the general education classroom, typically a process in which a student's strong performance in a special education class is seen as indicative of their preparedness for a *regular class*, has typically been referred to as ***mainstreaming***. The 1997 reauthorization of IDEA further emphasized this trend. However, in contrast to the notion of gradually moving students with disabilities into the general education classroom, the philosophical notion of ***inclusion*** presumes that the general education classroom is the most natural setting for all children (Gable & Hendrickson, 2000).

> Parents were the forefront.

> movements (still today)

> Working to move students w/ disabilit to genral curriculum classes.

THE SPECIAL EDUCATION CONTINUUM OF SERVICES

Figure 1.1. Continuum of Service and Placement Options

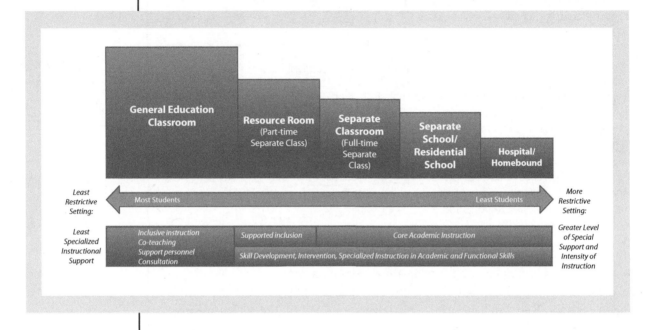

As legislation has changed over the years, schools have increasingly been held to a higher standard regarding the quality of educational services provided for students with disabilities (Katsiyannis et al., 2001). The most recent version of IDEA 2004 more closely aligns with the No Child Left Behind Act of 2001, taking one more significant step toward the education of students with disabilities in the general curriculum and holding schools accountable for their education (Gable & Hendrickson, 2000).

recent revision to IDEA

The Inclusion Argument: Where should we educate children with special needs?

A notable consideration of the contemporary idea of inclusion is how similar it is to the originally espoused goal of IDEA represented by the LRE principle. Essentially, general education classrooms (i.e., the regular school experience) should be the presumed learning environment for all children, and students who have disabilities should only be alternatively placed as their educational needs dictate. In contrast, many inclusion advocates suggest that the practical interpretation of the LRE in schools was to immediately remove students to alternative placements to meet their educational needs with little or no consideration of the general education classroom as a possible learning environment.

The most general and clear-cut definition of the term *inclusion* simply implies that we are educating students with disabilities in regular classrooms. Inclusion is also a term used to describe a broader social movement in the disability rights community reflecting the importance of individuals with disabilities living their lives as integrated and equal members of a pluralistic society. Research on inclusion is complicated, as there is no clear consensus on the goals of inclusion. For some advocates, a diverse learning environment where students with disabilities could be socially included and viewed as members of the classroom, is a positive outcome. Ultimately, though, special education is a process that demands results and improvement in the individualized educational experiences of children with disabilities. Left out of many discussions of inclusion is the need to provide truly specialized instruction to students with disabilities in general education classrooms. Inclusion that simply leaves children in regular classrooms without modifications or specialized planning is likely to fail to meet the needs of those children. In fact, some would argue that inclusion simply implies that we bring services to children rather than bringing children to services.

Numerous studies have validated the positive impact of inclusion on the academic and social experiences of children with disabilities when the educational experience has been designed with the needs of students with disabilities in mind. This requires careful planning, unique teaching methods, and often the support of special education professionals in the general education teacher's classroom.

Often, contemporary educators have extremely polarized positions on the value of inclusion based on their own experiences and observations. Too many educators have witnessed children with need for additional support, integrated into regular classes with no special education support or resources provided to the teacher. Sometimes this might even be the result of blanket policies on regular class integration that fail to evaluate whether a student's individualized educational needs can be met in the regular classroom. It must be noted that poor implementation of inclusion is not a good argument against the ideological orientation toward inclusion. Ultimately, research on inclusion suggests that children with disabilities can be successful in regular classrooms when they are given genuine opportunities to have *membership* in the classroom and the instructional supports they require, whether they are special learning accommodations (extended time, assistance with notes), special materials (computer-based materials, simplified texts), or the direct support of a highly trained special education teacher. One aspect that is often ignored

TRENDS IN PLACEMENT FOR STUDENTS WITH DISABILITIES

- Pre-1970s: Students lack access to regular schools. School districts not responsible for special support services.
- 1970s–1980s: Least Restrictive Environment (LRE) and continuum of services are dominant. Special education gradually develops as a separate community of professionals and researchers. Students experience special education as a *separate classroom* phenomenon.
- 1980s–1990s: REI and Mainstreaming movement emerges as critics suggest the distinction of special education as a separate physical place has resulted in segregation and lowered academic expectations for children with disabilities.
- 1990s–2000s: Mainstreaming gives way to more radical ideology of inclusion. Advocates with relatively extreme positions (in comparison to contemporary trends) argue for full inclusion of children with all levels of disabilities in regular schools and classrooms.
- Early to mid 2000s: No Child Left Behind holds public schools accountable for educating children with disabilities and demonstrating improved academic outcomes. Schools increasingly shift instruction to general education classrooms using emerging practices such as co-teaching to accommodate student differences.
- Late 2000s to present: Inclusion serves as a dominant framework for educating students with disabilities with highly variable interpretation and implementation across the nation base. Overall, significant emphasis is placed on education of most children with mild to moderate disabilities in general education classrooms for the majority of the school day with pull-out services used to augment instructional needs. Children with more significant disabilities remain largely excluded despite rare instance of highly effective inclusion and academic instruction.

in the process of making inclusion work is the philosophical orientation required of the professionals involved—an orientation that values the perspectives of children with disabilities and places high expectations for their school outcomes.

Fitch (2000) conducted a study that highlights the complexities of converting traditional exclusionary schools to more inclusive practice. He describes the outcomes of a qualitative investigation of students' perspectives on being in inclusive classrooms, integrated classrooms, and separate classrooms. The findings highlight the complicated nature of successful inclusion for children with disabilities. The following lists describe the contrast between what Fitch calls traditionalist and inclusive ideologies. His findings suggested that students with disabilities had the most positive sense of themselves and academic success when they were integrated in truly inclusive classrooms. Separation into special classes often led to a sense that they did not belong—a sense of marginalization and inferiority. There was, however, a sense of comfort and safety. Integration into classrooms that did not have an inclusive ideology as their foundation made students feel equally marginalized and inferior, suggesting that they might as well take advantage of the safety of special classrooms.

The findings from student comments affirm the need to integrate children with disabilities in regular classrooms to promote membership and academic outcomes, and the need for authentic investment in the interests of these children by all the educators and professionals involved. The second list portrays what Fitch describes as the ideology of inclusive teachers and schools. The contrasted belief systems presented here represent some of the greatest controversies and barriers for successful inclusion to take hold. It should be noted that the lists express extremes of positioning on this issue.

The Ideology and Philosophy of Inclusive Schools

Traditionalist Beliefs/Ideology (Fitch, 2003, p. 238)
1. Diversity in schools and society is problematic.
2. Disabilities are innate conditions of certain human beings. Those "with disabilities" are *essentially* different. Disability labels are inevitable, objective, fair, and beneficial.
3. Support and interventions are most appropriately and effectively provided in separate settings by special education experts. Progress is accomplished by professional expertise, technology, diagnosis, and intervention.
4. Special education and lower-achieving students will improve ("catch up") to their peers if they receive specialized, skill-based, intensive, individualized instruction in separate settings.
5. Learning is primarily developmentally linear; it takes place one sequential step at a time.
6. Competitive school structures are natural, fair, and expected; therefore, homogeneous grouping of students is inevitable.
7. Special education is a rational system of services that helps those individuals labeled or identified.

Inclusive Beliefs/Ideology (Fitch, 2003, p. 238)

1. Diversity is expected and valued. Individual and group diversity contributes positively to classroom climate, learning outcomes, and community quality.
2. Human commonalities cut across socially constructed categories of race, class, gender, sexual orientation, and disability. It is unnecessary and damaging to publicly label and group people according to how they differ from the norm.
3. It is in the interest of everyone to be in socially inclusive learning environments in which all individuals are valued. Teachers with different expertise can co-teach in inclusive settings while providing optimal social and academic results for all students.
4. Knowledge and competence are purposely constructed in a variety of ways.
5. Competitive structures and activities are socially constructed and not inevitable.
6. Collaboration, cooperation, and mutual support are preferred forms of interpersonal interaction.

[handwritten margin note: All individuals are valued!]

Thomas Hehir, former director of the Office of Special Education Programs, in his analysis of inclusive schooling and the role of special education in supporting children with disabilities, echoes the philosophical orientation of inclusion but positions issues of implementation in a practical context. In examining the relative strengths of different goals and trends in special education, Hehir (2006) considers "What should be accomplished by special education?" He concludes that the role of special education is "… to minimize the impact of disability and maximize the opportunities for children with disabilities to participate in general education in their natural community" (p. 49).

[handwritten margin note: "role of special Ed"]

Given this foundation, Hehir suggests several considerations for decisions regarding inclusion:

1. Educational decision-making must begin with the presumption that the general education classroom (the standard schooling experience) is the first placement consideration for all children with disabilities.
2. Placement considerations for children with disabilities should only emphasize separate settings when critical goals of the individualized education program cannot be achieved in general education classes.
3. Separate settings should not be justified by a school's refusal to provide services of accommodations in general education settings.
4. There is value in social inclusion for children with disabilities.
5. "Inclusion should be purposeful." (p. 81).

Notable in his guidelines is the idea that inclusion itself should not be the goal. Inclusion is a presumption, but the goal of special education, inclusive or not, is a strong academic/school experience for all children, with purposeful attention to the needs of children with disabilities. Given the balance of an ideological foundation which presumes inclusion to have intrinsic value and an explicit focus on the necessary practical issues relative to effectively educating children with disabilities, we begin to envision a flexible perspective on how to implement Hehir's philosophy on special education.

Understands both ways. →

For example, an educator with an inclusive philosophy believes that children with serious learning disabilities, hearing impairments, or blindness benefit from social and academic experiences in a natural, integrated school setting, but still understands that (1) students with learning disabilities often benefit from direct reading instruction in a resource room, (2) students with significant hearing impairments need instruction in American Sign Language or speech/language training, and (3) students who are blind benefit from Braille instruction, which is likely to be taught in a special classroom or in a resource room. Essentially, inclusion could be seen as the philosophical orientation that undergirds the practical actions and decision made on behalf of students with disabilities—*a way of valuing the educational experience of children with disabilities that presumes general education to be the standard expectation, but does not fail to recognize the importance of individualized instruction.*

WHY I VALUE SPECIAL EDUCATION AND INCLUSIVE EDUCATION.

I taught 6th, 7th, and 8th grade in a middle school in a diverse, urban, center-city community. Although the socio-economic status varied, the school was known for serving children from very low-income neighborhoods; many of the students grew up in communities characterized by generational poverty, high rates of crime, drug use, prostitution, and under-resourced young single-parent homes. Clearly, many of the students in our school brought with them the myriad challenges of their day-to-day lives. In my middle school, 24% of the students were placed in special education—a rate dramatically higher than would typically be expected. One of the greatest challenges with such a high rate of special education was to provide appropriate, individualized support necessary to help students actualize their potential in school. Placement decisions regarding inclusive and separate classes provided the greatest source of difficulty. Students entered 6th grade from various "feeder schools" (i.e., the smaller elementary schools in the local area that fed our large middle school). Among these feeder schools was considerable variability in expectations about whether children in special education could "make it" in regular classes. It depended on the belief systems of the teachers who taught them in elementary school and the way that the students compared to their peers in the elementary school. Generally speaking, our students entered 6th grade as timid, apprehensive, friendly children who wanted to figure out the middle school process. Our students in special education could be most easily described as students who struggled mildly or tremendously with reading, particularly reading in academic courses. The decision to place children in separate special education classes in our school had far-reaching implications. Although it is certainly not a universal problem, in our school, the separate special education classes were multi-grade (age 11-16) and offered in a completely separate part of the building. Often, the teachers assigned to teach these courses were non-licensed career-changers who were interested in making a difference in their community, but rarely had the knowledge or skills necessary to reach their students. The students in these classes rarely participated in field trips with the rest of the school. They experienced only special education courses with the same students all day. For students in the special program designed for children with emotional and behavioral disorders, there was virtually no academic instruction. One year, the students had a substitute teacher for 80% of the school year. They played video games in lieu of doing math or science providing they didn't cause problems for whatever new substitute teacher had been assigned to the class.

I was a special education teacher. My role was as a grade level "learning and inclusion specialist." For students deemed worthy, we used an approach called "supported inclusion." This meant that students in inclusive special education had one course with me each day called "Learning Strategies for Success in Middle School." Each day the students would read highly engaging grade-level books for pleasure while learning reading comprehension strategies. Also, I taught my students strategies for learning new vocabulary words in their general classes, strategies for note-taking, organization, writing, studying, and test-taking. The rest of the day, I co-taught their core courses, typically English and math, seeking to ensure that students used their new effective learning strategies in those classes. I also advocated for their learning modifications to ensure they experienced the same curriculum as their peers, while providing some additional supports and eliminating barriers—preferential seating for note-taking, shortened examinations, extended time to take tests and complete homework, etc. My students typically did very well in their courses despite considerable limitations in academic skills. At least 90% of my students passed their end-of-year tests (often at low levels of proficiency) and passed most if not all of their courses. Grade retention was almost never an issue for my students. I spent a considerable amount of my time providing effective instruction to these students to augment the remainder of their courses, advocating for them with their teachers, teaching the students to believe in themselves and work diligently, and communicating with parents. None of these services would have been provided without special education in public schools. They simply would have "floated" through school with little or no support. The fact that "my students" experienced so much more success than anyone expected they could is why I value special education. The fact that students in the separate special education program experienced a consistently non-academic school day, which undermined their ability to become fully developed, educated members of society, is why I value inclusive education.

– Chris O'Brien

WHAT IS SPECIAL ABOUT SPECIAL EDUCATION?

A critical assumption of special education is that it provides something more or something different than the mainstream educational experience and that it is designed to serve those students whose needs go beyond the needs of typically performing students. So, given all of the debate about how and where students with disabilities should be supported in schools, the critical question remains: *What is so special about special education?*

Ideally, it means carefully planned, skillful instruction tailored to a student's individual needs that results in rapid gains in academic performance. Unfortunately, in some schools, it is not that special. There is considerable variability. For some children, it means better student-teacher ratio (more one-on-one attention). For others, it may just be a sense of safety and comfort in a special class where at least one teacher "has their back" and doesn't make them feel inadequate.

The overarching emphasis of special education is on **intensive, individualized instructional interventions** based on the specific needs of children who fail to make typical progress in school settings (Hallahan and Kauffman, 2000). Cook & Shirmer (2003) defined what is intended to be special in special education and how the special education community generally defines the additional effectiveness provided to students with disabilities, emphasizing the vast contributions to research on instructional practices for students who struggle in school. Instructional practices have been devised for years, designed to specifically support the needs of learners who would otherwise struggle in school based on limitations in learning and behavior, in particular. Some of these include:

1. Direct instruction (particularly in the area of reading)
2. Self-monitoring strategies
3. Mnemonic instruction
4. Learning strategy training
5. Curriculum-based measurement
6. Applied behavior analysis
7. Functional assessment

Some in the profession have emphasized the importance of raising expectations for children with special needs as a core value in special education. When expectations are set high, students tend (with appropriate supports) to meet those expectations. It may take better or different techniques. It might not happen as quickly, but it is consistently clear that even those students with significant impairments can achieve great things given the appropriate level of instructional support and advocacy.

More recent strides include major movements in reforming general education such as **Response to Intervention, Positive Behavior Support,** and **Universal Design for Learning** (see Chapter 14 for more details). Even in the area of technology, many of the excellent examples of technology in education derived from earlier efforts at creating assistive technology for students with disabilities.

GLOSSARY IN PLAIN TERMS

Least Restrictive Environment (LRE): Students with disabilities should be educated as close to the general education classroom as possible while still meeting their individualized educational needs.

Special education: State and federally funded services provided by schools and school districts in response to federal legislation, IDEA, that mandates free and appropriate education individualized to the unique needs of students with disabilities.

Disability: Limitations in performing a given task based on an impairment or condition.

Exceptionality: Characteristic of an individual that is particularly unique when compared to the mainstream population.

IDEA: The Individuals with Disabilities Education Act most recently reauthorized by congress and the George Bush administration in 2004. Provides the foundation of rights and services for children with disabilities to receive special education in American public schools.

FAPE: Free Appropriate Public Education.

Continuum of services: A series of placement alternatives necessary to provide individualized special education services ranging from general education classrooms to an array of separate settings depending on the severity and intensity of needs of the student.

Zero reject: IDEA principle that prohibits schools from denying access to educational experiences in local public schools.

IEP: Individualized Education Program; A school district-developed document that outlines school-based needs, individualized goals, and an array of classroom accommodations and support services for a student in special education.

Inclusion: Special education philosophy that values social integration and access to general curriculum standards for children with disabilities by providing specialized services in regular classes.

REFERENCES

Blatt, B. (1970). *Exodus from pandemonium: Human abuse and a reformation of public policy.* Boston: Allyn & Bacon.

Blatt, B., & Kaplan, F. (1966). Christmas in purgatory: A photographic essay on mental retardation. Boston: Allyn & Bacon.

Cook, B.G., & Schirmer, B.R. (2003). What is special about special education? Overview and analysis. *Journal of Special Education, 37,* 200-205.

Fitch, F. (2003). Inclusion, exclusion, and ideology: Special education students' changing sense of self. *The Urban Review, 35*(3), 233-252.

Gable, R. A., & Hendrickson, J. M. (2000). Teaching all the students: A mandate for educators. In J. S. Choate (Ed.), *Successful inclusive teaching: Proven ways to detect and correct special needs.* (pp. 2-17). Boston: Allyn and Bacon.

Hallahan and Kauffman (2000). *Exceptional learners: Introduction to special education* (8th ed.). Boston: Allyn & Bacon.

Hardman, M. L., & Nagle, K. (2004). Public policy: From access to accountability in special education. In A. M. Sorrells, H. J. Rieth & P. T. Sindelar (Eds.), *Critical issues in special education: Access, diversity, and accountability.* (pp. 277-292). Boston: Pearson.

Hehir, T. (2006). *New direction in special education: Eliminating ableism in policy and practice.* Harvard Education Press: Cambridge, MA.

Levine, M. (1990). *Keeping a head in school: A student's book about learning abilities and learning disorders.* Cambridge: Educators Publishing Service.

Katsiyannis, A., Yell, M. L., & Bradley, R. (2001). Reflections on the 25th anniversary of the individuals with disabilities education act. *Remedial & Special Education, 22,* 324-339.

Olson, J. L., & Platt, J. C. (2004). *Teaching children and adolescents with special needs* (4th ed.). Upper Saddle River, New Jersey: Pearson.

Smith, J.D. (2004). The historical contexts of special education: Framing our understanding of contemporary issues. In A. M. Sorrells, H. J. Rieth & P. T. Sindelar (Eds.), *Critical issues in special education: Access, diversity, and accountability.* (pp. 1-15). Boston: Pearson.

Categories of Disability Under IDEA NICHCY, the National Dissemination Center for Children with Disabilities. www.nichcy.org April 2009.

Yell, M.L. (2005). The law and special education. Prentice Hall.

Yell, M. L., Drasgow, E., Bradley, R., & Justesen, T. (2004). Contemporary legal issues in special education. In A. M. Sorrells, H. J. Rieth & P. T. Sindelar (Eds.), *Critical issues in special education: Access, diversity, and accountability.* (pp. 16-37). Boston: Pearson.

QUESTIONS *for Reflection:*

"All children are different and have different profiles of ability—strengths and weaknesses." Given the assumption that the previous statement is true, what is the rationale for giving children disability labels in special education?

allow schools / systems to be able to group those students.

What categories of children in special education comprise the majority of students served by special education services in U.S. schools?

In your own words explain the idea of "demystification" as it relates to helping a child understand her disability.

How does the contemporary notion of inclusion contrast with the original idea of the LRE presented in the 1975 passage of the national disability legislation?

Why do some professionals suggest that the continuum of services legitimizes segregating students with disabilities from their peers?

To what extent does the history of oppressive treatment of individuals with disabilities reinforce the highly ideological and philosophical rhetoric of contemporary advocates of inclusion and disability rights?

NOTES

CHAPTER 2

Planning and Providing
Special Education Services

John Beattie and Jeremy Lopuch

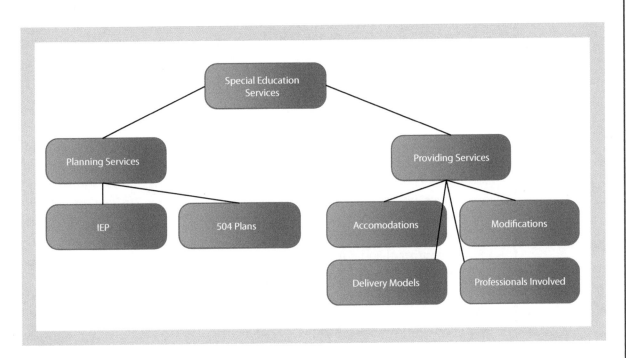

THE TOP TEN TERMS FOR CHAPTER 2:

The following key terms or big ideas are critical to your understanding of the content for chapter 2 and the in-class discussions to follow.

• 504 Plan	• Accommodations
• Consultation	• Co-teaching
• IFSP	• Modifications
• Resource Room	• Response to Intervention (RTI)
• Self-Contained classroom	• Transition

Chapter 1 told us that special education can be many things to many people. Each person involved with students with special needs, including the student, potentially brings his or her own interpretation of what IS and what SHOULD BE. This is why there are laws that govern what we do in our schools as we work with these learners. Regardless of one's interpretation or bias relating to students with disabilities, there are several underlying truths that guide just about everything that happens in special education in our schools. Toward the end of Chapter 1, we stated that students are likely to perform more effectively if and when the expectations for their performance are set high. Effective interventions and support are crucial to ensure that students reach the level of the expectations. Special education is not a "one size fits all" model; rather, special education emphasizes that it may likely take better or different techniques to help all students with disabilities perform at a higher level. This alternative instruction begins with the completion of the Individualized Education Program (IEP). How and where students with disabilities receive services and who provides these services are identified in the IEP. This "blueprint" consequently guides the instruction to be provided for all students with disabilities. Chapter 2 will discuss the elements of the IEP and the resulting impact this legal document has on the instruction implemented with students with disabilities.

TRADITIONAL PRACTICES OF REFERRAL TO SPECIAL EDUCATION

Why do students get referred? It is safe to say that the majority of students are referred for possible services in special education by their classroom teacher. Often, these teachers believe that their own efforts to help children who are struggling in their classes are less effective or appropriate than efforts by outside professionals (e.g., reading interventionists, separate classroom teachers, counselors). This often results in having many children who are experiencing difficulty referred to special education rather than addressing student needs in the general classroom setting (Soodak & Podell, 1994). Nonetheless, as teachers believe that they are ill prepared to meet the needs of the struggling students, these professionals often make referrals for special education services with little or no attempt to "solve the problem" in their classrooms (Gottlieb, Gottlieb, & Trontgone, 1991).

Occasionally parents request a special education evaluation for their children. The parents relate their experiences with the child and seek to find answers to the issues that confront them in their home environment. Given the teacher's experience with the child, the teacher may agree with the parent and initiate the referral process. Conversely, the teacher may not observe the challenges noted in the home environment and suggest that more observations may be necessary to ensure the greatest opportunity for the student to experience success.

How teachers have traditionally decided when to refer. Crowl, Kaminsky, & Podell (1997) suggested that teachers ask themselves a series of questions prior to referring students for special education services:

- Initially, classroom teachers should determine that all possible interventions and strategies have been implemented in an attempt to meet the needs of the struggling student(s).
- Next, teachers must ensure that they have collaborated with their colleagues and other professionals in an effort to find alternatives to the existing classroom instruction.
- Once the alternative instructional practices have been implemented, the teacher should then determine if the general education setting does indeed provide services appropriate to the needs of the student(s).
- Finally, after carefully considering the answers to the first three questions, the teacher should reflect on the situation and ***decide if a referral is in the best interests of the student***. If the teacher determines that additional services would be beneficial in helping the student(s) succeed, the referral for special education services should be made.

What traditionally happens after the special education referral process begins? Upon referral for special education, the student is assessed by professionals from various disciplines. These professionals administer a series of standardized tests designed to measure the student's intellectual ability, academic skills, verbal and written language, behavior, and any other area of concern (Algozzine, Christenson, & Ysseldyke, 1982). Historically, evidence suggests that the significant majority of referrals to special education will result in placement in special education programs (Algozzine, et al., 1982).

How final decisions are traditionally made to determine students eligible for special education? Upon completion of the test administrations noted above, the results of the student's performance on the battery of tests are scored, analyzed, and interpreted in an effort to determine the possibility of placement in a special education program. These results are compared to the specific criteria established by each state for each of the disability categories (e.g., learning disabilities, intellectual disabilities). For example, Chapter 5 describes the criteria used to identify a student as having intellectual disabilities. These criteria state that the student must have general intellectual ability that is significantly below average compared to the student's peers. The student must also experience difficulty with adaptive behavior skills such as counting money or riding a city bus. These difficulties must also occur before the child turns 18 (see Chapter 5 for more details regarding the identification criteria for students with intellectual disabilities). If it is determined that, prior to the student's 18th birthday, the student has an Intelligence Quotient (IQ) that is significantly below average (i.e., 70 and below) co-occurring with deficits in adaptive behavior, the individual qualifies to receive services in a program for students with intellectual disability. At this point, a meeting is arranged to produce a plan designed to meet the needs of the student throughout the academic year.

What traditionally happens before an individualized education program is developed? Students may struggle in the general education classroom for various reasons. Some students enter the school environment with limited exposure or experience in pre-academic and academic skills. These children begin their academic careers without the necessary skills displayed by the majority of their peers. It is possible that these students will lag behind their peers until they are exposed to and learn the skills exhibited by their peers upon entering school. These students will likely benefit from instruction and, with time, often "catch up" to their peers. This may be accomplished by entering into a summer enrichment program, or receiving support beyond the scope of the traditional school day (e.g., after school tutoring). These students will likely perform at a level commensurate to their peers and require no support.

However, there are students who function significantly below their grade level peers and demonstrate limited success in the general education setting. Students who are in this situation often require instruction that is different from that typically provided in the general education setting. When a student is identified as having significant academic or behavioral difficulty in the general education classroom, the student often receives intervention strategies specifically designed to meet his/her needs. The interventions are developed by a committee and incorporated into the general education classroom setting. These interventions are implemented by the general education teacher and data are collected as to the student's progress over a 2 or 3 week period. If the student makes progress as a result of the "new" interventions, the intervention technique(s) continues. However, if the student does not make progress and continues to struggle, further steps are taken. The student may receive more extensive support as his/her progress continues to be monitored. Once again, if the student makes appropriate progress, the intervention continues and no further services are required. If, however, the student fails to benefit from this instruction, the intervention team or committee proceeds with a referral for special education services. After obtaining parental consent, a traditional evaluation is completed and if the student meets the disability criteria established, the student may begin to receive special education services.

RESPONSE TO INTERVENTION (RTI)

Why RTI? Problems with the Traditional Evaluation Process

A recent innovation of the special education referral process has been presented to school systems that strongly emphasize prevention of school failure. The three-tier model referred to as RTI is an attempt to define efforts for monitoring student performance in school and providing interventions in areas of struggle with progressively greater intensity corresponding to student needs. The development of RTI was in response to a number of key issues related to general education service delivery. First, the role of instructional materials and practices used with the majority of students (core instruction) had been largely ignored as it related to inadequate student learning. For example, students received poor general instruction and were thought to be disabled because they did not perform well. These students were "instructional causalities" of the poor core instruction they received.

Second, general education classrooms lacked differentiation. Instruction in classrooms had primarily been delivered in whole group formats, with emphasis on teaching to the average student (Baker & Zigmond, 1990). In addition, struggling students were typically provided environmental adjustments, such as preferential seating or extra time on assignments, instead of instruction geared toward areas of need.

Lastly, instructional practices within general education lacked scientific evidence. In other words, teachers were using methods not proven to work for most students. All of these factors, have in part, lead to large numbers of students referred, evaluated, and found eligible for special education services due to the poor quality of instruction and limited range of services received through general education. As you can see, RTI is intended to provide more research-based and appropriate intervention techniques to students in an effort to reduce the number of students who are inappropriately identified as students with disabilities. This intervention takes place in tiers; IDEA suggests using a three-tiered approach (see Figure 2.1).

problem in general education setting.

How does RTI improve upon the Traditional Referral Process?

Traditionally, students with unique learning needs were referred by their teachers for evaluation. This process is discussed as "pre-referral." As mentioned above, this process had a host of problems ranging from poor instructional practices to subjective referrals for evaluation. In an RTI model, students move through the process in response to their learning. For example, in the traditional model, teachers were not required to collect data on direct student response to instructional practices. This led to teachers making referral decisions based on opinion rather than objective data. RTI systems are designed to improvement this problem by requiring data on student learning to make educational decisions. Core or Tier 1 instruction takes place in the general education classroom. Tier 1 consists of research-based instructional materials and strategies documented to be effective for most students. Nonetheless, it is important to recognize that attention to student diversity and differentiated instruction is incorporated into the Tier 1 setting. Primary prevention or Tier 2 requires more support from the classroom teacher and other professionals who have the training or background to provide more focused, intense support. See Table 2.1 for descriptions on how to make activities "more" intense. These interventions are typically provided in small group settings. If a student does not respond to these interventions, the student progresses to Tier 3. At this level, the student receives the most intensive level of support available. This means the student receives even more carefully designed instruction to match student needs. The delivery of Tier 3 instruction may vary (general or special education delivery) depending on local procedures and resources. Typically, if a student is not responsive to Tier 3 instruction, this begins the process designed to determine eligibility for special education services.

→ referred by teacher for evaluation

Figure 2.1.

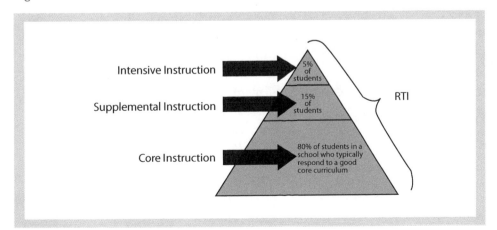

Table 2.1. How Instruction Can Become "More" Intense

"More" **explicit** and **clear explanations**
"More" exposure to **multiple instructional examples**
"More" **instructional time** in area(s) of need
"More" **error correction, feedback,** and **monitoring** procedures
"More" opportunities to **model instruction**, with **guided** and **independent practice**

Prereferral intervention
(Core instruction and primary prevention)
· This is essentially a tier 1–2 procedure relating to RTI;
· If the intervention is successful, the process stops;
· If the intervention is not successful, the student is referred for an evaluation.

Tier 3 instruction and multifaceted evaluation
· Daily, small group instructed tailored specifically to individual student needs;
· Appropriate assessment tools are used to determine student's academic performance, general intellectual ability, social skill development, hearing acuty, and visual acuity.

Determining student eligibility
· IF no disability is determined, special education services not needed;
· If disability is determined, student is eligible for special education services.

IEP is planned and developed
· IEP team meets to plan and develop the IEP.

Student is placed in least restrictive environment (LRE)
· Team decides the most appropriate educational placement for the child.

Special education services provided (FAPE)

Progress monitoring
· Data collected to determine student's progress wihtin the curriculum.

Annual review
· Review the IEP at least once per year to ensure that the document remains appropriate.

Reevaluation
· The multifactored evaluation must be completed at least every three years to determine if the student continues to require special education services.

Developing an Individualized Education Program

Now that the student has been identified as a student with a disability, the student's Individualized Education Program (IEP) must be developed. The IEP is a written statement for each child with a disability that is developed, reviewed, and revised in a meeting (34 C.F.R. 300. 320 (a)). As described in Chapter 1, a student with a disability may be classified in one or more of the 13 disability categories (see Chapter 1, pp. 9–12 for descriptions of the disability categories). ***All children who are ages 3–21 and have been identified as a student with a disability must have an IEP written to ensure that their individual needs are met.*** Regardless of the category of disability, the IEP is developed by a team of professionals, the parents of the student, and when appropriate, the student himself/herself (see Table 2.2 for a list of IEP team members). The IEP team meets to discuss the strengths and weaknesses of each individual student and ultimately identify the most appropriate placement and intervention strategies for that student (see Figure 2.2). It is important to note that the IEP focuses only on the areas that are affected by the child's disability, so if, for example, a child is academically competent, academic goals may not be included in his IEP.

Figure 2.2. Eligibility Process

Table 2.2. Members of the IEP Team

General participants to be invited:
Parents
At least one general education teacher
Child's special education teacher
School system representative (LEA)
Professional who can interpret evaluation results (School Psychologist)
Student, as appropriate
Where transition is a component, meeting should include:
Appropriate service agency and/or post-secondary representative(s)
Student aged 16 or older must be invited according to IDEA
Other participants that may be informed or invited by parents/school:
Related service providers
All teachers who work with the student
The principal, if other than the school representative
Other individuals who have knowledge or pertinent information to contribute
Parent advocate

© Dmitriy Shironosov, 2015. Used under license from Shutterstock, Inc.

As the team develops the IEP, several pieces of information must be included. These include:

1. A statement of the child's present levels of academic achievement and functional performance. This statement must indicate how the child's disability affects the child's involvement and progress in the general education curriculum (i.e., the same curriculum as for non-disabled children). For preschool children, the IEP must describe how the disability affects the child's participation in age appropriate activities;

2. A statement of measurable academic and functional annual goals. These statements outline the primary needs for educational performance based on the student's present level of performance. When possible, these annual goals should be aligned with the standardized curriculum experienced by non-disabled peers. When it has been determined that the student's progress will be most accurately measured using alternate assessments aligned to alternate achievement standards, a description of benchmarks or short-term objectives must also be included in the IEP;

3. A description of the process for measuring the child's progress toward meeting the annual goals. In addition, information must be provided that identifies when reports on the progress the child is making toward meeting the annual goals will be provided to parents, guardians, and other key stakeholders (e.g., general education teachers);

4. A statement of the special education and related services, and supplementary aids and services to be provided to the child, or on behalf of the child. Information must also be provided that describes the program modifications or supports to be incorporated into the child's educational setting. This provision is included to ensure, to the maximum degree possible, that the child is making appropriate progress toward attaining the annual goals established in the IEP. The overriding goal here is that the child is involved in and is making progress in the general education curriculum, thereby ensuring that the child will be educated and participate with other children with disabilities and non-disabled children in the activities described in this section;

5. An explanation of the extent, if any, to which the child will not participate with non-disabled peers in the general education class;

6. A statement of any accommodations necessary to measure the academic achievement and functional performance of the child on state and district-wide assessments. It is important to note at this time that should the IEP Team determine that the child must take an alternate assessment instead of the regular state or district-wide assessment of student achievement, it is necessary to provide a description of why the child cannot participate in the regular assessment, as well as the specific alternate assessment tool that will be used to measure the child's performance; and

7. The projected date for the beginning of the services, accommodations, and modifications described earlier, and the anticipated frequency, location, and duration of those services and modifications.

Individualized Programs for Young Children

As mentioned earlier in this chapter, all children ages 3–21 who have been identified as a student with a disability must have an IEP written to ensure that their individual needs are met. The Individuals with Disabilities Education Act (IDEA, Public Law 99-456, 1986) extends and enhances this age range to include children who are identified prior to their third birthday. IDEA encouraged states to provide early intervention services to children birth through age 2 but did not mandate these services. Instead, states that chose to participate in these birth-to-two programs were allocated additional funding to help defray the cost inherent to developing such programs. Participating states and individual programs continue to be responsible for meeting the needs of the children served under IDEA; to ensure that the needs were met and to maintain consistency, documentation is also required for children birth-to-two who are receiving special education services. An **Individualized Family Service Plan (IFSP)** must be completed for each child and family receiving services. The IFSP identifies the services to be provided to the child in cooperation with the child's family. Given the nature and age of the child, the IDEA authors recognize the vital role that parents and families play in the early development of all children. Consequently, the IFSP must also identify services designed to help families in their support of their young child with a disability. The most recent updates of IDEA further emphasize the importance of utilizing research-based intervention strategies as instruction is provided to help these young children develop pre-literacy and language skills crucial to school readiness (U.S. Department of Education, 2005).

Individualized Programs for Older Students

Previous discussion noted that students aged 16 or older must be included on the IEP team. As students near the end of their public school careers, it is critical that consideration be given to their future outside the schools. These students are continuing their transition from the public schools to the "real world." The success of this ongoing transition is enhanced through the IEP. As students with disabilities approach adulthood (i.e., age 16 and above), the IEP must identify individual goals for the student beyond the public school setting. These goals must incorporate age appropriate transition assessments focusing on training, education, employment, and, where appropriate, independent living skills that will increase the likelihood of success in the "real world."

ADDITIONAL LEGAL CONSIDERATIONS

The Individualized Education Program (IEP) is a significant part of the Individuals with Disabilities Education Act. Students with identified disabilities that meet the standards established in IDEA are consequently eligible for an IEP. However, there are many students with disabilities who need specific special education or related services but will not qualify to receive services under IDEA. Nonetheless, these students may require specific <u>accommodations</u> (see further description of accommodations later in this chapter) to enable them to work and achieve to the maximum of their ability. The needs and consequent accommodations of these students are often provided for under Section 504 of the Rehabilitation Act. Section 504 is a civil rights law that was developed to protect persons with disabilities from discrimination based solely on their disability. The goal of Section 504 is to ensure that the student with a disability has access to an education similar to that of students without disabilities (Chambers, 2008). The specific considerations provided for an individual student is documented in the "504 Plan." The 504 Plan, often referred to as an "Accommodation Plan," does not guarantee that the individual student will benefit from the services provided. Instead, the 504 Plan is the document that states that the student with a disability will have the same opportunity as other students <u>to benefit from</u> classroom <u>instruction</u> (Chambers, 2008).

SPECIAL EDUCATION SERVICES IN TODAY'S SCHOOLS

Special education services are provided in various classroom settings. As described in Chapter 1, the continuum of special education services ranges from the general education classroom to a homebound or hospital setting. At this point, we will consider the classroom settings in which the needs of students with disabilities are met.

General Education Classroom/Inclusion

As noted in the continuum of services model, services provided in the general education classroom setting take place "under the direction of the general education classroom teacher." The classroom teacher is often considered to be the "content expert." That is, the general education teacher knows and understands the specific elements of the particular content material presented to the students in that classroom setting. In other words, a third grade teacher has learned the curriculum involved in teaching third grade students to use prefixes or suffixes, make predictions about specific reading material, or to solve problems using measurement concepts. However, general education teachers often do not have the training or confidence to work with students with disabilities. One of the most significant comments from general education teachers is that they lack the knowledge and skills necessary to provide appropriate interventions for students with special needs (Soodak, Podell, & Lehman, 1998). Therefore, it is critical that general educators receive support from special educators who are trained to meet the special learning and behavioral needs of students in special education. The support is designed to provide intervention strategies directed to the content while taking into consideration the student's disability. It is important to recognize at this point that students with special needs placed in the general education setting are able to meet the requirements of this classroom setting with appropriate accommodations and/or modifications. These specific accommodations or modifications are often necessary in one or two academic content areas. For example, many students with learning disabilities may have difficulty with language arts or reading material but are superior mathematicians.

The accommodations or modifications would be incorporated into the instruction focusing on the language arts content with no such consideration necessary for math. More information regarding accommodations and modifications will be provided later in this chapter.

The additional support that is necessary to meet the needs of ALL students in the general education classroom setting is often provided by the special educator. It is important to remember that the student with special needs continues to receive instruction in the general education classroom setting along with his/her non-disabled peers. This support is typically provided in one of two broad models.

Consultative support. Once again, the general education teacher assumes the overall direction of the classroom and the activities and lessons that take place in the general education classroom setting. However, additional support is often provided via a consultative support model. The special education teacher does not provide direct services to the students with and without special needs. Rather, the special educator "consults" with the general educator regarding the specific needs of an individual student(s). This consultative support may involve specific intervention strategies, classroom management techniques, or simply providing resources for the general educator. While this consultation often takes place whenever it is possible for the general and special educators to meet, this approach is far more effective when designated times and places are arranged to meet to discuss the student(s) with special needs. This usually occurs on an "as needed" basis although consistent meeting times are likely to be far more beneficial. While not always true, this consultation model often takes place in small schools which do not have the population to warrant a full time special educator. In this situation, it is often determined that the most effective use of the limited availability of the special educator is to consult rather than co-teach. However, more and more schools are using the co-teaching model in their efforts to provide the best possible education to students with and without special needs.

Co-Teaching Model. This model implies that the general and special educators provide instruction in which each professional assumes and completes a specific role. This model is often incorporated into the inclusion classroom setting. As defined in Chapter 1, inclusion is the special education philosophy that values social integration and access to general curriculum standards for children with disabilities by providing specialized services in general education classes.

In other words, inclusion classrooms are designed to provide appropriate instruction to students with and without special needs. Students without disabilities are provided with the opportunity to interact with students with disabilities in both academic and social circumstances. This can only be accomplished when a strong partnership between the general education teacher and the special education teacher has been established. Initially, this suggests that both the general education and special education teachers want to be in a co-teaching setting. There may also be a need for additional training for each teacher. This training may focus on the unique needs of students with disabilities, typically provided for the general education teachers. Similarly, the special education teachers benefit from training that focuses on the specific content taught in the inclusion classroom (Beattie, Jordan, & Algozzine, 2006; Friend & Cook, 2004; Keefe, Moore, & Duff, 2004; Murawski & Dieker, 2004).

Effective co-teaching can be accomplished using various classroom approaches. An approach often used in the inclusion classroom identifies one teacher as the "lead" teacher who presents most of the instruction to the entire class. The second teacher observes the class members during the whole group instruction and is available to answer questions or provide small group instruction as needed (Beattie, Jordan, & Algozzine, 2006). Co-teaching may also involve certain models like Station Teaching, in which each teacher presents content to two groups located in different sections of the classroom. Station teaching is a means for providing differentiated instruction to the class. A third approach to co-teaching is referred to as Parallel Teaching. This is accomplished by dividing the class into two heterogeneous groups (Friend & Cook, 2003). Each teacher presents essentially the same content material to her/his "half" of the entire class. Team Teaching is the final approach to be considered in this chapter. Instruction in the team teaching approach is shared by the co-teachers. One teacher may be designated as the "lecturer" for the target content material, while the second teacher demonstrates or models the concept being discussed. This is not an exhaustive list of co-teaching approaches. Rather, these examples are presented in an effort to demonstrate the basic elements of co-teaching and to emphasize that co-teaching can only be effective when each professional assumes and adheres to the specific duties of the presentation model.

Resource Room

Regardless of the general classroom placement, there is often the need for additional instruction to ensure that each student with disabilities is provided with the most appropriate opportunity to learn and master the target skill. In some circumstances, it is necessary for students to be pulled out of the general education classroom. These students work with a special educator in a format designed to provide direct attention to specific academic skills. Support in a resource room is provided in a small group setting, which enables the teacher to focus on the specific areas of need for each student. This instruction usually emphasizes specific skill development or additional opportunity to learn class material. There are several approaches that may guide the instruction that takes place in the resource classroom. One common approach emphasizes the remediation of basic skills, which the students with disabilities have not mastered in the general education classroom. The special educator uses alternative instructional techniques designed to meet the unique learning needs of the individual students in the resource setting. For example, instruction may be directed to the remediation of basic reading or math skills. Alternatively, instruction in the resource room provides opportunities to teach students learning strategies that may facilitate success in their general education classroom. Students may learn strategies that enable them to learn specific content material (e.g., mnemonics such as HOMES to remember the Great Lakes) or to be more effective with classroom assignments (e.g., previewing techniques prior to reading new content material). Additional instruction in a resource setting might include tutorial support with particular attention to content material from the general education classroom. Oftentimes, students with disabilities do not learn the material from a general education classroom lesson. These students often have the wherewithal to do so but are unable to process the information at the rate at which the material is presented. Therefore, the resource room teacher may present the material using different stimulus information or at a reduced rate. The same material is emphasized simply using an alternative approach. Finally, resource room instruction is often directed at meeting the student's needs outside of the educational environment. The attention to functional skills, such as completing a job application, assists the student in making the transition to the "real world."

Separate or Self-contained Classroom

The overriding goal that guides all work completed with students with disabilities is driven by the Least Restrictive Environment (LRE) provisions of IDEA. Every effort is made to provide the most appropriate education possible for these students in a classroom environment that allows for the greatest exposure to students without disabilities. However, there are circumstances when the LRE is not the general education classroom. In these situations, students with disabilities receive instruction in what is often referred to as a separate or self-contained classroom. This separate setting reduces the opportunity for students with disabilities to interact with students without disabilities. However, this decision is made with the individual student's best interests at heart. If the IEP Team determines that an individual student will not benefit from instruction with non-disabled peers, the student may likely receive instruction in a separate or self-contained class. This placement option is one that requires considerable thought and caution. As noted previously in this chapter, one of the required components of the IEP is an explanation of why an individual student with a disability will not participate with non-disabled children in the general education class. Therefore, the IEP Team must ensure that the decision to place a student in a separate classroom is the least restrictive and one that will provide the student with the greatest opportunity to grow academically and socially.

When the decision is made to place a student with disabilities in a separate classroom, additional issues must be taken into account. The No Child Left Behind Act (2004) has established strict policies to ensure that all children will be taught by highly qualified teachers (HQT). One of many implications of this mandate for HQT may have an ever-increasing impact on instruction in the separate or self-contained classroom. The special educator assumes the responsibility for teaching specific content information to students with disabilities in the separate setting. This suggests that special educators teaching in the separate classroom setting must be highly qualified in the academic content area for which they are responsible. The implication of this may be that a teacher certified in special education who teaches math in a separate class environment, may be required to secure additional certification in math to continue to teach in the math self-contained classroom. These standards have not been established at this time; however, if there is such a mandate, the implications will be far reaching and likely have a significant impact on the separate/self-contained placement option.

WHAT IS DIFFERENT ABOUT INSTRUCTION FOR STUDENTS WITH DISABILITIES?

As noted previously in this chapter, students with disabilities can and do learn in a variety of academic situations. However, there are occasions in which specific consideration must be given to the nature and severity of the disability. There are circumstances during which a student with a disability may need some adjustment to the content material, the way in which the material is presented, the way in which the student responds, and/or the way in which the student is evaluated. These considerations are typically referred to as Accommodations or Modifications to the curriculum.

Accommodations

An accommodation involves taking the steps necessary to make something more suitable or appropriate to the needs of an individual. This is accomplished by making adjustments to the classroom instruction or assessment used with a student (Beattie, Jordan, & Algozzine, 2006). It is an attempt to "level the playing field," so students with disabilities have access to the same curriculum standards as their peers without disabilities (Beattie, Jordan, & Algozzine, 2006). That is, students with disabilities are exposed to content material that is as similar to their non-disabled peers as possible. Further, accommodations do not reduce the quantity of material for which students are responsible.

Accommodations are put into place for students with IEPs and/or 504 Plans. These documents identify the specific accommodations that will be available to the student. It is important to note that the accommodations may not be used in all circumstances or at all times. The key is that they are available to the student during all of the identified academic activities so as to provide equal access to those activities. These accommodations can be incorporated into a variety of daily tasks in which the student is involved. Students can receive accommodations related to the manner in which material is presented, to how the students respond, the location in which they receive services, and the timing and scheduling of specific academic activities (Thompson, Morse, Sharpe, and Hall, 2005). Specific accommodations are presented in Table 2.3.

Table 2.3. Examples of Possible Accommodations

Accommodation to the way material is presented:
Material at a lower reading level, focusing on same content
Utilize hands-on materials
Provide for multiple opportunities to respond
Use technology as needed/appropriate
Present information in a multi-sensory format whenever possible

Accommodation to the way students respond:
Provide alternatives to traditional response systems (e.g., oral v. written tests)
Use technology as needed/appropriate (e.g., computer to complete written assignments)
Incorporate a scribe into the classroom setting as appropriate
Reduce the number of items on homework assignments or on tests
Extend deadlines in consideration of specific areas of concern (e.g., processing disorders

Accommodation to the location of the service delivery:
Provide instruction in small group or one-to-one settings
Provide "quiet" zones in the classroom for ALL students to complete work, if necessary or desired
Enable student with disabilities to take tests in quiet setting
Allow students to move, sit on the floor, or doodle during class time
Incorporate peer tutoring into the classroom

Accommodation to the timing and/or scheduling:
Provide extended time for tests and other appropriate academic tasks
Break testing into segments, conceivably over a period of days
Attempt to schedule more content-intensive classes (e.g., reading and math at the elementary level) in the early part of the day
Break instruction into smaller segments (e.g., 30 minutes) followed by some hands-on, application activity
Provide breaks for students that enable them to move independently for a short period of time

Modifications

As noted above, accommodations are put into place in an effort to provide students with disabilities an equal opportunity to benefit from the curriculum and instruction that is available to their peers without disabilities. It is often necessary to provide further adjustments to a student's daily academic or behavioral activities. These are often referred to as modifications. Modifications are changes in the content material that change, lower, or often reduce learning expectations (Thompson, Morse, Sharpe, and Hall, 2005). These authors warn that the utilization of modifications may result in a more significant gap between the academic work of students with disabilities from their peers without disabilities. This concern is often exacerbated by the resultant lowering of expectations for students with disabilities. In other words, as the demands placed on students with disabilities are reduced, the expectations for future performance may likely also be reduced. Beattie, Jordan, & Algozzine (2006) note the potential Catch-22 that may occur as a result of implementing specific modifications; while the intent of modifying instruction is to provide access to the general education curriculum, the modifications often eliminate the possibility of such access. Thompson, Morse, Sharpe, and Hall (2005) make a similar observation; they note that

> Providing modifications to students during classroom instruction and/or classroom assessments may have the unintended consequence of reducing their opportunity to learn critical content. If students have not had access to critical, assessed content, they may be at risk for not meeting graduation requirements. Providing a student with a modification during a state accountability assessment may constitute a test irregularity and may result in an investigation into the school's or district's testing practices (p. 15).

When modifying instruction for students with disabilities, it is important to keep in mind that modifying content material should occur only if the modification will provide access to the content material used in the standard curriculum. It is also crucial to realize that not all students with disabilities will require modifications in all academic areas. Many students will benefit from modifications to one content area with no such consideration in other academic areas.

Who Is Involved in Delivering These Services

We have discussed the core factors that lead to effective interventions with students with disabilities. This section will briefly discuss the professionals who assume the responsibility of meeting the needs of students with disabilities in various settings.

Audiologist. The trained professional who administers various hearing tests in an effort to determine the potential presence of a hearing loss. If a hearing impairment is identified, the audiologist works closely with the child, family, and school to identify the most appropriate use of hearing aid technology and to facilitate the use of this technology in the classroom setting.

Counselors. These professionals are trained to assist all children with social and emotional issues that may have a negative impact on relationships in school. Issues and concerns are also considered in relationship to students' family life and life outside the school environment.

Interpreter. An interpreter is that professional who translates the verbal language occurring in the classroom for students with hearing impairments. Typically, the interpreter uses sign language to enable the deaf or hard-of-hearing student to function in the general education classroom.

Music/Art Teacher. These teachers, while not necessarily trained to work with students with disabilities, often provide exposure to the arts enabling students with disabilities to express themselves when they are unable to do so with verbal language. Students may express themselves by drawing a picture or "writing" a song to describe their feelings rather than discussing this with other professionals in the school.

Occupational Therapist (OT). The OT helps students improve their ability to perform motor tasks in the school environment. They work with students with mental, physical, developmental, or emotional conditions. Occupational therapists use treatments to develop, recover, or maintain the daily living and work skills of their patients. The therapist helps students to perform activities such as using a computer or caring for daily needs such as dressing, cooking, and eating.

Physical Education (PE) Teacher. Aside from the responsibilities to the entire school, the PE teacher may also provide adaptive support for students with disabilities. This may include work mobility or participation in leisure activities such as bowling or basketball. The Adaptive PE teacher is knowledgeable of the developmental and physical needs of students as well as the rules governing the target leisure activities, which are the focus of the PE class.

Physical Therapist (PT). Physical therapists evaluate and diagnose areas concerned with movement and use targeted interventions in their work with children and adults alike. In their work with students, PTs may use interventions including manual therapy techniques, functional training, and training in using assistive and adaptive devices and equipment. Physical therapists evaluate the students in an effort to develop treatment techniques to promote the ability to move, reduce pain, restore function, and prevent disability.

General Education Teacher. The general education classroom teacher is often responsible for providing instruction, with or without the support of the special educator, to students with disabilities. This instruction is intended to focus on content material that is as similar as possible to that of his/her peers without disabilities. This education professional typically works closely with special education and related services personnel in an attempt to meet the needs of the students with disabilities placed in the general education classroom.

School Nurse. The school nurse is ultimately responsible for the medical services provided to all children in the school setting. The role of the school nurse has changed somewhat over time as more and more students receive medical treatment for disorders such as ADHD, depression, or diabetes. The nurse is often responsible for administering the appropriate medication as well as monitoring the individual student's reactions to that medication.

School Psychologist. The role of the school psychologist has also changed over time. Given the nature and extent of the psycho-educational testing that exists in public schools today, the psychologist's primary role is to administer, score, and interpret students' test performance. In addition, the school psychologist typically serves on the IEP team, and interprets and explains the test results and the academic implications of these test results to the members of the IEP team.

Social Worker. These specially trained professionals help students who are having trouble in school. They might find a mentor or a learning expert with whom an individual student may work. Social workers often attend to individual student concerns that may include child abuse, poverty, and violence. They work closely with students and families in an attempt to help them understand and solve their problems and make plans to remedy the concerns.

Special Education Teacher. As noted earlier in this chapter, the special education teacher is specially trained in identifying and implementing alternative intervention techniques designed to meet the needs of students with disabilities. The special educator may work with students in an inclusion setting, a resource room, a separate or self-contained classroom, or in more restrictive settings. This work may include indirect services in which the special educator consults with the regular education teacher or in providing direct services to students in the various settings mentioned above.

Speech Pathologist. The speech pathologist, often called the speech teacher or speech therapist, is initially responsible for evaluating students' speech and/or language disorders. Once a diagnosis has been made, the speech pathologist provides direct speech therapy to students in the school setting. These services include therapy designed to meet the speech and/or language needs of the identified students. The speech pathologist may also provide consultative support for teachers. This support often results in the development of specific activities that the classroom teacher can incorporate into the daily classroom regimen.

GLOSSARY IN PLAIN TERMS

504 Plan: The document that is used for students who do not qualify for an IEP but still have disabilities that impact their academic, behavioral, or social behavior. It is often called an "Accommodation Plan" as it provides specific accommodations to the student's school activities.

Accommodations: Specific considerations that are taken into account as the student completes his/her daily work. The purpose of accommodations are to provide access for students with disabilities to material available to students without disabilities.

Consultation: A method of enhancing the instruction provided to students with disabilities. The special education teacher works with the regular education teacher to provide alternative instructional strategies that are in turn implemented by the regular educator. The special educator has no direct contact with students but merely serves as a consultant.

Co-teaching: The teaching process in which the regular and special education teachers plan and carry out lessons in the regular/included classroom setting. The class consists of both students with and without disabilities.

IFSP: The service program developed to meet students' needs who are identified prior to beginning the traditional public school Kindergarten program. These students must be identified as having specific disabilities or being at-risk for disabilities.

Modifications: These are adaptations to the content material that change, lower, or often reduce learning expectations for the target student. Modifications alter the curriculum to the degree that students with disabilities who receive the designated modifications are often no longer able to learn the same content material as their peers.

Resource room: The pull-out classroom in which students with disabilities are removed from the general education classroom setting to receive instruction that typically focuses on specific academic, learning, or behavioral skills. The students return to the regular classroom after a specific period of time (i.e., 45–90 minutes).

Responsiveness to Instruction (RTI). The IDEA mandate that incorporates a tier approach to working with students. RTI is designed to utilize research-based interventions in the general education classroom setting with progressively more support provided to the classroom teacher. The intent is to provide appropriate instruction to students in the general education classroom thereby reducing the number of students inappropriately identified as students with disabilities.

Self-contained classroom. The special education classroom setting in which the majority of academic content is delivered by the special education teacher. Students placed in this setting spend limited periods of time interacting with students without disabilities.

Transition. The term that describes the attempt to adequately prepare students with disabilities to move into the world of work or, in some circumstances, higher education (e.g., community college programs).

References

Algozzine, B., Christenson, S., & Ysseldyke, J. E. (1982). Probabilities associated with the referral to placement process. *Teacher Education and Special Education, 5*, 19-23.

Beattie, J., Jordan, L. & Algozzine, B. (2006). *Making inclusion work: Effective practices for all teachers.* Thousand Oaks, CA: Corwin Press.

Chambers, E.M. (2008). *IEP or 504 Plan: What difference does it make?* Retrieved from www.spedwatch.org on August 26, 2010.

Crowl, T. K., Kaminsky, S., & Podell, D. M. (1997). *Educational psychology: Windows on teaching.* Dubuque, IA: Times Mirror Higher Education Group, Inc.

Friend, M. & Cook, L. (2003). *Interactions: Collaborative skills for school professionals* (4th Ed.). New York: Longman.

Gottlieb, J., Gottlieb, B. W., & Trongone, S. (1991). Parent and teacher referrals for a psychoeducational evaluation. *Journal of Special Education, 25*, 155-167.

Keefe, E.B., Moore, V., & Duff, F. (2004). The four "knows" of collaborative teaching. *Teaching Exceptional Children, 36*, 36-42.

Murawski, W.W., & Dieker, L.A. (2004). Tips and strategies for co-teaching at the secondary level. *Teaching Exceptional Children, 36*, 52-58.

Soodak, L. C., & Podell, D. M. (1994). Teachers' thinking about difficult-to-teach students. *Journal of Educational Research, 88*, 44-51.

No Child Left Behind Act (2001). P.L. 107-110.

Soodak, L.C., Podell, D.M., & Lehman, L.R. (1998). Teacher, student, and school attributes as predictors of teachers' responses to inclusion. *Journal of Special Education, 31*, 480-497.

Thompson, S., Morse, A., Sharpe, M., & Hall, S. (2005). *Accommodations Manual.* Washington, D.C.: Council of Chief State School Officers.

U.S. Department of Education. (2005). *To assure free appropriate public education: Twenty-seventh annual report to congress on the implementation of the Individuals with Disabilities Education Act.* Washington, DC: Author.

QUESTIONS *for Reflection:*

Respond to the statement that "the career goal of special educators is to be unemployed." Will this likely ever occur?

What is the difference between accommodations and modifications? What impact does the difference have on students with disabilities?

In your own words explain what inclusion is. Then, describe what you anticipate happening in an inclusion classroom in which you co-teach?

What do you believe to be the advantages and disadvantages to inclusion?

Describe the difference between an IEP and a 504 Plan.

What purpose does the IEP Team serve? Ask a school member who is on an IEP Team her/his opinion of the process incorporated into the team meetings.

Select a professional who works with students with disabilities; please choose one that is different from your intended major area of study. Discuss why you would enjoy and why you would not enjoy the role.

Notes

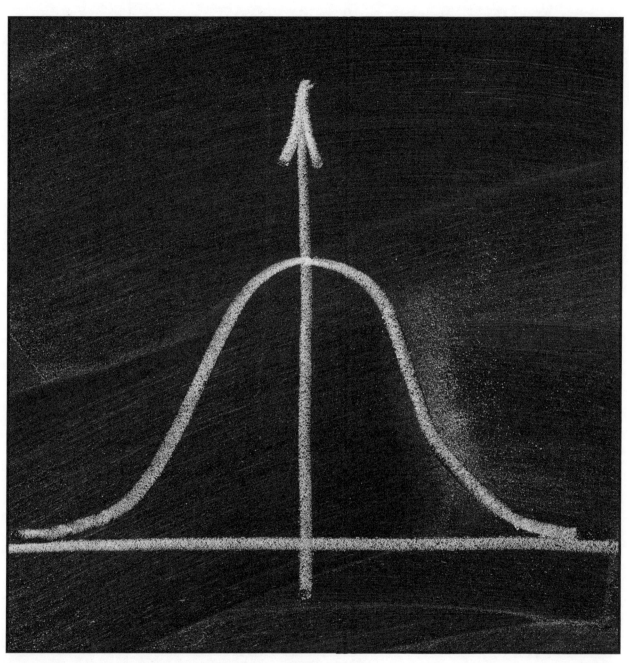

CHAPTER 3

Foundations of Academic Exceptionalities: Defining Normality, Disability, and Giftedness in School Settings

THE TOP TEN TERMS FOR CHAPTER 3:

The following key terms or big ideas are critical to your understanding of the content for chapter 3 and the in-class discussions to follow.

• Intelligence theories	• Multiple Intelligences
• Giftedness	• IQ testing
• Normal curve	• Intellectual disability
• Reading disability	• ADHD
• Phonemic awareness	• At-risk

This chapter will serve as a foundation to understanding the way schools measure student progress, evaluate normality and disability, and what we generally know about how children learn and demonstrate both academic and intellectual ability in schools. By the end of this chapter we hope you can answer the following questions, as they will be briefly addressed to provide appropriate background knowledge to understand issues and trends in special education in contemporary public schools:

- How are disability and exceptionality defined in schools?
- What are the commonalities among students identified with high-incidence disabilities that are important for teachers to know?
- Why do so many high-incidence disabilities in schools seem to be subjectively defined?
- Do all students learn differently? How important are "learning styles" to addressing the needs of students in special education?
- What is intelligence and what does it have to do with determination for special education?
- How do schools assess and measure student ability?
- Is giftedness part of special education? How is giftedness defined in schools?
- What does it mean to be "at-risk" and how does that differ from being in special education?

How are disability and exceptionality defined in schools?

Often, professionals in the field of special education take for granted that parents and members of society at large understand what they mean when they use terms like "students with disabilities." The concept is more conceptually ambiguous than it might initially appear. When you examine social trends like the "disability rights" movement, you tend to see significant attention paid to individuals with physical disabilities that inhibit movement or communication (e.g., Cerebral Palsy, paralysis, and other similar conditions) or sensory impairments like blindness and hearing loss. The disability rights movement in schools stems primarily from advocacy for individuals with significant levels of cognitive/intellectual impairment for whom few educational and life opportunities existed prior to the mid to late-20th century. One must note, however, that most children in contemporary American public schools who receive special education services and fall under various semantic headings like "Exceptional Children" or "students with disabilities," have what are often called *mild disabilities*. It is debatable whether it is condescending to refer to someone's disability as "mild" given the various levels of impact that disability might have on his or her life aspirations, but generally speaking it is fair to say that most children who are considered "disabled" in school, actually have prior limitations in what could be considered **school-related abilities**.

For the most part, students with disabilities appear to be very much like their peers. A common theme for children with disabilities in schools is that they tend to need more from schools: more instructional time, more intensive instruction, and more individualized instruction. A focus on this specific theme should reinforce and clarify the instructional focus of special education. The emphasis of special education should be on instructional effectiveness and intensity personalized to the unique needs of a small number of children—not a bureaucratic process of categorization that simply "names the problems" that a child has and ignores the instructional consequences. The latter is a common criticism of special education in American public schools.

Perhaps the most common scenario of a child with a disability in school today is that of a little boy who comes to school in Kindergarten without strong pre-literacy skills and some developmental lag in the areas of social skills, language development, and behavioral self-monitoring. This child might struggle with some fundamental skills required to acquire reading fluency in future grades. A common area of struggle relates to something called *phonemic awareness*—roughly, the ability to manipulate the sounds of language in a way that underpins early skills in sounding out words and early reading experiences. Children who have problems with phonemic awareness are typically poor at playing rhyming games or identifying multiple words that start with a certain phoneme (letter sound). As minor as it might seem, if the child's teacher is unaware of this problem, he may continue to struggle with basic skills in reading to the point that he is identified as a labored or slow reader. Without effective intervention, these challenges often lead to ongoing difficulty with schoolwork in which reading and language-based activities are fundamental. Many times, the child will be retained for a year so that he can have some additional time to mature and *catch up*. Of course, this can be a traumatic experience for many students and without additional intervention specific to the child's needs, it might not accomplish much. Given the passage of enough time in which the student struggles to perform as expected, he is likely to be referred to special education and would often fit the qualification criteria for special education in the category of **Specific Learning Disability** in reading.

This scenario has presented a number of questions for the field of education to address. *Do this child's problems really qualify as a disability?* If we simply mean that a child "cannot do something"—a very narrow definition of the term disability—then maybe they do. *How do we differentiate this child from the many other children who struggle in school, particularly in reading? Should all children who struggle in reading be in special education?* Another important question: *Is a specific learning disability a real concept or are we just punishing this child for learning differently or being a little behind other children?* Finally, a very important question: *Couldn't we have identified his reading problem early and prevented this little boy from being referred to special education by intervening when he needed it most?* The progression of an academic problem to a problem of ***motivation*** and ***poor affect*** toward school is a rapid one for young children. It doesn't take long for many children to decide that school is simply not a place where they will be successful.

> **Point of Clarification**: The term **affect** (and affective) used in psychology refers to an emotional state or emotional response.

Crowl, Kaminsky, and Podell (1997) suggest that the "disability is not in the student but in the *gap between the student and the educational environment*." In essence, it is only reasonable to expect that various attributes contribute to the unique makeup of each child in our classrooms. Some of these attributes will appear more or less typical or "normal" in school. Some of the child's positive attributes will not always show up clearly in an elementary classroom. For some children, their only weaknesses might be the qualities required for children to flourish in school (reading ability, motivation, memory, verbal ability). School disabilities, in this way, are complicated. They are most often a reflection of a child's inability to perform well in academic settings. That is not to say that performing well in academic settings doesn't matter; only that disabilities are not the full picture of the child. As there could be a multitude of measurable qualities that children possess, many of them are only observed in a minimal and superficial way. In contemporary schools, it is likely that children with gifts in visual arts, music, singing, physical agility, interpersonal skills, leadership potential, etc., that might define their success and life journeys, might be only marginally acknowledged in school contexts.

How do psychologists define disabilities and disorders?

To fully grasp the basis for how schools define and evaluate disabilities, future teachers must understand the dominant role that the field of psychology plays in defining disabilities and disorders in American society. The Diagnostic and

Statistical Manual of Mental Disorders (DSM), published by the American Psychiatric Association is something of a guidebook for psychologists/psychiatrists to examine and categorize disorders associated with various impairments in mental ability and behavior. Although the text is not without controversy, the terminology and assessment processes of psychologists are ubiquitous in American public schools. Most of special education research and policy stems from the earliest foundations of the field of behavioral psychology. It is critical for teachers to understand that much of the conversation of special education is built upon a foundation of psychological theory. Most notably, the DSM is used to diagnose mental disorders in much the same way that the special education referral process leads to the development of an IEP based first on the categorization of the child's disability. Rather than focusing purely on an area of need (e.g., reading failure), special education begins with a diagnosis that defines the problem to be addressed by special education professionals. Of course, most important are the actions taken after the evaluation process to ensure the child achieves his or her full potential in school and life.

WHAT ARE THE COMMONALITIES AMONG STUDENTS IDENTIFIED WITH HIGH-INCIDENCE DISABILITIES THAT ARE IMPORTANT FOR TEACHERS TO KNOW?

For most of the general public, the conceptualization of disability relates to physical or medical impairments. Complicating this preconceived notion is the fact that the *overwhelming* majority of children served by special education have what could be described as "academic" disabilities. These include learning, behavioral, attention, and mild cognitive disabilities. These children account for approximately 90% of children served by special education in American public schools and the primary commonality among them is **poor academic performance**.

Table 3.1. Students with mild disabilities account for approximately 90% of students with disabilities (ages 6–21) served by IDEA in American public schools.

High-incidence Disabilities in Special Education	
Specific Learning Disability	Approximately 90% of children in special education (see table in chapter 1 for most recent data)
Speech and Language Impairment	
Attention Deficit Hyperactivity Disorder or ADHD (under OHI)	
Mild Intellectual/Developmental Disability	
Emotional and Behavioral Disability	

Public policy in special education defines disabilities as those limitations that "affect educational performance." The consistencies across the above categories that comprise the great majority of students in special education relate largely to deficits in academic ability. Specifically, **the struggle to develop proficiency in reading** is probably one of the most common themes of students with high-incidence (or mild) disabilities. These disabilities are not obvious until students are placed in situations, typically school situations, which illuminate a child's weaknesses. The children in these groups are certainly heterogeneous. They rarely have clearly defined conditions to explain their difficulties and they represent a broad array of unique profiles of individuality. In school, they often appear relatively similar to each other and may represent a substantial overlap in their needs for assistance from special education. For some of these children, their difficulty with behavior or self-control might lead them to be poor readers and academically behind. For others, their difficulty with reading, rapid formal learning, or academic language proficiency might lead them to have problems with motivation and poor behavior. The commonalities among these children lead to a specialization of some special education professionals to intervene as reading interventionists, specialists in behavior management, and learning strategies teachers. Children with high-incidence disabilities have many needs in common from special education including explicit-intensive instruction in highly prioritized academic skills (e.g., reading fluency, written expression, reading comprehension, study skills).

WHY DO SO MANY HIGH-INCIDENCE DISABILITIES IN SCHOOLS SEEM TO BE SUBJECTIVELY DEFINED?

Psychological constructs can be problematic for casual observers, as some symptoms of disorders like ADHD, for example, seem like characteristics we see to some degree in everyone. Everyone has some manifestation of *inattention, hyperactivity, and/or impulsivity*, which can lead the general public to assume that children with ADHD are being "diagnosed" with a disorder that characterizes normal childhood behavior. The discussion of *normal* versus *typical* is important as a basis for further discussion of special education. Many in the field of special education and disability advocacy detest the use of the term *normal* when discussing children with disabilities. Essentially, use of the term normal to describe children's characteristics derives from the medical model of diagnosing illness and the use of terms like "norms," in which children's performance is compared to a cross section of other children who, when averaged together, create a picture of what we would normally expect to see children doing (at a certain point in time, developmental milestone, grade level, etc.). Of course, anyone who has been around very small children knows that they do not always perform every task right at the time that has been predicted. Because a child has not reached every milestone suggested by the pediatrician at one year of age, does not mean the child is not "normal." Often, parents are quick to observe that their child might appear to be ahead in some areas of development, on track in others, and maybe a little slower in others. This reflects the obvious nature of diversity of human characteristics. The term *normal* typically applies judgment of a child's ability being either "right or wrong." The term *typical* is much more accurate, because comparing a child to developmental norms is actually an effort to compare a child to what other children "typically" do by that age, grade level, etc.

At some point, however, a delay in a skill can become so thoroughly divergent from typical development that it appears that a child might have a disorder (or disability). One of the greatest challenges for professionals is to determine the "line" between difficulty or delay with a skill that could be easily remediated and an actual disorder that might require intensive intervention (or that might relate to a life-long attribute). ADHD is often a good example for discussion because it is true that children naturally exhibit varying degrees of inattention, impulsivity, and hyperactivity. Occasionally, terms like ADHD cross over from the psychology literature to the consciousness of the general public and then a full-scale culture debate ensues. The question becomes: *Is ADHD real or a made-up construct of the psychology community?* The pragmatic response is that both can be true to some degree depending on your perspective. All labels or categorizations of human behavior are, to some degree, "made-up," or socially constructed because it is human nature to create semantic labels for various human attributes.

ADHD is a term that was created as a description of behavior among a small number of children who exhibited extreme levels of inattention, hyperactivity, impulsivity, or a combination of the former. In that case, *the condition is clearly "real."* The children are real. The controversy inherent in the discussion relates to how the label should be applied and who really qualifies for this label. Some have argued that the increase in application of the label represents impatience with the naturally erratic behavior of some children. This might be true to some degree—boys are much more likely to receive the label and are typically more active in childhood; boys in the U.S. are the most likely to be prescribed stimulant medication as a treatment. These appear to be indicators of *over-identification*. Over-identification problems, however, do not negate the validity of the construct for some children. There are children who genuinely fit the evaluation criteria based on defined levels of severity or dysfunction in their environment and require intervention to be successful in school and life.

WHY DO SOME SCHOLARS REFER TO SCHOOL DISABILITIES AS "SOCIALLY CONSTRUCTED"?

Two extreme schools of thought come up often in discussions of disability in American public schools:

1. Because disabilities are simply descriptions of inability in certain skills, everyone must have a disability of some kind. These educators see disability everywhere. They use terms like Obsessive Compulsive Disorder (OCD) or Autistic tendencies in everyday conversation applying them to friends and colleagues.

2. Because it is logical to assume incredible genetic variance among children, it is not logical to define differences as disabilities (just differences). These educators see children in special education as victims of the dominance of psychology over school processes (Haberman, 2005) leading us to sort

children into unnecessary categories instead of accepting the natural array of differences. Some in this camp describe disabilities as *socially constructed*.

Point of clarification:

The term *social construction* can be simply defined as the perspective that a construct exists only to the extent that a social group agrees that it exists. Put another way, disabilities exist in schools because we define normal behavior and ability, and define disabilities as contrasts to socially accepted standards of normality.

SUBJECTIVITY IN ACADEMIC DISABILITIES

Skrtic (2004) explains that feelings of ambiguity and subjectivity regarding the complicated nature of special education categorization stem from a lack of a valid theoretical foundation in the field. He suggests the notion of special education disabilities proceeds based on a *confounded theory* that inappropriately integrates statistical and medical theory. The logic of statistics applies no value; data points are simply judged to be closer or further from mean or median values with no attribution of merit to that variance. In contrast, medical/biological theory judges conditions to be either normal/healthy or pathological (implying disease). The integration of these two distinct paradigms results in a statistical model that attributes pathology to characteristics that differ significantly from a mean value (Skrtic, 2005). Particularly questionable is the concept of labeling itself, as it has an effect of stigmatization and has long been viewed as a necessary evil in educational policy (Hardman & Nagle, 2004). Assigning a negative label to a child, indicative of a permanent substandard condition, can hardly represent the best intentions for the life of that child, but it is justified by the presumed consequences of individualized and effective intervention to help the child.

Some argue that the field of special education continues to be plagued by its foundation in a medically oriented perspective on disability that reflects a **deficit-based orientation** (i.e., the deficit model), viewing difference as abnormality rather than a feature of natural human diversity. The desire to designate every difference in human performance as a disorder or dysfunction and the subsequent need to "fix" these dysfunctions is foundational thinking in the medical or "pathological model," and pervasive in the perspectives of many special educators (Skrtic, 2004, p. 82). This philosophical viewpoint is evidenced in the desire of the special education field to create endless labels and semantic categories for discussing individuals—a desire to collapse unique human experiences into larger, more easily discussed categories (e.g., mild disabilities, severe disabilities). Although there is certainly a practical orientation involved in this kind of thinking, it may be problematic that special educators often accept, without any critical reflection, the undeniable accuracy of its labels (Skrtic, 2004).

The theory of **social construction** suggests that the special education process can never be entirely objective. In practice, this perspective suggests that children identified as having learning disabilities, for example, are only disabled to the extent that certain demands are placed upon them. In other words, a child with a learning disability may exhibit characteristic behaviors of a learning disability when asked to independently complete a 5-paragraph essay, but without this requirement he or she may exhibit no clear deficits or impairments. Therefore, the social construction of "essential skills for academic success" *creates* the disability in the child; the disability exists in the child only to the extent that the teacher makes certain demands (Dudley-Marling, 2004). Although this perspective has limited practical significance to teachers—children have no choice but to go to school and engage in academic activities—it does shed some light on the dramatic increase in attention to mild disabilities like SLD, ADHD, language impairment, and mild cognitive disabilities in recent years. As academic demands in our society have increased, more children have been identified for these disorders. Generations earlier, the need for agricultural work, work in factories and mills, and the limited emphasis on high-school graduation meant that schools did not have the level of academic intensity witnessed today.

Skrtic (2005) actually suggests that the categorization of students with learning disabilities represents a "perfect storm in the historical development of public education—the fateful convergence of a dramatic increase in student diversity and the extensive bureaucratization of schools in the first half of the 20th century" (p. 149). He explains that learning disabilities are better described as "organizational pathologies" (Skrtic, 1995, p. 190), in effect suggesting that the disability does not reside within the child but is instead generated by the defective organization of the schools and their inability to predict academic failure and respond to it effectively. Further, Skrtic (1995; 2005) argues that the "machine bureaucracy" structure of schools supported by the supposed efficiency of scientific management does not naturally serve to educate all children, but rather sorts them by ability as would an industrial machine or assembly line. Students whose skills, interests, or motivation conflict with the status quo are simply sorted out of the system. The system they are sorted into is called special education (Skrtic, 1995).

Critics charge that schools operate like factories.

© *Luiz Rocha , 2015. Used under license from Shutterstock, Inc.*

Do all students learn differently? How important are "learning styles" to addressing the needs of students in special education?

Earlier in this chapter, we discussed the idea that disability, to some extent, represents the interaction between the student's abilities and his learning environment. Essentially, he is only disabled to the point that the academic setting demands that he perform certain school-oriented tasks. The subjectivity of this description and the degree of burden it places on schools might encourage some educators to adopt the perspective that "every child learns differently," so there is no logical basis for academic disabilities in special education. The implications of how teachers think about learner diversity are significant as we consider the use of effective instructional strategies. There is no real problem with the statement that "every child learns differently." It is a logical assumption that every child brings different levels of readiness, life experiences, background knowledge, and different profiles of strengths and weaknesses to any given learning situation. In fact, differences in ability among the student population are the basis of special education eligibility. These factors are important for teachers to consider; however, if teachers are guided in their instructional decision-making by an assumption that children in their classrooms are endlessly diverse in the manner in which they learn, the education profession cannot be guided by the extensive, empirical evidence on effective instructional strategies that are broadly useful and positively impact all learners (Heward, 2003; Pashler, McDaniel, Rohrer, & Bjork, 2008).

Learning styles theory is a particularly problematic manifestation of misguided ideas about learner diversity. Learning styles theories promote the idea that effective instruction begins with a formal process of diagnosing a students' dominant learning style and subsequently designing instruction based on that learning style. Teachers are advised to plan lessons while making note of all of the identified learning styles in their classroom. Applied to special education, the assumption would be that students would show enhanced performance if instruction was simply matched to their learning style. The most commonly referenced perspective on *learning styles* suggests that everyone can be identified as a different type of learner based on modalities (e.g., kinesthetic, auditory, visual, and reading/writing learners) serving as a predictor of how they will experience success in the classroom (Fleming & Mills, 1992).

The problem with a concept like *learning styles* premised on the idea that "every child learns differently," is that it does not appear to have much supporting evidence or instructional relevance. A common resulting myth from this theory is that everyone is a particular "type" of learner. Evidence from psychology does not support the idea that students are purely any one kind of learner. We all have preferences for learning and habits for learning that work well for us. In fact, nurturing and developing these personal learning rituals is critical for children to be successful in school. (How successful would you be in high school if you never figured out how you best take notes, organize your homework, study for tests, etc.?) It is intuitive in our observations of our own learning habits that some of us learn well in lectures, while others need to do things that our "hands-on;" however, the notion that teachers must tailor each instructional opportunity to the learner's specific modality for learning is false. There is no empirical evidence to support this idea (Pashler, McDaniel, Rohrer, & Bjork, 2008). In fact, the most important consideration of whether an instructional opportunity should be visual, auditory, or hands-on is probably dependent on the content being taught. In some instances, reading and writing activities are not the best way to teach a concept in math (that benefits from hands-on manipulatives) or science (that benefits from experimentation and observation). For some instructional units, the use of videos and audio (music or recorded interviews) are instructionally appropriate given the content. Reading and writing activities focused on textbook instruction will be challenging for many students, but this is not the case because they are not "reading/writing" learners. They are likely struggling with those skills and need additional support.

Maybe a balanced perspective on the issue of learning styles would be to say that the case for instruction tailored to learning styles has been overstated and is generally unsubstantiated. In essence, the terminology is acceptable to the degree that it reflects a popular wisdom that all students are "individuals" with their own habits and preferences for learning.

A critique of learning style instruction does not negate the idea of differentiating instruction for student needs. Children experiencing reading failure may have increased chances for special education because they have received reading instruction that was (a) not sufficient, (b) not intensive, (c) uninformed by assessment data, and/or (d) not motivating for the child. Differentiated reading instruction that addressed their needs would have been appropriate and might actually prevent further decline in performance. Effective instruction with multiple opportunities for practice and ways of accessing content can be designed to meet the needs of students with multiple learning preferences or specific learning weaknesses, but it simply does not make sense to design an individual lesson for each child's learning style, whether it be visual, auditory, or other. A concerned teacher might attempt to integrate instructional opportunities over time that address a broad array of learner preferences and needs based on clearly relevant factors like reading ability, readiness for the content, sensory disabilities (hearing and vision problems), English language ability, and so on. Some have referred to the attempt to provide the greatest breadth of access to learning experiences by proactively designing for learner diversity as *Universal Design for Learning*. See Chapter 14 for more details on this topic.

WHAT IS INTELLIGENCE AND WHAT DOES IT HAVE TO DO WITH DETERMINATION FOR SPECIAL EDUCATION?

There are numerous unspoken beliefs about IQ scores and what they tell you about human potential. Further, the most significant assumption is that there is such a thing as "intelligence" that can be measured and that IQ scores—typically thought of as a singular, composite score—represent the extent to which someone is intelligent.

> IQ is an abbreviation of Intelligence Quotient. A single numerical representation of overall intelligence, the IQ score is derived from standardized tests of intelligence.

Notably, though, most educators and members of the general public rarely scrutinize the construct of intelligence or even hazard an attempt at a definition. It simply "is what it is." A call for scrutinizing IQ scores may stem most substantially from the extrapolation of IQ score data to broad views about the intelligence of groups of people or the extent to which IQ measures contribute to different educational opportunities and outcomes in school. For example, the categories, Mental Retardation (now referred to as Intellectual or Developmental Disabilities) and Specific Learning Disabilities in special education have traditionally required a school evaluator to obtain IQ scores in order to identify qualification for special education. Special programs for gifted children also rely heavily on IQ scores for identification. A challenge with this process has been the tendency for IQ scores to create pervasive bias in the evaluation processes. Specifically, school psychologists have established for several years that African-American children tend to perform at a lower level (15 points lower) on IQ tests which makes them more likely to qualify for programs for Mental Retardation and less likely to qualify for programs in gifted education (Warner, Dede, Garvan, & Conway, 2002). So embedded in the belief systems of American public school educators is the "sanctity" of IQ scores, that some professionals have even suggested that differences in IQ measures are illustrative of real, genetic, differences in intelligence among different racial groups in the U.S. Of course, most professionals find this proposal quite objectionable and clearly flawed, compelling numerous scholars to take a closer look at intelligence theory and how it contributes to identification for special programs like MR, SLD, giftedness, etc.

Traditional IQ testing researchers suggest that composite intelligence scores (IQ) can be compared and displayed as a normal distribution (see below). This curve suggests that most individuals have IQ scores closer to the middle (i.e., mean/average) score. Those whose scores deviate from the mean score (IQ=100) would be considered unusual (less common) in the population and often assigned labels in accordance with this deviation (e.g., Mental Retardation, Academic Giftedness). The normal distribution is often called a normal curve or bell curve. It is typical to use the normal curve figure to consider the distribution of numerous educational measures, particularly IQ scores.

Table 3.2.

Statistical Terminology in Educational Data
Mean – measure of central tendency; generally referred to as the "average"
Median – measure of central tendency; generally referred to as the middle number
Mode – the most frequently occurring number in a data set
Standard Deviation – the standard deviation represents approximately how much, on the average, each score differs from the group's mean

Figure 3.1. Cutoff of 70 IQ or below is used for eligibility for Intellectual Disability.

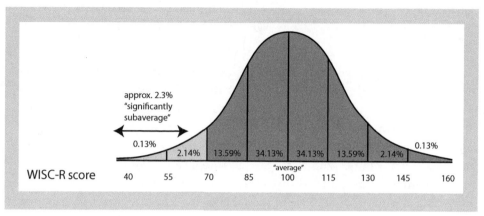

Figure 3.2. Cutoff of 130 IQ or above is used for eligibility for Intellectual Giftedness.

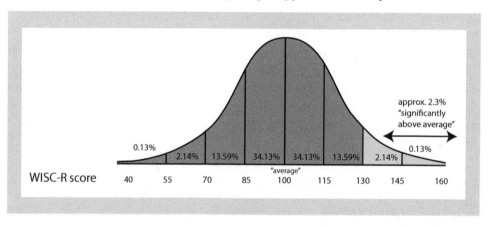

To interpret the normal curve relative to IQ scores, note how the frequency of scores is highest on the y-axis toward the middle of the curve. These scores are closest to the mean. The mean IQ score is typically 100. A score of 100 is also the most likely score that a child would receive in the sense that it is the most common score in the overall population (the **mode**). Further examination of the curve shows that the majority of individuals have IQ scores within one standard deviation of the mean of 100 either below to 85 or above to 115—suggesting that most children you teach in school (about 68%) would have an IQ between 85 and 115. Beyond that, almost all children (about 95%) score within two standard deviations of the mean. Two standard deviations below, IQ of 70, and above, IQ of 130, are actually considered sufficiently extreme in the overall population that they have traditionally been used as "cut points" for exceptionality. Below 70 classifies children for **intellectual disabilities**. Above 130 classifies children for **intellectual giftedness**. Of course, the definitions are more complicated than this, but the scores have traditionally served as a foundation of the eligibility process.

WHAT IS INTELLIGENCE, EXACTLY?

Most school-based discussions of intelligence are quickly extrapolated to assessments of the child's overall potential. The notion of intelligence, though, is largely unexamined and is premised on a conceptualization of intelligence as measured by intelligence testing. Definitions based on testing expertise might be referred to as "Psychometric Definitions of Intelligence," indicating that they are premised on the belief that specialists in psychological evaluation can measure psychological phenomena. In essence, this means that we would define intelligence by discussing how we measure it. This is the common discussion among professionals in schools. Intelligence testing includes certain kinds of items or tasks to evaluate intelligence and the ability of an individual to perform those tasks well, is the indicator of their intelligence. The problem with this discussion is that it leaves out the core phenomenon being evaluated. Instead, it suggests that the test "measures intelligence," so the performance score is intelligence—certainly a bit of logical feedback loop. The notion of intelligence and intelligence testing is so well integrated into our "modern" and psychology-oriented thinking about human characteristics that we rarely, consciously reflect on the idea that intelligence is an idea—a theoretical construct—not a physical "thing" that can be measured in the traditional methods of the natural sciences.

Some psychologists have attempted to define what the core concept of intelligence is. **Spearman** is credited for the psychological construct used in the field of psychology referred to as "g," which roughly represents the idea of a "general intelligence" or a general intelligence factor. Spearman's work proposed that intelligence could be defined as a measured combination of general intelligence factors and "s" factors that represent specific skills that apply to specific and varied tasks that an individual might perform (Crowl, Kaminsky, & Podell, 1997). Notably, Cattel and Horn added to the conceptualization of intelligence as "g" with the notion of two forms of intelligence: crystallized intelligence and fluid intelligence. *Crystallized intelligence* is that which an individual develops through their life experiences by interacting within a cultural context and learning the rules and values of their environment. *Fluid intelligence*, in contrast, is relatively culture-free and is seen to be a representation of an individual's ability to think and reason. The theory resonates with many people's intuitive understanding of intelligence—an intelligent person thinks and reasons out problems well (they are clever), but they also must possess some general knowledge about the world in which they live. A person who could solve complex riddles but did not know who was the president of the United States, would not typically be viewed as very bright. The challenge with ideas like crystallized intelligence is that it is inherently difficult to measure across cultural groups and culture has more levels than we commonly acknowledge. For example, American culture has a multitude of subcultures. Given the peer group, an intelligent person might be able to do well on "Jeopardy," whereas others might have a more practical orientation and know a great deal about the mechanical processes of a 1960s Ford Mustang (including what might go wrong with the engine, etc.).

Gladwell's (2007) article illustrates the last point very well as he shares the story of psychologist Michael Cole and colleagues who visited a traditional African tribe, the Kpelle, in Liberia, to administer a modified version of a test of similarities from a common American IQ test. The tribe members participating in the test of similarities were asked to take certain items and put them into logical categories. Various items were offered with the expectation that they would be sorted into the categories like a basket of food, tools, containers, and clothing. Instead, the Kpelle sorted the items in logical pairings according to how they would be used: a knife was paired with a potato rather than a fork because you need the knife to cut the potato if you want to eat it. According to the test, their pairings were incorrect. After probing from the psychologist, it became apparent that they understood that knives, forks, spoons, etc. were tools or eating utensils and thus could be sorted in that way, but it simply wasn't an intelligent thing to do because it made more sense to sort them functionally.

Observing what he called the "vicious circularity" of intelligence theory that focuses on testing, Sternberg (1985) sought to extend intelligence theory beyond psychometrics and developed a Triarchic Theory of Intelligence, which defines intelligence in three parts: componential, experiential, and contextual. He suggested that intelligence could be described as "mental activity directed toward purposive adaptation to, selection and shaping of, real-world environments relevant to one's life" (p. 45). The **componential aspect** roughly equates to more traditional psychometric theories of intelligence focusing on thinking processes, problem-solving ability, and general analytical intelligence. The theory broadens the perspective on intelligence by including the **experiential aspect**, which he relates to novel experiences and creativity, and the **contextual aspect** which could be summarized as "practical intelligence" that relates to everyday life in one's environment.

In recent years, Howard Gardner's theory of Multiple Intelligences became extremely well publicized and popular despite its significant departure from established theory in the psychology community. Gardner (1983) suggested that there was an inherent flaw in contemporary intelligence theory. Intelligence was too narrowly defined based on the weight that western society and schools place on linguistic and mathematical ability. Essentially, he pointed out that Americans, for example, consider an intelligent person to be someone who knows a lot, has a large vocabulary, does well in math, and generally excels in academic environments. The problem, he noted, was that his observation of human abilities, particularly observation of individuals with rare gifts in music and art, suggest that there are other intelligences that people might have that are undermined by a focus on the narrow definition (as measured by IQ tests). Gardner, in his original theory, offered a list of multiple intelligences including the traditional intelligences like linguistic-verbal and logical-mathematical, but added spatial, musical, bodily-kinesthetic, interpersonal, intrapersonal, and naturalistic intelligences, insisting that these not be viewed as mere "abilities" but instead be viewed with equal weight. Gardner's theory seemed to connect with many education professionals who had observed children identified as very intelligent who seemed quite impaired in many other domains of ability and children deemed to be intellectually limited who appeared to have wondrous abilities in other areas like music or art. In the long-term, Gardner's theory has not substantially impacted the way children are viewed in terms of intelligence or the way school evaluations are conducted. Many schools attempted to apply the theory to instruction, but like *learning styles*, the theory is more conceptual, compelling society to have a broader view of human potential, than it is a directive for instructional design.

CRITIQUE OF IQ AND THE INTELLIGENCE CONSTRUCT

There is no clear consensus on what intelligence is or if it can be quantified—even if there is a testing process that can measure human potential. The testing culture, however, is pervasive in schools and aptitude testing that leads to IQ scores is a major factor in identification of children in special education. Hilliard (2003) states that despite the general wisdom, "present science, technology, and mental measurement are fundamentally incapable of measuring human capacity" (p. 135). Hilliard proposes that intelligence tests should only be viewed as a different form of achievement testing that inevitably favors students who have had a "privileged opportunity to be exposed to those things being measured on the tests" (p. 135). As such, although IQ scores may inform educational professionals about a current state of general ability, the measures reflect achievement based on assumptions of what knowledge and skills are valuable. These measured knowledge and skills may not necessarily reflect general intelligence. In fact, Hilliard suggests that there is still no consensus on the meaning or definition of intelligence as a measurable construct, so extreme caution should be taken when schools integrate the use of intelligence testing into evaluation processes.

The National Research Council of the National Academy of Sciences (Donovan & Cross, 2002 cited in Hilliard, 2003) published a report stating that "no contemporary test author or publisher endorses the notion that IQ tests are direct measures of innate ability. Yet misconceptions that the tests reflect genetically determined, innate ability that is fixed throughout the life span remain prominent with the public, many educators, and some social scientists" (p. 136).

In contrast to the general misconceptions, the authors conclude that intelligence tests are measures of achievement and learning exposure to the point that they are examined. Although they might reflect broad assessments of achievement, they are also substantially rooted in cultural assumptions about mental processes and the nature of intelligence. The authors warn that the tests are not sufficiently effective in measuring school achievement to be used as integral components of the decision-making process for eligibility for special education or gifted programming.

Traditionally, IQ scores have been utilized with confidence (if not as measures of overall innate potential), at least as indicators of the likelihood that an individual would do well in school and likely go on to have success in life after school. Much research does support the idea that IQ correlates strongly with academic achievement (as the previous argument suggests), but even this is insufficient as a measure of children's likelihood to do well in school, overall. The measures have been referred to as "imperfect" and it is notable that many other factors contribute to success in school such as support networks, hard work, and motivation (Crowl, Kaminsky, & Podell, 1997).

HOW DO SCHOOLS ASSESS AND MEASURE STUDENT ABILITY?

Origins of Intelligence Testing

Alfred Binet, for whom the test was named, was called upon by the French government in the early 20th century to develop a testing procedure that would identify those children in need of remedial education. Although Binet did not suggest that the test result, which was expressed as a single score, could serve to summarize a person's overall ability, the testing procedure laid the foundation for intelligence testing. Notably, the assessment outcomes were intended to inform instructional interventions; not to establish a summary evaluation of intellectual ability that would be viewed as a truly measurable and fixed construct. The test was adapted for use in the United States and called the *Stanford-Binet*. The single score for the intelligence test was referred to as the child's "mental age." Binet, however, did not believe that IQ tests could accurately measure intelligence (Binet & Simon, 1905).

Later, the Stanford-Binet scores were computed by calculating the ratio of a student's mental age to their chronological age, then multiplying by 100. Because a ratio of mental and chronological age in which the scores are the same (1:1) results in a ratio of 1, the score multiplied by 100 is 100. Essentially, 100 is the expected score of a child whose mental age is perfectly consistent with their actual age. Scores of less or more than 100 are interpreted as lesser or greater levels of intelligence, 100 being the average score (Crowl, Kaminsky, & Podell, 1997).

The WISC (Wechsler Intelligence Scale for Children)–Fourth Edition (WISC–IV) is arguably the most commonly used intelligence test in schools today. Although there are 15 subtests in the WISC-IV, the standard administration is comprised of 10 individual subtests (See Table 3.3 for a description of the individual subtests). The scoring and analysis of a child's performance on these subtests results in an overall or Full Scale IQ score. In addition, various subtests are combined to provide four composite scores (Verbal Comprehension Index, Perceptual Reasoning Index, Working Memory Index, and Processing Speed Index). The items that constitute the Verbal Comprehension Index require the child to listen to verbally presented questions and produce an oral response. Perceptual Reasoning is the composite index that measures the student's ability to complete visual-motor tasks. Working Memory Index subtests focus on short-term auditory memory skills. The Processing Speed Index determines how quickly and efficiently a student can complete precise pencil/paper tasks within a specified time frame.

Table 3.3.

Subtest	Description	Composite Index Scores
Similarities	Child must identify how 2 words are alike (cat-mouse).	Verbal Comprehension (VCI)
Vocabulary	Child is asked to name a picture or to define a word.	VCI
Comprehension	Child must answer questions measuring general knowledge and social awareness.	VCI
Block Design	Child is asked to reproduce a design using several colored blocks; this is a time subtest.	Perceptual Reasoning Index (PRI)

Picture Concepts	Child is shown 2 or 3 rows of drawings and must choose one drawing from the top row that corresponds to the other row(s).	PRI
Matrix Reasoning	Child is presented with a matrix in which one drawing is missing; must then choose one of five drawings to accurately complete the pattern.	PRI
Digit Span	Child listens to a series of numbers read by the test administrator; the child must initially repeat the numbers in order. The second part of this subtest requires the child to repeat the numbers backwards.	Working Memory Index (WMI)
Letter-Number Sequencing	The test administrator reads a series of letters and numbers; the child must initially repeat the numbers in numerical order and then the letters in alphabetical order.	WMI
Coding	In this timed task, the child is presented with a code consisting of numbers and geometric shapes. Each number corresponds to a shape. The numbers are presented with a blank space under each number; the child must write the appropriate number in as many blank spaces as possible.	Processing Speed Index (PSI)
Symbol Search	In this timed task, the child is shown 1 (for younger children) or 2 symbols; the child must then determine if a symbol appears in a separate row of 3 (for younger children) or 5 symbols.	PSI
Supplementary Subtests	**Description**	**Composite Index Score (if used)**
Picture Completion	The child is presented with an incomplete drawing and asked to identify the missing part within a 20 second period of time.	PRI
Cancellation	Within a 45 second time limit, the child must locate target pictures presented among a number of pictures containing both the target pictures as well as other, non-matching pictures.	PSI
Information	The child is asked a series of general information questions to which s/he must produce a verbal response.	VCI
Arithmetic	A series of arithmetic problems are presented; the child must determine the answer without paper or pencil within 30 seconds.	WMI
Word Reasoning	A series of 1, 2, or 3 "clues" are read to the child. The child must use the clues to identify the target concept.	VCI

Table 3.4.

Testing Terminology (Crowl, Kaminsky, & Podell, 1997)

Norm-Referenced Tests. Tests comparing a student's performance to a representative sample of other children called the "norming sample" that suggest a predicted level of typical performance. Scores reflect comparison to other children such as percentile scores or grade equivalent scores. A child that scores at the 60th percentile scored better than 60% of other students in the norming sample.

Criterion Referenced Tests. Tests that specifically assess a student's ability to meet pre-determined criteria based on instructional objectives that have been expected to be achieved. These tests are relevant for attending to instructional achievements.

Formative Evaluation. A the effectiveness of instruction in producing desired outcomes. Extremely important for teachers to perform in order to modify instruction or provide "just-in-time" interventions.

Diagnostic Evaluation. Typically a broad battery of tests performed by special education professionals, specifically school psychologists, in order to determine special education placement and overall strengths and weaknesses in school performance.

THE INEVITABILITY OF CULTURAL EXPERIENCE IN ASSESSMENTS OF INTELLIGENCE

One of the greatest challenges of intelligence testing has been the issue of potential bias in the testing process or the test itself. Some have denied the likelihood of bias suggesting that intelligence "exists in a vacuum," but extensive evidence suggests there are multiple potentialities for bias in school testing. First, it is well established that children from both low socioeconomic backgrounds and families of minority backgrounds are likely to score lower than groups like White middle class children. This gap in performance has led many critics to conclude that the test items or testing experience favors the cultural experiences of certain groups of children (see Chapter 4 for a detailed analysis of bias in school testing and urban schools). Attempts have been made to make tests as free of culture as possible, but this is an extraordinary challenge as life experiences affect the ways in which we think, our communication styles, and vocabulary we use. Issues have arisen related to language used on tests, so attempts have been made to measure nonverbal intelligence. Other unexpected issues arise such as scorer bias, in which psychologists might be influenced by preconceived notions about students based on their gender, appearance, or race and score some students lower than they would others (Sattler, 1992). These issues may occur in moments of testing in which the individual administering the test has opportunities to make decisions about the acceptability of a response. Another notable issue is the impact of the interpersonal relationship between the student and the individual administering the test. Fuchs & Fuchs (1986) describe the effects of familiarity as relevant to scores, particularly for students of a low SES background. Similarities in class, race, and other factors appear to positively impact scores on these evaluations.

IS GIFTEDNESS PART OF SPECIAL EDUCATION?
HOW IS GIFTEDNESS DEFINED IN SCHOOLS?

A discussion of intelligence logically leads to a discussion of intellectual giftedness. We described earlier that giftedness typically indicates that a child has been regarded as particularly unique (on the positive end of the IQ spectrum) as it relates to our general notions of intelligence. Broader conceptualizations of giftedness include strengths in areas like creativity, music, art, etc.

Gifted students in American public schools are often referred to with language like "exceptional children." In fact, some professionals use the term "exceptional" specifically to reflect the unique qualities of children whose intellectual and creative gifts set them apart from their peers. Ultimately, though, gifted children do not participate in special education, nor do they receive an IEP. Although federal education funding changes over time, generally speaking, the Jacob K. Javits Gifted and Talented Students Education Act provides the funding and public policy foundation for gifted programming. The implementation and definition of gifted education is quite different from special education, as the practices and identification processes differ from state to state based on local decisions and funding sources. Federal guidelines are minimal and funding sources even less predictable than in special education (National Association for Gifted Children, 2010).

HOW ARE STUDENTS IDENTIFIED AS HAVING
INTELLECTUAL GIFTEDNESS?

Again, we must understand how intelligence is defined and evaluated among school-age children to understand how a child might receive "gifted education" in school. The Federal definition from the Elementary and Secondary Education Act, states that gifted students are those

> Students, children, or youth who give evidence of high achievement capability in areas such as intellectual, creative, artistic, or leadership capacity, or in specific academic fields, and who need services and activities not ordinarily provided by the school in order to fully develop those capabilities.

The National Association for Gifted Children suggests that is difficult to estimate the number of children who are gifted in U.S. K-12 public schools because there is not an official requirement to maintain statistics in the manner that it occurs in special education. The estimate, though, is approximately 3 million children.

Most estimates and definitions of giftedness emphasize intelligence as measured by an IQ score. A high IQ score is typically prerequisite for receiving special gifted services in schools, although there are broader models that include characteristics such as talent and creativity in non-academic areas.

The National Association for Gifted Children uses the educational term **differentiation** to describe the most effective opportunity to address the unique learning needs of gifted students. Clarifying the need for students who are gifted to receive specialized instructional opportunities, the NAGC emphasizes the need to modify instruction in accordance with students' unique intellectual and/or creative gifts, ultimately avoiding the tendency for gifted children to feel a lack of challenge and general tedium in school (a common experience for gifted children). Effective instruction centered on differentiation includes opportunities for **accelerated instruction**, more **intensive study** in selected subject matter, learning **challenging content** with greater complexities, and greater variety of instructional and curricular opportunities. The greatest criticisms of poor quality differentiation for gifted children focus on teachers that simply give more work (at the same level of challenge) when students finish early. Table 3.5 describes what Frasier et al. (1995) describe as core attributes of giftedness that describe not only how gifted children vary from the typical population, but why standardized instruction is often insufficiently motivating.

Table 3.5.

General Descriptions of the 10 Core Attributes of Giftedness	
Motivation	Evidence of desire to learn
Communication skills	Highly expressive and effective use of words, numbers, symbols, etc.
Interest	Intense (sometimes unusual) interests
Problem-solving ability	Effective (often inventive) strategies for recognizing and solving problems
Imagination/Creativity	Produces many ideas; highly original
Memory	Large storehouse of information on school or non-school topics; exceptional ability to retain and retrieve information
Inquiry	Questions, experiments, explores method or process of seeking knowledge, understanding, or information
Insight	Quickly grasps new concepts and makes connections; senses deeper meanings
Reasoning	Logical approaches to figuring out solutions
Humor	Conveys and picks up on humor well

Adapted from Frasier, M. M., Hunsaker, S. L., Lee, J., Mitchell, S., Cramond, B., Krisel, S., García, J. H., Martin, D., Frank, E., & Finley, V. S. (1995).

One of the greatest criticisms of the extension of intelligence theories and intelligence testing to the creation of the giftedness construct relates to the likelihood of bias and under-identification for children from low SES and minority backgrounds. This is based on the many pitfalls of psychological processes and social dynamics. The National Research Center on the Gifted and Talented identifies several challenges that limit the likelihood of more equitable identification practices in gifted education for students who are from low SES backgrounds, minority backgrounds, or are English Language Learners (ELLs). Some notable challenges include

1. Standardized test bias
2. Diverse indicators of giftedness among different cultural groups
3. Divergent use of standardized English (e.g., limitations of academic language proficiency among ELL students and use of subcultural language like Ebonics), and
4. Expectations bias toward subcultural groups assumed to be disadvantaged

(Frasier, M. M., Hunsaker, S. L., Lee, J., Finley, V. S., Frank, E., García, J. H., & Martin, D., 1995).

WHAT DOES IT MEAN TO BE "AT-RISK" AND HOW DOES THAT DIFFER FROM BEING IN SPECIAL EDUCATION?

An important observation to make about the majority of children in special education is the considerable similarity in what is an otherwise heterogeneous population of children. What do most students in special education have in common? They have extreme difficulty in school and are **at-risk** for both school failure and school dropout. These risks are due to problems with academic skills—those skills which make children successful in a school setting. Many people who become teachers have tremendous strengths in these "school" skills. What are they?

- Reading fluency – the ability to decode new words and breeze through text to make meaning
- Reading comprehension – the ability to grasp the "big picture" ideas conveyed in text, make inferences, and generally grasp the nuanced, high-level meaning of text
- Written expression – the ability to clearly and accurately express complete thoughts in writing
- Oral expression – the ability to clearly express ideas verbally in a manner that is organized and meaningful to an audience
- Social skills – a set of abilities that relate to functioning in social groups by appropriately using language, *proxemics*, and other "hidden curriculum" concepts like on-task behavior, respect for authority, etc.

The definition of disability is somewhat different in school than it is in general life and that is important to understand in a teaching situation. Generally speaking, the children who comprise the great majority of children in special education require a greater intensity of instruction with a greater breadth of skills, in order to be successful in school. Another group that struggles in school is the population identified as *at-risk*. At-risk students could be easily defined as those students who are likely to do poorly on standardized tests and have a higher-than-typical risk of dropping out of school. Of course, the era of high-stakes testing has put even greater emphasis on student performance on standardized tests and accordingly schools assess a large number of students as "low-performing," with little regard for the statistical likelihood of distribution of performance across each age-group of children. Of course, due to the weight of standardized tests, at-risk students might also be those students who are likely to be retained in school and often repeat grades, particularly in elementary school. Alternatively described as "low achievers" in school, there is a substantial population of students in school who experience challenges very similar to those placed in special education, but who may not fit the evaluation criteria. Considerable debate has occurred over this "marginal" population. Some would argue that they have been spared the labeling and separation of special education. Others would argue, particularly in schools that have high-quality special education programs, that these children have been left in "limbo" with insufficient support systems to overcome their school challenges.

Unlike students with learning disabilities whose challenges in school typically stem from deficits in specific learning domains like reading, low achieving or at-risk populations often experience difficulty across the curriculum due to myriad challenges that inhibit their school performance. For some students, poor performance could derive from problems at home including a family environment that does not promote school performance as a value or undermines school performance, a lack of motivation due to a poor track record of school performance, or perhaps a pattern of school absence or transiency that has led to inadvertent gaps in the student's skills over time (Crowl, Kaminsky, & Podell, 1997).

Numerous factors have been examined that relate to disadvantage in the school experience (National Center for Education Statistics, 1992).

The most notable risk factors include:
- Low-socioeconomic background/status
- Background of minority cultural/racial group
- Lack of parental involvement in schooling

The National Center for Education Statistics (1992) suggests that an at-risk child is "generally defined as a student who is likely to fail at school" (p. 2). It is quite difficult to separate that description from the majority of children identified with high-incidence disabilities. Perhaps the root cause is the most significant source of the differences in labels and processes for intervention, but ultimately there appears to be considerable overlap among the needs of students with high-incidence disabilities and those students deemed to be at-risk.

It might appear challenging to differentiate between those students who are at-risk or disadvantaged in school and those who are placed in special education. In either case, the focus should not be on the label we choose, but on the *school's ability to intervene for these children with effective instruction and support services*. Often, students identified as "at-risk" are overlooked by schools and represent a large proportion of children who drop out of school, particularly in high-poverty communities. One cannot help but examine the extent to which there are meaningful differences between at-risk populations and the large population of students with "high-incidence disabilities" in schools. Presumably, the special education system provides a level of advocacy and intervention for children in special education, so what qualifies these children for special attention while other students who are "at-risk" remain in the mainstream population? Typically, for each area of disability, there are specific and detailed observational and evaluative processes used to "qualify" children for special education services. For example, placement in the category of Specific Learning Disability has traditionally required that a school psychologist administer an intelligence test and an achievement test. If there is a "significant discrepancy" between the student's ability in a certain area of achievement and his overall intelligence, a specific learning disability has been "detected." A problem, however, with this conceptualization of a specific learning disability is that school psychologists generally acknowledge that the main criteria for placement in the SLD category is *poor academic performance*. Specifically, 80-90% of children in the category of specific learning disability are placed on the basis of a history of reading failure (Lerner, 1989). Some have suggested that specific skill weaknesses like difficulty with **phonemic awareness** can be directly linked to deficits in the school's reading curriculum and subsequent failure in reading by some subgroups of children in school (who later get placed in special education).

Some authors have suggested there are few substantial differences between students identified as SLD and students who could be described as low achieving or at-risk in school (Algozzine & Ysseldyke, 1983). Although it is a very controversial perspective, Spear-Swearling and Sternberg (1996) note that making a distinction between a student who struggles with reading and a student with a **"reading disability"** involves acceptance of a set of "erroneous, potentially damaging assumptions that are embedded in the concept of reading disability," ultimately diminishing the student's potential for academic success (p. 1). In that vein, numerous authors call for prevention strategies in reading performance based on the anticipation of reading failure among a large number of students. Again, there becomes an emerging logic to the examination of trends among low achievers, at-risk students, and students with high-incidence disabilities relevant to instructional practices and the ubiquity of need for certain interventions for problems in areas such as reading, writing, math computation, study skills, and social skills.

SPECIAL EDUCATION AS AN INTERVENTION THAT IMPROVES ACADEMIC PROGRESS

Notably, the efforts made to address the needs of at-risk and low achieving students are often very similar to what would be typically defined as special education services. Students at-risk often benefit from strategically implemented ***direct instruction reading programs***, courses in ***learning strategies*** that teach *study skills, reading and other strategies* in balance with a model of advocacy that promotes a positive affect toward schooling. Crowl, Kaminsky, and Podell (1997) articulate the "expectations" argument associated with students at-risk for school failure: "If you do not expect low achievers to learn, they may fall into the trap of a **self-fulfilling prophecy**."

One of the strongest commonalities among students at-risk and students with high-incidence disabilities is poor performance in reading and basic skills in elementary school. Increasingly, public policy and school decision-making has sought to proactively address these common challenges. As mentioned in the previous chapter, the Response to Intervention Model is one of the major methods of addressing the predictable struggle to develop reading proficiency among so many school-age children. Much of the attention to contemporary models of assessment and intervention like RTI, stem from concern over **the performance gap in reading** (see Figure 3.3).

School professionals and school leaders commonly refer to challenges in schools using terms like performance gap, literacy crisis, or achievement gap. Often, the term *achievement gap* is used to refer to the gap in school performance between privileged student populations (e.g. White middle class children from suburban communities) and students from high-needs communities and culturally, linguistically diverse backgrounds (more on this in Chapter 4). There is also a significant *performance gap* between students with "mild" disabilities (and at-risk students) and their non-disabled peers. The performance gap indicates that students who have disabilities or extreme difficulties based on limitations in reading (e.g., students with Specific Learning Disability) come to school with limited readiness and basic skills, which initially accounts for small, but significant delays in academic performance. Students who struggle at the early levels in school, particularly with "learning to read," are likely to fall further behind their peers as they transition to "reading to learn" (Deshler, 2004). In essence, early deficits in basic skills like decoding skills, can result in adolescents who fall substantially behind their grade-level peers. Early limitations in literacy act as an ongoing barrier to learning content in middle and high school. The term *Matthew effects* is sometimes used to refer to the long-term impact of early reading failure. The term, a reference to the biblical gospel of Matthew, implies that the rich get richer while the poor get poorer. Applied to poor readers in elementary school, who proceed without proper remediation of difficulties, we observe that poor reading predicts academic weaknesses in related areas. Students are likely to have limited vocabulary and overall language development along with difficulty in developing higher-level content knowledge due to their lack of ability to access information from print (Siegel, 1999; Stanovich, 1986). Ultimately, deficiencies in reading can predict an overall inhibited opportunity to become educated and prepared for life after school, making early intervention a critical consideration.

Later chapters in this text will elaborate on how RTI models can be used to assess student progress and intervene appropriately to prevent the expansion of the performance gap for students with significant reading problems (see Chapter 14) and how effective instruction centered on adolescent literacy needs may mean that it is never too late for students to close the gap (see Chapter 6).

Figure 3.3. Common Representation of the Performance Gap for Students with High-Incidence Disabilities Typically Resulting from Early Reading Failure

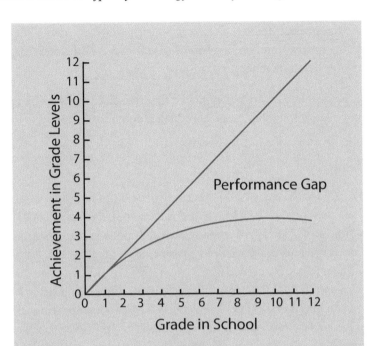

GLOSSARY IN PLAIN TERMS

Intelligence theories: Varying definitions of what it means to be functional in school and life; or what it means to be "smart," typically related to some idea of how the brain functions.

Giftedness: The idea of advanced intellectual ability or exceptional abilities in certain skills; often based on IQ scores that are 2 standard deviations above the average.

Normal curve: Representation of the distribution of human characteristics (including IQ) best known as a "bell curve."

IQ testing: A formalized practice in which a trained evaluator asks questions and provides prompts suggested to measure language development, thinking skills, and general knowledge.

Reading disability: Extreme deficits in the basic skills that support reading development including phonological processing skills.

Phonemic awareness: Related to the ability to recognize the sounds represented by alphabetic letters and manipulate the sound structure of language.

ADHD: Substantial and chronic challenges with inattention, hyperactivity, and impulsivity.

Intellectual disability: Substantial limitations in cognitive development translating to difficulty performing intellectual or academic tasks.

Multiple intelligences: Intelligence theory that suggests a broader set of human abilities which comprise intelligence (not limited to the traditional academically-oriented measures of intelligence).

At-risk: A term used in educational policy to describe children who are likely to fail in school due to various challenges and/or difficult circumstances.

REFERENCES

Algozzine, B., & Ysseldyke, J. (1983). Learning disabilities as a subset of school failure: The oversophistication of a concept. *Exceptional Children*, 50(3), 242-246.

Binet, A., & Simon, T. (1905). Methodes nouvelles pour le diagnostique du niveau intellectuel des anormaux. *L'annee psychologique*, 11, 245-336.

Crowl, T. K., Kaminsky, S., & Podell, D. M. (1997). *Educational psychology: Windows on teaching*. Dubuque, IA: Times Mirror Higher Education Group, Inc.

Deshler, D.D., Schumaker, J.B., & Woodruff, S.K. (2004). Improving literacy skills of at-risk adolescents: A schoolwide response. In D.S. Strickland & D.E. Alvermann (Eds.), *Bridging the literacy achievement gap grades 4-12* (pp. 86-104). New York: Teachers College Press.

Dudley-Marling, C. (2004). The social construction of learning disabilities. *Journal of Learning Disabilities*, 37(6), 482-489.

Fleming, N. D., & Mills, C. (1992). VARK a guide to learning styles. Retrieved October 11, 2005, from http://www.vark-learn.com/English/index.asp.

Frasier, M. M., Hunsaker, S. L., Lee, J., Mitchell, S., Cramond, B., Krisel, S., García, J. H., Martin, D., Frank, E., & Finley, V. S. (1995). *Core attributes of giftedness: A foundation for recognizing the gifted potential of economically disadvantaged students* (RM95210). Storrs, CT: The National Research Center on the Gifted and Talented, University of Connecticut.

Frasier, M. M., Hunsaker, S. L., Lee, J., Finley, V. S., Frank, E., García, J. H., & Martin, D. (1995). *Educator's perceptions of barriers to the identification of gifted children from economically disadvantaged and limited English proficient backgrounds* (RM95216). Storrs, CT: The National Research Center on the Gifted and Talented, University of Connecticut.

Fuchs, D., & Fuchs, L.S. (1986). Test procedure bias: A meta-analysis of examiner familiarity effects. *Review of Educational Research*, 56, 243-262.

Gardner, H. (1983). *Frames of mind: The theory of multiple intelligences*. New York: Basic Books.

Gladwell, M. (2007, December). None of the above: What I.Q. doesn't tell you about race. *The New Yorker*. Retrieved from www.newyorker.com.

Hardman, M. L., & Nagle, K. (2004). Public policy: From access to accountability in special education. In A. M. Sorrells, H. J. Rieth & P. T. Sindelar (Eds.), *Critical issues in special education: Access, diversity, and accountability*. (pp. 277-292). Boston: Pearson.

Heward, W. L. (2003). Ten faulty notions about teaching and learning that hinder the effectiveness of special education. *Journal of Special Education, 36*(4), 186-205.

Hilliard, A. G. (2003). No mystery: Closing the achievement gap between africans and excellence. In T. Perry, C. Steele & A. Hilliard (Eds.), *Young, gifted, and black: Promoting high achievement among African-American students.* Boston, MA.: Beacon Press.

Lerner, J. (1989). Educational intervention in learning disabilities. *Journal of the American Academy of Child and Adolescent Psychiatry, 28*, 326-331.

National Association for Gifted Children. (2010). *What is gifted?* Retrieved from http://www.nagc.org.

National Association for Gifted Children. (2010). Differentiation of Curriculum and Instruction. Retrieved from http://www.nagc.org.

Owings, J. (1992). *National Education Longitudinal Study of 1988: Characteristics of At-risk Students in NELS: 88.* National Center for Education Statistics: Washington, D.C.

Pashler, H., McDaniel, M., Rohrer, D., & Bjork, R. (2008). Learning styles: Concepts and evidence. *Psychological Science in the Public Interest, 9*(3), 105-119.

Sattler, J.M. (1992). *Assessment of children (3ʳᵈ ed.).* San Diego: Jerome M. Sattler.

Siegel, L. S. (1999). Learning disabilities: The roads we have traveled and the path to the future. In R. J. Sternberg & L. Spear-Swerling (Eds.), *Perspectives on learning disabilities: Biological, cognitive, contextual.* Boulder, CO: Westview Press.

Skrtic, T. (1995). *Disability and democracy: Reconstructing (special education for post-modernity).* New York: Teachers College Press.

Skrtic, T. M. (2004). The crisis in special education knowledge: A perspective on perspective. In S. Danforth & S. D. Taff (Eds.), *Crucial readings in special education* (pp. 80-95). Upper Saddle River, New Jersey: Pearson.

Skrtic, T. M. (2005). A political economy of learning disabilities. *Learning Disability Quarterly, 28*(2), 149.

Soodak, L. C., & Podell, D. M. (1994). Teachers' thinking about difficult-to-teach students. *Journal of Educational Research, 88*, 44-51.

Spear-Swerling, L., & Sternberg, R. J. (1996). *Off-track: When poor readers become "Learning disabled".* Boulder, CO: Westview Press.

Stanovich, K. (1986). Matthew effects in reading: Some consequences of individual differences in the acquisition of literacy. *Reading Research Quarterly, 21*, 360-407.

Sternberg, R. J. (1985). *Beyond IQ: A Triarchic Theory of Intelligence.* Cambridge: Cambridge University Press.

Warner, T. D., Dede, D. E., Garvan, C. W., & Conway, T. W. (2002). One size still does not fit all in specific learning disability assessment across ethnic groups. *Journal of Learning Disabilities, 35*(6), 500-508.

QUESTIONS *for Reflection:*

How are disability and exceptionality defined in schools (as opposed to society in general)?

How do concepts like "learning styles" and multiple intelligences inform or misinform instructional design?

In your own words, what is intelligence and how is it assessed in schools?

How do students who are gifted fit within the paradigm of exceptional children?

What does it mean to be "at-risk" and how does that differ from being in special education?

NOTES

CHAPTER 4

Providing Special Education Supports in Urban Schools: High-Needs Communities and Culturally, Linguistically Diverse Students

Shaqwana Freeman, Chris O'Brien, Lan Kolano, and Theresa Perez

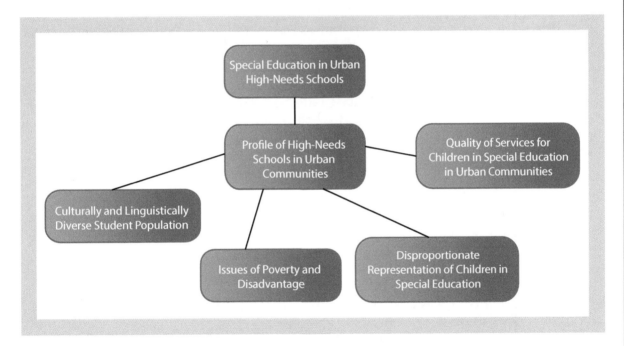

THE TOP TEN TERMS FOR CHAPTER 4:

The following key terms or big ideas are critical to your understanding of the content for chapter 4 and the in-class discussions to follow.

• Disproportionality	• Culturally and linguistically diverse
• ELLs	• Cultural incongruity
• Achievement gap	• Assessment bias
• Socioeconomic status	• Early intervention
• Deficit model	• Title I

Chapter 4 offers a unique perspective on special education services that you would rarely find in an introductory text of this nature. The purpose of this chapter is to provide a final piece of background knowledge related to the school context or the realities of special education in *actual* schools. Specifically, because an assumption of this text is that a large number of students preparing to be teachers will be desperately needed in the schools of large, urban centers, and many of these future educators have only a preliminary understanding of the nature of high-needs, urban schools (Haberman, 2005), a more in-depth analysis of the context is beneficial. There are a few reasons that this chapter is significant for advancing the understanding of future educators:

- Urban schools in high-poverty communities with diverse student populations have the highest rates of identification of children for special education.
- Students of culturally, linguistically diverse backgrounds are disproportionately represented in special education; meaning some CLD students are over-identified as having language and behavior disabilities and some under-identified as being gifted.
- Critics of special education in urban schools suggest that urban students are victims of low expectations and cultural incongruity based on the contrasts between student demographics and teacher demographics.
- Critics of special education in urban schools suggest that problems with limited district resources and persistent teacher shortages undermine the likelihood that special education will offer students genuine opportunities for improvement (i.e., labeling is justified on the basis of intervention, but schools may label without the ability to meaningfully intervene).

The remainder of this chapter will address the contextual issues of teaching in urban schools in high-needs communities with culturally, linguistically diverse students, the barriers that persist for improving student outcomes, and the need to focus efforts on helping students in the most challenging circumstances to fully actualize their considerable potential.

The Context of High-Needs Urban Schools

In his well-known work *Savage Inequalities*, urban schools activist, Jonathan Kozol describes his earliest teaching experiences in Roxbury, a neighborhood of Boston, Massachusetts, that served as the foundation for a life of advocacy for children in high-needs, urban schools across the United States. His classroom in 1964 was racially segregated, overcrowded, and comprised exclusively of children from the lowest socioeconomic strata of the city. He explains that as a new teacher in the school, he did not even have a classroom for his students. His 35 4th grade students were already approximately 2 grade levels behind in their reading abilities. Prior to his arrival, the children had yet to have a regular classroom teacher; instead they were taught by a series of substitute teachers. These are *hardly the conditions that one would imagine in order to actualize all of the lofty ideals of effective and equitable instruction that we have discussed so far.* We cannot assess student progress, intervene for student difficulties, differentiate and/or individualize instruction for a diverse population of children, when they don't even have a permanent teacher.

Often, educators lament the era of poor-quality urban schools that existed during Kozol's time as a teacher when schools were so severely segregated by race and socioeconomic status. It would be a mistake, however, to assume that the example of his classroom is simply a memory of a troubled time in the history of American schooling. In urban, high-poverty communities across the United States, including large urban centers (e.g., Chicago, Los Angeles, New York, Philadelphia, Washington, D.C., Milwaukee), scholars and observers like Kozol have observed the continuation of trends that leave schools in high-needs urban communities to have disproportionately limited resources, fewer qualified teachers, and school populations that are sometimes more segregated by race, culture, language, and level of income than they were during the civil rights movement (Haberman, 2005; Kozol, 1991; Kozol, 2005).

It might be important to consider the actual resources and contextual factors that exist for children in urban community schools. As noted previously, students in high-needs communities enter school having already experienced a less privileged existence than their middle class counterparts, but rather than the egalitarian system that so many Americans envision to "equalize the playing field," students in urban schools often enter the classroom that Kozol described from his early years in Boston in the 1960s. Haberman (2005), a noted scholar of urban education, describes the classrooms of challenged schools in the Milwaukee school district, characterized by high poverty rates and an extreme level of racial isolation, as follows:

- Class sizes over 30
- Limited availability of quality curriculum or even basic content materials
- Insufficient resources like dictionaries or paper, pencils, chalk, etc.
- Computers that lack Internet access
- No funds for teacher supplies

Ultimately, the difficult conditions of urban schools and the challenging circumstances of their students lead to observations of gaps in academic performance when compared to peers in other more "privileged" schools (e.g. middle class, suburban communities). Numerous explanations have been offered over the years to explain why it appears that children from high-needs urban communities tend to lag behind. Well-known works by authors such as Jonathon Kozol (1991) and Ruby Payne (2005), among many others, have described numerous contextual factors of high-poverty, urban communities that inevitably create barriers for children to actualize their full potential.

Some challenges noted include:

- A culture of poverty that is sufficiently distinct from school culture and requires children to learn "middle class" school culture (suggested by Payne).
- Use of subcultural language such as Ebonics that require children to "code switch" in order to acclimate to academic language use in school.
- Family contextual barriers including homes in which there might be insufficient resources available for children to learn at the rate of peers.

- Environmental contaminants that contribute to high rates of childhood health problems, particularly more severe cases of asthma that occur due to concentration of undesirable industries (e.g., chemical plants, waste incineration facilities) in low-income communities.
- Community blight that can contribute to unhealthy psychological exposure to high rates of violent crime, prostitution, and abuse of drugs and alcohol (see Kozol's 1991 description of East St. Louis for case example).
- High rate of children born to young, single mothers who may have insufficient support networks or maturity for parenting. This is also referred to as the *cycle of poverty* in which children are likely to repeat the same difficult circumstances of their families with few resources or opportunities for improvement.

AVOIDING THE DEFICIT MODEL IN URBAN EDUCATION

Ruby Payne's 2005 work, *A Framework for Understanding Poverty*, has been identified as both an excellent resource for expanding the contemporary teacher's ability to understand the unique needs of students in high-poverty communities and attacked as perpetuation of the **"Deficit Model"** approach to urban schooling (Kunjufu, 2006). In a "deficit model" orientation, educators focus on excuses for the low performance of students in challenged schools instead of *raising expectations* and focusing on variables of quality teaching.

> *Deficit model* – common approach in schools in which teachers and evaluators seek to blame poor school performance on the child or the child's circumstances; leads to lowered expectations and fails to seek out assets that children bring with them to school that might offset barriers.

Payne's text is a guidebook for thousands of educators in urban schools, as it claims to help teachers understand the lives and unique challenges of children who live in a "culture of poverty" that emphasizes *immediacy of needs* and may undermine the value of educational experiences. The framework compares the shared values of individuals living in poverty versus those who are middle class or wealthy and seeks to clarify how differences in family life and value systems may account for poor performance in school. From this premise, teachers would be able to identify barriers of poverty and help students overcome them by developing the assets valued most in middle class, school culture. The counterpoint to the "framework for understanding poverty" is that teachers are most likely to see the "culture of poverty" as a rationalization for low performance of their urban students in a manner that undermines what the children truly need—effective, intensive, rigorous education from highly skilled teachers (Kunjufu, 2006).

Many urban educators view most of the previously mentioned social challenges as "double-edged" swords. On one hand, the arguments seek to explain why otherwise bright, capable children tend to lag behind their own potential in school, but they also perpetuate negative stereotypes about urban schools. Many future educators, rather than being inspired to teach children who need great teachers, tend to look at such barriers as a rationale for why they won't teach in urban schools. Also, despite facts to support the existence and relevance of previously mentioned challenges, inordinate focus on these barriers promotes a persistent problem of lowered expectations for children in urban communities.

Although we would all like to see social problems in high-needs, urban communities solved, they are unfortunately out of the control of schools and teachers. An optimistic outlook is to examine barriers that exist for children in high needs communities teaching children coping skills and strategies for overcoming their more difficult circumstances. Ultimately, though, students are most likely to benefit from teachers holding ***high expectations*** for the children in their classes in a manner that dismisses the tendency to use these barriers as excuses for failure. Although teachers will ultimately have to view their students as products of their life experiences, that should never lead to a preconceived notion of potential outcomes.

CHILDREN FROM CULTURALLY, LINGUISTICALLY DIVERSE BACKGROUNDS

Cultural and linguistic diversity is certainly not unique to urban schools, but it would be unrealistic to examine the context of urban schools without a closer examination of the unique demographics in urban communities. Within urban and other demographic landscapes, **English Language Learners** (ELLs) with diverse racial, cultural, and linguistic backgrounds have historically impacted schools and continue to challenge educators across the U.S. Current demographics show that the Hispanic student population has grown to over *4.5 million*, as reported in the 2000 U.S. census. Wainer (2004) reports large urban communities in states like North Carolina, have the fastest growing immigrant populations in the nation. Unlike the six states that have been historically identified as primary destination points (i.e., CA, NY, TX, FL, IL, NJ), these new growth areas in the Southeast, are populated by newcomers; with a majority of immigrants who have arrived mostly since 1995 (Fix & Passel, 2003). For children of immigration, school remains the primary site for the development and acquisition of English. In North Carolina and other new growth areas, where the increase of Latinos and Asians has begun to dramatically change the racial composition of the classroom, the need to understand how to work with them becomes even more important. With support from the literature, we know that a teacher's ability to successfully meet the needs of students who are ethnically, culturally, and linguistically diverse is dependent upon their attitudes and prior experiences with diverse cultures and the quality of teacher education training. However, much data reports that ELLs often enter schools and classrooms with teachers who feel underprepared to meet their complex needs (Waxman, Tellez, & Walberg, 2004).

As frustration mounts, classroom instruction is ultimately impacted. Recent research shows that much of the ELL population typically receives ineffective and often inappropriate classroom instruction, particularly in reading and writing. When students struggle to complete fundamental classroom assignments, teachers and administrators look to alternative placements for students who struggle. English language learners are often not placed in appropriate environments where they can participate to their fullest potential and have a challenging academic experience. One of the most challenging issues for a mainstream classroom teacher is to successfully differentiate emergent second language development from learning problems, particularly if the child has good communicative competence but struggles in reading and writing (Klingner & Artiles, 2006). Thus, at minimum, teachers need to understand second language acquisition in order to properly consider the learning needs of their students. Teachers may have students who can communicate effectively with a teacher but cannot read a passage and answer basic reading comprehension questions. Without an understanding of the basic process of second language acquisition and development, a teacher can mistakenly underestimate the child's potential or even make an inappropriate referral for special education services.

Second Language Acquisition

It is important for all educators to understand the following basic tenets of second language development as they observe and assess ELLs in their individual classrooms. First, teachers need to know that language development is not random. It progresses along a continuum over several stages. Just as children cannot jump from emergent readers to fully comprehending a novel, ELLs cannot transition from learning basic vocabulary to completing an End-of-Grade or End-of-Year assessment at the same level as their native English speaking peers. Although there is variation among learners, the acquisition of language occurs rather systematically. Second, there is a distinction between acquiring and learning language. According to Stephen Krashen (1982) as part of his *Monitor Theory*, **acquisition** of a language is a natural process; whereas **learning** a language is a conscious process. Third, there are five basic stages of second language (L2) development: **Pre-production, Early Production, Speech Emergence, Intermediate Fluency,** and **Advanced Fluency**. While there is great variation in the amount of time children spend at each stage, all students will move through these stages as they learn English. Fourth, knowledge of a first language supports L2 development. Students who are functionally literate (those who can read and write with fluency and proficiency) in their native languages will learn English more quickly and with more ease. The preservation of native languages is critical in learning and should be used to support the development of academic English development (Gutierrez-Clellen, 1999; Cummins, 1991, 2001; Nguyen, Shin, & Krashen, 2001).

Finally, there is a clear distinction between conversational and academic language. Understanding this distinction is critical for educators across the K-12 context. According to Cummins (1981), second language learners develop *basic interpersonal communication skills* **(BICS)** before they acquire *cognitive academic language proficiency* **(CALP)**. Cummins asserts that students develop phonological skills and basic communicative fluency before literacy and vocabulary knowledge is fully developed. The time it takes to develop academic language varies, but research shows that while students acquire BICS between 2-3 years, CALP or *academic language* requires much more time. Students need between 5-7, and sometimes 10 years to fully develop their academic language proficiency.

This delay in development of academic language proficiency is a factor in determining if a student has learning problems and certainly complicates matters. Of course, there are certainly instances in which a student who is developing second language proficiency will also demonstrate a need for special education. In this instance, Artiles & Ortiz (2002) emphasize the following for teachers who work with ELLs with special needs:

- Instruction works best for ELLs when the activities they engage in build on their home languages and affirm their cultural backgrounds.
- ELLs can learn within classroom contexts with native English speakers who are good models, there is rich language input and opportunities for output, there are multiple forms of literacy practices and print materials.
- ELLs must be exposed to a variety of instructional strategies (interactive activities, Socratic methods, and direct teaching) and organizational structures that include opportunities for group work and individual instruction when possible.

It is when students' linguistic resources are considered in the learning process and their cultural backgrounds are affirmed, that instructional strategies and other classroom interventions prove to be most successful.

TITLE I INTERVENTIONS FOR DISADVANTAGED STUDENTS

Our discussions in the text so far have focused on the manner in which academic failure leads to a high likelihood of special education referral and ultimately, a specialized process of support and intervention by special education professionals. By no means, however, is special education the only process for schools to address the needs of students who struggle in school. As discussed previously, students who are considered "at-risk" or "disadvantaged" often become eligible for special support to enhance their educational opportunities. Interventions for students in schools in "disadvantaged communities" across the nation are supported at the federal level by *Title I of the Elementary and Secondary Education*. **Title I** funds are a substantial source of support for high-needs schools across the nation who might not otherwise have sufficient resources to address the breadth and intensity of their students' needs. Title I initiatives (Improving the Academic Achievement of the Disadvantaged) includes the following statement of purpose:

> *The purpose of this title is to ensure that all children have a fair, equal, and significant opportunity to obtain a high-quality education and reach, at a minimum, proficiency on challenging state academic achievement standards and state academic assessments* (20 U.S.C. 6301 et seq. SEC 1001).

Although there are a considerable and lofty set of goals associated with Title I, the general understanding is that the federal initiative *addresses the educational needs of students demonstrating poor academic progress in high-poverty schools.* Most notably, the Title I initiatives are intended to meet the needs of students experiencing negative environmental effects of high-poverty and under-resourced communities, students who have limited English proficiency, migrant status, and/or fit the general profile of at-risk. Another well known goal of Title I funding and interventions is to address the ***achievement gap*** between minority and non-minority students and similarly between students of different social strata. Essentially, long-standing gaps in academic performance have been observed between two theoretical sets of students: (a) culturally linguistically diverse students in low SES communities and (b) students in predominately White-European middle and upper SES communities. According to the report on the *National Assessment of Title I*, the number of participants in Title I programs across the nation has increased dramatically to approximately 20 million students in 2004-05. Title I programming is extensive in U.S. schools with 56% of schools receiving funds. The great majority of students receiving Title I program supports and interventions are minority students (African-American children are the largest subgroup), typically in the early grades. Commonly, schools identified as ***high-poverty*** (rate of free or reduced lunch program above 50%) receive the bulk of Title I intervention funds to support the development of special instructional programs with appropriate support personnel (Stullich, Eisner, & McCrary, 2007).

Caution should be taken in evaluating the profiles suggested by the achievement gap. The American population obviously represents a diverse array of communities: rural, urban, suburban, mixed development; some socially, racially segregated and others more diverse. There are no absolute correlates between race, poverty, and performance. In fact, despite disproportionate rates of poverty in many large urban centers occupied primarily by non-White populations, the substantial effects of poverty in the United States persist in rural, predominately White-European communities.

The Achievement Gap Debate in Urban Schools

To this point we have examined external influences on the lives and schooling of children in high-needs urban communities that could contribute to gaps in academic performance. Given the background knowledge established in chapter 3 related to intelligence, as a construct, and intelligence testing, the deepest debate regarding the ***achievement gap*** stems from an ongoing debate about intrinsic differences in ability between the races. The well-known text, *The Bell Curve: Intelligence and Class Structure in American Life* by Richard Herrnstein and Charles Murray, is notorious for its bold and controversial assertions that there are evident genetic gaps between White Europeans and African Americans that account for differences in school performance. Defending the authenticity of intelligence testing against indictments of bias toward low SES and minority groups, the authors reinforced the findings of intelligence testing data that supports the idea of fixed, unchangeable differences in intelligence. In support of their perspective, the authors direct attention to the phenomenon of the 15 point score difference which disadvantages African American children on intelligence tests. Whereas other scholars have acknowledged this "15 point" phenomenon as evidence of score bias in the testing process, Herrnstein and Murray defended intelligence theory and pointed to the score difference as proof that efforts to address minority and SES-related achievement gaps are ultimately futile. The "Bell Curve" mentality appears repugnant to most educators, but it would be naïve to assume that the evidence of intelligence testing does not influence the expectations of racial minority children in high-needs communities.

Of course, there is a huge body of literature criticizing and refuting the points made in *The Bell Curve*. Authors like Kunjufu (2006) argue for social causes of the achievement gap defending the environmental argument by noting the nature of the gap such as it widens over time. Kunjufu suggests that if the problem of the achievement gap was purely genetic, we wouldn't observe the gap between White and minority children growing as children proceed through different life and schooling processes. Considerable evidence supports the discussion of differential environmental exposure as a source of performance gaps, reinforced or exacerbated by differential exposure to high-quality education.

A publication of the Economic Policy Institute, *Inequality at the Starting Gate: Social Background Differences in Achievement as Children Begin School* (Lee & Burkam, 2002), summarizes the important differences in readiness for school that exist across lines of race, ethnicity, and socioeconomic status before children even begin school. The report indicates the differences in school readiness between children in high-poverty (in contrast to upper SES communities) are evident prior to school and are even more dramatic than some would suspect. In fact, upper SES children demonstrate average measures of cognitive ability that are approximately 60% higher than children from low-SES backgrounds.

Although there appear to be cultural comparisons embedded in the discussion, disproportionate rates of poverty among minority populations make it difficult to scrutinize any correlations with race. There do also appear to be some associations with differences in family structure and household expectations for children's academic achievement. Although a controversial discussion steeped in complicated family variables, there do appear to be differences by race relative to the percentage of children raised in single-parent homes. According to the same report by Lee and Burkam, greater than half of African-American children are raised in single-parent homes, as compared to about 15% among Whites. A logical consequence to single-parent homes is a tendency toward reduced household income (notably reflective of the comparison to a two working parent household in the U.S.). Perhaps the greatest area for concern based on the notion of schools having an "equalizing effect" on differences in community resources, is the data that indicates the children from high-poverty communities with the lowest levels of school readiness, are the most likely to enter low-performing elementary schools. Despite assumptions of the equality of offerings of public schools, data suggest that disadvantaged children are much more likely to attend the *poorest quality public schools* with limited resources to respond to the vast needs of their students. The school quality issue actually results in replication and reinforcement of inequalities that existed prior to school age and can be observed over the span of the child's school experiences (Lee & Burkam, 2002). Notably, **early intervention programs** have been shown to counteract the differences in educational opportunity by supporting families in using intellectually enriching home activities and honing social skills, pre-literacy, and pre-numeracy skills in community-based pre-schools. Rigorous analysis of social programs by economists reveals that early intervention and high-quality, early school experiences have long-lasting, positive impacts on the life outcomes of participating children (Lynch, 2004).

Hilliard's (2003) critique of the achievement gap, as described by Herrnstein and Murray, is premised on the notion that intelligence tests actually assess achievement. He scrutinizes the *achievement gap* construct pointing out racially-condescending undertones embedded in such attention to the gap between the achievement of African-Americans and European Americans, in particular. A concern of Hilliard's is the assumption that the performance of White Europeans is automatically set as the standard of a "universal norm" for comparison (p. 137), as if White performance is the logical "high point" of achievement. Like Kunjufu, Hilliard focuses the argument relevant to the achievement gap on a state of inequality suggesting that among different groups in American schools, "*equal opportunity to learn does not yet exist*" (p. 138). Hilliard suggests that a more productive argument for educators would be the gap that exists between current achievement of African-Americans and the excellent performance that they are capable of achieving. *The real gap to be addressed is between the student's current performance and the student's true potential.*

ISSUES OF ACCESS TO QUALIFIED TEACHERS

Haberman (2005) shifts the argument of student performance in urban schools away from "what is wrong" with the students to an indictment of the inability of urban school districts, which he describes as dysfunctional bureaucracies, to offer equitable educational opportunities. Focusing much of his analysis on the key variables of **teacher quality** and teacher attributes, rather than student background, Haberman summarizes one of the major challenges of urban, high-needs schools as a problem of "teacher shortage" and "teacher quality." Specifically, there is a shortage of *the right teachers* for the schools of children in urban communities. Haberman explains that despite the apparently sufficient supply of qualified teachers prepared by universities across the country, there is a consistent shortage of qualified teachers in urban schools. Often, the teachers who enter the teaching profession in urban communities are new to the profession and may not be prepared for the unique circumstances they will confront. Consequently, children in urban communities are left without a teacher after the school either cannot find a qualified teacher or the teachers leave the school. He describes this process as a "churn of teachers into and out of schools, serving diverse children in poverty" (p. 4) and clarifies that African-American children in urban public schools are far more likely to experience this phenomenon with a 50% chance of having two or more teachers during the school year.

Similarly, the population of English Language Learners within urban and other school contexts may lack access to qualified ESL teachers (National Center for Education Information, 2000). ELLs are often taught in the mainstream and even ESL classrooms by teachers with little to no knowledge of multicultural issues or specific training in ESL. Given the lack of knowledge or understanding to work with students with cultural and linguistic diversity, language development is often mistaken for learning problems and academic needs remain unaddressed.

Special education classrooms are likely the most severely impacted classrooms in urban high-poverty schools. McLeskey, Tyler, and Saunders Flippin (2004) report what could be considered a national crisis in teacher shortages and attrition (i.e., teachers leaving the profession) for special education teachers. Essentially, the data indicate that a considerable number of students in special education have *inconsistent access* to highly-qualified special education teachers with the necessary knowledge and skills to intervene for children and produce meaningful improvements in their school performance. The authors note that separate classrooms for children with emotional and behavioral disorders and classrooms called "multi-categorical" (i.e., students with various disabilities in the same, self-contained classroom) have extreme shortages of qualified teachers and statistics do not indicate the situation will improve any time soon.

CULTURAL INCONGRUITY BETWEEN TEACHERS AND STUDENTS IN URBAN SCHOOLS

Many teachers in urban schools, often novice teachers trained in state university programs, have little ability to "connect" with students in diverse, urban, high-poverty schools (Haberman, 1995). Due to the typical demographic characteristics of elementary school teachers being White, middle-income females from suburban communities, there are often some considerable incongruities between the identity and life experiences of teachers and their students. Haberman (2005) describes how these incongruities can lead teachers, particularly novice teachers, to attribute their initial poor experiences with teaching to negative qualities and lack of ability among their students. They seek out tricks or quick ways to fix their kids out of a sense of desperation. Often, students are pushed out of the classroom due to a sense that someone else can or should fix the child. Among many novice teachers, there is a sense that the children in their classrooms are "defective" in ways they cannot hope to resolve.

Haberman (2005), quite controversially, faults the dominance of psychologists over the evaluation of student performance and the nature of "normal" behavior in schools, for perpetuating a school culture in which teachers seek to define and sort children. He notes that the psychological orientation compels teachers to seek outside professional intervention for students who do not meet their expectations. The school psychology perspective, Haberman claims, confuses "normal" with "desirable," leading to the over-identification of problems and abnormalities among urban populations. He explains that many large school districts have identification rates for special education as high as 1 in 4 children. Some districts are even higher.

For students who come from different cultural, racial and linguistic backgrounds, cultural incongruity is particularly relevant. These students bring different norms, values, and practices to mainstream classrooms. These differences often conflict with the dominant culture on multiple levels and can create a mismatch between the culture of the student and the culture of the school. In addition to lack of cultural understanding, the lack of a shared language makes the teaching of ELLs even more challenging for teachers. Students who are learning English are often taught by classroom teachers who are either monolingual or unable to speak the language of their students. Without shared linguistic referents, communication breaks down, making instruction difficult. As a result, teachers often report feeling frustrated in teaching ELLs because of this lack of communication. This often limits their ability to provide good instruction to students who cannot understand them. Thus, the diverse cultures of students and teachers, coupled with failure to communicate in a shared language, often create an environment of frustration. Many researchers argue that this situation, compounded by negative attitudes held by some teachers toward culturally different students, negatively affects the academic, social, and psychological success of non-white minority students (Delpit, 1995).

It is often the case that ELL students are perceived by the school community as low achievers, with the result that these children begin to see themselves as having little competence. If they feel they have little worth, they do not see themselves as legitimate members of the classroom, and often become passive learners. Not only are these ELLs seen as deficient, but there is also a prevalent view that their parents have no valued cultural knowledge and need remediation. These views are so pervasive that even when teachers note that these students are capable, they are still seen as having deficits (Colombo, 2007). Teachers often base their notions on what they see as families who are poor, with little to no education, and as being unfamiliar with the U.S. school system, without investing in getting to know these families. Thus, parents are perceived as not having the background to help their children. With these attitudes, trust between home and school is often diminished (Amitia, Cooper, Garcia, Ittel, Johnson, Lopez, & Martinez, 1994). If teachers got to know these families, they would learn that while their cultural knowledge does not match the school's institutional knowledge, there is rich cultural knowledge in these homes. Much discussion and interaction occurs between children and their parents regarding school activities, providing evidence that parents do want to be involved in their childrens' education.

As a direct consequence of cultural contrasts between school and home, many ELL's are encouraged to discard their first language by the schools. Teachers and administrators often tell children and their families that speaking their native languages in the home will somehow negatively impact their learning of English. The emphasis schools place on learning English at the cost of ELL's native language becomes a critical issue for these children. When ELLs develop their native language and place value on their culture, it enhances English literacy, and, conversely, when children lose their first language, their ability to read and write in English is stalled (Peterson & Heywood, 2007). There is convincing evidence that many important values are lost when native language is lost. Bonds between parents and their children are broken when children lose their language and parents have not learned English. These children experience trauma and often become alienated from both family and school. Teachers need to be aware of the alienation process these children are encountering in becoming American (Fillmore, 2000).

BIAS AND OVERREPRESENTATION ISSUES IN SPECIAL EDUCATION

In 2005, Jawanza Kunjufu published a book titled, *Keeping Black Boys Out of Special Education*. The title should raise several questions to a future educator. Are there too many Black boys in special education? Why would we want to keep them "out of special education?" That sentiment makes it sound like "Black boys" have been sentenced to a punishment, but special education is supposed to help children who are having difficulty in school. So what is the problem?

Figure 4.1 demonstrates a commonly known, but worrying trend in special education. Although there are not more African-American children in special education than other groups, there are more than there logically should be. That's confusing, of course. In the figure, you can observe the percentage of children who are African American in the overall student population. You can also see the percentage of children in the category referred to as "Serious Emotional Disturbance" (a.k.a. ED, EBD, BED, behavior disorder). The concern is that the percentage of children who are African-American in the SED category is much higher than the percentage of children who are African-American in the general population. This is referred to, alternatively, as **overrepresentation** and **disproportionality**.

Essentially, the term *disproportionality* is used in reference to a review of statistics on referral to and placement in special education, with particular attention to the likelihood that being a member of certain racial, cultural groups might suggest a greater chance of being placed in special education. Because disabilities have traditionally been viewed as intrinsic conditions that a child *has*, many professionals have questioned why any one minority group would be more likely to be identified as disabled. This is viewed as a major challenge by educators who advocate for children in culturally, linguistically diverse urban schools where, as previously mentioned, there can be rates of identification for special education over 25%.

Hispanic students and English language learners (ELLs), who are the largest and fastest growing student populations in U.S. schools, are, on an average, underrepresented nationally, yet both groups are frequently over- and underrepresented at state and district levels to varying degrees (Artiles, Rueda, Salazar, & Higareda, 2005; Sullivan, 2011). The issue of overrepresentation or over-referral is also evident related to the learning problems of English Language Learners in grade 3 and above. Recent findings suggest that the overrepresentation of ELLs occurred most often in large urban school systems with substantial numbers of CLD students (Artiles, Rueda, Salazar, & Higareda, 2005). In fact, these researchers found that the odds for special education placement increased as language support was reduced. ELLs in English Immersion programs were almost three times as likely to be placed in special education programs than ELLs in Bilingual Education programs. Moreover, they found that the most vulnerable ELL subgroup included those with limited proficiency in both their native languages and English. Specifically, ELL students with little formal education are often referred for special education.

The over-identification issue in urban schools seems to most egregiously affect African-American male students and specifically for referral in two special education categories: Mild Mental Retardation/Intellectual Disability and Serious Emotional Disorder (SED). Although the disproportionality is observed nationwide, the problem does not appear to follow any clear patterns of geography or regionalism (Webb-Johnson, 2003). There is also a related under-identification for programs that assume intellectual talents (Hilliard, 2003). The table below illustrates the nature of disproportionality as it existed at the time of the 2004 reauthorization of IDEA. Despite national attention to this challenge many states have actually witnessed further growth in the disparate representation of African American males identified with behavioral disorders (Sullivan & Bal, 2013).

Figure 4.1. Statistics Demonstrating Rates of Identification of African American Students for EBD and the Actual Representation of African American Students in the Public Schools

Percentages of African American Students with Emotional Disturbance in General and Special Education

States Representing the Greatest Disparity	General School Population	Emotional Disturbance	Disparity
All 50 States and Outlying Areas	17.00	27.30	+10.30
New York	20.40	45.29	+24.89
North Carolina	31.20	52.16	+20.96
Louisiana	47.70	66.80	+19.10
Kentucky	10.40	27.64	+17.24
California	8.40	24.75	+16.50
Delaware	30.40	46.54	+16.14
Nebraska	6.50	21.28	+14.78
New Jersey	18.10	32.55	+14.45
Maryland	36.60	51.04	+14.44
Florida	25.41	39.40	+13.99
Illinois	21.40	34.44	+13.04
South Carolina	42.00	54.98	+12.98
Missouri	17.30	28.87	+11.57

Note: Data from U.S. Department of Education (2002).

EXPLAINING THE OVERREPRESENTATION OF MINORITY GROUPS IN SPECIAL EDUCATION

The disproportionality of students from diverse racial, cultural, linguistic, and economically disadvantaged backgrounds served in special education has been a topic evoking much discussion for over four decades. The reasons cited for the larger representation of ELLs in special education programs include a variety of factors in and outside of school that include: lack of first-language proficiency, poverty, functional literacy in a child's native language, inconsistent assessment procedures, referral bias, and lack of opportunity to learn within the mainstream classroom context. Before making a referral, teachers need to inquire as to whether the behavior or assumed delay is exhibited in the child's native language and in the home. A student acquiring a second language may be losing his/her first language in the process and this can be interpreted as a language delay. Also, one needs to ask if the assistance team includes members of the community, who have knowledge of the student's language and culture.

Although the issue confronts numerous groups in CLD communities, the overrepresentation of African-Americans in high-incidence disability categories has become a nationwide issue with roots of this issue dating back to the 1960s (Dunn, 1968). Because the diagnosis of high-incidence disabilities are not determined by biological factors, clear operationalized definitions are difficult to establish, leaving room for ambiguous and biased decisions with regard to diagnosis (Artiles, Kozleski, Trent, Osher, & Ortiz, 2010).

Inequalities such as ***special education referrals, assessments***, and ***placement processes*** have all been identified as contributing factors for the overrepresentation of African-American males receiving special education services (Harry & Anderson, 1994). The irony that a program (i.e. special education) designed to address the civil rights of individuals with disabilities could also create an inequality among those same groups of individuals is puzzling and has plagued the field of special education for years.

THE REFERRAL PROCESS

Referral for intervention or eligibility testing is a key predictor of placement in special education (Artiles & Trent, 1994). For example, Hosp and Reschly (2003) conducted a meta-analysis to compare special education referral rates to population rates of students from different ethnic backgrounds. The data showed that the referral rate for students varies significantly between ethnic groups. Also, results indicated that for every 100 Caucasian students referred for consideration for intervention or assessment, 132 African-American and 106 Hispanic students are being referred. For every 100 Caucasian students found eligible, 118 African-American and 89 Hispanic students are found eligible for special education services. This meta-analysis provided support to previous literature justifying the variability of referral rates between ethnic groups.

The argument was made that since special education was meant to have a positive effect on individual students, then the percentage of that population should not be a major factor considering that the needs of the different groups are being addressed. Patton (1998) countered this argument suggesting that there are obvious problems inherent to the special education referral and eligibility processes premised on a history and belief system that marginalizes the interests of African-American learners.

Some educational professionals have pointed to the history of "cultural incongruity" between teachers and White, middle class teachers and CLD students living in poverty children as a factor that promotes problems with the referral process. Surprisingly, there is not uniform agreement that the school experiences of African-American children were improved by school desegregation during the Civil Rights Movement. In fact, a core challenge of that era was the movement of African-American children into White schools that educated primarily White children without a consequent integration of the teaching workforce. Tyler, Yzquierdo, Lopez-Reyna, and Saunders (2004) report that 38,000 African-American teachers lost their jobs during the civil rights movement setting the tone for generations of African-American students to be taught in public schools in which their teachers were unlikely to live in their communities. Their teachers were likely to differ from them in sociocultural experience and race. Although we would prefer to assume that this cultural incongruity is insignificant, research suggests that it is relevant to the referral process. At the earliest points of the school desegregation movement, schools assigned special labels for African-American learners who appeared to lag behind their typically middle-class, White peers including mental retardation and *cultural deprivation*. Currently, 70% of the nation's teaching workforce are women with the largest majority in elementary schools, so gender incongruities are equally worth consideration. Most referrals originate in the elementary grades; however, African American men constitute only 0.4% of elementary and 2.2% of secondary special education teachers (Nettles & Perna, 1997). Further, despite considerable cultural linguistic diversity in American schools, concentrated at extremely high rates in urban communities, 40% of American schools have no faculty of culturally and linguistically diverse backgrounds (Riley, 1998).

The primary reason that cultural incongruity is mentioned as a challenge in the overview of disproportionality relates to the tendency for special education referral to result in placement (and even permanent segregation in school) and the indication that teachers might refer students at a higher rate who are different from their own cultural identity. Tobias, Cole, Zibrin, and Bodlakova (1982) found that general education teachers, regardless of their race, were more likely to recommend students from ethnic groups other than their own, for referral to special education. Because the majority of the nation's teachers are European American, some consideration should be given to the idea that inappropriate referral can be related to cultural incongruity and contribute to overrepresentation of minorities in special education.

Assessment Bias

Selecting appropriate intelligence tests when considering eligibility for special education placement is equally as important in order to avoid overrepresentation of minority groups. Intelligence tests are designed to produce score variability between individuals and groups of individuals (Valencia & Suzuki, 2001), which deems it necessary to closely examine the information about mean standard score differences between subgroups with regard to the examinees' parental educational level, gender, and ethnicity. Currently, the data for mean IQ difference by ethnic group is no longer being provided by test developers (Edwards, 2006). Unbiased information about which intelligence tests fairly and reliably represent minority group scores is needed to determine which test to administer. According to Jensen (1998), it is possible to have up to a 10-20 point difference between ethnic groups on different intelligence tests. Selection of intelligence tests with information regarding mean score differences for ethnic groups may aid to avoid adverse consequences for the lower scoring groups (Edwards).

Case example of bias in the Woodcock Johnson III in an urban school setting: An examiner (a co-author of this chapter) was administering the Woodcock Johnson III to an African American high school student who was going through the assessment process because a referral for special education services had been made. While administering the test, the examiner noticed that some of the student's "wrong" answers tended to be "correct" answers depending upon who you asked and their cultural background. For example, the student was asked to give a synonym for the word, *restrained*. The student confidently replied, *arrested*. Although the examiner could make the connection to what the student was referring to, "arrested" was not one of the correct answers on the test, so the examiner asked the student if she could think of another word other than *arrested* that meant the same thing as *restrained*. The student again confidently answered, *handcuffed*. As you may have come to realize by now, *arrested* and *handcuffed* were not acceptable answers for the response to be counted as correct on the Woodcock Johnson, so the examiner had to score the student's response as incorrect, indicating that the student did not know the meaning of the word, *restrained*. A few questions later the student was asked to give a synonym for the word, *blaze*. The student replied, *smoke*. The examiner again looked at the student and had to ask the student for another word other than *smoke* that also meant *blaze*. This time the student was not able to come up with another word for *blaze*, so again her initial response was scored as incorrect. As a future educator, do you think that this student indeed did not know the meaning of the words *restrained* and *blaze*?

Do you think the examiner should have scored the responses as incorrect even though the examiner knew what the student was referring to when she gave her answers?

Would you have scored her responses as incorrect? This case study is an example of how different cultural experiences in life can lead to testing bias and thus influence the decision making process of placement into special education.

How often have students been labeled with disabilities because their cultural background and life experiences differed from the standardization of the assessment tool?

THE PLACEMENT PROCESS

Once students are identified as having a disability, the next step in the process is determining the individualized, education program that is least restrictive and provides the most appropriate access to typically developing peers. This process includes determining where the child is to be taught and by whom. It has been found that students from minority groups are more likely to be placed in a more restrictive setting and receive related services than their Caucasian peers in the same disability category (Artiles, et al., 2010; Harry & Anderson, 1994). Also, data from the National Institute for Urban School Improvement (2008) reported that African-American students were less likely to be placed in general education classrooms than their Caucasian peers (Artiles, et al., 2010). From Blackorby and colleagues (2005) it was reported that *students with disabilities who were placed in general education classrooms, as opposed to pull-out or separate settings, performed closer to grade level, were absent less, and achieved higher test scores.*

IS DISPROPORTIONALITY REALLY A PROBLEM?

It has been argued that the disproportionalities among ethnic groups in special education are justifiable because special education has many desirable features (e.g.

small class sizes, individualized education, specialized teachers, and funding allocations), from which the minority students can benefit, particularly if they come from economically disadvantaged backgrounds (Artiles, et al., 2010). Also, since minority groups perform more poorly than their Caucasian peers on academic measures and as stated previously, come from economically disadvantaged backgrounds resulting from high poverty rates, they would seem to need special education services more than their Caucasian peers who come from more advantaged backgrounds (Artiles, et al., 2010; Hosp & Reschly, 2003). With this argument, four assumptions concerning the influence of poverty on disproportionality can be formed (Skiba, Poloni-Staudinger, Simmons, Feggins-Azziz, & Choong-Geun, 2005):

1. Minority students are disproportionately poor and hence are more likely to be exposed to a variety of sociodemographic stressors associated with poverty.
2. Factors associated with living in poverty leave children less developmentally ready for schooling and ultimately yield negative academic and behavioral outcomes.
3. Students who are *low achieving* or *at-risk* for negative behavioral outcomes are more likely to be referred to, and ultimately found eligible for, special education service.
4. Therefore, poverty is an important contributing factor that increases the risk, presumably in a linear fashion, of special education placement for minority students. (p. 131)

As Skiba and colleagues (2005) point out, from the above assumptions, if the first three assumptions are proven true, then the fourth assumption could be inferred based on logical sequencing. The researchers conducted a study that explored the relationships between race, poverty, and special education identification to estimate the contribution of poverty to racial disparities. The findings from the current study were consistent with previous research in that it failed to establish a reliable relationship between poverty rates and overrepresentation of minority groups in special education. This suggests that poverty is not the center of the overrepresentation issue concerning minority groups in special education.

Another factor used to aid in explaining the disproportionalities in special education is culture. A child either learns information and skills that are not useful for school learning or their culture prevents school success by inhibiting them from learning certain skills, habits, or values (Artiles, et al., 2010). There is the premise that "living under certain conditions exposes children to cultural practices that limit the acquisition of normative bodies of knowledge, dispositions, as well as skills, and limits access to experiences that are valued by the dominant society (Artiles, et al.)." The list can continue on and on with relevant factors that may influence overrepresentation in special education, but one question still remains.

DOES SPECIAL EDUCATION IMPROVE OUTCOMES FOR MINORITY CHILDREN IN URBAN SCHOOLS?

From the seemingly beneficial advantages of being placed in special education; how successful has it been for minority groups? According to current research and data on poor post school outcomes of students with disabilities the answer is: ***not very successful*** (Artiles, et al., 2010; Blackorby & Wagner, 1996; Blackorby, et al., 2005). Although there has been some improvement from the minority groups, the academic performance gap between students with and students without disabilities still remains substantial (Wagner, Newman, Cameto, Levine, & Garza, 2006). An example of this improvement for students with disabilities came from data from the National Assessment of Education Progress (NAEP) in 2007. Cortiella (2007) reported that students with disabilities were performing at a faster rate than students without disabilities even though they were still below the basic level in reading and math. The author attributed these positive increases to the changes in the Individuals with Disabilities Education Act (IDEA), increased access to the general education curriculum, and the accountability resulting from the "Adequate Yearly Progress" requirements of the No Child Left Behind (NCLB) Act. Given evidence that minority students are less likely to have access to general education classrooms once placed in special education (Blackorby et al., 2005) and special education classrooms in high-poverty schools, particularly those for students with emotional and behavioral disorders, cannot be filled by professional special education teachers (McLeskey, et al., 2004), it appears difficult to defend special education as a dependable source of intervention and support for minority children in urban schools.

While there are no easy answers, an abundant amount of research over the past 40 years has been conducted that delved into the issue of overrepresentation of African-Americans in special education. From the literature we have learned that there are a multitude of factors that can contribute to the disproportionality issue. There is a need for change in the referral, assessment, and placement processes of all students referred to special education. Artiles et. al. (2010) suggested examining culture to inform future research priorities and policy making in general and special education documenting its practice, research, and policy in schools and the community.

REVISITING THE REFERRAL PROCESS AND PRE-REFERRAL INTERVENTION

In chapter 2, we discussed some key points that teachers should consider in the pre-referral process including two issues of particular relevance in this chapter:

1. whether alternative classrooms strategies and school resources have been exhausted prior to referral, and
2. consideration of whether the referral to special education is in the best interest of the child and will result in an improved situation.

More needs to be done to ensure that the processes by which make educational decisions for students to receive special education services are effective and appropriate. Classroom teachers should be aware of the cultural incongruities that exist between them and their students. Being aware of these incongruities will be important when making educational decisions regarding a student by being able to distinguish between those characteristics that Haberman described as "normal" versus "desirable." Further, teachers may need to consider whether referral to special education will truly result in improved outcomes for the child or if further intervention might have promise in the general education classroom. Teachers play a role in determining the options available for students who struggle in urban schools and a critical examination of the contextual factors that exist in high-needs schools is relevant to the decision-making process. We must ensure that the goal of a truly *special* education is equally accessed across contexts including schools in high-needs, CLD communities.

GLOSSARY IN PLAIN TERMS

Achievement gap: The difference between the academic performance of minority and non-minority students.

Assessment bias: Refers to content in an assessment that is not familiar or appropriate to all students that might negatively impact the students' performance on the assessment.

Cultural incongruity: Having values, beliefs, or behaviors that differ from others affecting interactions between teachers and students.

Culturally and linguistically diverse: Refers to individuals whose first language is not English or who may be members of distinct subcultural groups.

Deficit model: Blaming low academic performance on the child or their circumstances without looking at the quality of instruction in the classroom or other possible contributing factors.

Disproportionality: Refers to the over placement of students from certain racial or cultural groups into special education.

Early intervention: Programs designed to prevent infants and young children who have disabilities or who are at-risk for developing disabilities from experiencing academic failure.

ELLs: Students whose first language is not English and who are in the process of learning English.

Socioeconomic status: Based on family income, parental education level, parental occupation, and family social status in the community.

Title I: A federal program that provides funds to improve academic achievement for disadvantaged students who are not performing at grade-level on standardized tests and are of a lower socioeconomic background.

REFERENCES

Artiles, A. J., & Ortiz, A. (2002). *ELLs with special needs: Identification, placement, and instruction.* Washington D.C.: Center for Applied Linguistics.

Artiles, A. J., Kozleski, E. B., Trent, S. C., Osher, D., & Ortiz, A. (2010). Justifying and explaining disproportionality, 1968-2008: A critique of underlying views of culture. *Exceptional Children, 76*(3), 279-299.

Artiles, A. J., & Trent, S. C. (1994). Overrepresentation of minority students in special education: A continuing debate. *Journal of Special Education, 27*(4), 410-437.

Blackorby, J., & Wagner, M. (1996). Longitudinal postschool outcomes of youth with disabilities: Findings from the national longitudinal study. [Article]. *Exceptional Children, 62*(5), 399-413.

Blackorby, J., Wagner, M., Camerto, R., Davies, E., Levine, P., Newman, L., et al. (2005). *Engagement, academics, social adjustment, and independence*. Palo Alto, CA: CRI.

Cortiella, C. (2007). NAEP: What is it and why should you care. *Exceptional Parent, 37*(12), 38-40.

Dunn, L. M. (1968). Special education for the midly retarded – Is much of it justifiable? *Exceptional Children, 35*, 5-22.

Edwards, O. W. (2006). Special education disproportionality and the influence of intelligence test selection. *Journal of Intellectual & Developmental Disability, 31*(4), 246-248.

Haberman, M. (1995). Selecting 'STAR' teachers for children and youth in urban poverty. *Phi Delta Kappa, 76*(10), 777-781.

Harry, B., & Anderson, M. G. (1994). The disproportionate placement of African American males in special education programs: A critique of the process. *Journal of Negro Education, 63*(4), 602-619.

Hilliard, A. G. (2003). No mystery: Closing the achievement gap between Africans and excellence. In T. Perry, C. Steele & A. Hilliard (Eds.), *Young, gifted, and black: Promoting high achievement among African-American students*. Boston, MA.: Beacon Press.

Hosp, J. L., & Reschly, D. J. (2003). Referral rates for intervention or assessment: A meta-analysis of racial differences. *Journal of Special Education, 37*(2), 67-80.

Jensen, A. R. (1998). The g factor and the design of education. In R. J. Sternberg & W. M. Williams (Eds.), *Intelligence, instruction, and assessment: Theory into practice*. (pp. 111-131). Mahwah, NJ US: Lawrence Erlbaum Associates Publishers.

Klingner, J., & Artiles, A. J. (Eds.). (2006). English Language Learners struggling to learn to read. *Journal of Learning Disabilities, 39*, 99-156; 386-398.

Kozol (1991). *Savage inequalities: Children in America's schools*. New York: Crown Publishers.

Kozol, J. (2005). *The shame of the nation: The restoration of apartheid schooling in America*. New York: Three Rivers Press.

Kunjufu, J. (2005). *Keeping black boys out of special education*. Chicago, Illinois: African American Images.

Kunjufu, J. (2006). *An African centered response to Ruby Payne's poverty theory*. Chicago, Illinois: African-American Images.

Lee, V. E., & Burkam, D. T. (2002). Inequality at the starting gate: Social background differences in achievement as children begin school. Retrieved from http://www.epi.org.

Lynch, R. (2004). Exceptional returns: Economic, fiscal, and social benefits of investment in early childhood development. Washington, D.C.: Economic Policy Institute.

McLeskey, J., Tyler, N. C., & Saunders Flippin, S. (2004). The supply of and demand for special education teachers: A review of research regarding the chronic shortage of special education teachers. *Journal of Special Education, 38*(1), 5-21.

National Center for Education Information. (2007). *Number of Emergency Teaching Licenses, by State, 1985 – 2003*, retrieved on June 30, 2008, from http://ncei. com/statistics/html.

Nettles, M. T., & Perna, L. W. (1997). *The African American education data book: Volume 1. Higher and adult education.* Fairfax, VA: Frederick D. Patterson Research Institute.

Ortiz, A. (2002). *English language learners with special education needs: Identification, placement, and instruction* (pp. 107–132).Washington, DC: Center for Applied Linguistics.

Patton, J. M. (1998). The disproportionate representation of African-Americans in special education: Looking behind the curtain for understanding and solutions. *Journal of Special Education, 32*(1), 25-31.

Payne, R. K. (2005). *A framework for understanding poverty.* Highlands, TX: Aha! Process, Inc.

Riley, R. (1998). Our teachers should be excellent, and they should look like America. *Education and Urban Society, 31*(1), 18-29.

Skiba, R. J., Poloni-Staudinger, L., Simmons, A. B., Feggins-Azziz, L. R., & Choong-Geun, C. (2005). Unproven links: Can poverty explain ethnic disproportionality in special education? *Journal of Special Education, 39*(3), 130-144.

Stullich, S. Eisner, E. & McCrary, J. (2007). Report on the National Assessment of Title I, Volume I, Implementation of Title I, Washington, D.C.: U.S. Department of Education, Institute of Education Sciences.

Sullivan, A. L., & Bal, A. (2013). Disproportionality in special education: Effects of individual and school variables on disability risk. *Exceptional Children, 79*, 475-494.

Tobias, S., Cole, C., Zibrin, M., & Bodlakova, V. (1982). Teacher–student ethnicity and recommendations for special education referrals. *Journal of Educational Psychology, 74*, 72-76.

Tyler, N. C., Yzquierdo, Z., Lopez-Reyna, N., & Saunders Flippin, S. (2004). Cultural and linguistic diversity and the special education workforce: A critical overview. *Journal of Special Education, 38*(1), 22-38.

Valencia, R. R., & Suzuki, L. A. (2001). *Intelligence testing and minority students: Foundations, performance factors, and assessment issues. Racial and ethnic minority psychology series.* Thousand Oaks, CA: Sage.

Wagner, M., Newman, L., Cameto, R., Levine, P., & Garza, N. (2006). *An overview of findings from wave 2 of the national longitudinal transition study-2 (NSTS2). (NCSER 2006-3004).* Menlo Park, CA: SRI International.

Waxman, H., Tellez, K. & Walberg, H. (2004). Improving Teacher Quality for English Language Learners: Reports and Next-Step Recommendations from a National Invitational Conference. *The Laboratory for Student Success*, 3(1), 1-3.

Webb-Johnson, G. (2003). Behaving while black: A hazardous reality for African American learners? *Beyond Behavior, 12*(2), 3-7.

QUESTIONS *for Reflection:*

What are some of the contextual factors of high-poverty urban communities that create barriers for children to achieve their full potential?

Explain the "Deficit Model" and how it relates to your philosophy of teaching.

How is federal intervention in schools used to counteract the "achievement gap" for students in schools in disadvantaged communities?

If the typical demographic characteristics of elementary school teachers are White, middle-income females from suburban communities, what are some of the incongruities that may exsist between the teacher and the students? (Think: "desirable" versus "normal") How would you respond to those incongruties in your own classroom?

Since special education referrals, assessments, and placement processes have all been identified as contributing factors for the overrepresentation of African-American males receiving special education services, what would you do differently to address the concerns in each of these areas?

NOTES

CHAPTER **5**

Teaching Children with Intellectual and Developmental Disabilities

Melissa Hudson and John Beattie

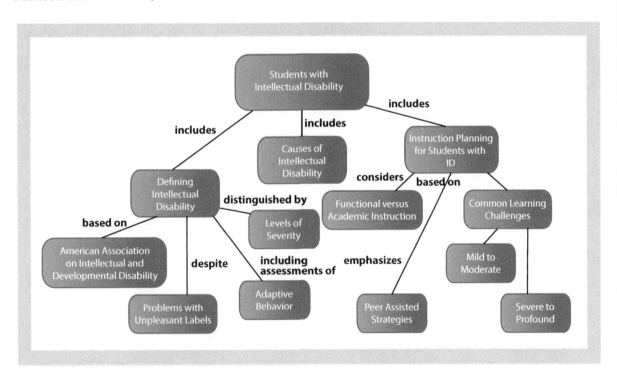

THE TOP TEN TERMS FOR CHAPTER 5:

The following key terms or big ideas are important to your understanding of the content for chapter 5 and the in-class discussions to follow.

• Adaptive behavior	• Person-first language
• Functional skills	• Generalization
• Down Syndrome	• Alternate Assessment based on Alternate Achievement Standards (AA-AAS)
• General curriculum access	• Intellectual Disability
• Peer-assisted Strategies	• Levels of support

Defining Disability in Intellectual Development: A Diverse Group of Children

Historically, children with intellectual development significantly lower than their typically functioning peers have been referred to as children with mental retardation. In fact, the Individuals with Disabilities Education Improvement Act (IDEIA, 2004) continues to use the term mental retardation as one of the 13 disability categories in which special education supports and services can be provided to eligible students. IDEA describes students identified as having mental retardation as exhibiting *"significantly subaverage general intellectual functioning, existing concurrently with deficits in adaptive behavior and manifested during the developmental period, that adversely affects a child's educational performance."* States may choose to add to the requirements of federal law and provide services beyond the scope of the law, but cannot provide fewer services than the law requires. Individual states must incorporate the basic elements of the law into the definitions they develop. For example, the state of North Carolina's definition of intellectual disability clearly mirrors the federal law but differs in the terminology used to describe the disability category, using the term *intellectual disability* instead of mental retardation.

North Carolina's Definition of Intellectual Disability

Intellectual disability means significantly subaverage general intellectual functioning that adversely affects a child's educational performance existing concurrently with deficits in adaptive behavior and manifested during the developmental period.

http://www.ncpublicschools.org/docs/stateboard/meetings/2007/revisions/1001attachrev.pdf

---

While some states have recently chosen to use alternative terms to describe these students, some professional organizations have long advocated for a philosophical shift from the term mental retardation, to less stigmatizing terms such as intellectual disability. Not only have professional organizations opted for differing terminology, but one organization changed its name to reflect the philosophical shift. Originally called the American Association on Mental Retardation (AAMR), the organization changed its name to reflect the preferred terminology; AAMR became the *American Association on Intellectual and Developmental Disabilities* (AAIDD) in 2006. Similarly, AAIDD also provided an alternative definition utilizing the new, more preferred term of intellectual disability. The AAIDD definition is presented in the text box below.

AAIDD Definition for Intellectual Disability

Intellectual disability is a disability characterized by significant limitations both in intellectual functioning and adaptive behavior, which covers many everyday social and practical skills. This disability originates before the age of 18.

http://www.aamr.org/content_100.cfm?navID=21

Saying Goodbye to Mental Retardation: The Difficulty with Labels for Children with Intellectual Disability

Many labels are used to describe children with intellectual disability and a negative stigma can be attached over time because the term is associated with something undesirable. For example, "mental retardation" has acquired such a negative connotation that removing all references in federal law to "mental retardation" and "mentally retarded individual" is the focus of a bipartisan senate bill, Rosa's Law (Pecquet, 5/23/10). Rosa's Law would replace the terms *mental retardation* and *mentally retarded individual,* with *intellectual disability* and *individual with an intellectual disability.*

The words used to describe a person with intellectual disability can change over time, but regardless of the words used, ***it is important for educators to use person-first language.*** Person-first language names the person before the disability to acknowledge that the person is more important than the disability (e.g., a person *with* autism rather than autistic person). Some of the labels used in the past to describe individuals with intellectual disability with current labels are described in the text box.

Table 5.1. Comparison of Past and Present Labels and Examples of Person-First Language

Past Labels	Present Labels	Person-first Language
Autistic	Autism Spectrum Disorder	A person with autism
Imbecile	Intellectual disability	A person with intellectual disability
Cretin	Developmental delay	A person with a developmental delay
Mongoloid	Down Syndrome	A person with down syndrome
Feeble-minded	Extensive support needs	An individual with extensive support needs

It is important to emphasize that the term *intellectual disability* is, for all intents and purposes, synonymous with the term *mental retardation.* Nonetheless, the shift to the new term is significant. As noted in a previous chapter, IDEA has mandated the use of "person-first" language when referring to students with disabilities.

This seemingly insignificant change can result in a very significant, real change in one's perception of an individual with a disability. The disability is not the defining element of the individual; rather, the individual is a "person first" who also happens to evidence some type of disability. Perhaps more than any category of disability, the impact of the language used to describe students with intellectual disability is clear and sometimes unintentional. An example of this can be seen in the text box below.

The "R" Word by John Beattie

My son and I were recently talking with a friend of his. His friend responded to an overheard comment by saying, "That's just retarded." My son cringed and said, "Don't ever use that word around my dad. It really makes him furious." The friend looked surprised, clearly not understanding what all the commotion was about. I recognized the look, as I have seen it many times before, and asked him, "Why did you use the word 'retarded'?" His friend thought about it and replied, "Because that comment was really stupid and embarrassing." I took a breath, trying to decide if it was the time and place to stand up for what I believed and, to my son's chagrin, I decided it was. I said to the friend, "That's exactly why I don't like using that word. When someone talks about a 'retarded person,' the natural assumption is that person can't understand or do anything because he is 'retarded.' When you use the word in that way, you probably don't mean to be hateful, but that's what many people hear who care about someone with an intellectual disability." The friend looked at me, obviously thinking, "I sure wish I hadn't said that." He said, "I really didn't mean it like that. I didn't even think about, but I can see why that would be hurtful and I will make sure I stop using that word."

The definitions mentioned above, regardless of the origin, are intended to provide a framework for identifying students with intellectual disability. The identification of these, and all students with disabilities, is a critical step in the process of providing services in the public school setting. Any definition ultimately considers three major factors in defining and identifying students with intellectual disability (a) **intellectual functioning**, (b) **adapted behavior skills**, and (c) **age of onset**.

Intellectual functioning refers to general mental capacity, such as reasoning, learning, or problem solving. Students with intellectual disability generally exhibit "significantly subaverage general intellectual functioning" when compared to their non-disabled peers (see the definitions mentioned earlier in this chapter). Students are classified in one of four broad categories and referred to as *students with mild, moderate, severe,* or *profound intellectual disability*. This distinction is made based upon the individual student's performance on some type of intelligence test. *Students with mild intellectual disability (ID) include a range of IQ scores from 55 to 70/75.* This constitutes those students who fall 2 to 3 standard deviations below the mean IQ score of 100. *Students with moderate ID exhibit an IQ range of 35 to 55.* This is essentially the same as a score that falls 3 to 4 standard deviations below the mean. *Students identified as having severe ID score at an IQ range of 20 to 35,* which is 4 to 5 standard deviations below the mean. Finally, *students with profound ID have IQ scores below the 20-25 range.*

Special education labels and IQ scores may provide a common language for research and funding, but they tell teachers little about the students they are teaching. Chapter 3 describes the limitations of intelligence testing in detail. Given these limitations, teachers should keep in mind that labels and IQ scores do not describe what a student is capable of learning or the supports they need to learn. The AAIDD uses *levels of support* to define students with intellectual disability. In other words, while recognizing the importance of the classification system ranging from mild to profound, AAIDD suggests that using criteria involving levels of support is a more accurate means of classifying students with intellectual disability.

There are four levels of support that may be necessary in meeting the needs of students with intellectual disability. *These levels include intermittent, limited, extensive, and pervasive.* Raver (2009) relates the levels of support to the four broad categories of functioning based on IQ scores. Students in need of intermittent support may not require support on a day-to-day basis; instead, support is provided when specific support is necessary for the student to function appropriately in the academic setting. The intermittent support is similar to the student with mild intellectual disability. The limited level of support, which is similar to moderate intellectual disability, is provided to students for a limited period of time. For example, this support might be provided as a student makes the transition from the school to the work place. The third level of support is more extensive in that the support may be required on a daily basis for an extended period of time. The student with a need for an extensive level of support may need assistance in the home for longer periods of time. The extensive level of support is similar to the category of severe intellectual disability. Finally, the pervasive level of support requires constant assistance across all environments. This parallels the profound level of intellectual disability. A summary of this information is provided in the text box.

Table 5.2.

Classification based on IQ scores	Classification based on level of support
Mild intellectual disability; IQ range from approximately 55 – 70/75	Intermittent level of support
Moderate intellectual disability; IQ range from approximately 35 – 55	Limited level of support
Severe intellectual disability; IQ range from approximately 20 – 35	Extensive level of support
Profound intellectual disability; IQ range approximately from 20/25 and below	Pervasive level of support

The second part of the federal definition for mental retardation describes deficits in **adaptive behavior**. Adaptive behavior refers to the social and practical skills people use every day and include communication, motor, self-help, self-determination, or social skills. To learn adaptive behavior skills, students with intellectual disability may need individualized instruction while in school. For example, they may need instruction on how to use an **alternative augmentative communication (AAC)** device to talk with their peers, make choices that reflect their preferences, or show what they know about a science concept. Simple communication rules like turn-taking and reciprocity may also need to be explicitly taught. It would be easy for teachers to focus on what students with intellectual disability cannot do, but as advocates for all children, it is important to see beyond the disability to the unique abilities of each individual student.

Recognize the Abilities of Every Child
- intelligence is not a single characteristic
- all students have unique strengths on which educators can build
- all students can and should indicate preferences and make choices
- all students can and should learn with their peers
- there is value in being meaningfully involved in activities with peers
- if a student fails to learn, the effectiveness of instruction should be questioned, not the student's ability to learn (Jorgensen, 2005)
- people learn best when they are valued, when people have high expectations for them, and when they are taught and supported well

---

CAUSES OF INTELLECTUAL DISABILITY

When considering potential causes, it is important to recognize that many students with intellectual disability are *classified without any clear-cut, identifiable cause.* It is estimated that a specific cause can be identified in only 25% of the individuals with intellectual disability (Shapiro & Batshaw, 2007). The majority of these identifiable causes are evidenced in individuals with severe or profound intellectual disability. It has been further estimated that over 350 possible causes of intellectual disability have been identified (Luckasson et al., 2002). When causes can be identified, they typically focus on risk factors or a specific time period in the individual's life (Schalock et al., 2010).

Risk factors that may cause intellectual disability include biomedical, social, behavioral, and educational factors. These factors are often considered together because it is difficult to determine which of these factors is the specific cause of intellectual disability (Turnbull, Turnbull, & Wehmeyer, 2010). Risk factors may occur during a specific period of time during the development of the individual with intellectual disability, including before (prenatal), during (perinatal), or after birth (postnatal). Examples of causes and the times at which they may occur in the developmental process are described in the text box below. The most commonly noted congenital causes of intellectual disability include **Down Syndrome, Fetal Alcohol Syndrome,** and **Fragile X Syndrome** (CDC, 2010).

Table 5.3.

Common Causes for Intellectual Disability	
Causes	**Examples**
Prenatal (before birth)	Fragile X Syndrome Down Syndrome Fetal Alcohol Syndrome (FAS) Low socioeconomic status Violence in the home Parental issues (drug abuse, smoking) Limited parenting skills
Perinatal (during birth)	Prematurity Asphyxiation Low socioeconomic status Lack of health care
Postnatal (after birth)	Head injury Stroke Meningitis Low socioeconomic status Abuse or neglect Delayed inception of services
Adapted from Encyclopedia of Mental Disorders http://www.minddisorders.com/kau-Nu/mental-retardation.html and Centers for Disease Control and Prevention http://www.cdc.gov/ncbddd/dd/mr3.htm	

PLANNING SERVICES FOR CHILDREN WITH INTELLECTUAL DISABILITY

Functional and Academic Instruction

Functional and academic skills are important to all students with intellectual disability, regardless of the severity of the disability. **Functional skills** are the skills that are meaningful and immediately useful in a child's life and include the skills that someone would have to do for the child if they did not learn to do it for themselves. To identify which functional skills are most important for students to learn, teachers assess the child's current and future environments (e.g., home, school, community) and teach the most important skills. Functional skills continue to be valued and promoted for students with intellectual disability, but recent legislation has emphasized the importance of academic instruction for all students. For this reason, most teachers provide instruction on both functional and academic skills for their students with intellectual disability.

The IDEA amendments of 1997 first required students with disabilities to have **general curriculum access** and be included in large scale assessments. **General curriculum access** is the opportunity to learn and be provided the instructional supports needed to demonstrate learning in grade-level reading, math, science, and social studies content. Providing access to the general curriculum also gives students with intellectual disability an opportunity for (a) improved adult competence, (b) high expectations for learning, (c) equal educational opportunities, and (d) means and opportunities for self-determination (Browder, Wakeman, Flowers, Rickelman, Pugalee, & Karvonen, 2007). IDEIA (2004) reinforced general curriculum instruction for students with intellectual disability and specifically stated that students with intellectual disability must (a) have *access to*, (b) *be involved in*, and (c) *progress in* the general education curriculum. With these goals in mind, students with intellectual disability must be provided with every opportunity to achieve academic goals while also considering the functional and social skills they will need to become successful, participating members of society.

CHILDREN WITH MILD/MODERATE INTELLECTUAL DISABILITY

Common Learning Challenges. Students with mild/moderate intellectual disability often receive part of their instruction in regular classroom settings. The U.S. Department of Education (2005) reported that 15% of students with intellectual disability spend a significant portion of their academic day (i.e., 80%) in the general education classroom. More and more students have academic goals that are the same as or similar to students without disabilities. Consequently, any academic intervention involving students with mild/moderate intellectual disability should focus on the general education curriculum or a state approved standard course of study. In addition, instruction must also consider the unique needs of each student. Students with mild/moderate intellectual disability have difficulty with several elements of the cognitive process required to learn and retain information presented in today's schools. These elements include **attention, memory, generalization,** and **motivation** (Rosenberg, Westling, & McLeskey, 2008; Turnbull et al., 2010).

Difficulty with attention may be evidenced in a student's inability to focus on directions, filter out extraneous information, and maintain attention on the target activity (Rosenberg, et al., 2008). This lack of attention may cause the student with mild/moderate intellectual disability to misunderstand or misinterpret classroom directions, focus on irrelevant environmental stimuli not associated with the target lesson, or fail to complete tasks due to the inability to stay focused on the class topic.

Students with mild/moderate intellectual disability also experience difficulty with tasks involving short-term memory. These students have difficulty remembering math facts or lists of information. However, it is crucial to recognize that these students can enhance their memory skills by introducing specific strategies. **These strategies may include rehearsal, verbal prompts, or mnemonic techniques** (Turnbull et al., 2010; Rosenberg et al., 2008).

Generalization is the skill that enables students to understand and use information in settings other than the primary classroom setting or with materials or tasks other than those used in the classroom. For example, a student may be very successful with learning money skills (e.g., making change) in the classroom using paper and plastic money. However, this skill is not **generalized** if the student is not able to make change in a grocery store where the skill is ultimately needed. While it is important to learn a skill, it becomes far less significant, if not worthless, if the skill cannot be generalized to *natural settings*. An example of generalization is featured in the text box.

Recently, a fifth grade general education class was observed. The class was working on map skills that involved locating certain cities using latitude and longitude. The majority of students were able to successfully complete this task and identify the exact locations of the target cities. However, the co-teachers in this class had planned an alternative for two students with moderate intellectual disability. Rather than learn the coordinates of cities like Paris or London, the students with intellectual disability learned how to use coordinates to find specific places in their own community. They used community maps to determine the location of the school, the library, and their individual homes. They were clearly a part of the class activity as they learned skills similar to their non-disabled peers as well as valuable map skills that would help them in their daily lives.

Motivation is a truly misunderstood concept. *It is the trait that enables a person to do, to the best of her/his ability, that which s/he is capable of doing* (Lavoie, 1989). One can be extremely motivated to complete a task but fail to do so without the necessary skills. Students with mild/moderate intellectual disability often are or appear to be less motivated than their peers without intellectual disability. Over time, these students can develop an awareness of the tasks they can or cannot successfully complete. Consequently, students with mild/moderate intellectual disability may approach a task with little or no enthusiasm or motivation because they know the task will be hard. This limited motivation may also occur because students have learned that others (e.g., teachers, parents, fellow students) will help them with their work or simply do the work for them. Essentially, these students with mild/moderate intellectual disability have "figured out" that if they approach the right person, many times they can avoid the assigned task altogether.

CHILDREN WITH SEVERE/PROFOUND INTELLECTUAL DISABILITY

Common Learning Challenges. Students with severe/profound intellectual disability may have learning challenges including (a) *language and short-term memory*, (b) *generalization of learned skills*, (c) *responding to instruction*, (d) *motivation and focus*, and (e) *social skills and peer relationships* (Copeland & Cosbey, 2008-09). Teachers can provide instruction to help students overcome common learning challenges. For example, Wolery and Schuster (1997) found that using authentic materials (e.g., real vs. play money) and teaching in the actual places where the skill is needed (e.g., paying for lunch in the school cafeteria) helped students learn and generalize money-handling skills. Breaking complex tasks into smaller steps and teaching the steps systematically (i.e., task analyzed instruction) can also help students learn. For example, Collins, Branson, Hall, and Rankin (2001) taught three high school students with moderate and severe disabilities in an inclusive secondary writing class to write letters (e.g., date, greeting, body, and closing) using an 11-step task analysis, systematic instruction, and peer tutoring. Common learning challenges and some instructional practices and strategies teachers can use to address them in their classrooms are described in the box.

Table 5.4.

Common Learning Challenges of Students with Moderate and Severe Intellectual Disability (adapted from Copeland & Cosbey, 2008-2009)	
Challenge	Effective Instructional Practices and Strategies
Language and short-term memory	• Task analyzed instruction (i.e., breaking a complex task into smaller steps and teaching these steps). • Use visual supports (e.g., a picture list of activities to be completed in sequential order). • Provide multiple opportunities to practice skills within a varied range of activities requiring the skills.
Generalization	• Use authentic instructional materials (i.e., real money instead of Monopoly money). • Employ in vivo instruction (i.e., teaching in settings where knowledge or skill is needed). • Use general case instruction (i.e., teaching with examples that represent the range of possible situations a student may encounter). • Provide quality simulated instruction at school along with instruction in actual community sites* in mixed ability groups (i.e., community-based instruction). *Leaving school to receive instruction is not generally age appropriate for younger students.
Responding to instruction	• Embed multiple opportunities within naturally occurring activities to practice a new skill across the student's school day. • Equip students who are nonverbal with augmented communication devices they can use easily.
Motivation and focus	• Provide opportunities to make choices about materials and instructional activities. • Provide instruction with peers in inclusive settings. • Use peer mediated interventions (i.e., peer tutoring, peer supports, classwide peer tutoring, student learning dyads and triads). • Promote active student engagement during instruction (choral responding, student response systems, yes/no response cards, think-pair-share activities).
Social and communication skills	• Provide opportunities for students to interact with peers (i.e., general education classroom). • Use peer mediated interventions (i.e., peer tutoring, peer supports, classwide peer tutoring, student learning dyads and triads). • Provide Direct Instruction. • Utilize Peer Modeling.

Adapted from Copeland & Cosbey, 2008-2009.

Alternate Assessment based on Alternate Achievement Standards (AA-AAS). The No Child Left Behind Act of 2001 (NCLB, 2002) require schools to demonstrate high levels of learning in reading, math, and science for all students. Both the NCLB Act and IDEA (1997) require schools to include all students in state and district assessments and allow schools to use an **alternate assessment based on alternate achievement standards (AA-AAS)** linked to grade-level content standards for students who are unable to take the assessment with accommodations. Even though the AA-AAS is based on alternate achievement standards, the alternate achievement standards must be aligned with a state's academic content standards, promote access to the general curriculum, and reflect the highest achievement standards possible. All states have developed alternate assessments based on alternate achievement standards to assess students who meet eligibility requirements. For example, the North Carolina Department of Public Instruction has designed the NCEXTEND1 alternate assessment for reading and math in grades 3-8 and 10, science in grades 5, 8, and 10, and writing in grades 4, 7, and 10. The eligibility requirements for the NCEXTEND1 are described in the text box.

North Carolina AA-AAS Eligibility Requirements

The NCEXTEND1 alternate assessment is designed for students with disabilities who:
- Have a current IEP
- Are enrolled in grades 3–8 or 10 according to the Student Information Management System (e.g., SIMS/NCWISE)
- Are instructed in the North Carolina *Standard Course of Study* Extended Content Standards in ALL assessed content areas
- Have a SIGNIFICANT COGNITIVE DISABILITY (i.e., exhibit severe and pervasive delays in ALL areas of conceptual, linguistic and academic development and also in adaptive behavior areas, such as communication, daily living skills and self-care)

http://www.ncpublicschools.org/docs/accountability/policyoperations/ncextend1/ncextend-1eligibilitycriteria20071212.pdf

---

For students to demonstrate learning on state assessments like the AA-AAS in content areas like English/ language arts and mathematics, they need opportunities to learn academic content (i.e., access to the general curriculum). For many students with severe intellectual disability, opportunities to learn adapted grade-level academic content may happen best in the general education classroom. Earlier in the chapter, we learned that general curriculum access is a common course of study for all students, not a place where instruction is received. Although the general curriculum can be accessed in self-contained, special education classrooms when special education teachers are highly qualified (i.e., has full state certification in each subject he or she teaches), many special education teachers are not highly qualified to teach content areas (Downing, 2008). Additionally, research has indicated that instruction in separate settings is less focused on the general curriculum (Helmstetter, Curry, Brennan, & Saul, 1998; Palmer, Wehmeyer, Gipson, & Agran, 2004). For example, Palmer et al. (2004) and Helmstetter et al. (1998) compared the instruction received by students with disabilities in the general and special education classrooms and confirmed that students received more exposure to the standardized general curriculum when they participate in the general education classroom.

Including students with severe intellectual disability in general education classes requires professionals and the school to work together. Nolet and McLaughlin (2000) emphasize the importance of collaboration between general education and special education teachers. By combining the special education teacher's expertise in differentiated instruction with the general education teacher's expertise in academic content, big ideas and key concepts from the general curriculum can be made accessible to students with severe/profound intellectual disability. In addition to professional collaboration, the school environment must be flexible to allow changes in critical resources to meet student needs. The text box describes ways general curriculum access can be promoted for students with severe intellectual disability.

Promoting General Curriculum Access for Students with Severe Intellectual Disability

(Adapted from Nolet & McLaughlin, 2000.)

- School staff share a foundational expectation that all students will benefit from access to the general curriculum.
- The school environment is flexible, allowing critical resources, such as teachers and time, to change in response to student needs.
- Teachers share knowledge of the general curriculum and have opportunities to discuss the most important aspects of the curriculum to teach.
- Teachers (and other specialists) are able to describe what they expect a student to be able to do as a result of instruction in the curriculum.
- Teachers have a shared language and knowledge of subject matter content, as well as the skills needed to make student accommodations.

Peer-assisted Strategies

To meet the needs of all students with intellectual disability, it is crucial to consider alternatives to the traditional "teacher-student" setting. One such alternative that has proven effective for students with intellectual disability is peer-assisted strategies. **Peer-assisted strategies** involve students with disabilities learning from peers without disabilities in inclusive settings and have been effective in promoting academic learning for students with intellectual disability (Winokur, Cobb, & Dugan, 2007). Peers can be a powerful resource to general education teachers by helping to provide general curriculum access for students with intellectual disability. Many different types of peer-assisted strategies exist and three commonly used in general education classrooms are described in the following examples (i.e., partner learning, classwide peer tutoring, and peer tutors). First, McDonnell, Thorson, Allen, and Mathot-Buckner (2000) used partner learning to improve the spelling test performance for four elementary students with severe disabilities when they were grouped into triads with peers, and members rotated between the roles of word wizard, word conjurer, and word keeper two times a week during spelling class. Spelling words were taken from the general education spelling curriculum for two students and the Edmark Reading program for a third student.

Second, Van Norman and Wood (2008) taught six kindergarten students at risk for mild intellectual disability (e.g., reading difficulties) to tutor each other and provide accurate feedback using prerecorded sight words from a voice output device. The reading skills of these students improved significantly using peer tutoring during classroom instruction. Third, McDonnell, Mathot-Buckner, Thorson, and Fister (2001) used classwide peer tutoring to supplement weekly instruction for three junior high students with severe disabilities. Students were grouped into triads and members rotated the roles of tutor, tutee, and observer during two 15-min. classwide peer tutoring sessions each week. A multi-element curricula was developed cooperatively by the general and special educators that focused on pre-algebra, physical education, and history objectives from the general curriculum (i.e., converting percentages to decimals and determining a percent of a given number using a calculator; chest passing the ball to a peer from 20 feet and dribbling the ball with one hand for 20 feet; identifying a Conestoga wagon, Utah's state bird, state flower, and a picture of Jim Bridger). Accommodations were developed by the general and special educators as needed.

Fourth, McDuffie, Mastropieri, and Scruggs (2009) investigated the effects of peer tutoring in co-taught and non-co-taught classes on science content learning for students with and without disabilities and found that students receiving peer tutoring performed better than students receiving traditional instruction on unit tests. Fifth, Gilberts, Agran, Hughes, and Wehmeyer (2001) also found middle school peer tutors improved classroom survival skills for five students with severe disabilities. During the last 10-15 min of Spanish, reading, art, or U.S. History class, peer tutors taught students 11 classroom survival skills rated very important by general education teachers (e.g., in-class when bell rings, bring appropriate materials to class, greet the teacher) using examples and nonexamples. After students learned the survival skills, peer tutors taught students how to self-monitor their own behavior using a self-recording sheet.

Last, Jameson, McDonnell, Polychronis, and Riesen (2008) used middle school peers to embed systematic instruction (i.e., constant time delay) into on-going general education class activities to teach students with significant intellectual disability academic targets aligned to content standards in health (e.g., effects of smoking on the body) and art (e.g., definitions related to hand building ceramic forms). Peers were trained in 30 min. and delivered instruction with high levels of procedural fidelity.

Simple Ideas That Future Teachers Should Understand about Supporting Students with Intellectual Disability in School

A final thought about working with students with intellectual disability; while there is no single intervention technique or strategy that will work with ALL of these students, ALL techniques or strategies will work with someone! In that light, the bulleted list below provides some general suggestions that may be applicable to your work with students with and without intellectual disability.

First and foremost, we must **hold high expectations for student performance.** The reader will notice that each of the chapters that provide recommendations for practice will include this statement as the first thought and reminder. The success of students with disabilities is often built upon a foundation of a teacher's beliefs that they can accomplish great things in school and in life. Other suggestions include:

- Use language appropriate to the student(s)
- Repeat information as much as necessary to ensure student understanding
- Provide training in social skills
- Make sure that the classroom rules and procedures are understood and monitored on a daily basis
- Present material in a sequential manner
- Make instruction practical and related to "real life"
- Make instruction hands-on
- Ensure that students are actively engaged
- Provide appropriate, systematic feedback
- Always focus on the generalization and maintenance of skills
- Utilize material that is high-interest but at the appropriate level
- Be realistic, yet challenging
- Practice, practice, practice
- Task analyze as much as possible

GLOSSARY IN PLAIN TERMS

Adaptive behavior: The social and practical skills people use every day.

Alternate Assessment Based on Alternate Achievement Standards (AA-AAS): The achievement test based on adapted academic standards to measure progress in the general curriculum taken by students for whom the typical standardized achievement tests are not appropriate, even with accommodations.

Down Syndrome: A problem with the chromosomes that often causes moderate to severe intellectual disability. Individuals with Down Syndrome also exhibit certain physical characteristics unique to the syndrome.

Functional skills: Skills that are meaningful and immediately useful.

General curriculum access: The opportunity to learn and instructional support to demonstrate learning on grade-level reading, math, science, and social studies content.

Generalization: The ability to learn a skill, then use that skill when completing a different task. It also involves using skills learned in one setting across different settings.

Intellectual disability: Significantly subaverage general intellectual functioning that adversely affects a child's educational performance existing concurrently with deficits in adaptive behavior and manifested during the developmental period.

Levels of support: There are four levels of support that may be necessary in meeting the needs of students with intellectual disability. These levels include intermittent, limited, extensive, and pervasive.

Peer-assisted strategies: Students with disabilities learn from peers without disabilities through peer tutoring, peer instruction, or cooperative learning in inclusive settings.

Person-first language: Names the person before the disability to acknowledge that the person is more important than the disability (e.g., person with severe/profound intellectual disability).

REFERENCES

Browder, D. M., Wakeman, S. Y., Flowers, C., Rickelman, R. J., Pugalee, D., & Karvonen, M. (2007). Creating access to the general curriculum with links to grade-level content for students with significant cognitive disabilities: An explication of the concept. *The Journal of Special Education, 41,* 2-16.

Collins, B. C., Branson, T. A., Hall, M., & Rankin, S. W. (2001). Teaching secondary students with moderate disabilities in an inclusive academic classroom setting. *Journal of Development and Physical Disabilities, 13,* 41-59.

Copeland, S. R., & Cosbey, J. (2008-2009). Making progress in the general curriculum: Rethinking effective instructional practices. *Research and Practice for Persons with Severe Disabilities, 33-34,* 214-227.

Downing, J. E. (2008). *Including students with severe and multiple disabilities in typical classrooms.* Baltimore: Paul H. Brookes.

Gilberts, G. J., Agran, M., Hughes, C., & Wehmeyer, M. (2001). The effects of peer delivered self-monitoring strategies on the participation of students with severe disabilities in general education classrooms. *The Journal of the Association for Persons with Severe Handicaps, 26,* 25-36.

Helmstetter, E., Curry, C. A., Brennan, M., & Saul, M. S. (1998). Comparison of general and special education classrooms of students with severe disabilities. *Education and Training in Mental Retardation and Developmental Disabilities, 33,* 216-227.

Individuals with Disabilities Education Act Amendments of 1990, 20 U.S.C. §1400 *et seq.* (1990) (amended 1997).

Individuals with Disabilities Education Improvement Act of 2004, 20 U.S.C. §1400 *et seq.* (2004) (reauthorization of the Individuals with Disabilities Education Act of 1990).

Jameson, J., M., McDonnell, J., Polychronis, S., & Riesen, T. (2008). Embedded, constant time delay instruction by peers without disabilities in general education classroom. *American Association on Intellectual and Developmental Disabilities, 46,* 346-363.

Jorgensen, C. (2005). The least dangerous assumption: A challenge to create a new paradigm. *Disability Solutions, 6(3),* 1, 5-9.

Lavoie, R. (1989). *How difficult can this be: FAT city.*

Luckasson, R., Coulter, D. L., Polloway, E. A., Reiss, S., Schalock, R. L., Snell, M. E., . . . Stark, J. A. (2002*). Mental retardation: Definition, classification, and systems of supports (10th ed.).* Washington, D.C.: American Association on Mental Retardation.

McDonnell, J., Thorson, N., Allen, C. & Mathot-Buckner, C. (2000). The effects of partner learning during spelling for students with severe disabilities and their peers. *Journal of Behavioral Education, 10,* 107-121.

McDonnell, J., Mathot-Buckner, C., Thorson, N., & Fister, S. (2001). Supporting the inclusion of students with moderate and severe disabilities in junior high school general education classes: The effects of classwide peer tutoring, multi-element curriculum, and accommodations. *Education & Treatment of Children, 24,* 141-160.

McDuffie, K. A., Mastropieri, M. A., & Scruggs, T. E. (2009). Differential effects of peer tutoring in co-taught and non-co-taught classes: Results for content learning and student-teacher interactions. *Exceptional Children, 75,* 493-510.

No Child Left Behind Act of 2001, 20 U.S.C. 70 § 6301 *et seq.* (2002).

Nolet, V. & McLaughlin, M.J. (2000). *Accessing the general curriculum: Including students with disabilities in standards-based reform.* Thousand Oaks, CA: Corwin Press.

Palmer, S. B., Wehmeyer, J. L., Gipson, K., & Agran M. (2004). Promoting access to the general curriculum by teaching self-determination skills. *Exceptional Children, 70,* 427-439.

Pecquet, J. (5/23/10). *Bipartisan senate bill aims to take 'retarded' out of federal lexicon.* The Hill, Retrieved from http://thehill.com/homenews/senate/99391-senate-bill-aims-to-take-retarded-out-of-federal-lexicon.

Raver, S.A. (2009). *Early Childhood Special Education – 0 to 8 Years: Strategies for Positive Outcomes.* Upper Saddle River, NJ: Pearson Education, Inc.

Rosenberg, M.S., Westling, D.L., & McLeskey, J. (2008*). Special Education for Today's Teachers: An Introduction.* Upper Saddle River, NJ: Pearson Education, Inc.

Schalock, R.L., Borthwick-Duffy, S.A., Bradley, V.J., Buntinx, W.H.E., Coulter, D.L., Craig, E.M. . . .Yeager, M.H. (2010). *Intellectual disability: Definition, classification, and systems of supports (11th ed.).* Washington, D.C.: American Association on Intellectual and Developmental Disabilities.

Shapiro, B.K., & Batshaw, M.L. (2007). Mental retardation (intellectual disability). In R. M. Kliegman, R.E. Behrman, H. B. Jenson, & B.F Stanton (Eds.), *Nelson textbook of pediatrics* (18th ed.). Philadelphia, Pa: Saunders Elsevier.

Turnbull, A., Turnbull, R., & Wehmeyer, M. (2010). *Exceptional lives: Special education in today's schools.* Upper Saddle River, NJ: Pearson Education.

U.S. Department of Education. (2005). *To assure free appropriate public education: Twenty-seventh annual report to congress on the implementation of the Individuals with Disabilities Education Act.* Washington, DC: Author.

Van Norman, R. K., & Wood, C. L. (2008). Effects of prerecorded sight words on the accuracy of tutor feedback. *Remedial and Special Education, 29,* 96-107.

Winokur, M. A., Cobb, R. B., & Dugan, J. J. (2007). *Effects of academic peer assistance interventions on academic outcomes for youth with disabilities: A systematic review.* Fort Collins, CO: School of Education, Colorado State University.

Wolery, M., & Schuster, J. W. (1997). Instructional methods with students who have significant disabilities. *The Journal of Special Education, 31,* 61-79.

QUESTIONS *for Reflection:*

What is the difference among the classifications of students with intellectual disability?

What are the criteria used to identify students with intellectual disability?

What are adaptive behavior skills? What are examples of these skills?

List and describe the levels of support for students with intellectual disability identified by AAIDD.

Select one "common learning challenge" for students with mild/moderate intellectual disability; compare/contrast that with one "common learning challenge" for students with severe/profound intellectual disability.

What can/should teachers do to ensure access to the general curriculum for students with intellectual disability?

Select 5 suggestions provided in the chapter that may likely be applicable to your future work with students with and without disabilities. Briefly describe these items.

NOTES

CHAPTER **6**

Teaching Children with Specific Learning Disability

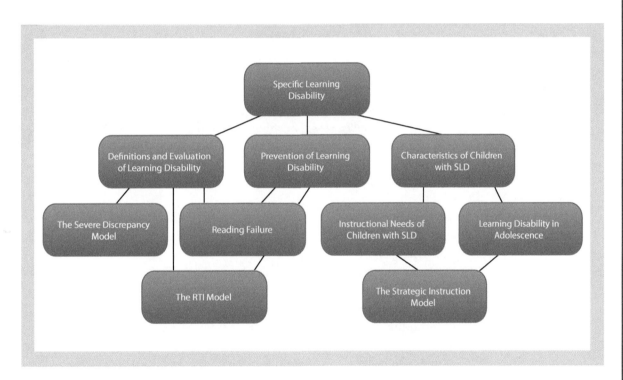

THE TOP TEN TERMS FOR CHAPTER 6:

The following key terms or big ideas are critical to your understanding of the content for chapter 6 and the in-class discussions to follow.

• Specific Learning Disability	• RTI
• Dyslexia	• Severe discrepancy
• Dysgraphia	• Dyscalculia
• Phonological processing	• Exclusionary definition
• Explicit Instruction	• Learning Strategy Instruction

Defining Learning Disability

IDEA Definition of Specific Learning Disability – term used to describe a

> disorder in one or more of the basic psychological processes involved in understanding or in using language, spoken or written, that may manifest itself in the imperfect ability to listen, think, speak, read, write, spell, or to do mathematical calculations. This term does not apply to students who experience learning problems due to other disabilities.

The definition provided in IDEA has led to a dominant view of learning disability as a disorder that is *intrinsic to the child* in contrast to theories that describe the disability as the result of a social system phenomenon (Wagner & Garon, 1995). According to the National Center for Learning Disabilities (NCLD), a learning disability should be viewed as a real disorder. The NCLD definition, which varies slightly from the IDEA definition, clarifies that a learning disability is

> a neurological disorder that affects the brain's ability to receive, process, store and respond to information. The term *learning disability* is used to describe the seeming *unexplained difficulty a person of at least average intelligence has in acquiring basic academic skills* [emphasis added]. These skills are essential for success at school and work, and for coping with life in general. LD is not a single disorder. It is a term that refers to a group of disorders (NCLD, 2009, www.ncld.org).

Specific deficit areas that have historically been associated with specific learning disability based on psychological evaluations include **dyslexia, dysgraphia,** and **dyscalculia**.

- **Dyslexia**—neurologically based disability that reflects intrinsic, often persistent, deficits in fundamental reading skills (e.g., phonological processing, word recognition, fluency/decoding).
- **Dysgraphia**—a learning disability that impacts written language based on difficulty with language formulation and organization and, often, limitations in fine motor skills.
- **Dyscalculia**—a learning disability associated with the inability to understand or manipulate mathematical concepts including retaining math facts and performing computations.

These disabilities could be seen as the "specific" in specific learning disability. It is relatively uncommon for public schools to make reference to these terms in the referral or eligibility process, as they derive from work in psychological evaluation and medical research. Some learning disability advocacy groups continue to use the terms to clarify how and why a student is struggling.

One of the challenges associated with developing clear definitions of learning disability relate to the "exclusionary" nature of most definitions. In other words, definitions of LD focus on the idea that a child is experiencing inexplicable difficulty with learning in school. Based on the IDEA perspective on learning disability established in American public schools, learning problems are not necessarily learning disabilities. A child whose learning problem can be attributed to an underlying condition, syndrome, sensory limitation, or lack of opportunity to learn cannot be accurately described as a learning disability. Although some have suggested that the primary indicator of learning disability is generally poor school performance, exclusionary factors are those factors that might typically explain the poor performance in school. The following problems cannot serve as the etiology of learning disability:

- Severe emotional or behavioral problems
- Hearing impairment
- Visual impairment
- Physical disability
- Intellectual impairment
- Environmental or economic disadvantage
- Immigrant or second language status

> *Etiology* – an identified cause or set of causes for a medical condition or disorder.

Ruling out all of these common sources of difficulty in learning, the child with a specific learning disability would be the child experiencing severe difficulty with a specific academic skill, typically reading (Lerner, 1989), that cannot be logically explained. The word *inexplicable* is used commonly to describe the observations of parents and school professionals in observation of a young child experiencing a learning disability.

Despite exclusionary factors associated with the definition, it is possible to have concomitant disorders.

> *Concomitant* – accompanying; term used to describe characteristics or disorders that can co-occur.

For example, the linguistic basis of learning disability suggests that some children are likely to receive services for both learning disability and impairment in language development. Language impairments are often associated with difficulty in oral and written expression, formulation of ideas to express clear thoughts in conversation, and listening comprehension. There is considerable overlap between these characteristics and those of learning disability. Neither is it uncommon to see concomitant identification of learning disability and problems with attention and focus in school (e.g., ADHD). It is possible that a child with a disability, such as a physical disability, could also have a learning disability, but the exclusionary factors cannot be the source of eligibility for learning disability.

> *Confusion about the LD definition*
>
> A few years ago, a student told me about a little boy in her clinical placement who had a learning disability and was experiencing many of the problems I had described in class. Later in our conversation she described how his physical impairments required him to use an electronic wheelchair, multiple computerized communication devices, and some tools for holding a pencil and drawing in class. The continued conversation revealed that the little boy was quite bright, receiving great support in school and performing quite well. Of course, he had cerebral palsy (CP). That was the clear source of his special learning needs in school. *He did not have a specific learning disability (SLD).*

Probably the most common misconception about learning disability leads to the greatest confusion in diagnosis: children with learning disabilities are typically quite bright. By traditional evaluation procedures, they must have at least average intelligence to qualify for special education in this category. Because children with learning disabilities tend to be generally intelligent and possess various accompanying gifts or talents (like all children), it can come as a shocking and traumatic experience for families to witness their children enter school and suddenly struggle to translate their myriad gifts into classroom success. Although there are often numerous areas of academic struggle for children with learning disabilities, difficulty with language-based skills (i.e., native language development and academic language development) tend to create a major "bump in the road" in the development of children with learning disabilities. Children with reading problems often have difficulty with underlying linguistic abilities that might go unnoticed prior to school. For example, strengths in the area of ***phonological processing*** or ***phonemic awareness*** tend to be reliable precursors for reading success in school. Children who excel in these skills can look at a letter and tell you what sound that letter makes. The sound of the letter is much more important than the name of the letter, if a child is to develop early reading abilities that require "sounding out" of words. Rhyming games are also reflective of phonemic awareness, as they require a child to be able to manipulate sounds in words and see patterns in phonemic sequencing that underlay the structure of words in reading. Although these activities are common in childhood, difficulty might not be seen as a problem, and the intellectual abilities and vibrant personalities of children with reading-based learning disabilities are likely to "mask" any established weaknesses with pre-literacy skills.

The subjectivity of the learning disability definition has led to years of debate about the authenticity, validity, reliability, and political motives of having a learning disability category in special education. There are various ideological "camps" in the fields of study related to learning disability, but most advocacy groups like the *Learning Disability Association of America* or the *International Dyslexia Association* have spent years advocating to the general public that **learning disabilities are real and intrinsic to the child.** Given that premise, the current dispute is associated with rate of identification and ensuring that only children with "real" learning disabilities are determined to be eligible. *Prevention* of inappropriate referral and eligibility is a major goal of contemporary educational leaders (see description of RTI in this chapter).

CONTROVERSY IN THE LD DEFINITION

Despite the notion that disability labels are stigmatizing, services for specific learning disability have often been seen in a more positive light by the general public. The services are viewed as *genuinely beneficial* due to the extensive network of support that special education can offer when a family understands the rights associated with IDEA and advocates for those rights at their community school. A common criticism of the learning disability construct in American schools relates to the tendency to under- or over-identify children based on the ambiguity of the construct. Depending upon the perception of learning disability eligibility in school as either: a) a beneficial opportunity to receive special education that will result in a child receiving additional and individualized support in school or b) a process of defining typical reading failure as a disability and ingraining that failure by naming rather than remediating it; you will find differences of opinion about the eligibility process and rates of identification. Some scholars have noted that the definition of learning disability, which excludes children who have experienced environmental, cultural, or economic disadvantage, creates an identification process that favors eligibility for children of the majority American culture (i.e., White, middle class children) and thus, a less stigmatizing way of receiving special education that will aid the child in navigating the educational bureaucracy. In a potentially correlated manner, students of color and students from disadvantaged communities are much less likely to be identified for SLD and more likely to be identified for special education programs like Intellectual Disability in the mild range or to be called "at-risk," a quasi-category that affords no clear educational benefit without special school programming being developed. On the other hand, many theorists have noted that the term *learning disability* is overgeneralized and should not be applied as often as it is. Essentially, the idea that learning disability has been consistently referred to in the literature as virtually synonymous with *reading disability*, reading disabilities tend to stem from an interaction between intrinsic deficits in phonological processing and school programs that are insensitive to the needs associated with those deficits, and there is a natural variance in propensity for phonological processing, suggests that it is virtually impossible to find the "real" learning disability. Instead, the focus should be on broad efforts at identifying and addressing reading problems in schools.

THE SEVERE DISCREPANCY

Traditionally, one of the easiest ways to explain a learning disability to someone who has never worked with this population was to say, "Learning disabilities are related to gaps between perceived *aptitude* and actual *achievement*." In other words, there is an inexplicable failure to perform at the level that would otherwise be expected. The gap between these two areas was often referred to as a "severe discrepancy." This definition is reinforced by the most commonly used method of evaluation of learning disabilities in schools. School psychologists determine eligibility for special education in public schools by administering a battery of tests which include an intelligence test (e.g., the WISC-IV) and an achievement test (e.g., the Woodcock-Johnson Tests of Achievement). Achievement tests administered in schools assess the student's abilities in specific areas relevant to school performance. These skills include, but are not limited to spelling, reading and writing fluency, passage comprehension, and vocabulary knowledge. Once scores have been determined for overall intelligence and performance in specific academic achievement areas, the psychologist can determine whether a "severe discrepancy" exists between the student's assumed ability (IQ) and their specific level of achievement. The determination of what qualifies as "severe" depends on state and school district regulations for evaluation. Typically, a 15-20 point discrepancy is sufficient to establish a severe discrepancy.

For a number of years, scholars and social critics have noted the inherent challenges with *the severe discrepancy model*. Most notable among educators was the tendency to see a student's needs neglected if they did not qualify with a severe discrepancy in their scores. Unfortunately, a lack of attention to a student's failure in an academic area would ultimately result in their achievement score becoming increasingly discrepant with their IQ as time passed. IDEA 2004 included language to support alternative means of evaluating learning disability. Prior to the IDEA change, greater than 90% of U.S. states used evaluation procedures based on severe discrepancy from IQ (Hynd, Clinton, & Hiemenz, 1995). Concerns about IQ testing and flaws, and contradictions in evaluation procedures contributed to recent changes in perspective regarding the validity of the severe discrepancy model's use for clear and valid determination of specific learning disability. A common complaint among psychologists relates to the flawed belief that achievement and IQ tests measure different things and are measuring sufficiently distinct constructs such that comparison of scores would be valid (Sternberg & Grigorenko, 2002). In contrast, Spear-Swerling (1995) explains that the two constructs corrupt each other. Although ability can predict achievement (the basis for discrepancy evaluation), a lack of achievement and exposure to rigorous academic experiences is likely to influence IQ measures with the result of suppressing scores. Ultimately, it becomes clear that the severe discrepancy process is unreliable due to correlations that exist between the scores that are being compared. As such, artifacts of the testing process influence determination more than the student's characteristics and potential to benefit from special education (Spear-Swerling; Sternberg, 1995).

The process was further criticized for using evaluation procedures that were substantially distinct from the actual definition of SLD, which implies an intrinsic condition at the root of the problem. The testing procedures that school districts used (and often still use) resulted in purely *algorithmic* determinations and explained nothing about the origins of failure. In fact, differing requirements for discrepancy scores (e.g., 15 vs. 20) meant that a student could have an identified learning disability, move to a school in a new state where the formula is different, and no longer have an identified learning disability. These problems led to students missing out on needed services if they could not meet this rather arbitrary discrepancy criteria (Wagner & Garon, 1995).

Consensus around testing procedures among numerous theorists involved in the study of learning disability suggest that IQ testing is generally not a useful process for determining learning disability. In contrast, numerous researchers have suggested that tests of phonological processing would be an improvement in identifying the characteristic difficulties associated with reading-based learning disabilities (Sternberg, 1995).

CHARACTERISTICS ASSOCIATED WITH LEARNING DISABILITIES

The characteristics of students with learning disabilities generally reflect the components of the definitions used to describe this population. The single, defining characteristic of students with learning disabilities is the presence of specific and significant achievement deficits in the presence of adequate overall intelligence.

While not all encompassing, Table 6.1 below provides a list of characteristics that are often observed in students with LD and essentially reflect the defining characteristic mentioned above.

Table 6.1.

Students with Learning Disabilities may:
demonstrate gaps in critical skills for school
demonstrate performance limitations in basic literacy
have problems with self-monitoring of attention and on-task behavior
seem to be capable of more than they are achieving in school
require additional time to determine the meaning of a question
require additional time to produce a response
be inconsistent in his/her academic performance (e.g., may appear to understand a skill one day only to be unable to complete the same task the next day)
have difficulty establishing and maintaining interpersonal relationships
behave inappropriately DUE TO the frustration experienced with academic difficulties
have difficulty grasping a concept presented in one format while understanding the same concept presented in an alternative format (see text box)
master math facts but have difficulty with problem solving tasks
have difficulty expressing himself/herself in a written format even though he/she can do so verbally

Perspective from John Beattie, co-author of this book:

I have been identified as an adult with a learning disability in reading. Several years ago, I was working with my son, trying to teach him a specific learning strategy. As he described how he learned most effectively, it became clear that this was another area in which we were different. My son can look at a table or graph and remember every specific detail of the information. He can read a story, close his eyes, and clearly describe the specific details of the story. He never understood why I was unable to do the same thing...until one day when he said to me, "Dad, just close your eyes and picture what you read." I did what he asked and waited for his next instructions. He then said, "When you closed your eyes, could you 'see' the stuff from the story in the way the author described it?" I looked at him and simply said, "No, I did not." He was getting frustrated with me; he then asked, "Well, what DID you see?" I stopped and thought for a moment and replied, "The backs of my eyelids!" For some reason, my son seemed to have a greater understanding of how I learned.

READING FAILURE AND LEARNING DISABILITY

When people think about reading, their thoughts are affected by their past experiences (positive or negative) with reading tasks. Some think of reading as a wonderful process that opens new worlds to us as we "glide" through the printed material. Others think of reading as an incredibly difficult, embarrassing chore that the "lady in the dress makes me do every day" in school. Regardless of our experiences or our success with reading, it is a crucial skill that enables students to gain knowledge from numerous sources about numerous topics... that is, if there are no problems in the "learning to read" process. Unfortunately, this is not always the case.

Reading is an extremely complex process that involves decoding letters/sounds in an effort to ultimately gain an understanding of the target material. In other words, reading requires us to recognize that our language is made up of sounds, which is referred to as *phonological awareness*. This knowledge leads readers to recognize that words are formed by combining individual sounds into words (i.e., *phonemic awareness*). Once this recognition is well established, a child can identify a variety of words by "reading" them in a book, magazine, or paper in school. This process must be completed in an automatic manner so that students can read each word quickly. This finally allows the students to identify the meaning of the printed material. However, even this complex process is not sufficient to ensure that a student will truly understand the content of the classroom's reading material.

The complex reading process is further complicated due to the nature of the language involved. The definition described earlier stated that learning disabilities result from difficulty "involved in understanding or in using language, spoken or written, that may manifest itself in the imperfect ability to listen, think, speak, read, write, spell, or to do mathematical calculations." Students with learning disabilities, by definition, have problems understanding and using language skills. In reading the sentence, "I will walk around the block tonight to get some exercise," a student with learning disability may be able to read/decode the word "block," but struggle to understand the context in which it is used. The student may ask, "Why is it healthy to walk around the block?" This student may recognize a block as the wooden cube used in many tasks in school, not the area in their neighborhood. The student with a learning disability in reading may well become more confused with this process called reading because he has learned that there are errors that occur even if he "knows all the words." The elements of language exacerbate the already difficult reading process. Not only must we be able to decode the individual words and recognize their place in sentences or passages, we have to be able to differentiate the meaning of the words relative to how they are used in the passage. A classic example of the complexity of our language is apparent in the silly poem in the text box below.

> She threw the ball through a window pane,
> And suffered a really major pain,
> She heard the owner,
> Who had a beard and
> Who also sounded very weird!
> His threat was so great that she ran in fear,
> As if being chased by a bear (not beer).
> The owner stopped and began to laugh
> At his very real social gaff.
> "It's OK," he finally said.
> "Don't worry, just forget it and go to bed."

There seems to be little wonder as to why **reading failure is the characteristic most commonly identified in students with learning disabilities**. Not only must students recognize the difference between tough and dough (see above), they must also understand that the meaning of these odd sounding words may change from one sentence to the next. There are far too many examples of the potential confusion that all readers might experience to discuss here. However, it is critical that the professional working with students with and without learning disabilities remember how confusing this process can be and find ways to ensure that students learn to read to the maximum of their ability.

SOCIAL SKILLS

An area that is often overlooked in working with students with LD is the impact the learning disability can have on the child's social behavior. Many students with LD find difficulty in making real friends. Although, it might seem unrelated to learning problems, Kavale and Forness (1996) report that 75% of students exhibit social skill deficits in three categories:

- pure skill deficits due to the lack of acquisition of a particular social skill
- deficits in performance in which students fail to use social skills they have previously learned in the appropriate social situations, and
- deficits in self-control that result in demonstration of negative patterns of behavior.

Further, although learning disabilities are not characterized by characteristics of ADHD like hyperactivity and impulsivity, there are in fact relatively high rates of comorbidity between the two disabilities that could contribute to perceptions of social difficulties.

According to the National Center on Learning Disabilities, many students with learning disabilities including dyslexia may experience language development-based challenges that extend into the area of communication with peers and perceptions of social deficits. It is not uncommon to hear anecdotal descriptions of students failing to get jokes their friends make, possibly due to difficulties with the subtleties of language in humor including sarcasm. Students also struggle with "storage and retrieval" in language processing, so they may appear to stumble and struggle for words in conversation. In general, students with learning disabilities experience the most notable social challenges in academic experiences, but it is reasonable to consider the myriad ways that expressive and receptive language development can impact social competence in daily interactions, whether that be in daily communication or even expressed in a lack of desire to e-mail or message with friends due to hesitation regarding written communication. Once the social issues/concerns are identified and understood, students with LD will benefit from intervention focusing on specific and unique aspects of the behavior and the tactics that can help avoid future concerns.

Why Do Students with Learning Disabilities Struggle with Mathematics?

By Shaqwana M. Freeman, Illinois State University

It is no secret that many students struggle with mathematics, but it is especially true for students with learning disabilities (LD). The data from the 2005 National Assessment of Education Progress (NAEP) indicated that only 2% of the students in the United States attained advanced levels of mathematics achievement by the 12th grade (*National center for education statistics*, 2006). Additionally, on a national assessment of mathematical proficiency Lee, Grigg, and Dion (2007) reported that only 8% of students with disabilities in grades 4 and 8 were performing at or above proficiency level. It has been determined that between 3% and 14% of children have mathematical disabilities (Dowker, 2005; Shalev, Manor, & Gross-Tsur, 2005). One thought is that these apparent difficulties in mathematics are due to the increased demand in the content knowledge required for students with and without disabilities.

The standards for teaching and learning mathematics as developed by the National Council of Teachers of Mathematics (Mathematics, 2000) now place greater emphasis on conceptual understanding, mathematical reasoning, and problem-solving skills which require a greater understanding of math concepts. However, *students with LD often struggle with mathematics because of their difficulty with skills not directly related to math. These may include perceptual skills, language deficits, reasoning skills, and memory deficits* (Ginsburg, 1997). Additionally, Maccini and Gagnon (2000) reported *information processing, self-monitoring, and basic arithmetic computational deficits* as additional factors contributing to students' struggles with mathematics. The previous findings have also been supported by Bryant, Bryant and Hammill (2000) and Bryant, Hartman and Kim (2003) who found that students who struggle in math often struggle with memory, poor calculation skills, number reversals, and difficulty understanding procedural processes. Given the research-based evidence, one might assume that teachers are equipped with the knowledge base to successfully remediate mathematics deficits in students with learning disabilities; however, this is often not the case.

Students with LD continue to struggle with mathematics. There could be numerous reasons that would provide insight as to why students with LD struggle with mathematics, but the one reason that comes into question the most is the adequacy of instruction that the students receive and their teacher's ability to teach the subject.

In the past, general education teachers taught students without disabilities and special education teachers taught students with disabilities. As the number of students with disabilities included in the general education classrooms increases, the distinction between the roles and responsibilities of general and special education teachers have become less apparent. As stated previously, teachers are expected to follow the standards set forth by the NCTM; however, in a study conducted by Maccini and Gagnon (2000) almost half of the special education teachers were unaware of what the NCTM standards were.

General and special educators each have areas of expertise that complement each other when applied to a specific instructional setting; one teacher's strengths work to fill in the gaps that the other teacher may have (Friend & Cook, 2006). Nonetheless, far too many elementary students fail to acquire skills involving the basic operations and applications of mathematics that are requisite for success with higher level mathematic skills (Jones, Wilson, & Bhojwani, 1998). The need for effective high-quality instruction is at an all-time high.

Factors that may contribute to low-quality instruction include poorly designed and managed instruction and unskilled teachers (Stein, Kinder, Silbert, & Carnine, 2006).

Having a clear understanding of what goals and objectives need to be taught is the first step in teaching students how to "do" math. When designing a lesson, the teacher should take five things into account: (1) sequence of skills and concepts, (2) explicit instructional strategies, (3) preskills, (4) example selection, and (5) practice and review (Stein, et al., 2006). Once teachers are aware of the considerations necessary for an effective lesson, it is imperative to identify the specifics of "what and how" to teach the content to meet the needs of students. This can be accomplished through diagnosis of the problem experienced by the student, data collected from an initial assessment, ongoing progress monitoring, error-correction procedures, knowledge of appropriate presentation techniques, as well as alternative remediation techniques (Stein, et al., 2006).

Management of mathematics instruction can be looked at from three aspects: 1) teacher-directed instruction, 2) student independent work, and 3) teacher workcheck (Stein, et al., 2006). A lesson that has been well-designed offers teacher-directed instruction that produces high rates of student-teacher interaction in a briskly paced instructional lesson. Independent work should cover skills that the students have demonstrated that they are able to complete independently and should include the majority of practice from the most recently acquired materials with previously learned material embedded as a review. Workcheck is also an important process in which the teacher should correct the students' errors during independent work time; the quicker weaknesses or deficits are identified, the easier it is to remediate the skill (Stein, et al., 2006).

Providing students with disabilities classroom teachers who are qualified to teach the content area is a high need. Having every classroom staffed with a "highly qualified teacher," as required by the No Child Left Behind Act (NCLB) of 2001, will hopefully result in increased academic achievement and improved post school outcomes for students with disabilities.

CAUSES OF LEARNING DISABILITIES

Controversy related to the definition of learning disabilities relates strongly to the debate over etiology. The origin or cause of learning disabilities is highly debatable. For years, there has been considerable disagreement about whether medical professionals could specifically isolate the condition that leads to a learning disability. Although research using fMRI and PET scans does indicate unique "processing signatures" in individuals determined to have learning disabilities in reading, the nature of causes is still quite unclear (see Figure 6.1 below).

Figure 6.1.

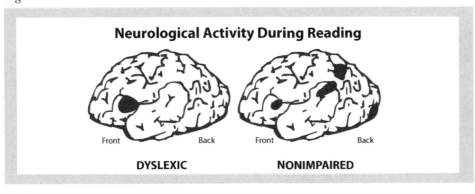

There is some consensus among specialists in psychological and medical fields that the vast majority of poor readers do not have an intrinsic disorder or syndrome at the root of their reading failure. Wagner and Garon (1995) suggest that the search for a specific disorder, condition, or syndrome leading to reading disability is inappropriate. They explain that learning disability is best viewed as the interaction between intrinsic characteristics (e.g., varying levels of propensity with phonological processing) and the educational practices of their school. Students who demonstrate deficits in phonological processing are more or less likely to have identified learning disabilities in reading, depending on how the school assesses reading performance and provides targeted supports and intervention in areas of difficulty. In other words, it is likely that a number of children will come to school at-risk for reading failure due to a mismatch between the ways in which they process linguistic information (pre-literacy abilities) and the manner in which their school teaches children to read. Wagner and Garon (1995) suggest reading skill should be viewed like IQ or other academic characteristics that are dispersed along a normally distributed continuum of performance. There will also be some children for whom reading skills are substantially limited (on the lower end of the continuum); however, it is a relatively arbitrary distinction to be made between poor reading and disabled reading. Theorists have acknowledged that although most children with reading problems do not appear to have clear conditions that cause the failure, that does not stop reading failure from being a genuine and significant problem for children experiencing that reading failure. Ultimately programs must be developed by schools to respond to reading failure, particularly on the basis of characteristics like phonological processing deficits that predict difficulty.

What is the core characteristic contributing to learning disability in reading?

Deficits in phonological processing ability: phonological awareness, phonological memory, and phonological naming/rapid naming (Wagner & Garon, 1995).

Are learning disabilities genetic? Do they run in families?

Yes. Whether you view learning disability as a disorder or a characteristic of the child that leads to reading problems, family members tend to demonstrate similar profiles. Like so many human characteristics, LD may be viewed as the result of an interaction between genetic predisposition and environmental context (Sternberg, 1995).

Do more boys have learning disabilities than girls?

Yes and no. Theorists who advocate for the intrinsic and severe disorder of learning disability suggest there should be an equal prevalence between genders. In schools, however, numerous factors lead to boys being over-referred for learning disability and identified at higher rates (e.g., lower expectations about school performance among boys; the tendency for boys to act out when struggling, whereas girls tend to hide their difficulties) (Wagner & Garon, 1995).

Do children with severe learning disabilities have genuine differences in neurological processing?

Yes. Children with severe reading disabilities exhibit different language processing effort in the brain as viewed by neurological processing signatures measured with fMRI and PET scans (Shaywitz & Shaywitz, 2004). Further, there have been suggestions that subtle neuro-anatomical variation could exist (Hynd, et al., 1995).

Prevalence and Notable Statistics for Learning Disability in American Schools

The 35th Annual Report to Congress on the Implementation of the IDEA (2011) estimated that 2.9 million American children had identified specific learning disabilities and received special education services in public schools. More recent statistics suggest a decline in these numbers coinciding with an increase in *Other Health Impairment,* a category comprised mostly of students with Attention Deficit Hyperactivity Disorder (ADHD).

*The common estimate of prevalence trends suggest that approximately **5% of children in American public schools are found to be eligible for special education on the basis of a learning disability, which tends to account for nearly 50% of the overall special education population**.* These statistics tend to vary from year to year, but there are relatively consistent trends that indicate large numbers of students with learning disabilities in schools. Despite lack of biological evidence to support gender differences in learning disability prevalence, the National Center for Learning Disabilities estimates that close to four times as many boys are identified for learning disability, particularly for reading problems.

Ultimately, students with learning disabilities are commonly included in general education classroom instruction. According to the same 2013 report, approximately 66.2% of students with learning disabilities are educated primarily in general education classes (80% of the day or more), while another 31.8% spend between 21 and 60% of their day in separate settings. Less than 2% of students with learning disabilities served in public schools are educated in fully separate schools or educational settings.

Trends suggest that students with learning disabilities who are eligible for special education are unlikely to be "dismissed" from special education or "lose" the disability label, as about only 9% of students do so. Post-school outcomes, although not consistent with typically-achieving peers, have improved in recent years. Students with learning disabilities have decreased in high school dropout rates of 12.5% from 43% within the past decade.

RESPONSE TO INTERVENTION MODEL

Despite the fact that many states and school districts have their own interpretations of the RTI process, the following overview of RTI is provided based on the work of the National Research Center on Learning Disabilities (NRCLD) and specifically the center's summary provided by Mellard titled, "Understanding Responsiveness to Intervention in Learning Disabilities Determination." An overview of RTI is intended to help future educators understand the nature of RTI as a school policy for evaluating academic performance and providing multiple levels of instructional intensity and intervention for children as they progress through school. For a more detailed explanation of what RTI can look like at the practical classroom level, see the section of Chapter 14 describing general education classroom methods of reading assessment and intervention.

At its core, the fundamental difference between RTI and traditional assessment practices for learning disabilities is the tremendous emphasis on monitoring and *prevention of failure*. Many in the education field have described the traditional processes used by school psychologists as a "wait to fail" model in which teachers and other professionals delayed special education evaluation in order to give the child time to "catch up" to his peers. Unfortunately, reading failure is not easily resolved and it is rare that children experiencing difficulty will teach themselves. Side effects of the "wait to fail" model could include: a) the student's reading problems becoming more established, b) student affect towards reading and school, in general, is likely to decline precipitously, and c) the student is likely to be retained in their current grade level due to inability to master the curriculum that is so heavily focused on reading proficiency.

Although there is almost universal consensus on the RTI premise of preventing reading failure in the manner proposed, there remains controversy regarding the way in which RTI methods will be used to make LD determination. In other words, how will monitoring and prevention strategies lead to accurate measures of determining that a child has a genuine learning disability? Because of the multitiered approach, the general consensus is that a child meeting eligibility for special education in the category of specific learning disability, would be that child who has experienced multiple tiers of academic intervention including small group and intensive academic intervention programs, and yet still lags substantially behind in an academic area like reading performance. Presumably, the focus on multiple instructional strategies, ongoing assessment, and intensive interventions would meet the needs of vast population of children who would currently be placed in special education, and result in a small number of children meeting eligibility criteria such that they would be considered "learning disabled" and in need of ongoing special education. Certainly, this process is more ambiguous, subject to problems of fidelity, and time-consuming than traditional practices that simply required comparison of intelligence and achievement test scores.

Theorists in the field of learning disability have long suggested that there is a real construct of Specific Learning Disability that can be identified from neuropsychological, biological, and neurological evidence. Notably, though, many of the key scholars in learning disability research distinguish the research-based phenomenon from the over-identified and "over-generalized" construct used in American public schools that eventually led to such elevated identification rates that as many as 51%

of children in special education were considered to have Specific Learning Disability (or approximately 5% of the total school-age population). In contrast, (1995) note that a truly severe reading disability that would more accurately match the idea of a "medical-model-type disability" is likely to substantially more rare; perhaps as low as 1% of the total school population, but probably no more than 3% (p. 100). An assumption of the RTI process is that this smaller number of children with verifiable and substantial disabilities in reading would be least responsive to even the most effective and targeted reading interventions, resulting in a small number of children receiving special education for learning disability. Wagner and Garon (1995) echo this sentiment suggesting that school programs that intervene in the area of phonological processing, for example, tend to be effective for promoting basic reading skills among many children with reading problems, but there remain a small number of children who appear not to respond as would be expected. Despite effective programming, some children appear to have substantial reading problems that are more resistant to remediation and may, consequently, require the civil rights protections and academic accommodations, justifiably, provided by IDEA. Historically, the lack of valid school-based identification processes has impeded progress in distinguishing between poor readers and the reading disabled.

RTI reflects a genuine departure from traditional practices in reading instruction. The concept of RTI derives from an established public health model that employs primary, secondary, and tertiary interventions. Each of the tiers of RTI represents progressively increasing intensity of intervention for students. Essentially, the instructional responsibilities of RTI rely on improved and enhanced responsibilities of general classroom teachers in assessing reading performance and delivering instruction based on evidence-based practices in teaching reading rather

Figure 6.2.

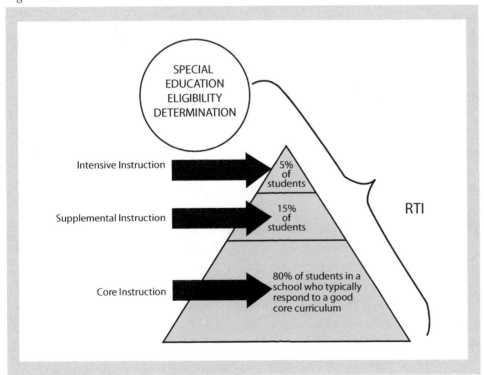

than relying on "conventional wisdom." Historically, reading programs have had inconsistent or limited evidence of effectiveness across the full population of school children. In some cases, any random reading program could produce desirable outcomes for a large number of children who simply have a strong predisposition for reading ability. Unfortunately, these reading programs were ineffective for a large number of children.

At the primary level of the RTI "triangle," there is an expectation of improving the reading instruction that all children receive in school. Presumably, about 80% of children will make expected reading progress based on whole-class quality reading instruction. The secondary level of intervention assumes a small number of students (perhaps 15% of students) considered at-risk for reading failure will require more supplemental instruction in reading strategies beyond what is offered to the full population. At the tertiary level of intervention, approximately 5% of students in the school population will require a very intensive level of reading intervention.

CRITICAL FEATURES OF RTI

1.   Ensuring that instruction provided by general education classroom teachers reflects high quality instructional methods known to address the needs of most students.
2.   Research-based instruction guides general classroom instructional practices.
3.   Assessment of performance by the general education teacher.
4.   Universal screening by school staff.
5.   Progress monitoring to track student performance.
6.   Intensive reading interventions based on research on interventions for struggling readers.

PLANNING INSTRUCTION AND SUPPORTS FOR CHILDREN WITH LEARNING DISABILITIES

Educational Approaches – Interventions used with students with learning disabilities must endeavor to present material in a manner that is as clear as possible, maintaining an approach that is "short, sweet, and to the point." This is best accomplished using techniques that emphasize ***explicit instruction***. Explicit instruction involves the teacher serving as the party responsible for providing the information. This is crucial in working with students with learning disabilities who, for a variety of reasons, may experience difficulty in learning new or complex material. Consequently, teachers must present content material in a clear format that focuses directly on the content to be learned (Mercer & Mercer, 2005). Explicit instruction requires the teacher to present a model of the target material. The teacher next guides the student(s) through activities designed to enable the student(s) to appropriately apply the skill in various contexts. Finally, the teacher develops activities designed to enable the student(s) to independently apply the skill to ensure mastery and generalization (Mercer & Mercer, 2005). Teachers who effectively implement explicit instruction *provide a sufficient range of examples to illustrate a concept.* This often involves providing models of proficient performance to ensure that the student(s) understands what the solution "looks like." In an effort to further ensure student understanding, teachers incorporating explicit instruction into their lessons ask students to explain how and why they made the decisions to identify a solution. Inherent in this approach is the need for adequate practice opportunities followed by frequent, positive feedback for student performance.

Content enhancements are also utilized in working with students with learning disabilities. Teachers use content enhancements in their instruction in an effort to foster students' ability to identify, organize, understand, and remember content material (Lenz, Bulgran, & Hudson, 1990). There are several techniques that help students identify, organize, understand, and remember content material. Guided notes can be utilized in a variety of classroom settings with a variety of content material. Teachers use their "lecture" notes as a frame of reference as they develop the guided notes. For example, in presenting a lesson on Christopher Columbus, the teacher might provide the following "guided notes" for the class to use as the teacher discussed Columbus' voyage to the New World:

1. Money from Queen of _____
2. Sailed with ___ ships.
3. They were the _____, _____, and the _____ _____.

Graphic organizers and visual displays are also potentially invaluable techniques designed to enhance the content knowledge of students with and without learning disabilities. An excellent example of such a technique is provided at the beginning of each chapter in this book. The graphic organizer provides a "flow chart" format that identifies the focal points of the chapter as well as information about the various elements of the chapter. Students can learn to use this technique with almost any academic content material.

Mnemonic instruction is an approach to content enhancement that helps students remember classroom material (Fontana, Scruggs, & Mastropieri, 2007). We have all learned that the first-letter mnemonic **HOMES** is a technique to help remember the Great Lakes (i.e., **H**uron, **O**ntario, **M**ichigan, **E**rie, **S**uperior). Mnemonics can be used in helping students remember specific content information (as with HOMES). This enhancement is also beneficial when working with specific academic tasks.

Students with learning disabilities who are learning to produce sentences, paragraphs, and stories in a written format often have difficulty with the "nuts and bolts" of the writing process. They exert so much energy and attention to the content of the written product that they often neglect to consider the grammatical elements of writing. Teachers remind their students to "Watch out for the COPS" after finishing a writing assignment. The students remember that they need to make sure that the appropriate word is **C**apitalized, that the **O**verall appearance of the story is as it should be (some teachers tell students that the 'O' is for Organization), that the **P**unctuation is accurate, and that they have **S**pelled the words correctly.

ADOLESCENTS WITH LEARNING DISABILITIES AND THE STRATEGIC INSTRUCTION MODEL

Although prevention models like RTI seek to identify and remediate early reading difficulties, reading problems often linger throughout the schooling process for children with learning disabilities. As mentioned in chapter 3, students with learning disabilities often experience a "ceiling effect" in their reading performance that translates to a need to learn rigorous secondary curricula despite reading performance that plateaus at the 4th grade level. High-level reading comprehension tasks and rapid acquisition of content knowledge reflect the unique requirements of adolescents with learning disabilities. Many educators specialize in interventions that focus on the secondary schooling experience for students with learning disabilities.

THE STRATEGIC INSTRUCTION MODEL AND THE CONTENT LITERACY CONTINUUM

The University of Kansas Center for Research on Learning (KUCRL), founded by Donald Deshler and Jean Schumaker, is dedicated to improving the performance of students with learning disabilities and has paid particular attention over the years to the performance of all adolescents demonstrating extreme difficulty with reading and academic performance such that they lag behind grade level peers. The center is responsible for the concept of strategic instruction and is most notable for advocacy in the area of explicitly teaching children to use "learning strategies." According to the center, a **Learning Strategy** is "an individual's approach to a task, including how to approach and do the task and evaluate performance of the task." Learning strategies can develop through a student's experiences with learning in life and school, but due to gaps in use of appropriate learning strategies across academic and social settings, many students can benefit from receiving instruction from a trained teacher on using learning strategies.

STRATEGIC INSTRUCTION

In its early work, the KUCRL focused heavily on the development of a learning strategies curriculum intended to be a strategy-by-strategy response to the academic limitations of students struggling in school. Students have difficulty with remembering extensive vocabulary, so the center developed a vocabulary acquisition strategy (i.e, the LINCS Vocabulary strategy). Students had difficulty with reading comprehension, so the center developed myriad comprehension strategies addressing everything from paraphrasing to visualizing and making inferences. In recent years there has been a push to embed these strategies in content classrooms to avoid the infrastructural challenges of creating separate classes for learning strategies instruction and risking a lack of generalization into content classrooms.

Strategy instruction is an appropriate instructional approach to negate the tendency toward minimizing educational experiences of students with learning

Table 6.2.

Commonly Used Strategies to Support Students with Reading Comprehension or Acquisition of Knowledge
Word Identification Strategy
Self-Questioning Strategy
Visual Imagery Strategy
Paraphrasing Strategy
The Inference Strategy
Commonly Used Strategies for Storage or Retention of Key Information
FIRST-Letter Mnemonic Strategy
Paired Associates Strategy
LINCS Vocabulary Strategy
Commonly Used Strategies for Demonstrating Knowledge
Assignment Completion Strategy
The Sentence Writing Strategy
The Paragraph Writing Strategy
Test-taking Strategy
Essay Test-Taking Strategy

University of Kansas Center for Research on Learning: Common Learning Strategies (Lenz, Deshler, & Kissam, 2004).

disabilities—sometimes referred to as *watering down* the curriculum (King-Sears, 1997). Rather, the ***Strategic Instruction Model*** (including **the learning strategies curriculum** and **the content enhancement series**) is an approach that assists students in overcoming areas of deficit in their skill repertoire and improving their metacognitive practices to improve performance in academic content. In contrast, this process has been referred to as "watering up the curriculum" (Ellis, 1997, p. 407). There is an expectation of content learning and effective learning strategy usage.

Student-focused interventions involve the development, among students, of specific strategic approaches to learning content by addressing areas of deficit. The larger collection of these learning strategies is referred to as the Learning Strategies Curriculum and includes a continuum of strategies to address skills in *acquisition of knowledge, storage or maintenance of knowledge*, and *expression or demonstration of knowledge*. Strategies in this curriculum include strategies for reading comprehension (e.g. The Word Identification Strategy, The Paraphrasing Strategy), memorization of information (e.g. The FIRST-Letter Mnemonic Strategy, The LINCS Vocabulary Strategy), written expression (e.g. The Sentence Writing Strategy, The Paragraph Writing Strategy), and demonstration of competence (e.g. The Test-Taking Strategy) which have been shown to be effective in improving student learning and performance (Lenz, Deshler, & Kissam, 2004).

Another example of a learning strategy that is commonly learned by students with learning disabilities as they transition to secondary schools, is the classroom participation strategy called SLANT. Based on the premise that students with learning disabilities a) project a negative affect toward school by using poor posture and looking uninterested, and b) fail to actively process the critical information taught in their classes, a key learning strategy for students with learning to implement focuses on both "teacher-pleasing" behaviors and a systematic way to think and listen in class. The SLANT strategy is taught by pre-testing students' current approach to participating in class, which tends to be underdeveloped, and is followed by a description of SLANT, modeling of the strategy, and verbal practice with the mnemonic device that represents the steps involved. The students also practice using the strategy and eventually make commitments to generalize the strategy to all of their school experiences, which require extensive interaction with teachers and peers and the ability to focus attention on content acquisition.

The **SLANT** Strategy
Sit up
Lean forward
Activate your thinking
Name key information
Track the talker

THE SIM CONTENT ENHANCEMENT SERIES

Part of the *Strategic Instruction Model*, the Content Enhancement series focuses again on the use of mnemonic devices and graphic organizers/concept maps to make rigorous content more conceptually explicit. Content Enhancement Routines are used to organize the "big ideas" of a course so that students can systematically learn and interact

© AVAVA, 2015. Used under license from Shutterstock, Inc.

with the critical ideas in a content presentation and remember the key information. The content enhancements also help teachers organize their content strategically such that they must consider learner diversity in the process of planning. A commonly used example of a content enhancement is the Unit Organizer Routine, which includes a concept map to explicitly present only those aspects of the content that everyone should know, organized around overarching essential questions. Many teachers also begin by using the Course Organizer Routine. This is an approach used to explicitly discuss and justify the relevant concepts that will be taught throughout the year. As an educator, this can be equally beneficial as a means of examining what you believe are the critical questions or ideas of your course. (Example, Are you just trying to get to the end of the year, or do you believe there are certain core ideas that your students must know before they leave your course?)

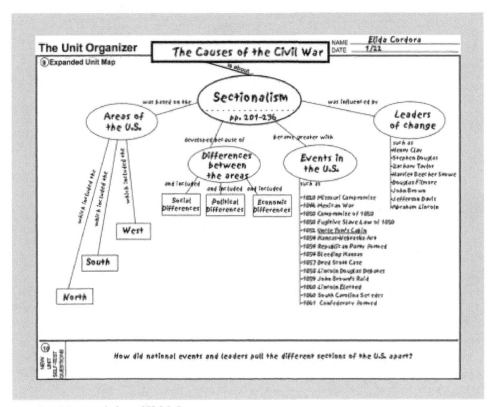

Reprinted by permission of Keith Lenz.

There are also content enhancement routines for teaching concepts and increasing performance (Lenz, Deshler, & Kissam, 2004). Key routines include the *Concept Anchoring Routine, Concept Comparison Routine,* and *Concept Mastery Routine.* The routines make conceptually ambiguous content more explicit by using graphic organizers to clarify examples, non-examples, and key characteristics. Effective implementation has typically resulted in substantial improvement in academic performance by students with learning disabilities.

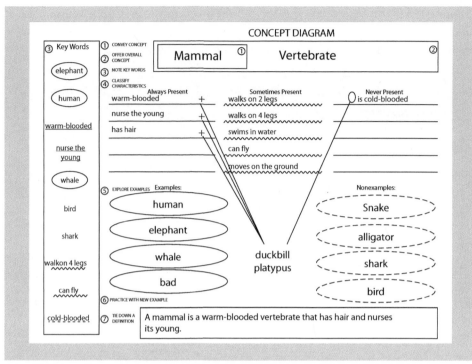

© *The Concept Mastery Routine, Bulgren, J.A., Schumaker, J.B., Deshler, D.D., Edge Enterprises, Inc. 2005, Lawrence, KS. Reprinted by permission.*

The Content Enhancement graphic organizers are instructional tools developed and researched at the University of Kansas Center for Research on Learning. These are examples of a number of teaching devices designed for teachers to use as they teach content information to classes containing diverse student populations. They are data-based teaching instruments have been found effective when used with a planning routine as well as a teaching routine that combines cues about the instruction, specialized delivery of the content, involvement of the students in the cognitive processes, and a review of the learning process and content material.

Table 6.3.

Content Enhancements for Planning
Course Organizer Routine Unit Organizer Routine Lesson Organizer Routine
Content Enhancements for Supporting Comprehension in Text and Explaining Key Topics
Clarifying Routine Framing Routine Survey Routine
Content Enhancements for Explicit Content Instruction
Concept Mastery Routine Concept Anchoring Routine Concept Comparison Routine

Improving Student Performance
Recall Enhancement Routine
Question Exploration Routine
Quality Assignment Routine
Vocabulary LINCing Routine

Most recently, the Center for Research on Learning has emphasized the need to focus on adolescent literacy and content acquisition in order to actualize the potential of students with learning disabilities who would otherwise be inhibited by reading problems. **The Content Literacy Continuum** (Ehren, Lenz, & Deshler, 2005) summarized in Table 6.4 emphasizes a multi-leveled or multi-layered approach to remediating the gaps in academic performance observed among adolescents with learning disabilities. At the fundamental level, students with learning disabilities who struggle with reading are likely to experience difficulty with language development. Students who still struggle with this level of reading development in adolescence will likely benefit from therapeutic intervention from a Speech-Language Pathologist. Beyond this level of support is the most intensive intervention provided by special educators in the form of Direct Instruction programs that systematically teach students the basic skills of reading including decoding, fluency, and comprehension strategies. Each level of instruction builds upon the foundation of more intensive instruction in more discrete and fundamental skills. The remainder of the continuum reflects the Strategic Instruction Model's emphasis on both intensive learning strategy instruction in separate classrooms and embedded in general education classes. Finally, the Content Enhancement Series fills in the remaining gaps in academic content acquisition by using explicit instructional techniques known to be effective for students with learning disabilities.

Table 6.4.

The Content Literacy Continuum to Improve Adolescent Literacy	
Level 1: Content Enhancements in General Education Classes	Prioritizing "Big Ideas" of content instruction, general education teachers use content enhancement routines as a form of explicit instruction.
Level 2: Embedded Learning Strategy Instruction in General Education Classes	General education teachers weave learning strategies into general education courses in a manner that immediately promotes application of the strategies to the relevant content area.
Level 3: Intensive Learning Strategy Instruction	Characteristic of a "supported inclusion model," students are taught a range of learning strategies that can eventually be generalized to content-area courses. Instruction is intensive and requires a separate classroom to ensure sufficient time and practice.

Level 4: Intensive Instruction in Basic Skills	For students who have not developed sufficient skills in reading to access advanced content, students are provided direct instruction in reading fluency, decoding, and comprehension.
Level 5: Therapeutic Intervention in Language Development	Support is provided in the form of language therapy and/or intervention provided by professionals like speech language pathologists.

Postsecondary Success for Students with Learning Disabilities: What Does It Take?

By Debra Holzberg, University of North Carolina at Charlotte

Why, when school presents such significant challenges for students with learning disabilities (LD) in K-12 schools, are more students choosing to attend postsecondary institutions? According to the National Center for Learning Disabilities (Cortiella & Horowitz, 2014), in 1990, approximately 30% of students with LD matriculated to college. Fifteen years later, in 2005, that number increased to 48%. Much of the drive to attend institutions of higher learning is born out of the fact that an individual's earning potential is positively correlated to their level of education (United States Department of Labor, 2014). Additionally, due to the advent of and access to technology (i.e., e-learning experiences), what once may have been a nearly insurmountable task, is now within reach.

With increased enrollment of students with LD, comes the need to identify what it takes for those students to achieve success. The greater demands of postsecondary education pose a formidable task for students with LD as they call upon fundamental skills students with LD often lack. For example, according to the International Dyslexia Association, 70–80% of students with specific LD have deficits in reading (http://www.interdys.org/). An integral part of most coursework, proficient reading is a prerequisite for college-level classes. Additional challenges presented by postsecondary education involve difficulty in organization of tasks for both life and learning, difficulties in written expression and math, skill set deficits in studying and test-taking, and social skill deficits (Skinner, 2004). Compounding the skill set deficits inherent with LD is the fact that accommodations once provided by law, are no longer guaranteed to college students. While postsecondary institutions must grant certain accommodations (providing the student has proper documentation) in order to comply with the American with Disabilities Act and Section 504, there is a degree of flexibility in the extent to which accommodations will be offered. In essence, institutions are obligated to do the bare minimum (if they want to retain federal funding); however, they are not required to go above and beyond. Finally, while schools (up through high school) are mandated to find students with disabilities, that is no longer the case in postsecondary education. Therefore, students with disabilities must self-identify; often students elect to forgo the accommodations to which they are entitled and which will improve their chance of success. It is interesting to note that according to the National Longitudinal Transition Study, 69% of young adults in postsecondary schools "did not consider themselves to have a disability" while 24% of students self-identified and informed the school. Additionally, 7% acknowledged their disability but chose not to inform their schools (2011).

Research clearly indicates the need of students with LD to actively advocate for their educational accommodations in order to facilitate their success. Students with LD experience a 34% graduation rate from four-year colleges and universities versus a 51% graduation rate of their non-disabled peers (Cortiella & Horowitz, 2014).

We know that there are a number of strategies or themes shown to increase the likelihood of a student's success. Included in those themes are the following: knowledge of one's disability and the accommodations appropriate for that disability; an understanding of one's psychoeducational evaluation; knowledge of disability laws designed to protect the student; the student's ability to effectively self-advocate (which involves understanding one's disability and the law); access to appropriate support systems; and the student's ability to persevere or persist when faced with challenges (Skinner, 2004). Add to the aforementioned strategies or themes, an understanding of the available technology and the ability to leverage the technology in one's learning.

Technology has the ability to level the playing field for students with LD (as all accommodations are designed to do). With the advance of both accurate and easy *speech-to-text* and screen readers, students with language-based LD are more easily able to meet the demands of the college curriculum. There is an established sense in the scholarly literature that computer technology can and will serve as an "electronic curb-cut" to borrow from the language of Universal Design suggesting a trend in which barriers to postsecondary learning will be reduced given the ability to offer more accessible materials in more accessible courses (Fichten, Asuncion, Barile, Fossey, & de Simone, 2000).

Online learning environments enable students to take courses at times more suitable to their learning; a "morning" person may choose to take their classes online in the morning when they are most productive. Utilizing calendars that sync across devices enables students to stay organized and helps meet deadlines. There is a multiplicity of available technologies to help students succeed; of paramount importance for the student with a LD are the understanding of what is available and the willingness to adopt the strategies designed to facilitate their success. Both high schools and colleges must to work to provide students with the tools in order to bridge the gap to better prepare students with LD for a twenty-first century college education so they may achieve their potential.

Simple Ideas that Future Teachers Should Understand about Supporting Students with Learning Disability in School

Hold high expectations for student performance
1. Regularly assess academic performance (i.e., progress monitoring)
2. Teach learning strategies to promote academic performance
3. Provide direct, intensive interventions in targeted reading skills (e.g., phonemic awareness)
4. Teach using explicit instruction
5. Teaching learning strategies to promote academic performance
6. Use assistive technology to compensate for academic deficits (see chapter 14 on UDL for details)

GLOSSARY IN PLAIN TERMS

Specific learning disability: a disability characterized by inexplicable difficulty with specific academic skills like reading or writing, despite typical intelligence.

Dyslexia: disability in reading.

Dysgraphia: disability in writing.

Dyscalculia: disability in mathematics.

Severe discrepancy: a numerical gap between a score on an intelligence test and a score on an achievement test; reflects the gap between aptitude and achievement associated with learning disability.

RTI: Response to Intervention (or Instruction); a classroom level and schoolwide model of reading instruction that emphasizes ongoing assessment, effective reading instruction, and reading intervention for students who experience difficulty.

Phonological processing: general ability to recognize and manipulate the sound system of language; predictive of early reading skills like decoding.

Exclusionary definition: suggests that the SLD definition (or eligibility) is based on the exclusion of multiple factors that could logically explain a student's failure in school (e.g., intellectual disability, emotional disturbance).

Explicit Instruction: a direct instruction approach to teaching characterized by instructional clarity that emphasizes guided practice, modeling, highlighting critical information, and offering numerous examples and non-examples when teaching new information.

Learning strategy instruction: explicit instruction in tactics for succeeding in school including approaches to classroom participation, reading, writing, test-taking, etc.

REFERENCES

Bryant, D. P., Bryant, B. R., & Hammill, D. D. (2000). Characteristic behaviors of students with LD who have teacher-identified math weaknesses. *Journal of Learning Disabilities, 33*(2), 168.

Bryant, D. P., Hartman, P., & Kim, S. A. (2003). Using explicit and systematic instruction to teach division skills to students with learning disabilities. *Exceptionality*, 11(3), 151-164.

Cortiella, C. and Horowitz, S. H. (2014). The State of Learning Disabilities: Facts, Trends and Emerging Issues. New York: National Center for Learning Disabilities. Retrieved September 12, 2014.

Dowker, A. (2005). *Individual differences in arithmetic: Implications for psychology, neuroscience and education.* New York, NY US: Psychology Press.

Ehren, B. J., Lenz, B. K., & Deshler, D. (2005). The content literacy continuum: A school reform framework for improving adolescent literacy for all students. *TEACHING Exceptional Children*, 37(6), 60-63.

Ellis, E. S. (1997). Watering up the curriculum for adolescents with learning disabilities: Goals of the knowledge dimension. *Remedial and Special Education*, 18(6), 326-346.

Fichten, C. S., Asuncion, J. V., Barile, M., Fossey, M., & Simone, C. D. (2000). Access to Educational and Instructional Computer Technologies for Post-secondary Students with Disabilities: lessons from three empirical studies. *Journal of Educational Media*, 25, 179–201.

Fontana, J. L., Scruggs, T., & Mastropieri, M. A. (2007). Mnemonic strategy instruction in inclusive secondary social studies classes. *Remedial and Special Education*, 28, 345-355.

Friend, M., & Cook, L. (2006). *Interactions: Collaboration skills for school professionals* 5th ed.. Boston, MA: Allyn & Bacon.

Ginsburg, H. P. (1997). Mathematics learning disabilities: A view from developmental psychology. *Journal of Learning Disabilities, 30*(1), 20.

Hynd, G. W., Clinton, A. B., & Hiemenz, J. R. (1995). The neuropsychological basis of learning disabilities. In R. J. Sternberg & L. Spear-Swerling (Eds.), *Perspectives on learning disabilities: Biological, cognitive, contextual.* (pp. 60-79). Boulder, CO: Westview Press.

Jones, E. D., Wilson, R., & Bhojwani, S. (1998). Mathematics instruction for secondary students with learning disabilities. In D. P. Rivera (Ed.), *Mathematics education for students with learning disabilities: Theory to practice.* Austin, TX Pro-Ed.

Kavale, K. A., & Forness, S. R. (1996). Social skill deficits and learning disabilities: A meta-analysis. *Journal of learning disabilities, 29*(3), 226-237.

King-Sears, M. E. (1997). Best academic practices for inclusive classrooms. *Focus on Exceptional Children, 29*(7), 1-22.

Lee, J., Grigg, W., Dion, G., & National Center for Education Statistics, W. D. C. (2007). *The nation's report card™: Mathematics 2007 – National assessment of educational progress at grades 4 and 8. Nces 2007-494:* National Center for Education Statistics.

Lenz, B.K., Bulgran, J.A., & Hudson, P. (1990). Content enhancement: A model for promoting the acquisition of content by individuals with learning disabilities. In T. Scruggs & B. Wong (Eds.), *Intervention research in learning disabilities.* (pp. 122-165). New York: Springer-Verlag.

Lerner, J. (1989). Educational intervention in learning disabilities. *Journal of the American Academy of Child and Adolescent Psychiatry, 28*, 326-331.

Maccini, P., & Gagnon, J. C. (2000). Best practices for teaching mathematics to secondary students with special needs. *Focus on Exceptional Children, 32*(5), 1-22.

Mercer, C.D. & Mercer, A.R. (2005). *Teaching students with learning problems (7th ed.).* Upper Saddle River, NJ: Pearson Education, Inc.

National Council of Teachers of Mathematics. (2000). *Principles and standards for school mathematics.* Reston, VA: National Council of Teachers of Mathematics. *National center for education statistics* (2006). Washington, D.C.: U.S. Government Printing Office.

Shalev, R. S., Manor, O., & Gross-Tsur, V. (2005). Developmental dyscalculia: A prospective six-year follow-up. *Developmental Medicine & Child Neurology, 47*(2), 121-125.

Shaywitz, S. E., & Shaywitz, B. A. (2004). Reading disability and the brain. *Educational Leadership, 61*(6), 6-11.

Skinner, M. E. (2004). College Students with Learning Disabilities Speak Out: What It Takes to Be Successful in Postsecondary Education. *Journal of Postsecondary Education and Disability, 17*, 91–104.

Spear-Swerling, L. (1995). Can we get there from here? Learning disabilities and future education policy. In R. J. Sternberg & L. Spear-Swerling (Eds.), *Perspectives on learning disabilities: Biological, cognitive, contextual.* (pp. 250-273). Boulder, CO: Westview Press.

Stein, M., Kinder, D., Silbert, J., & Carnine, D. W. (2006). *Designing effective mathematics instruction: A direct instruction approach* (Fourth ed.). Upper Saddle River, New Jersey: Pearson.

Sternberg, R. J. (1995). Epilogue: Toward in emerging consensus about learning disabilities. In R. J. Sternberg & L. Spear-Swerling (Eds.), *Perspectives on learning disabilities: Biological, cognitive, contextual.* (pp. 277-282). Boulder, CO: Westview Press.

Sternberg, R. J., & Grigorenko, E. L. (2002). Difference scores in the identification of children with learning disabilities: It's time to use a different method. *Journal of School Psychology,* 40(1), 65-83.

United States Department of Labor, Bureau of Labor Statistics (2014) [Chart of earnings and unemployment rate by educational attainment in 2013]. Retrieved from http://www.bls.gov/emp/ep_chart_001.htm

Wagner, R., K., & Garon, T. (1995). Learning disabilities in perspective. In R. J. Sternberg & L. Spear-Swerling (Eds.), *Perspectives on learning disabilities: Biological, cognitive, contextual* (pp. 84-105). Boulder, CO: Westview Press.

QUESTIONS *for Reflection:*

Why is it so hard to find consensus on a clear definition of a Specific Learning Disability?

How does the RTI model impact the nature of eligibility for Specific Learning Disability?

Describe how the academic and social setting demands of classrooms in American public schools serve as the basis for learning strategy instruction.

Based on the characteristics of students with Specific Learning Disability, what classroom accommodations might be necessary to support students in a general education classroom?

NOTES

CHAPTER 7

Teaching Children with Attention Deficit Hyperactivity Disorder

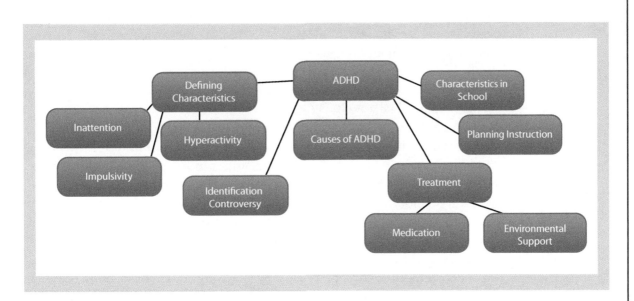

THE TOP TEN TERMS FOR CHAPTER 7:

The following key terms or big ideas are critical to your understanding of the content for chapter 7 and the in-class discussions to follow.

• Inattentiveness	• Chronicity
• Hyperactivity	• Stimulant
• Impulsivity	• Non-stimulant
• Dopamine	• Comorbidity
• Neurotransmitter	• 504 Plan for ADHD

Defining Attention Deficit Hyperactivity Disorder (ADHD)

ADHD is a term that is used in many conversations in our country today, is omnipresent in the print media, and is frequently the "hot topic" on many of our television and radio stations. It is so prevalent that it is rare to speak to an adult who has not used or at least heard the term used at some point in time. Unfortunately, the common use of the term does not translate to a strong understanding of what ADHD really is. This lack of understanding is at least partially due to the fact that there is not a clear definition for ADHD. While we do not suggest that we have "the definition," we will attempt to consider this disorder in a way that will enable us all to have a better sense of what ADHD is and what it "looks like" in children.

According to *The American Heritage Science Dictionary* (2005), ADHD is a syndrome that is usually diagnosed in childhood. It is characterized by a persistent pattern of impulsiveness, a short attention span, and sometimes hyperactivity, and interfering especially with academic, occupational, and social performance. Another medical definition suggests that ADHD is a neurobiological disorder that results in a child having difficulty regulating activity (referred to as hyperactivity), inhibiting behavior (impulsivity), and attending to tasks (inattention) in developmentally appropriate ways (CDC, 2010).

The Individuals with Disabilities Education Act (IDEA) does not formally define ADHD. Rather, IDEA considers ADHD as a part of the category "Other Health Impairments" (OHI). Children identified as having other health impairments are children who have limited strength, vitality or alertness due to some type of health condition (e.g., asthma, epilepsy, sickle cell, attention deficit hyperactivity disorder). As a consequence, these children are often extremely sensitive to environmental stimuli, which results in a limited alertness or awareness of events in the educational environment. This lack of awareness causes the individual child to experience difficulty with appropriate academic work (IDEA regulations, 2006). A student with ADHD who receives services under the category of OHI must have an IEP, which, as we know, stipulates the services required to meet the individual needs of the student.

Many students who are identified as having ADHD do not meet the standards established in IDEA. As a result, many students receive services for ADHD under Section 504 of the Rehabilitation Act (1973); these services follow the accommodations listed in what is commonly referred to as a 504 Plan. The 504 Plan is a document that is designed to "level the playing field" by providing the same educational opportunities for the student with ADHD as her/his peers. Regardless of the law under which children with ADHD are served, the identification process involves the administration of a series of tests. These tests might include measures of cognitive ability, tests focusing on academic achievement, behavior rating scales, checklist information provided by teachers or parents, and/or other specific types of procedures that are judged to be appropriate in meeting the needs of the individual child.

ADHD is often identified along with other disabilities; this is referred to as **comorbidity**. Consequently, it is beneficial to conduct an evaluation that determines the presence or absence of other disorders or disabilities. For example,

ADHD is often identified in students with learning disabilities (LD). Students with LD often fail to attend to classroom lectures or other activities. This may be due to an attention deficit; however, it may also be due to the fact that the student does not understand the material being studied in class and fails to pay attention because he/she has learned that there will be little benefit to paying attention. While these students may not be attending to the material, this inattentiveness occurs for potentially different reasons than the student with ADHD. As you can see, it is extremely important to determine the reason a student has difficulty focusing and attending to the target stimulus. As such, the diagnostic process used to identify students with ADHD should involve collecting data to determine the possible presence or absence of other disabilities (e.g., LD, behavior disorders) along with the assessment tools used to identify ADHD.

Further, symptoms for ADHD are often confused with those symptoms that are also characteristic of other disorders or disabilities and an attempt should be made to ensure that another factor is not present. For example, children with auditory processing disorders often fail to benefit from listening to lectures or other verbal classroom activities. The child who does not process information presented orally, does not attend because he/she has learned that there is little reason to do so. Therefore, the child does not appear to be paying attention to verbal directions, lessons, or assignments. This is different than the child with ADHD who does not attend due to the impact of the ADHD. These distinctions may seem to be insignificant; however, the opposite is true. Treatment for ADHD is conceivably very different than the interventions used to treat auditory processing disorders.

Ultimately, children are identified as having ADHD as a result of meeting specific criteria. These criteria have been developed by the American Psychiatric Association (APA) and are published in the *Diagnostic and Statistical Manual of Mental Disorders* (DSM-V-TR, 2000). As noted in the above definitions, identifying ADHD must consider three behavioral areas: inattentiveness, hyperactivity, and impulsivity. Specific behaviors are delineated in each of these areas. These are provided in Table 7.1. Because there are many children who would conceivably meet the established criteria without careful consideration, the DSM-V criteria emphasize that the individual must exhibit behaviors that are significantly different from the behaviors of other like-aged children. In addition, the DSM-V criteria stress the fact that the behavior must be chronic and on-going, and not simply the short-term result of some stressful event experienced by the child. The DSM-V criteria emphasize that at least 6 of the 9 behaviors must be present (i.e., significant inappropriate behavior patterns) for a period of 6 months or longer (chronicity). These factors are considered and included in the DSM-V criteria in an attempt to reduce the number of individuals who might be falsely identified. By requiring 6 behaviors to be present for at least 6 months, the DSM-V criteria attempt to identify individuals with significant and on-going difficulties with attention, activity level, or impulsive behavior.

Methods of Evaluation for ADHD

The behavioral criteria may be identified by evaluating specific tasks designed to measure a child's ability to focus and maintain attention to the target activity.

Occasionally, computer-based measures are utilized in an effort to collect objective information. Continuous Performance Tests (CPT) may be used in the evaluation process. CPTs require the child to perform computer generated, unexciting tasks for an extended period of time (i.e., 10 minutes). The degree to which the child maintains focus is taken into consideration in determining the possible presence of ADHD. While CPTs are not always utilized in identifying individuals with ADHD, data are typically identified as a result of a series of observations/experiences with the target child in various settings. Parents, teachers, and others having long-term exposure to the child will typically complete a checklist that considers each of the behaviors noted in Table 7.1. According to the National Resource Center on ADHD, when identifying ADHD, checklist information is often collected from teachers and parents. Several of the most commonly used checklists include the Vanderbilt Assessment scales, Conners Rating scales, Barkley Home Situations Questionnaire (HSQ) and the Barkley School Situations Questionnaire (SSQ), and ACTers. The questions on the checklists typically provide a series of possible responses. The person completing the checklist is asked to read the item and select the response that is most like the child being evaluated. The response choices generally range from "Not at all/Never" to "Very Often/Most of the time" (see Table 7.1 for examples). If the child is observed as displaying these behaviors beyond what might be expected of his/her chronological age, a diagnosis of ADHD may be indicated. Finally, it is critical to recognize the potential impact of the ADHD on a child's academic performance. If the child meets the DSM-V criteria but does not experience difficulty with school related tasks, s/he will not be identified as a child with ADHD in the school setting.

Table 7.1. ADHD criteria from DSM-V (CDC, 2014).

Children, adolescents, and adults (*please note the different symptom requirements for children aged 4–16 and individuals aged 17 to adult**emphasis added*) with ADHD show a persistent pattern of inattention and/or hyperactivity-impulsivity that interferes with functioning or development:

1. **Inattention:** Six or more symptoms of inattention for children up to age 16, or five or more for adolescents 17 and older and adults; symptoms of inattention have been present for at least 6 months, and they are inappropriate for developmental level:
   * Often fails to give close attention to details or makes careless mistakes in schoolwork, at work, or with other activities.
   * Often has trouble holding attention on tasks or play activities.
   * Often does not seem to listen when spoken to directly.
   * Often does not follow through on instructions and fails to finish schoolwork, chores, or duties in the workplace (e.g., loses focus, side-tracked).
   * Often has trouble organizing tasks and activities.
   * Often avoids, dislikes, or is reluctant to do tasks that require mental effort over a long period of time (such as schoolwork or homework).
   * Often loses things necessary for tasks and activities (e.g., school materials, pencils, books, tools, wallets, keys, paperwork, eyeglasses, mobile telephones).
   * Is often easily distracted.
   * Is often forgetful in daily activities.

2. **Hyperactivity and Impulsivity:** Six or more symptoms of hyperactivity-impulsivity for children up to age 16, or five or more for adolescents 17 and older and adults; symptoms of hyperactivity-impulsivity have been present for at least 6 months to an extent that is disruptive and inappropriate for the person's developmental level:

- Often fidgets with or taps hands or feet, or squirms in seat.
- Often leaves seat in situations when remaining seated is expected.
- Often runs about or climbs in situations where it is not appropriate (adolescents or adults may be limited to feeling restless).
- Often unable to play or take part in leisure activities quietly.
- Is often "on the go" acting as if "driven by a motor."
- Often talks excessively.
- Often blurts out an answer before a question has been completed.
- Often has trouble waiting his/her turn.
- Often interrupts or intrudes on others (e.g., butts into conversations or games).

In addition, the following conditions must be met:

3. Several inattentive or hyperactive-impulsive symptoms were present before age 12 years.

4. Several symptoms are present in two or more setting, (e.g., at home, school or work; with friends or relatives; in other activities).

5. There is clear evidence that the symptoms interfere with, or reduce the quality of, social, school, or work functioning.

6. The symptoms do not happen only during the course of schizophrenia or another psychotic disorder. The symptoms are not better explained by another mental disorder (e.g., Mood Disorder, Anxiety Disorder, Dissociative Disorder, or a Personality Disorder).

Based on these criteria, three types of ADHD are identified:

IA. ADHD, *Combined Type*: if both criteria IA and IB are met for the past 6 months.

IB. ADHD, *Predominantly Inattentive Type*: if criterion IA is met but criterion IB is not met for the past six months.

IC. ADHD, *Predominantly Hyperactive-Impulsive Type*: if Criterion IB is met but Criterion IA is not met for the past six months.

Once the results of the data collection have been reviewed by a licensed psychologist, psychiatrist and/or medical doctor and it has been determined that the individual has met the diagnostic criteria, a more specific type of ADHD is identified. There are three different types of ADHD that may result from the interpretation of the data. These three (3) types or presentations of ADHD are:

Predominantly Inattentive Type. As humans, we typically complete certain processes to focus or pay attention. We must initiate the process by directing our attention to the target stimulus. We then sustain this attention for as long as is necessary for the target task. In so doing, we also inhibit the tendency to pay attention to something other than the target stimulus. Finally, we shift our attention from one task to another (Fowler, 2002). A child who experiences difficulty with these processes may be identified as exhibiting a **Predominantly Inattentive Type** of ADHD. This child is identified in this category if s/he evidences 6 or more of the attention symptoms listed in Table 7.1. This child has difficulty paying attention to details, following instructions or conversations, or organizing or finishing a task. Generally, this child is easily distracted or forgets details of daily routines.

Predominantly Hyperactive-Impulsive Type. Typically, children are active in their daily lives, especially young children. However, there are children who are significantly more active than their peers. This child fidgets and talks a lot and has a great deal of difficulty sitting still for long. Young children may run, jump or climb constantly. Similarly, a child who may be identified as having ADHD may respond without recognizing or thinking about the consequences of a particular behavior. Because this child struggles with delaying gratification, s/he may fail to wait for his/her turn or to hear all of the directions. The individual feels restless and consequently responds in an impulsive manner. Someone who is impulsive may excessively interrupt others, grab things from people, or speak at inappropriate times. It is hard for these children to wait their turn or listen to directions, which often results in more accidents and injuries than others. A child is identified in this category if s/he evidences 6 or more of the hyperactive-impulsive symptoms listed in Table 7.1.

Combined Type. A child is identified in this category if s/he evidences 6 or more of the attention symptoms <u>as well as</u> 6 or more of the hyperactive/impulsive symptoms listed in Table 7.2.

Table 7.2. Sample Items from the Vanderbilt Assessment Scale

Symptoms of Inattention
Has difficulty keeping attention to what needs to be done.
Has difficulty organizing tasks and activities.
Is easily distracted by noises or other stimuli.
Symptoms of Hyperactivity
Fidgets with hands or feet or squirms in seat.
Leaves seat when remaining seated is expected.
Talks too much.
Symptoms of Impulsivity
Blurts out answers before questions have been completed.
Has difficulty waiting his or her turn.
Interrupts or intrudes in on others' conversations and/or activities.

The ADHD Identification Controversy in U.S. Schools

The rise in the number of children who have been diagnosed with ADHD has resulted in some backlash. The sheer number of children identified has caused many to be suspicious of the over-identification of the disorder. While the exact number of children who have been identified as having ADHD is difficult to specifically pinpoint, it has been estimated that anywhere from 2 to 18% of school-aged children have been diagnosed with ADHD (Rowland, Lesesne, & Abramowitz, 2002). In 2011–2012, the Center for Disease Control (CDC) published the Summary Health Statistics for U.S. Children. One of the statistics reported was the prevalence of school-aged children with ADHD. The CDC reported that 7.4% of children ages 5 to 11 have ADHD and that 9.7% of children between the ages 12 to 17 exhibit the symptoms of ADHD. Another study (Smith, Barkley, and Shapiro, 2007) reports that 3 to 8% of children have been identified as having ADHD. Although there is variability in the exact number of children with ADHD, it is clear that a significant portion of the population has been identified with this disorder. The high prevalence of children with this disorder has led some to question the legitimacy of the diagnosis. Why are so many children being identified now? If a child can concentrate on a video game for hours, can he still have ADHD? Are parents and teachers just looking for an excuse to justify children's inappropriate behavior? These questions are topics of conversation in individual family homes, schools, and doctors' offices throughout the country. While the answers to these concerns may vary from child to child, there are growing numbers of factors that substantiate the diagnosis of ADHD.

Causes of ADHD

Although there is often no clear-cut cause for the presence of ADHD in many children, there is a growing research base for the diagnosis. There are essentially three potential causes for ADHD: genetics, brain anomalies, and environmental.

Genetics. There appears to be a strong family factor related to the presence of ADHD in children. Recent research suggests that ADHD is due to genetic influences in approximately 75% of individuals identified with the disorder (Faraone, Perlis, Doyle, Smoller, Goralnick, Holmgren, & Sklar, 2005). Children whose parents are identified as having ADHD are far more likely to exhibit characteristics of the disorder. It has been estimated that there is a 40 to 57% chance that children of an adult(s) with ADHD will also be diagnosed with the disorder (Barkley, Murphy, & Fischer, 2007).

Brain Anomalies. Technological advancements have enhanced much of the research being conducted with children with ADHD. These advancements have enabled researchers to determine that the brains of individuals identified with ADHD have less brain activity and a decreased flow of blood than do their peers (Castellanos & Swanson, 2002). The reduced brain activity and blood flow occur in the parts of the brain that enable children to maintain attention and inhibit behavior, critical factors related to ADHD (Castellanos & Swanson, 2002).

Castellanos & Swanson (2002) have also conducted research that strongly suggests that individuals with ADHD may lack certain chemicals that may result in greater chances of inattention, hyperactivity, and impulsivity. These chemicals, called neurotransmitters, enable brain cells to communicate. Dopamine is a neurotransmitter that appears to be involved in individuals with ADHD.

Environmental. Children born to parents who smoke or use alcohol during pregnancy are more likely to experience symptoms of ADHD (Linnet, Dalsgaard, Obel, Wisborg, Henriksen, Rodriguez, Kotimaa, Moilanen, Thomsen, Olsen, & Jarvelin, 2003; Mick, Biederman, Faraone, Sayer, & Kleinman, 2002). Additionally, young children who have been exposed to lead often found in paint or older plumbing fixtures are at a higher risk for developing ADHD (Braun, Kahn, Froehlich, Auinger, & Lanphear, 2006).

TREATMENT

Once a child has been diagnosed with ADHD, it is critical for the professionals involved to develop a treatment plan that provides interventions that will enable the child to increase attention and reduce the overactivity and impulsive behavior patterns. The treatment plan should never consist of a single intervention. Rather, the most successful treatment plan involves several key factors.

Stimulant medication is the preferred treatment for almost 60% of children diagnosed with ADHD (Center for Disease Control, 2005). It is somewhat obvious but nonetheless important to remember that medications can only be prescribed by a medical doctor. The doctor uses the information provided by parents, teachers, school psychologists, and other individuals involved in the identification process. Once the decision is made to incorporate medication into the treatment procedure for the child, the medical doctor must decide upon the most appropriate medication to use with each child. Because each child is different, the decision as to the most appropriate medication should be made carefully. These medications may be taken in a pill or capsule as well as in a liquid form. Recently, stimulant medications have been developed so as to be used in a skin patch. Medications may also be administered as a short-acting, long-acting, or extended release dose. The ingredients in the medication do not change; however, the manner in which it is released into the body is different. Long-acting or extended release forms often allow a child to take the medication just once a day before school, so they don't have to make a daily trip to the school nurse for another dose. The doctor, parents, and teachers should work together in an effort to determine which medication is best for the child and whether the child needs medication only for school hours or for evenings and weekends.

There are numerous medications potentially used with children with ADHD (see Table 7.3 for a list of many of these medications). Regardless of the specific medication prescribed, the intended outcome of the intervention remains constant; medication is implemented with the goal of helping the child attend to the target stimuli, reduce the overactive behaviors, and limit the impulsive reactions to typical environmental events. Stimulants are used with children with ADHD because they are effective shortly after taking the medication and leave the body relatively quickly as well. But the biggest reason stimulants are used is, they work!

Table 7.3. Selected Medications for ADHD Treatment

Trade Name	Generic Name	Approved Age
Adderall®	Amphetamine and dextroamphetamine	3 and older
Adderall XR®	Amphetamine-Dextroamphetamine Extended Release	6 and older
Concerta®	Methylphenidate extended release	6 and older
Daytrana®	Methylphenidate patch	6 and older
Desoxyn®	Methamphetamine	6 and older
Dexedrine®	Dextroamphetamine	3 and older
Dextrostat®	Dextroamphetamine	3 and older
Focalin®	Dexmethylphenidate	6 and older
Focalin XR®	Dexmethylphenidate extended release	6 and older
Metadate ER®	Methylphenidate extended release	6 and older
Metadate CD®	Methylphenidate extended release	6 and older
Methylin®	Methylphenidate chewable tablets and oral solution	6 and older
Ritalin®	Methylphenidate	6 and older
Ritalin SR®	Methylphenidate extended release	6 and older
Ritalin LA®	Methylphenidate extended release	6 and older
Vyvanse™	Lisdexamfetamine	6 and older

Source: http://adhd.emedtv.com/adhd/adhd-medications.htmlxetine

The application of medication as a treatment measure for children with ADHD is more and more a part of our culture. However, all involved with these children (e.g., parents, teachers, doctors) must ensure that the medication is working effectively with little or no side effects adversely affecting the child. Side effects of stimulant medication may include one or more of the following symptoms: loss of appetite, weight loss, slower growth, headaches, stomach pains, insomnia, irritability, sad or depressed behavior, and/or nervousness. If any of these side effects are present, the parents should be encouraged to talk to the child's doctor to determine if the specific medication is best suited for the child or if another type of medication is more appropriate.

Given the potential impact and side effects that might occur through treatment with stimulant medications, alternative or non-stimulant medications have been developed and are used with many children. Strattera® (hydrochloride) was the first non-stimulant medication approved to treat ADHD. Although Strattera is not a stimulant medication, it must be prescribed by a doctor. This medication has indications that may reduce the potential side effects noted above. Nonetheless, there are potential side effects with Strattera. These include dry mouth, stomach pain, insomnia, loss of appetite, and/or nausea. Strattera is approved for use in children, teenagers, and adults. Intuniv is another non-stimulant drug and is actually a long-acting version of guanfacine, a blood pressure medication. It was approved for use with individuals with ADHD in 2009. Intuniv is administered in an extended-release tablet and is taken once a day. Side effects may include fatigue, drowsiness, and headache.

Although medication is the most common intervention used with children with ADHD, medication alone is often not enough. The medication does not make the child more intelligent, more organized, or a better reader. Instead, it helps the child focus more effectively on the tasks presented throughout the day. Consequently, it is often important to incorporate some type of behavior plan into the child's daily regimen. The specific type of behavior plan should be developed based on the individual needs of the child. However, the behavior plan should endeavor to help the child be successful in carrying out the activities in and out of the school setting. Put simply, it is quite possible that the child with ADHD had never truly been aware of the school or classroom rules or "learned" how to behave appropriately to the satisfaction of the teacher. A behavior plan should assist the child, teacher, and parent in finding strategies that allow the child to function as part of the class and the entire school community.

Any intervention implemented with students with ADHD should always consider the environment in which the child is placed. Generally speaking, it is beneficial to reduce the extraneous stimuli evident in the classroom environment. While it is important to have an appealing classroom, teachers should remember to limit the number and degree of stimulating decorations in the classroom. Similarly, parents should consider the opportunities the home environment offers the inattentive, overactive child to be involved in activities unrelated to the target material. The list below is a starting point for teachers and parents to consider in setting up the school and home space used by children with ADHD. Please do not misinterpret this list as suggesting that the classroom or bedroom be void of any color, pictures, slogans, mottos, or school rules; rather, it is a recommendation that caution be implemented as the classroom itself is organized and decorated.

School

- develop and implement clear rules & expectations;
- reduce student down time to help ensure that students are focused on the target material;
- keep students actively engaged even during time when a transition is made between classroom activities;
- limit pictures, art work, or academic work posted in the child's immediate environment;
- keep doors and windows closed when introducing new information or during test situations;
- seat students with ADHD away from the doors and windows;
- seat students with ADHD in close proximity to the teacher to help direct students' attention;
- use the student's name to direct attention to the target information;
- use a light touch on the student's shoulder to secure his/her attention.

Home

- establish, post, and maintain a schedule;
- keep televisions, computers, and cell phones out of child's room unless being explicitly used for academic work;
- help the child with organization by keeping all school related materials in the same location (this will also help with other items not related to academics as well);
- to the maximum degree possible, assure that "recreational" items (e.g., video games, pool table) are in a room separate from where the child completes academic work;
- work in short time periods (e.g., 20 - 25 minutes) and allow a brief break (e.g., 5 minutes) during which the child can participate in activities that involve movement (e.g., shoot free throws in basketball, kick a soccer ball, get a drink of water, use the restroom).

Again, this list should not be considered to be all inclusive; instead, it is intended to provide a general selection of tasks that teachers and parents have found to be affective in working with students with ADHD. If there are specific behavioral concerns that may exist in your classroom, communicate with your school mentor or administrators who might have experience with the inappropriate behaviors you are experiencing.

CHARACTERISTICS OF CHILDREN WITH ADHD IN SCHOOL SETTINGS

Characteristics of children with ADHD can generally be traced to the symptoms identified in the DSM-V criteria. The characteristic behaviors of children with ADHD show themselves as inattentive behavior, overactive behavior, and/or impulsive behavior. These behaviors are described below.

Inattentive behaviors. Children who are inattentive evidence many of the following behaviors. The child may:
- be easily distracted,
- miss details during academic work,
- forget or lose things like pencils, notebooks, or homework,
- frequently switch from one activity to another,
- have difficulty focusing on one thing,
- become distracted when not working on something they like,
- have difficulty organizing a task,
- not complete a task,
- not complete or turn in homework assignments,
- not appear to listen,
- daydream, and
- have difficulty processing information as quickly and accurately as others.

Overactive behaviors. Children who are overactive evidence many of the following behaviors. The child may:

- fidget or squirm in the seat,
- talk continuously,
- move around the room with no apparent purpose,
- touch or play with anything in the environment,
- have trouble sitting still,
- be constantly in motion, and
- have difficulty doing quiet tasks or activities.

Impulsive behaviors. Children who are impulsive evidence many of the following behaviors. The child may:

- be very impatient,
- blurt out inappropriate comments,
- show their emotions without restraint,
- act without regard for consequences,
- have difficulty waiting for things they want,
- have difficulty waiting their turn in any activity, and
- interrupt others' conversations or activities.

In reading through these characteristic behaviors, it likely becomes clear as to why children with ADHD have difficulty in school, at home, or in social settings. These children are not purposely trying to be "bad" or to create problems in the school or home setting; they simply cannot control their behaviors without the appropriate intervention mentioned earlier in this chapter.

PLANNING INSTRUCTION FOR CHILDREN WITH ADHD

A professor in our graduate schoolwork once said, "Good instruction is good instruction." He meant that if teachers are effective and consistent in what they do and how they do it, instruction makes a difference in students' learning in any classroom setting. It is imperative to remember that in teaching students <u>with and without</u> ADHD, teachers must never forget to provide appropriate models, different examples of the concept, multiple chances for students to learn the material, and ample opportunity to practice the newly learned skill. There are, however, some additional considerations that teachers may wish to take into account in working with students with ADHD.

Simple Ideas Future Teachers Should Understand about Supporting Students with ADHD in School

Hold high expectations for student performance.
- provide structure in every element of the child's life,
- limit the distracters in the child's environment,
- provide clear and simply stated directions,
- reduce the amount of work presented (i.e., chunk information),
- provide extra time for tests and assignments, *   ——
- maintain consistency in implementing class rules and consequences,
- incorporate hands-on materials whenever possible,
- use physical contact to help the child focus, **
- get child's attention before introducing any new information,   ——
- maintain the same routine every day,
- post schedules in clear sight,
- discuss any changes to the posted schedule as soon as possible PRIOR to the change,
- help the child organize items used every day in the classroom,
- incorporate notebook organizers into the daily class work,
- teach students with ADHD how to use the notebook organizers,
- praise or reward when rules are followed.

*extra time is often inappropriately incorporated into classroom activities. Extra time should be utilized only when that time enables the child with ADHD to complete a task that might not be otherwise completed.
**Physical contact in this situation suggests that the teacher gently touch the arm or shoulder of the student in an effort to help the child direct his/her attention to the teacher.

GLOSSARY IN PLAIN TERMS

Inattention: difficulty or lack of ability to form and maintain attention on the target task.

Chronicity: the description used when a behavior is present over an extended period of time.

Hyperactivity: lack of ability to limit one's activity level for an extended period of time.

Stimulant: category of medications that are most often used in treatment of ADHD. This type of medication is known to increase the actions of the central nervous system.

Non-stimulant: category of medications that may be prescribed for use with individuals with ADHD. These medications may be prescribed because of the reduced risk of dependency, the potential for them to be effective for longer periods of time, and the reduced likelihood of insomnia.

Impulsivity: inability to think or consider the consequences of a behavior before responding.

Neurotransmitter: chemicals that enable brain cells to communicate through the synapse.

Dopamine: a neurotransmitter that appears to be associated with ADHD.

Comorbidity: a disability or disorder that exists with another disability or disorder.

504 Plan: a legal document that comes from the Rehabilitation Act of 1973. The 504 Plan lists accommodations that are appropriate to the needs of the student with ADHD.

REFERENCES

American Psychiatric Association. (2013). *Diagnostic and Statistical Manual of Mental Disorders*, (5th Ed), Arlington, VA: American Psychiatric Association.

Center for Disease Control and Prevention. (2014). *Symptoms and diagnosis: DSM-V criteria for ADHD.* Washington, DC. Retrieved from http://www.cdc.gov.

Barkley, R.A., Murphy, K.R. & Fisher, M. (2007). *ADHD in adults: Original research and clinical implications.* New York: Guilford Press.

Barkley, R.A. & Murphy, K.R. (1998). *Attention Deficit Hyperactivity Disorder: A Clinical Workbook,* (2nd Ed), Guilford Publications, New York.

Braun J, Kahn RS, Froehlich T, Auinger P, Lanphear BP. Exposures to environmental toxicants and attention-deficit/hyperactivity disorder in U.S. children. *Environmental Health Perspectives*, 2006 Dec; 114(12):1904–1909.

Castellanos, F. X., & Swanson, J. (2002). Biological underpinnings of ADHD. In S. Sandberg (Ed.), *Hyperactivity and attention disorders of childhood* (2nd ed., pp. 336–366). Cambridge, England: Cambridge University Press.

Center for Disease Control (September 2007). *Vital and Health Statistics.* U.S. Department of Health and Human Services.

Center for Disease Control, (Sept. 2, 2005). Morbidity and Mortality Weekly Report (MMWR).

Faraone, S.V., Perlis, R.H., Doyle, A.E., Smoller, J.W., Goralnick, J.J., Holmgren, M.A., & Sklar, P. (2005) Molecular genetics of attention-deficit/hyperactivity disorder. *Biological Psychiatry 57*:1313–1323.

Fowler, M. (2002). *Attention-deficit/hyperactivity disorder.* Washington, DC: NICHY, the National Dissemination Center for Children with Disabilities. Retrieved September 5, 2010.

Individuals with Disabilities Education Act regulations (IDEA), 34 C.F.R. 300.8 (2006).

Linnet KM, Dalsgaard S, Obel C, Wisborg K, Henriksen TB, Rodriguez A, Kotimaa A, Moilanen I, Thomsen PH, Olsen J, Jarvelin MR. Maternal lifestyle factors in pregnancy risk of attention-deficit/hyperactivity disorder and associated behaviors: review of the current evidence. *American Journal of Psychiatry*, 2003 Jun; 160(6):1028–1040.

Mick E, Biederman J, Faraone SV, Sayer J, Kleinman S. Case-control study of attention-deficit hyperactivity disorder and maternal smoking, alcohol use, and drug use during pregnancy. *Journal of the American Academy of Child and Adolescent Psychiatry*, 2002 Apr; 41(4):378–385.

National Resource Center on ADHD, http://www.help4adhd.org/en/treatment/scales. Retrieved August 10, 2010.

Rowland, A.S., Lesesne, C.A., & Abramowitz, A.J. (2002). The epidemiology of attention-deficit/hyperactivity disorder (ADHD): A public health view. *Mental Retardation Developmental Disability Research Review 8*, 162–70.

www.medterms.com/script/main/art.asp?articlekey=22329

QUESTIONS *for Reflection:*

Define ADHD in a manner that would help you describe the disorder to parents.

Describe a 504 Plan; include what it is and what it is designed to accomplish.

What is comorbidity?

Describe the impact and importance of the DSM-V criteria in identifying ADHD. What cautions must be taken into account with these criteria?

List and <u>describe</u> 5 characteristics of individuals with ADHD.

What is the most common treatment used with individuals with ADHD? What other factors should be taken into account?

List and <u>describe</u> 5 considerations teachers should take into account in their classroom.

NOTES

CHAPTER 8

Teaching Children with Speech and/or Language Impairments

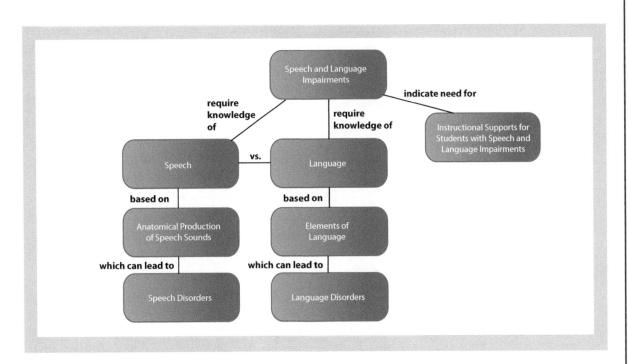

THE TOP TEN TERMS FOR CHAPTER 8:

The following key terms or big ideas are critical to your understanding of the content for chapter eight and the in-class discussions to follow.

• Phonology	• Morphology
• Semantics	• Syntax
• Pragmatics	• Articulation disorder
• Fluency disorders	• Voice disorders
• Expressive language disorder	• Receptive language disorder

The chapter will briefly summarize the critical elements of speech and language impairments including the specific difficulties that would be addressed in collaboration with an expert in Speech-Language Pathology. As a teacher, you will sometimes collaborate with Speech and Language Therapists/Pathologists. You will certainly have students in your class who struggle with speech and/or language problems. Developmental speech and language delays are very common in young children. The idea of *disorder* comes later when children have not made appropriate growth out of this *delay*.

The Relevance of Speech and Language Impairments in Schools

According to IDEA, a speech or language impairment is a disorder of communication related to the ability to create speech sounds (e.g., stuttering, articulation problems, or voice disorders) or process linguistic information (both expressively and receptively). The primary professional responsible for addressing intervention in these speech and language disorders is the Speech-Language Pathologist who works at the school or for the local school district. A Speech-Language Pathologist (SLP) has extensive training in child development, anatomy and physiology, and therapeutic intervention, particularly related to the development of communication—speech, language, and hearing (to a lesser extent). The term "speech teacher" is a bit misleading, as SLPs are actually prepared as therapists, similar to physical therapists, in a manner that reflects a healthcare perspective on intervention. Full qualifications for the profession include an advanced degree (Master of Arts; Master of Sciences) and both state and national certification by the American Speech-Language-Hearing Association (ASHA). Although SLPs practice with all age groups, school-based therapy sessions can range from direct speech training to address inappropriate development of speech sounds to language therapy sessions that resemble the academic support experiences offered by special education.

Speech and language impairments are often concomitant problems to other disorders. It would certainly not be unusual to see students with most special education disabilities (e.g., learning disability, Autism, Intellectual disability, Traumatic Brain Injury) experiencing deficits in speech or language production (Owens, 2009). The category of speech and language impairment, even as a distinct special education category, represents ***the second largest population of children requiring special education supports*** with some estimates approaching 20% of the special education population. It is fair to say that although most speech and language impairments are not severe in nature, they are certainly widespread in schools and have a meaningful impact on educational performance.

Unlike other disability categories, students receiving special education services for speech and language impairments are very likely to be found eligible, receive services, and subsequently be dismissed from special education when they are found to no longer require services. The 27th Annual Report to Congress on the Implementation of the IDEA (2005) reports that 34% of children in speech and language programs are "declassified" from special education following remediation of difficulties.

WHAT IS THE DIFFERENCE BETWEEN SPEECH AND LANGUAGE?

Speech and language, despite being synonymous in the common vernacular, are related, but different processes. Relevant to this chapter, differences between speech and language ultimately translate to differences between speech and language *disorders*. In fact, the best way to understand childhood disorders in speech and language is to have an in-depth understanding of the manner in which children produce speech and language, the normative development processes (i.e., milestones and age ranges), and factors that could interrupt development.

According to the American Speech-Language-Hearing Association (ASHA), **Speech** is limited to the verbal component of communication. Speech includes articulation of sounds, voice, and fluency. Essentially, speech is the process of making speech sounds—little noises called *phonemes*. Although humans have an amazing repertoire of speech sounds, the ability to create speech-like sounds is not unique to humans. Assigning meaning to those speech sounds makes us human and contributes to the richness and capacity of language (Owens, 1996). **Language** is a system of "socially shared rules" necessary for effective communication. Although speech is typically a key part of language, the complexity of linguistic interactions among conversational participants includes a mutual understanding of word meanings, structure and organization of words, and the practical use of certain language interactions that fit a given context (ASHA, 2010). Language reflects perhaps the most advanced of human abilities and neurological development—symbolic representation of reality. Owens (1996) suggests that "humans may be the only animals with a productive communication system that gives them the ability to represent reality symbolically without dependence on immediate context support" (p. 26).

The Mechanics of Speech

Although speech is a commonly accepted prerequisite for complex language (not including methods of manual communication), non-verbal communication is actually a key component of human interaction in face-to-face situations. The way someone looks when they are speaking—their body language, facial expressions, proximity to the other person, and hand gestures may say as much as, if not more than, the words coming out of their mouth (Owens, 1996).

Having established that speech is the verbal component of communication, it is productive to examine the *physiology of speech* (i.e., the way in which anatomical features of humans contribute to the creation of speech sounds). Owens (1996) describes *speech* as the "result of planning and executing specific motor sequences… that requires very precise neuromuscular coordination" (p. 7). Notably though, the precise coordination of these motor sequences builds upon actions that occur in a fairly natural way in humans. To that point, babies produce their first speech sounds without intentionality; instead, sounds are playful and result from experimentation with breathing, "voicing," and moving the tongue, teeth, and lips. This early experimentation evolves to articulation of specific, speech sounds to make certain words and control of voice quality, intonation, rate, and the rhythm or fluidity of speech (Owens). Speech is separate from the rules of language that assign meaning to speech. Young children go through an extensive developmental process in which early experimentation with sounds they can make evolves into early successes with "meaning making" as a result of speech sounds (i.e., "mama" makes mother happy and helps communicate a need in a manner that is better and more precise than crying). Without that attached meaning, the speech sounds that we produce are nothing more than strings of random noises.

Anatomy and Physiology of the Speech Mechanism

For the sake of clarity, speech can be explained as a very mechanical operation easily broken down into a fewer critical operations. Although neuromuscular control involving complex nerve innervations is certainly relevant to speech production a basic representation of speech can be described in the stages of **respiration, phonation, articulation,** and **resonance.**

Figure 8.1.

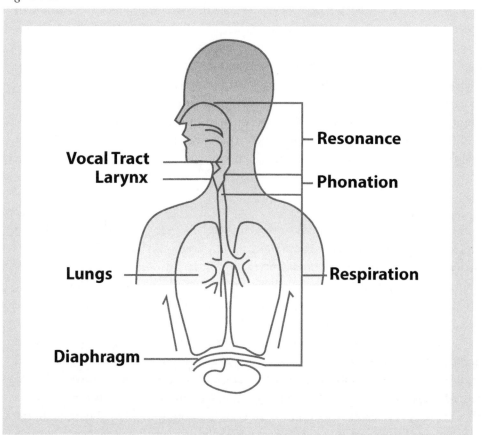

The Respiration Phase

The first step in speech is inspiration of air into the lungs. Of course, respiration is a key biological process for keeping us alive, but the air that feeds the lungs must also be expired from the lungs. As we breathe out the air, it flows out of the lungs into the trachea (or "wind pipe") and the larynx (or "voice box").

Figure 8.2.

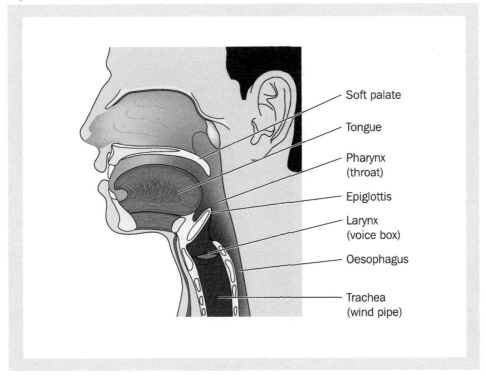

© *Blamb, 2015. Used under license from Shutterstock, Inc.*

THE PHONATION PHASE

Next, the air must pass through the larynx where two little flaps of skin called Vocal Folds (or Vocal Chords) are caught in the motion of airflow. The vocal folds, again, serve a primarily biological purpose (keeping food and liquid out of the lungs), but in a resting state, they are quite supple. They flap back and forth like butterfly wings. This fluttering action makes a simple buzzing sound (like the sound of a cell phone on vibrate). The buzzing sound creates "voice." Speech can occur without "voicing," if the air passes through the larynx without the effect of the vocal folds.

ARTICULATION AND RESONANCE PHASE

Next, the buzzing sound waves created by the rapid fluttering of the vocal folds are disbursed into the air through the oral and nasal cavities (your mouth and your nose). As the sound waves pass out, they pass through the narrow cavities of your nose creating the *resonant qualities* of your voice. They also bounce off your teeth, tongue, and lips as they leave. The manner in which a person stops and shapes that release of air in the oral cavity is referred to as *articulation*. Articulation occurs as a result of moving the teeth, tongue, and lips. For example, sounds like [p] and [b] are called "bilabial plosives" by linguists and this name literally refers to the fact that the production of these sounds results from the closure of the lips, trapping of air, and "explosion" of air from the pursed lips that creates a [p] if the air passes without voice and [b] if the air passes with voice.

Anatomy and Speech Disorders

It should be immediately clear that the mechanical process of speech could be interrupted anywhere along the way and create a speech disorder. Damage or limitations to the vocal folds would impact speech and result in what is called a **voice disorder**. Inability to manipulate the tongue, teeth, or lips appropriately to make precise speech sounds could lead to an **articulation disorder**. The articulation disorder could result from neurological processing problems, difficulty with neuromuscular control, or simple dysfunction in the anatomical features (e.g., malformation of tongue, teeth, or lips). A common speech problem called **anklyoglossia**, or being "tongue tied," results from an insufficient length of the frenum or frenulum under the tongue, which is the little piece of skin that limits the mobility of the tongue by anchoring it in the mouth.

A picture of success, Davis had multiple surgeries to repair his cleft palate and has made incredible strides in his speech development. This is very important, because he has so many things to say to friends and family.

    Cleft lip would be an example of a malformation of the lips that could affect articulation, but is typically much less severe than a **cleft palate**. Cleft palate, a cranial malformation affecting the hard and soft palate (roof of the mouth), is likely to result in severe limitations to effective speech production in the areas of articulation and resonance. Examination of Figure 8.3 should provide clues to the

Figure 8.3. Cleft Lip and Palate

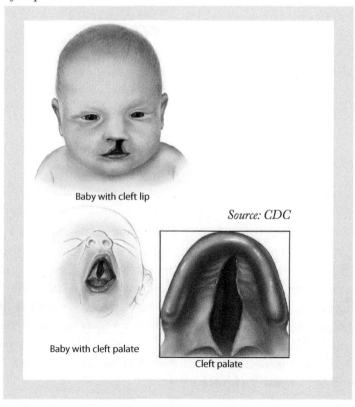

Baby with cleft lip

Source: CDC

Baby with cleft palate

Cleft palate

difficulty in creating speech sounds, as the openings in the mouth prevent adequate control of airflow and exaggerated nasal airflow that inhibit neuromuscular precision. Fortunately, extensive medical procedures and surgeries are available to children entering American public schools, which combined with intensive speech therapy sessions, are likely to ameliorate the most substantial impact on speech development.

TERMINOLOGY ASSOCIATED WITH SPEECH DISORDERS

Problems with speech are typically referred to as: (1) Articulation Disorders, (2) Fluency Disorders, (3) Voice Disorders, or (4) Resonance Disorders. **Fluency disorders** are more commonly known as *stuttering* or *cluttering* and related to the rate and rhythm of speech, particularly the fluid and comprehensible production of speech. **Voice disorders** typically manifest as hoarseness brought on by overuse of voice or illness. **Resonance disorders** occur due to improper airflow through the nasal cavity. **Articulation disorders** are problems with accurate creation of specific sounds (Van Riper & Erickson, 1996).

Fluency disorders refer to stuttering and cluttering, but it is notable that ***stuttering*** (also known as stammering) is one of the more common speech disorders confronted by young children. In fact, most children experience minor difficulty with fluidity and proper rate of speech. It would not be uncommon to hear an excited young child repeating a word again and again while struggling to complete a thought, but this is not the true disorder of stuttering that can be a severe and even lifelong challenge (ASHA, 2010).

The speech disorder, stuttering, is characterized by "stuttering moments" in which an individual will likely become "blocked" and either *repeat a speech sound* multiple times with difficulty moving on in the communication (i.e., I went to see a m, m, m, mmovie, movie) or become fixed on a sound and *prolong* the articulation of that sound (i.e., I went to see a mmmmmmmmm, mmmm, movie). Although most children outgrow stuttering or benefit from therapeutic intervention, children who continue to experience the difficulty over an extended period of time will likely develop substantial problems. As they get older in school, they are likely to develop concomitant anxiety associated with their speech problems such that the psychological consequences of stuttering and social anxiety can overshadow the severity of the condition itself. Many stutterers develop coping mechanisms that might include limited communication or social participation, creative avoidance of problem sounds (circumlocution), or use of pre-planned scripts in which they can be more confident in successful speech. Circumlocution, for example, can truly mask the challenges the individual experiences, but does not completely solve the problem, as there is a constant need to communicate using words selectively. For example, an individual experiencing moments of stuttering primarily with plosive sounds like [m], [p], [b], [w] would struggle with the sentence "Would you please give me that basketball?" and would instead have to create an alternative way of conveying this need as in "I appreciate your help getting me that, thanks." More unfortunate coping mechanisms include the use of body movements to "break out" of stuttering moments, which can begin with an "eye twitch" and lead to large motor movements like clapping hands or banging a hand on a table. Ultimately, these coping mechanisms are more socially dysfunctional than stuttering could ever be. Interaction with stutterers in the classroom should center on the reduction of anxiety (Bloodstein, 1995). Demands to finish sentences or "spit it out" produce the opposite effect and attempts to complete sentences for the person stuttering are generally considered rather disrespectful (ASHA, 2010).

Articulation disorders are common especially among young children. This can be due to specific problems like cleft lip or palate, lack of teeth, large or inflexible tongue, malformed lips, or general oral-motor weakness. For many children, it is simply difficult to reproduce the sounds they hear around them. This can be particularly challenging when children have undiagnosed ear infections. Ear infections (e.g., otitis media), or middle ear fluid, cause speech to sound muffled and generally unclear, which in turn causes children to learn an inaccurate model of speech and language usage.

Students will exhibit four major types of articulation errors including substitutions, omissions (or deletions), distortions, and additions (Van Riper & Erickson, 1996). The first three are certainly the most common and reflect typical issues in speech development for most children. These terms used in discussions of speech therapy refer to substantial and prolonged speech problems characterized as follows:

- **Substitutions:** substitution of sounds the child CAN say for sounds the child cannot say (e.g., "wabbit" for "rabbit")
- **Omissions:** simple deletion or omission of problem sounds such that a spoken word might have no first sound (e.g., "_abbit" for "rabbit")
- **Distortions:** approximation of the sound that sounds close to the desired phoneme (e.g., "wrwabbit" for "rabbit")
- **Additions**: the addition of an extra sound or syllable to ease in production of the desired sound (e.g., "ruhabbit" for "rabbit")

FUNDAMENTALS OF LANGUAGE DEVELOPMENT

Owens (1996) describes language as a "socially shared code or conventional system for representing concepts through the use of arbitrary symbols and rule-governed combinations of those symbols" (p. 8). Owens suggests that the complexity of language as a system necessitates an analysis of language according to specific components. The five components include *phonology, morphology, syntax, semantics,* and *pragmatics.* Generally speaking, these building blocks of useful, meaningful language production can be described using three themes of communication: form (structure and organization of language), content (the words/vocabulary we use), and use (social/functional process of communication). Although, each is equally important to create language, Owens emphasizes the functional use of language as paramount in effective communication.

Phonology essentially represents the component of language associated with speech sounds. Although language can be described and understood separately from speech, speech sounds or **phonemes** do contribute to the making of meaning in a linguistic system predicated on oral communication (Owens, 1996). The rules of phonology in a language dictate how speech sounds can be ordered and how words will be structured to create meaningful language. Owens suggests that the English language has approximately forty-five phonemes. Agility and accuracy with speech production that begins with simple babbling and evolves into dexterous control of subtle speech sounds in multi-syllabic words contributes to effective use of language.

Morphology relates to the structure of actual word parts comprised of **morphemes**. Without going into an elaborate description, morphemes are easily understood as word parts that can be joined together to create meaning in words. The easiest representation of this idea is to observe the differences in meaning that can be created by adding prefixes and suffixes to simple words. Certainly, <u>un</u>happy is quite different than happy. Consider, "big, bigger, biggest" or dog and dog<u>s</u>. These prefixes and suffixes are referred to as *bound morphemes* (make meaning when added to other words), whereas the root words like "big" are *free morphemes* (can stand alone).

Syntax is the last structural component of language. Together, syntax, morphology, and phonology make up the *form* of language. Syntax is commonly compared to our understanding of the grammar of a language. Syntax relates to the organization of meaning in communication governing rules of word order, sentence types, and use of nouns, verbs, adjectives, etc. To consider the importance of syntactic accuracy in English, consider how odd it would sound if someone asked you for "the hat red" rather than "the red hat." In Latin-based languages, the first syntactic structure would be correct, as in "le chapeau rouge" in French. The rules of order and structure add considerable clarity to the process of communicating.

Semantics might be the first concept you would imagine when thinking about what makes up a language. Of course, a language is made up of words or vocabulary. These are essentially symbolic representations of ideas or "things" that exist in the world. The word "cat" is not a cat. It is a representation in the English language of a cat that only exists because highly evolved human beings use "symbolic thinking" to represent the word around them. Two communicating participants of an English language conversation share the knowledge that "cat" or the phonemes [k –a- t] represent the animal that is a cat (or even a vast array of small animals that embody "cat" characteristics). Language is comprised of vast sets of words to describe ideas, actions and characteristics. Some are only subtly different from each, as in synonyms. We all have our own repertoire of words that we use effectively and probably a larger vocabulary that we understand or almost understand even if we would struggle to define it. The sum of words that you "know" is your lexicon and it obviously begins as a small set of words like "mama" and "eat" when we are very young and probably grows to an incredible 50-80,000 words by high school given an adequate educational experience (Owens, 1996).

Finally, **Pragmatics** is the functional piece of the language puzzle and can be a bit harder to describe as it has such broad implications for communication in daily life. Binding together all of the other elements of language, pragmatics is not just about word choice or structure; it is about following social rules of language use and communicating in a manner that demonstrates social competence given a particular communicative context.

For example, every language has cultural elements and every cultural group has different rules for:

- answering the phone
- engaging a friend in conversation
- interrupting a conversation
- asking for help
- addressing someone of a superior status (e.g., student to teacher)

Often, language interactions among a group of individuals follow a predetermined script, as in daily greetings and pleasantries. The communication is more habitual than meaningful (e.g., the phrase "How are you?" is rarely considered and answered with sincerity). Failure to acknowledge and follow these rules can have substantial implications for an individual's ability to effectively communicate.

The five dimensions of language:

- Phonology: sounds or phonemes of a language
- Morphology: small meaningful word parts in a language (e.g., prefixes and suffixes)
- Syntax: word order, the types of sentences used, use of parts of speech
- Semantics: elements of language that affect meaning
- Pragmatics: functional dimension of language emphasizing the social nature of language

---

LANGUAGE IMPAIRMENTS

Owens (2009) defines impairments of language as

> A heterogeneous group of developmental and/or acquired disorders and/or delays principally characterized by deficits and/or immaturities in the use of spoken or written language for comprehension and/or production purposes that may involve the form, content, and/or function of language in any combination (p. 22).

Despite the common association of "language" with *foreign languages* and second language acquisition, there is no explicit association between the idea of a language impairment and English Language Learners. Although the experiences of second language learners may seem similar to the challenges experienced by children with language impairments in their native language, the simple fact that a child is an English Language Learner cannot qualify a child as having a language impairment (Owens, 2009).

To put it simply, language disorders result from dysfunction in the aforementioned elements of form, content, and function in language. Limitations in semantic elements relate to limited capacity for vocabulary development. A lexicon that is significantly limited in comparison to age appropriate norms could reflect a language disorder. The same is true with the structural elements of language (i.e., morphology and syntax) and the functional use of language (i.e., pragmatics). Students with language disorders might have trouble with proper use of morphological elements like use of the possessive or plural final "s" or use of past tense morphemes (-ed). Pragmatics, as it has huge impact on language use in daily life, can be a source of difficulty for many children. Children with language disorders associated with pragmatic language might need help with issues like turn taking in conversations or appropriate proximity and eye contact in communicative situation.

In a broader sense, language disorders can be categorized as either expressive or receptive language disorders. Expressive language disorders relate to difficulty with clearly communicating ideas by planning your thoughts and ideas and communicating them clearly. Receptive language disorders are the opposite and relate to difficulty with understanding the communication of others including following directions. Both types of language disorders relate to limitations/weaknesses in the components of language development/use (Owens, 2009).

TYPICAL SPEECH AND LANGUAGE DEVELOPMENT

In order to detect delays and/or disorders of speech and language among your students, it is critical that you understand the typical developmental milestones or "norms." Researchers have determined at what age most children develop speech and language skills. This information is particularly relevant to early childhood educators.

Figures 8.4 and 8.5 summarize the age range of phoneme development in young children (there is a considerable range). You may not recognize all of the sounds, as they are phoneme representations from the phonetic alphabet (Cartier & Todaro, 1983) as opposed to the standard English alphabet. Figure 8.4 serves to clarify the relationship between phonetic symbols in Figure 8.5 and the sounds we recognize in spoken English.

Figure 8.4.

Phonetic Symbols for Consonants in the English Language			
English Phonetic Symbol	Example English Word	English Phonetic Symbol	Example English Word
p	pig, pop, pond	j	yes, yellow, your
m	mop, mill, mom	r	roar, wrong, ring
h	hat, hill, hot	l	loud, love, ball
n	night, not, nine	s	save, bass, sour
w	wall, witch, wild	ʃ	shower, shave, fish
b	big, ball, bob	tʃ	child, chicken, couch
k	kite, keep, seek	z	zero, buzz, zesty
g	goal, big, gone	dʒ	judge, jury, jealous
d	dog, done, sod	v	vowel, five, very
t	tool, ton, hot	θ	thing, bath, tooth
ŋ	sing, song, doing	ð	these, those, bathe
f	father, fix, if	ʒ	fusion, vision, beige

Figure 8.5.

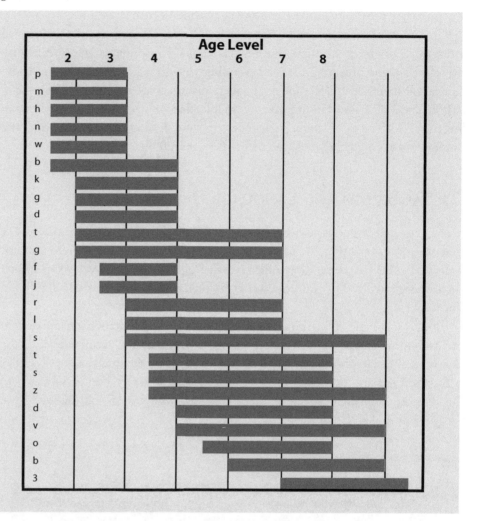

Owens, *Language Development: An Introduction,* Figure 3.3, "Average Age of Acquisition of English Consonants" p. 98. © 1996. Reproduced with permission of Pearson Education, Inc.

LANGUAGE NORMS

Table 8.1.

Typical Development Norms in Speech and Language (ASHA, 2010)
Birth to 3 Months • Cooing and gooing sounds emerge • Cries to make needs met • Shows response to known faces by smiling
4 to 6 Months • Emergence of babbling that resembles speech sounds from his/her language • Giggling and laughing • Communicates happiness, excitement, joy

7 Months to 1 Year
- Emergence of developed syllable babbling
- Transition to speech sounds rather than crying to gain attention and desired objects
- Development of communication using gestures (bye-bye waving, etc.)
- Imitation of sounds made in the environment including speech sounds
- By 12 months, develops use of basic words as a growth of syllable babbling (e.g., dada, mama, doggie, etc.); accuracy of speech sounds vary

1 to 2 Years
- Addition of new words to the child's lexicon
- Emergence of short phrases using one or two words such as "Where mama?" "Go bye-bye." "More juice."
- Considerable expansion of use of consonant sounds

2 to 3 Years
- Knows labels for items in every day life
- Considerable expansion of vocabulary
- Can ask questions and converse with parents using two-three word sentences
- Becomes proficient with common consonant phonemes like n, k, g, f, t, d.
- Although speech is not necessarily clear, child is able to communicate needs and is generally understood by family and familiar listeners
- Names objects in the environment

3 to 4 Years
- Begins to develop proficiency with speech such that he or she can be understood clearly by people outside of family and friends
- Develops sentences of 4 or more words to communicate
- Communicates ideas and interests related to every day life at home and in school

* Based on the age at which most children attain milestones if they speak only one language.
Table adapted from the American Speech-Language-Hearing Association.

One reason that communication norms are increasingly relevant is the increased attention to early identification of autism spectrum disorders (ASD). Because ASDs are primarily associated with deficits in communication and social development, considerable attention should be paid to any significant departures from incremental milestones related to language use and parent interactions.

For more information on developmental norms refer to public information sites:
- http://www.firstsigns.org/
- http://www.firstwords.fsu.edu

Supporting Children with Speech and Language Impairments

We have established that most speech and language impairments (in the absence of a primary disorder like an intellectual disability) are likely to be remediated given appropriate intervention from a highly-trained Speech-Language Pathologist. Also, these disorders are not typically of a severe nature. Still, difficulties can have relevant impact on classroom performance. Students with both speech disorders and expressive language disorders are much less likely to participate with confidence in your classroom. Like a learning disability, difficulty with expressive language planning might lead to a child exhibiting characteristics that mask the actual difficulty (e.g., being overly reserved; appearing unmotivated; disrupting class). Perhaps the most challenging situation a teacher could create for children with speech disorders is something traditionally called "Round Robin" reading in which all of the students in class take turns reading for the rest of their peers. For students who stutter or have substantial articulation disorders, this could be the most anxiety-ridden experience of their day. Although it is appropriate for teachers to be encouraging of improvements in speech, the classroom should not be used as a high-stakes opportunity to improve speech.

Language disorders have broad impact on school performance. The characteristics associated with language disorders in the classroom are best compared to the difficulties of students with learning disabilities. Students with language disorders are at a much higher risk of experiencing difficulty with reading, particularly if they have similar deficits in phonological processing that we would expect to see in students with a learning disability in reading (ASHA, 2010). Students with expressive language disorders are likely to have difficulty with verbal demonstrations of comprehension of academic content and difficulties will often extend into difficulty with written expression. Students with expressive writing problems (not associated with physical/motor delays) benefit from intensive-explicit instruction in the fundamentals of the writing process and strategies for pre-writing and formulating ideas on paper. Unlike a student who might "pour their thoughts" onto the page and edit them later, students with expressive language disorders struggle with developing clearly understandable thoughts in writing that follow the standard form of written language.

Classroom support for students with speech and language disorders should emphasize support, generalization, and maintenance of gains made in the speech and language therapy sessions conducted with the speech-language pathologist. For a student with a language impairment, it is important to consider the specific areas of difficulty that the student is working to improve. It is likely the students will need extensive support in vocabulary development including contextual support for unknown vocabulary during lessons. Building background knowledge and pre-teaching key vocabulary would be proactive strategies to support the students with language impairment. Much of therapeutic intervention focuses on guided opportunities for practice with corrective feedback. This can be easily continued in the general education classroom. The teacher should keep in mind that language-based tasks require an additional level of "information processing" on the part of the students with a language impairment. Intensive instruction in unknown language rules will be required and ongoing reinforcement for progress toward therapy goals will foster growth (Choate, 2004).

Simple Ideas Future Teachers Should Understand about Supporting Students with Speech and Language Impairments in School

Hold high expectations for student performance.

- Shape improvements in speech with low-stakes practice. Reduce anxiety around speech problems, particularly for stutterers for whom speech is a high-anxiety practice.
- "Start small and work big"; Rather than starting out with longer, more complex sentences for example, start with the basics and then expand. For example, ask the student to describe or label a picture of an object common to the child (e.g., car). Start by saying, "This is a car." Then ask the student to add a word that describes the car in greater detail; "This is a blue car." This process will continue as the student(s) expand their sentences/verbalizations without the prompts.
- Use student's existing language as a foundation for future attention to language activities. For example, if a student understands the language used in a particular area (e.g., sports), use the target term in other contexts. If the child does not understand "first", use the concept of a "first down" in football to illustrate that first is "at the beginning".
- Work on classification skills with students. Provide concepts and ask students to identify items that are part of the target concept. For example, the concept may be "function"; students try to think of words that describe "games we play" or "foods we eat". This helps children think of words that are similar relative to the concept being considered.
- Help students with previewing activities. Before they read a passage, for example, ask individual students to identify words they do not know. The teacher might also ask a student to describe a picture in the story; after the student has completed the task, ask others to think about why the picture was included in the reading material. This can be expanded to the degree that students learn to look for bold printed words, pictures and the captions, questions at the end of the section, or any other "clues" as to the meaning of the passage.
- Encourage students to use mnemonics whenever it helps them. HOMES is a mnemonic for the 5 Great Lakes or ROY G BIV is a first letter mnemonic for the colors in a rainbow.
- Use Graphic Organizers like we have done at the beginning of each chapter. This helps us all as we begin learning about a new concept or idea.

GLOSSARY IN PLAIN TERMS

Phonology: aspect of language that has to do with speech sounds or phonemes

Morphology: small word parts that contribute to the structure and subtle meanings of words

Semantics: vocabulary; word meanings in language

Syntax: organization, structure, or order of words in language to have clear meaning

Pragmatics: functional use of language as a tool for social communication

Articulation disorder: problem with making speech sounds that might include substituting an easy sound for a hard sound or simply leaving the sound out

Fluency disorders: problem with maintaining easy, fluid speech; typically refers to stuttering

Voice disorders: problem with the vocal folds—damage or weakness—that causes a weak or hoarse voice

Expressive language disorder: inability to clearly express thoughts or ideas to others

Receptive language disorder: inability to clearly understand the thoughts, commands, or directions of others

References

American Speech-Language-Hearing Association. (2010). What is language? What is speech? Retrieved from http://www.asha.org.

American Speech-Language-Hearing Association. (2010). How does your child hear and talk? Retrieved from http://www.asha.org.

American Speech-Language-Hearing Association. (2010). Speech and language disorders and diseases. Retrieved from http://www.asha.org.

American Speech-Language-Hearing Association. (2010). Reading and writing (literacy). Retrieved from http://www.asha.org.

Bloodstein, O. (1995). *A handbook on stuttering* (6th ed.). San Diego, CA: Singular Publishing Group.

Cartier, F., & Todaro, M. T. (1983). *The phonetic alphabet.* Dubuque, Iowa: Wm. C. Brown Company Publishers.

Choate, J. S. (2004). *Successful inclusive teaching: Proven ways to detect and correct special needs* (4th ed.). MA: Allyn & Bacon.

Owens, R. (1996). *Language development: An introduction.* Boston, MA: Allyn & Bacon.

Owens, R. (2009). *Language disorders a functional approach to assessment and intervention.* Boston, MA: Allyn & Bacon.

Van Riper, C., & Erickson, R. L. (1996). *Speech correction: An introduction to speech pathology and audiology.* Boston: Allyn and Bacon.

QUESTIONS *for Reflection:*

Briefly describe the speech mechanism using basic anatomical terminology as if you were explaining it to a school colleague.

What is the difference between speech and language?

How does a speech disorder differ from a language disorder?

What should teachers consider most seriously when working with children with speech disorders in everyday classroom situations?

How might expressive and receptive language disorders translate to classroom difficulties?

Expressive:

Receptive:

DeAndre is a 4 and 1/2 year-old child in your Kindergarten class. He mispronounces numerous words making it necessary to pay careful attention to what he is saying. Close analysis of his speech patterns reveals that he has difficulty with a few initial phonemes, particularly in conversation, causing his speech utterances to sound as follows:
"Chin" sounds like [tIn]
"Run" sounds like [wrun]
"Show" sounds like [so]
"Thick" sounds like [tIk]

What articulation problems characterize DeAndre's speech patterns? Would you refer him for speech therapy or work with him on this in the classroom?

NOTES

CHAPTER

Teaching Children with Emotional or Behavioral Disorders

Alicia Brophy

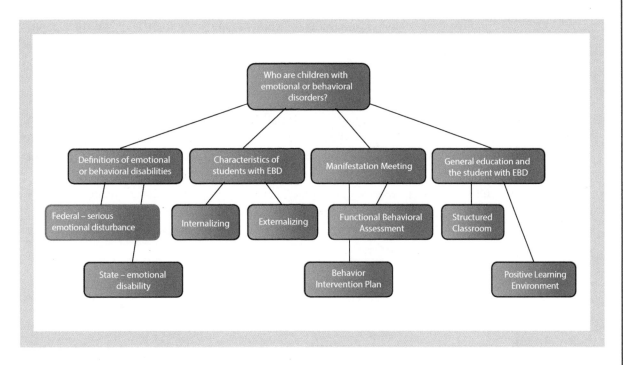

THE TOP TEN TERMS FOR CHAPTER 9:

The following key terms or big ideas are critical to your understanding of the content for chapter 9 and the in-class discussions to follow.

• Serious emotional disturbance	• Emotional disability
• Internalizing behavior	• Externalizing behavior
• Manifestation determination	• Functional behavior analysis
• Behavior Intervention Plan	• Behavior Intervention Specialist
• Behavior goals	• Proximity control

Chapter 9 provides information about one of the most challenging aspects of teaching students with disabilities, dealing with problem behaviors. The purpose of this chapter is to define the characteristics of students with emotional or behavioral disorders and provide strategies for assessing students' behavioral needs in order to plan for their academic success accordingly. Additionally, this chapter will offer effective teaching strategies for students of this particular population within the context of the general education classroom and information pertaining to placement decisions.

Defining Disability in Emotional or Behavioral Disorders

Of all students ages 6 through 21 who are currently receiving special education services, almost half a million children and youth have been identified as having an emotional or behavioral disability, or approximately 6% to 10% of the total population of students with special needs (see Chapter 1). However, less than 1% are actually identified as emotionally disturbed. (U.S. Department of Education, 2013). Many experts contend that this population of students is one of the most underidentified, estimating that they represent 3 to 6% of the total school-age population, and the most recent figure released from the U.S. Department of Education reinforces this assumption However, less than 1% of the overall student population is identified as having an emotional or behavioral disability (U.S. Department of Education, 2013), so there may be many students out there who have yet to be identified in order to receive appropriate services. While the states differ on how they prefer to label students with this type of disability, according to the Individuals with Disabilities Education Act, the term utilized is **serious emotional disturbance**. The following federal definition is provided:

> ...a condition exhibiting one or more of the following characteristics over a long period of time and to a marked degree that adversely affects educational performance –
>
> (A) An inability to learn that cannot be explained by intellectual, sensory, or health factors; (B) An inability to build or maintain satisfactory interpersonal relationships with peers and teachers; (C) Inappropriate types of behavior or feelings under normal circumstances; (D)A general pervasive mood of unhappiness or depression; or (E) A tendency to develop physical symptoms or fears associated with personal or school problems. (Individuals with Disabilities Education Act §300.7[b][9]).

Additionally, schizophrenia is included within the definition provided by the IDEA (1997); however, serious emotional disturbance is not applicable to children who are socially maladjusted, unless they are determined to be eligible for serious emotional disturbance under one of the aforementioned qualifications.

Schizophrenia – a mental disorder distinguished by degeneration of emotional responsiveness and thinking processes usually occurring in young adulthood; persons with this disorder may have difficulty organizing thoughts, engage in repetitive movements (i.e., pacing, wringing hands, etc.), experience hallucinations/delusions, experience difficulty with decision making, have a "flat affect," exhibit catatonia, have limited speech, experience difficulty paying attention or focusing, or lack the ability to retain and apply information learned.

It is important to differentiate a child with an emotional or behavioral disability from one who is ***socially maladjusted***. A child with an emotional or behavioral disability who meets the federal criteria above, is usually diagnosed with a mental health condition that severely impacts their ability to experience success in the academic environment, and has difficulty controlling one's behavior or making appropriate choices due to the aforementioned mental health condition. A child who is socially maladjusted is a student who seems to be aware of and purposely breaks societal norms, such as a student who engages in truancy or substance abuse. Some educators believe social maladjustment involves "willful" rule violations.

According to Center (1990), social maladjustment is described as socialized aggression that occurs as "an adapted response to environmental circumstances that leads to support and acceptance from a specific sub-culture." For example, if a student feels like they don't belong to a school or group, they may chose to purposely display inappropriate behavior to show their frustration of being in said circumstance. Merrell and Walker (2004) provided some common characteristics of students with social maladjustment: a) meet criteria for diagnosis of Conduct Disorder or Oppositional-Defiant Disorder in the Diagnostic and Statistical Manual of Mental Disorders (DSM-IV), b) chose to engage in problem behavior they could stop if they chose to, c) utilize problem behavior to get what they want, d) engage in rebellious and criminal behavior within the context of deviant peer groups, e) maintain social status within their peer group by engaging in problem behavior, f) believe rules are not applicable to them, and g) do not have mental health problems or internalizing/emotional difficulties.

While the North Carolina definition is almost an exact duplicate of the federal definition, it does differ with regard to the name of this disability category. North Carolina legislation prefers to use the term ***emotional disability*** while the federal government uses the term *serious emotional disturbance*. In the state of North Carolina, the following definition of this disability is provided:

> (5) Serious emotional disability (hereafter referred to as emotional disability)
> (i) means a condition exhibiting one or more of the following characteristics over a long period of time and to a marked degree that adversely affects a child's educational performance:
>> (A) An inability to make educational progress that cannot be explained by intellectual, sensory, or health factors.
>> (B) An inability to build or maintain satisfactory interpersonal relationships with peers and teachers.

(C) Inappropriate types of behavior or feelings under normal circumstances.

(D) A general pervasive mood of unhappiness or depression.

(E) A tendency to develop physical symptoms or fears associated with personal or school problems.

(ii) Serious emotional disability includes schizophrenia. The term does not apply to children who are socially maladjusted, unless it is determined that they have an emotional disturbance under paragraph (b)(5)(i) of this section. (NCDPI, 2010)

CHARACTERISTICS OF CHILDREN WITH EMOTIONAL OR BEHAVIORAL DISORDERS IN SCHOOLS

Do any of the following statements sound familiar? "You can't turn your back on Bryan for a minute, if you do, all heck will break loose. He's like a bull in a china closet." "Sarah can be sweet at times; just don't get on her bad side. Her personality can flip on a dime." "Nathan knows how to press all my buttons. He is smart and knows exactly what to say to get his classmates and teachers angry at him." "Mia is a hard-worker but she gets frustrated doing her class work occasionally. She cries and throws her books and papers on the floor. I think she does this to get attention." "Jamar is very shy most of the time. He never raises his hand or talks aloud in class. He seems to enjoy being in his own world."

Children with emotional or behavioral disabilities (often called EBD) have many characteristics which can make them stand out in the classroom environment… if you know what to look for. Students who exhibit **externalizing behavior** are easy to spot, as this type of behavior is outwardly visible. Some examples of externalizing behavior are the following: non-compliant to teacher directions, verbally or physically aggressive toward staff and peers, physically destructive toward material objects, self-destructive (e.g., use of illegal drugs, lying, stealing, cutting oneself), argumentative, and blatant disregard for classroom rules. Another term for externalizing behavior typically used in the classroom setting is "acting out" behavior. Students who have emotional and behavior disorders tend to have a poor self-concept and by "acting out," they let their teachers know that they are not happy or comfortable with themselves.

While externalizing behavior is very apparent, **internalizing behavior** is characterized by withdrawal, isolation, sadness, and shyness. While there are visible signs of internalizing behavior, the students who exhibit this type of behavior tend to be the ones who are least likely to be identified as EBD due to their predominately quiet and non-disruptive natures. Some examples of internalizing behavior are the following: avoidance of group and classroom activities, anxious, fearful of new situations, apathetic, self-depreciative, sad, self-conscious, and may appear to be inattentive or preoccupied.

PhotoDisc

Whether a student with an emotional or behavioral disability exhibits an internalizing or externalizing behavior disorder, there are still many characteristics that are shared between the two. Students with EBD are habitually a population with the worst academic outcomes when compared to other students; they experience academic underachievement, have more absences, lower grades, higher course failure, higher retention rates, and more frequent suspensions or expulsions (Bullis & Cheney, 1999; Greenbaum et al., 1996, Kortering & Blackorby, 1992; Sutherland & Singh, 2004; Wagner, 1995). In fact, youth with emotional or behavioral disabilities are most at risk of students across all disabilities to drop out of school prior to completion; 44% of students with EBD drop out, the highest dropout rate within disability categories (Wagner, Newman, Cameto, Levine, & Garza, 2006). Additional characteristics of students with EBD are that they experience alienation and social rejection, can be inattentive/highly distractible, are rarely popular with peers, are not leaders within their peer group, and arouse and induce negative feelings in others.

FUNCTIONAL BEHAVIOR ANALYSIS AND INTERVENTION PLANS

In the 1997 Individuals with Disabilities Education Act Amendments (IDEA 1997), two terms emerged that many special educators were previously unaware of, Functional Behavioral Assessment (FBA) and Behavior Intervention Plan (BIP). The underlying reason for the inclusion of the aforementioned terms was due in part to a need for all students to be educated within safe academic environments and for teachers and school administrators to have access to tools necessary for addressing problem behaviors appropriately. Essentially, there needed to be a way for educators and administrators to discipline students who had disabilities within the realm of emotional and behavioral disorders in an effective and appropriate manner. In the past, many of these students were suspended or excluded from academic activities due to ongoing discipline problems. The discipline process for students with disabilities changed according to IDEA 1997, as this population of students may now be disciplined using regular disciplinary procedures with some minor exceptions. Local education agencies (LEAs) can utilize regular disciplinary measures with students with disabilities as long as the following occur: a) discipline procedures must be nondiscriminatory (i.e., the same for students with or without disabilities); b) discipline procedures do not result in a change to a student's IEP placement (i.e., suspended for more than 10 days indicative of a pattern of exclusion, or change in IEP placement by school administrators rather than the IEP team); and c) a consequence of discipline procedures cannot be a termination of educational services (Yell & Katsiyannis, 2000).

In IDEA 1997, Functional Behavioral Assessments were expected to be completed within 10 school days of the removal of a student with disabilities for more than 10 school days, whether the behavior was related to their disability or not. In the reauthorization of IDEA (2004), if a student's problem behavior results from their disability, an FBA is required if one has not been conducted prior. However, administrators can exercise the option not conduct one if the behavior is unrelated to the student's disability. If a student with disabilities is suspended for more than 10 days, a school's IEP team must conduct what is called a **manifestation determination** meeting. If the IEP team concludes that the inappropriate behavior exhibited by the student is related to the student's identified disability, then the IEP team must decide how to plan for the student's behavior effectively in order to decrease the likelihood of this inappropriate behavior reoccurring. A way for school staff to investigate a student's problem behavior is to conduct a functional behavioral assessment (FBA) and to create a behavior intervention plan (BIP).

Functional Behavioral Assessment is a process in which school staff gather information about certain behaviors that a student is exhibiting and discover environmental variables which may have an impact on these behaviors, to enable staff to problem-solve and determine why the behavior is occurring (Ryan, Halsey, & Matthews; 2003). The FBA process can be summarized as a problem-solving strategy that includes the following: a) identify the problem, b) collect and analyze information, c) plan for an intervention, and d) monitor and evaluate (Sugai, Lewis-Palmer, & Hagan-Burke, 1999-2000). Data about the problem behaviors of the student can be collected through either formal or informal means. When data is collected informally, it can include record reviews (e.g., review of student's academic, medical, and special education folders), report cards, discipline reports, interviews (e.g., teacher, parent, and student interviews), checklists, questionnaires, behavior or social skill rating scales, prior behavior contracts, and grade level assessments. Formal data collection measures include direct observations of the student, anecdotal recording (written narrative of behavior as occurring), duration recording (how long behavior occurs), scatter plot recording (time of day behavior occurs), and event recording (how often behavior occurs) (McConnell, et. al, 2001).

Figure 9.1.

Sample Behavior Contract

DAILY GOALS:

1. I followed the teacher's directions.	🙂	🙁
2. I completed all my class work.	🙂	🙁
3. I kept my hands and feet to myself.	🙂	🙁
4. I cleaned up my workspace.	🙂	🙁
5. I raised my hand to ask for help.	🙂	🙁

To have a good day, I need 4 happy faces.
I had __4__ happy faces today.
I had a (good) bad day.

The main reason why educators need to complete an FBA is to increase the probability that the Behavior Intervention Plan (BIP) they develop for a student will be effective and relevant (Foster-Johnson, & Dunlap, 1993; Horner, 1994; O'Neill et al., 1997; Repp, 1994; Sugai, Horner, & Sprague, 1999). A **Behavior Intervention Plan** is created by school staff following a functional behavioral assessment; it contains interventions, strategies, and supports that can be used to reduce or replace a student's inappropriate behaviors (McConnell, et. al, 2001). Parents, general educators, and students (when appropriate) should be involved in the development of the Behavior Intervention Plan alongside the special educator. The FBA process should be an entire team-collaborative effort. In some school systems, the person assigned to facilitate the FBA process is a **Behavior Intervention Specialist**. For students who are identified as having an emotional or behavioral disability, the FBA and BIP should be completed on a yearly basis prior to the annual review of the student's IEP. An example of a completed FBA and a BIP is provided on the following pages to assist your understanding following the case study.

Case Study: Tyler James

Tyler is a student in the seventh-grade at a local middle school. His exceptional children's teacher, Miss Katz has Tyler in her resource classroom for three periods of the day. The periods for which he receives resource support are math, English, and reading. The rest of his classes occur in the general education setting and comprise social studies, science, physical education, and band. He rarely finishes work he starts either in group activities or independently and often forgets to turn in his assignments (even if they are complete). According to Mrs. Smile, his science teacher, he frequently yells out answers to questions she asks during class instruction, and leaves his seat without permission constantly. Mr. World, his social studies teacher reports that Tyler is very rude to his peers and has even called him inappropriate names on occasion. Tyler has received frequent office referrals and has been suspended for 10 days this school year, even though school just started in August. His teachers are beginning to wonder if Tyler is receiving the appropriate academic and social support he needs.

Sample Functional Behavioral Assessment

Name: Tyler James
Student ID#: 123456
Date of Birth: 01/05/97
Date of Report: 10/05/10
Age: 13 years, 9 months

Purpose

This assessment is being completed as part of the IEP Meeting process to review Tyler's progress toward IEP goals/objectives, to identify specific services and needed interventions, and to make future program recommendations for Tyler. Information contained within this functional behavior assessment was gathered through direct observation, record review, and staff survey, and contains the following three major components/sections.

- Description of Tyler's behaviors, including behaviors that occur together, and any noticeable patterns of behavior.
- Identification of antecedents: events, times, and situations that seem to increase/provoke certain negative or positive behaviors;
- Identification of the consequences that increase or diminish the problem behaviors.

Information contained within this functional behavioral assessment will be used as the basis for establishing and refining a behavior intervention plan to promote Tyler's success in school.

Description of Behaviors

Behavior can be characterized by distracting behaviors to self and others, laughing at inappropriate times, not raising hand before talking, getting out of his seat without teacher permission, yelling at his classmates and staff, shifting of attention, a lack of persistence with tasks done independently, inappropriate reactions to tension, inappropriate responses with peers (verbal threats toward peers, name-calling, cussing), physical aggression toward peers (kicking, pushing), non-compliance to classroom directions, a need to accept school routines and procedures, inability to take responsibility for own behavior, disrespectful at times to staff/peers.

Sample Functional Behavioral Assessment (continued)

Patterns and predictors of Identified Behaviors:

Certain times of day – 1st period (P.E.,) mostly during/after lunch, passing time between classes, unstructured activities

Certain settings – any classroom setting with the exception of band, lunch, hallway

Predictors – when working independently, group work situations, when another student makes a comment about him (or if he perceives someone is talking about him), when trying to gain peer or adult attention

Consequences that seem to Influence Identified Behaviors:

- Misses activities
- Adult requests to stop
- Upsets or annoys those around him
- Proximity control used (i.e. teacher stands near Tyler to discourage inappropriate behavior)
- Gets others involved or contaminated
- Escalation of behavior
- Redirection and task completion
- Gets adult one-on-one time
- Time-out of class (Transitions/Alternative Structure Class - ASC)
- Removal of distractible items
- Earning of points on a behavior contract resulting in privileges within a behavior management system
- Tangible rewards
- Clearly set limits with clear consequences
- Positive feedback on work and behavior

Sample Behavior Intervention Plan

Based on Tyler's identified strengths and needs, a behavior intervention plan was implemented during Tyler's enrollment at Serenity Middle School. This intervention plan for was built on the following components:

- Tyler will respond constructively to frustration/anger
- Increase Tyler's knowledge of peer relationships
- Tyler will participate appropriately in social activities
- Tyler will improve his problem solving skills

Deliberate and consistent application of comprehensive interventions including proactive and responsive strategies:

- Continuously review the rules of the program with Tyler
- Continuously review the established consequences for behaviors with Tyler
- Increase Tyler's control over his own behavior by the use of verbal prompts, visual signals, proactive counseling, and tangible rewards and consequences linked to specific behaviors
- Use of full continuum of surface management techniques
- Contracting/point sheets

Sample Behavior Intervention Plan (continued)

- Use of reinforcement bank
- Use of alternative structure
- Coordinated expectations and reinforcers between teachers
- Coordinated expectations and reinforcers between home and school
- Reinforcement of group standards and individual goals
- Infused social skill instruction into class learning activities
- Assigned seating

<u>Structured reinforcement for student success and hierarchy of consequences in response to student behavior</u>:

- Tyler receives positive recognition through established behavior management system (daily points on point sheet, recognition for successful days, etc.)
- Tyler can move through the level system to earn additional school privileges, participation in special events, tangible reinforcement, and positive phone calls home

<u>Clear understanding and consistent implementation of plan by all staff working with Tyler</u>:

- Staff will review the plan at periodic staff meetings
- Staff will continuously communicate with Tyler to review the plan and promote consistency between home and school
- The case manager and other educators will review the plan with Tyler to promote ownership and responsibility
- Staff will review progress to make modifications as needed
  - The first follow-up and review date will be on <u>11/5/10</u>.

The comprehensive services and interventions provided to Tyler within a special education resource program continue to be appropriate; however, he needs additional behavioral and academic support as outlined in the above behavior intervention plan.

<u>Participants in this FBA/BIP Meeting</u>

<u>Name</u>	<u>Role</u>
Ali Katz	Exceptional Children's Teacher
Sara Smile	General Education Teacher
Melissa Lee	Exceptional Children's Coordinator
Byron James	Father
Layla James	Mother
Tyler James	Student

INSTRUCTIONAL PLANNING AND PLACEMENT CONSIDERATIONS FOR CHILDREN WITH EBD

For students identified as having emotional or behavioral disabilities, one of the most important aspects of their IEPs is planning for *both* their academic and social success within the school environment. While the FBA process is not entirely what guides decisions the IEP team makes, it does provide useful information to the team as they begin to construct both academic and **behavioral goals** for the student with emotional or behavioral disabilities. Additionally, the information provided by the FBA can be used to help guide the IEP team toward making decisions regarding the student's special education eligibility, whether a problem behavior is a manifestation of a disability, and where the student's needs can best be addressed (Sugai, Lewis-Palmer, & Hagan-Burke, 1999-2000). On the following table, it is shown that the majority of students with emotional or behavioral disabilities (about 55%) will spend almost half of each school day in the general, also called regular, education classroom.

Table 9.1.

Time outside of the Regular Classroom				
Disability	<21 percent of the day (%)	21-60 percent of the day (%)	>60 percent of the day (%)	Separate environments*
Emotional disturbance	43.1%	18%	20%	18.2%
All disabilities	61.1%	19.8%	14%	5.1%

*The category of separate environments includes public and private residential facilities, public and private separate schools and homebound/hospital environments.
Source: U.S Department of Education, 2013. Thirty fifth annual report to Congress.

While 18.2% of students with EBD are educated within separate placement settings such as public and private residential facilities, separate schools, and homebound/hospital environments, the greatest majority will be seen daily by general educators. With this in mind, it is important for the general educator to have some "tricks of the trade" when teaching this population of students. When observing general education teachers to provide guidance in creating an atmosphere of academic success for students with EBD, a problem that consistently crops up is lack of structure within the classroom environment. While a structured classroom is integral for all students, it is even more so for children with emotional or behavioral disabilities due to their unique characteristics such as inattention or high distractibility.

The first part of a structured classroom is to have an appropriate classroom arrangement. During creation of an appropriate classroom arrangement, there are four variables which must be taken into consideration. In organizing the classroom environment, the teacher must be aware of visibility during instruction time (e.g., Is the teacher visible to students at all times? Can the teacher see all of his/her students at once?), accessibility of classroom materials, distractible items, and the teacher's proximity to students. Teachers should organize student desks in such a way that students' vision is not hampered. Likewise, the teacher's desk should be facing outward on his/her classroom at all times so that if the teaching is helping students at the desk, all students are in eyesight. Bookshelves, computers, work center tables, etc. may need to be placed near walls so that students are unable to hide behind these objects. Classroom materials should be placed in a central location so that all students will have access to them at any given time. If there are distractible items, these may need to be placed behind the teacher's desk so that students must obtain permission prior to usage or in an area away from students who have EBD, so that they will not be easily accessible. Aisles and walkways in the classroom should be clutter-free to enable the classroom teacher to maintain **proximity control** within the classroom environment to potentially ward off troublesome behaviors (Gallagher, 2010).

© *Monkey Business Images, 2015. Used under license from Shutterstock, Inc.*

The second part of a structured classroom is to have clear rules and consistent consequences for students who are in violation of the rules. Many schools have clearly outlined and established expectations of student behavior within the school environment. A way to involve students in their knowledge of the school and classroom rules is to allow them the opportunity to help the classroom teacher "create" classroom rules at the beginning of the school year. The teacher can provide scenarios to guide students toward stating the appropriate classroom/school rules. These can be written on a poster and signed by all of the students, so they can acknowledge that they were active participants in the creation of the rules and that they agree to follow said rules. A teacher may also want to post consequences for breaking the rules and discuss these with students prior to violation of rules. The consequences should also be reiterated with students if, and when, they do break the classroom or school rules.

The final part of creating and maintaining a structured classroom involves classroom routines. Students with emotional and behavioral disabilities tend to experience difficulty accepting changes to their daily routines, especially during times of transition. In order to keep students aware of daily activities, it is a good idea to post a daily agenda and a weekly agenda (to highlight activities such as specials, assemblies, featured guests, etc.). It is also a good idea to have specific break times outlined (i.e., bathroom breaks) due to the necessity of some students with EBD to be under constant adult supervision.

While the classroom teacher hopes that all students will be able to maintain their composure in the classroom environment, this may not always happen with students with EBD. The IEP team and the general education teachers with whom the student with EBD will have contact, need to take into consideration situations which may arise where the problem behavior of the student with EBD may affect the learning environment in a negative manner. A strategy that may be helpful for students with EBD is to provide them a place to "cool off" when they become agitated or frustrated (Gallagher, 2010). This may be in the physical classroom environment (i.e., desk near the back of the classroom, a study carrel, a reading corner, etc.) or the student with EBD may be given a "flash pass," so that the student can temporarily escape the conditions that are contributing to the frustrating situation.

It may also be important to consider that there could be situations in which the safety of other students in the classroom may be compromised by the aggressive or volatile behavior of the student with EBD (i.e., hitting, kicking, throwing objects, etc.). In these situations, it is important to contact a member of the school's "Crisis Intervention Team," usually comprised of a school safety officer, school administrators, school staff who are not classroom-bound (reading specialists, staff development teachers, school counselors , etc.), and special educators. General educators need to have a plan in place to safely remove other students from the classroom and provide for the supervision of the student with EBD who may be experiencing difficulty or emotional trauma. A teacher should not ever place hands on a student with EBD who is in crisis except in situations where the child is inflicting injury on oneself, inflicting injury on another person, or severely damaging school property (i.e., destroying a computer, breaking a window, throwing a desk across the classroom), and preferably only with another adult in the classroom.

There are specific guidelines recommended by Horner and Sugai (2009) for seclusion and restraint use in the school environment which include the following: a) most circumstances involving a student's problem behavior in which seclusion and restraint are used, could be preventable through early identification and intervention; b) seclusion and restraint can be incorporated as a safety response, but not used in a behavior intervention plan without previous conduction of a formal FBA; and c) seclusion and restraint should only be utilized as safety measures within a BIP and implemented by highly trained personnel. The "Crisis Intervention Team" members have been trained to efficiently and effectively deal with students during times of crises in the safest manner, so they should be the ones predominately dealing with a student who has EBD, and contacted as quickly as possible. If the general educator is involved in a situation where they are unable to contact the school's office, a responsible student can be given this task.

There are additional ways to create a climate conducive to the learning of students with emotional and behavioral disabilities. The classroom should be a safe, caring, and nurturing learning environment. To facilitate a pervasive mood of positivity and acceptance of all students, it is important for the classroom teacher to serve as a role model for his/her students by providing positive feedback and comments to students on a daily basis. In *Teaching Students with Behavior Disorders,* Gallagher (2010) provides some guidelines for positive feedback; here are some examples:

1. Feedback should be given immediately, whenever possible.

2. Feedback should be given in an animated and genuine manner.
3. Feedback should be given on a frequent basis.
4. Feedback should be personalized.
5. Teachers should serve as positive feedback models for students to increase their usage of positive remarks to peers.
6. Feedback can be used to provide corrective directions.
7. Feedback should be provided for academic and social tasks.

While students with emotional and behavioral disabilities are not entirely unlike their same age peers, due to the problem behaviors they exhibit at times, they can be become the most challenging population to teach within the confines of the general education classroom setting. The first part of integration into the classroom setting begins with the functional behavioral assessment process culminating in the creation of an appropriate behavior intervention plan. The BIP will assist the IEP team in planning for the student with EBD and in determining the appropriate placement for this student. General educators are important members of the IEP process because they will be involved facilitating the student's progress toward achieving their behavioral goals within the general education setting. In order to be successful, general educators need to have strong knowledge of appropriate classroom structure and techniques for constructing a positive learning environment.

Simple Ideas Future Teachers Should Understand about Supporting Students with Emotional and Behavioral Disabilities

Hold high expectations for student performance.
1. Provide structure and consistency in classroom procedures.
2. Provide immediate and positive feedback.
3. Maintain clear rules and consistent consequences for students who violate the rules.
4. Use proximity control as a preventive strategy for troublesome behaviors.
5. Provide a place for students to "cool off" in times of frustration or agitation.

GLOSSARY IN PLAIN TERMS

Serious emotional disturbance: federal classification of a student who has an emotional or behavioral disability (e.g., students who have poor social relationships, experience depression, have abnormal behavior/feelings, develop physical symptoms/fears exacerbated by school or personal problems).

Emotional disability: the term the state of North Carolina uses within its legislation to describe students who have emotional or behavioral impairments, the initial term within the State's definition is "serious emotional disability," however, after the first appearance within the law, it is called "emotional disability."

Externalizing behavior: problems that are outwardly manifested through behavior and can signal a child's negative reactions to their environment (e.g., non-compliance to teacher directions, work refusals, delinquency, aggression toward staff and peers).

Internalizing behavior: inclusive of behaviors that reveal difficulties within a child's inner emotional environment (e.g., depression, anxiety, self-consciousness, negative self-comments, withdrawal).

Manifestation determination: an IEP meeting held to determine if the inappropriate behavior exhibited by a student with disabilities is related or not related to their identified disability.

Functional Behavioral Assessment (FBA): a procedure used to gather information about student behavior and determine environmental variables surrounding its occurrence to enable staff to problem-solve; composed of the following: a) identify the problem, b) collect and analyze information, c) plan for an intervention, and d) monitor and evaluate.

Behavior Intervention Plan (BIP): a behavior plan developed by school staff containing interventions, strategies, and supports used to reduce or replace a student's inappropriate behaviors.

Behavior intervention specialist: school staff member who has specialized training in the implementation of evaluations and development of interventions for students who exhibit challenging behaviors within both special and general education settings.

Behavior goals: goals written for a student's IEP specifically related to social behaviors where a change is expected in order for the child to be successful within the context of the learning environment; consist of the following: a) condition under which the target behavior should occur, b) target behavior to be performed, and c) a measurable ideal level of achievement or outcome.

Proximity control: the teacher moves near students who are starting to engage in inappropriate classroom behaviors while continuing to provide instruction to the rest of his/her students.

REFERENCES

Bullis, M., & Cheney, D. (1999). Vocational and transition interventions for adolescents and young adults with emotional and behavioral disorders. *Focus on Exceptional Children, 31*, 1-24.

Center, D. B. (1990). Social maladjustment: An interpretation. *Behavioral Disorders, 15*, 141-148.

Foster-Johnson, L., & Dunlap, G. (1993). Using functional assessment to develop effective, individualized interventions for challenging behavior. *TEACHING Exceptional Children, 60*, 294-309.

Gallagher, P., A. (2010). *Teaching students with behavior disorders* (3rd ed.). Denver, CO: Love Publishing Company.

Greenbaum, P.E., Dedrick, R. F., Friedman, R. M., Kutash, K., Brown, E. C., & Lardieri, S. P., et al. (1996). National Adolescent and Child Treatment Study (NACTS: Outcomes for children with serious emotional and behavioral disturbance. *Journal of Emotional and Behavioral Disorders, 4*, 130-146.

Horner, R. H. (1994). Functional assessment: Contributions and future directions. *Journal of Applied Behavior Analysis, 27*, 401-404.

Horner, R. H., & Sugai, G. (2009). *Considerations for seclusion and restraint use in school-wide positive behavior supports.* Washington, DC: OSEP Center on Positive Behavioral Interventions & Supports. Retrieved on Sept 28, 2010, fromhttp://www.pbis.org/common/pbisresources/publications/Seclusion_Restraint_inBehaviorSupport.pdf.

Kortering, L. J., & Blackorby, J. (1992). High school dropout and students identified with behavioral disorders. *Behavioral Disorders, 18,* 24-32.

Individuals with Disabilities Education Act Amendments of 1997, P.L. No. 94-142, 20 U.S.C. Section 300.

McConnell, M. E., Cox, C. J., Thomas, D. D., & Hilvitz, P. B. (2001). *Functional behavioral assessment: A systematic process for assessment and intervention in general and special education classrooms.* Denver, CO: Love Publishing Company.

Merrell, K. W., & Walker, H. M. (2004). Deconstructing a definition: Social maladjustment versus emotional disturbance and moving the EBD field forward. *Psychology in the Schools, 41,* 899-910.

North Carolina Department of Public Instruction: Exceptional Children's Division. (2010). *Policies governing services for children with disabilities.* Retrieved July 25, 2010 from http://www.ncpublicschools.org/docs/ec/policy/policies/policies-62010.pdf.

O'Neill, R. E., Horner, R. H., Albin, R. W., Sprague, J. R., Storey, K., & Newton, J. S. (1997). *Functional assessment and program development for problem behavior: A practical handbook* (2nd ed.). Pacific Grove, CA: Brooks/Cole.

Office of Special Education Programs (OSEP). Questions and answers (1999, March 12). *Federal Register, 64* (48), 12553-12555.

Repp, A. C. (1994). Comments on functional analysis procedures for school-based behavior problems. *Journal of Applied Behavior Analysis, 27,* 409-411.

Ryan, A. L., Halsey, H. N., & Matthews, W. J. (2003). Using functional assessment to promote desirable student behavior in schools. *TEACHING Exceptional Children, 35,* 16-21.

Sugai, G., Horner, R. H., & Sprague, J. (1999) Functional assessment-based behavior support planning: Research to practice to research. *Behavioral Disorders, 24,* 223-227.

Sugai, G., Lewis-Palmer, T., & Hagan-Burke, S. (1999-2000). Overview of the functional behavioral assessment process. *Exceptionality, 8,* 149-160.

Sutherland, K. S., & Singh, N. N. (2004). Learned helplessness and students with emotional or behavioral disorders: Deprivation in the classroom. *Behavioral Disorders, 29,* 169-181.

U.S. Department of Education. (2006). *Twenty-eighth annual report to Congress on the implementation of the Individuals with Disabilities Education Act, 2006.* Washington, DC: Author. Retrieved March 1, 2010 from http://www2.ed.gov/about/reports/annual/osep/2006/parts-b-c/28th-vol-1.pdf.

Wagner, M. M. (1995). Outcomes for youth with serious emotional disturbance in secondary school and early adulthood. *The Future of Children, 5,* 90-111.

Wagner, M., Newman, L., Cameto, R., Levine, P., & Garza, N. (2006). *An overview of findings from wave 2 of the National Longitudinal Transition Study-2 (NLTS2).* Menlo Park, CA: SRI International. Retrieved on Oct 24, 2008, from www.nlts2.org/reports/2006_08/nlts_report_2006_08_complete.pdf.

Yell, M., & Katsiyannis, A. (2000). Functional behavioral assessment and IDEA '97: Legal and practice considerations. *Preventing School Failure, 44,* 158-162.

QUESTIONS *for Reflection:*

"Students who exhibit **externalizing behavior** are easy to spot, as this type of behavior is outwardly visible." Assuming this statement is correct, what are some examples of externalizing behavior?

Why do you think the Federal Government mandated the usage of Functional Behavioral Assessments and Behavior Intervention Plans for students with disabilities?

How does the completion of a Functional Behavioral Assessment contribute to the effectiveness of a Behavior Intervention Plan for a student with an emotional or behavioral disability?

Who bears the responsibility of implementing the Behavioral Intervention Plan and if there is more than one individual, explain the roles of those involved?

What are some ways that a general educator can prepare to effectively and efficiently teach a student with emotional or behavioral disabilities while retaining a learning environment that is appropriate for his/her students without disabilities?

NOTES

Author

CHAPTER **10**

Teaching Children with Autism Spectrum Disorders

Julie L. Thompson and Victoria Knight

(Kids will be kids catalog)

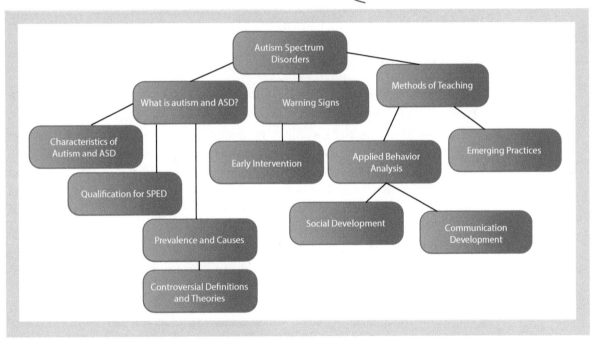

THE TOP TEN TERMS FOR CHAPTER 10:

The following key terms or big ideas are critical to your understanding of the content for chapter 10 and the in-class discussions to follow.

• Autism	• Reinforcement
• Autism Spectrum Disorder (ASD)	• Social Communication
• Asperger's syndrome	• Joint attention
• Applied Behavior Analysis (ABA)	• Evidence-based Practices
• Early Intervention	• Restricted interests/behaviors

What is autism?

Autism spectrum disorder (ASD) is a neurodevelopmental disorder that is identified by deficits in social communication/interaction and restricted, repetitive interests (American Psychiatric Association, 2013). Characteristics are observable in early childhood and cause significant impairment in life functioning. Although the symptoms may diminish over time, autism is a life-long disability.

What are the characteristics of ASD?

Characteristics of the disorder are variable, and range from mild to severe depending on the individual. Table 10.1 illustrates some characteristics of ASD. Despite some of the common characteristics they share, the symptoms may vary greatly from child to child. The overarching diagnostic characteristics include:

- deficits in social communication and social interaction
- restricted, repetitive behaviors and/or interests

Social Communication and Interactions

Individuals with ASD have communication problems that include both verbal (spoken) and non-verbal (non-spoken) interactions. For example, students with ASD may have difficulty initiating or sustaining a conversation, or they may have challenges engaging in reciprocal conversations (i.e., they may engage in one-sided conversations). Delays in language are common for individuals with autism, and may include *receptive* and/or *expressive* delays. **Receptive language** refers to the process of understanding what is said. **Expressive language** refers to the use of words and sentences to communicate thoughts, needs, and wants. The distinction between a receptive and an expressive difficulty is important because students with ASD may understand what is being said to them (i.e., receptive) without having the ability to communicate that they understand (i.e., expressive). Some individuals with ASD will lack spoken language while others may have difficulty with the pragmatics of language. Educators should know that these students will likely take literal meanings to idioms. "A bird in the hand is worth two in the bush" will have little meaning to an individual with ASD unless it is explained. Additionally, students with ASD may have echolalia, meaning they repeat entire phrases or parts of phrases. Finally, children with ASD may not engage in pretend play or the imitation of others.

In addition to difficulties with communication, individuals with ASD also have challenges in social interactions. Often communication and social deficits go hand in hand and can be difficult to discern. Difficulties initiating or sustaining a conversation are common. Further, this population of students requires instruction to engage in reciprocal conversations (i.e., they may engage in one-sided conversations). Even when students with ASD have strengths in verbal communication, as is the case for students with AS, non-verbal communication (e.g., eye contact, understanding facial expressions and gestures) can be lacking. Joint attention is another form of non-verbal communication. **Joint attention** refers to the shared experience of observing an object or event. For example, when a small child sees a dog, he/she will often look at the parent, point at the dog, and look back at the parent. As a result of these combined social deficits, students with ASD may have a difficult time developing appropriate peer relationships. The lack of peer relationships can lead to bullying, isolation, and lack of friendships unless the deficits are addressed.

RESTRICTED, REPETITIVE BEHAVIORS AND/OR INTERESTS

Another characteristic of individuals with ASD is engagement in restricted, repetitive behaviors and/or interests. Teachers and parents may notice that the child with ASD plays in a repetitive manner (e.g., stacking blocks the same way) or has intense interests in particular objects or parts of objects. Students with ASD may develop an interest in a certain unusual topic, which can tend to dominate conversations with others. Topics may range from dinosaurs to trains, football statistics to washing machines. The distinction between this characteristic and the development of a hobby is the abnormal intensity or focus for the topic or object. Repetitive behaviors may also manifest as repetitive motor behaviors such as finger flicking, repeating sounds or phrases, or spinning objects. In addition to repetitive behaviors, the child may seem to be inflexible or have a need to maintain a self-imposed schedule and react disproportionately to what may seem like minor changes in environment or schedule. For example, parents may notice that the child becomes upset when the table is set differently than it is usually set during the breakfast routine. Finally, students may have high or low thresholds of responses to sensory input and/or display an atypical interest in environmental sensory stimuli. For instance, a child may show indifference to pain or an unusual interest in textures such as sandpaper.

WHAT ARE THE WARNING SIGNS OF ASD?

Warning signs or "red flags" for ASD may be observable as early as 12–18 months of age (Boyd, Odom, Humphreys, & Sam, 2010). The warning signs include delayed use of speech, unusual speech (e.g., atypical prosody such as speaking with an odd cadence, using a high-pitched tone of voice, using a monotonous tone), limited or no eye contact paired with speech, not responding to name or simple verbal instructions (e.g., delayed receptive language), using object atypically (i.e., repetitive, idiosyncratic use of objects such as spinning or lining up), delayed or lack of joint attention, lack of pointing, and other use of gestures; flat affect (i.e., limited facial expressions), limited social smiling, avoidance of looking at faces; and unusual intense focus on objects or interests (Boyd et al 2010; Wetherby et al 2004). It is important to note that these warning signs may also be indicative of other neurological disorders (Wetherby et al 2004). It is imperative that teachers do not conclude a child has autism based on observing one or more of these warning signs. Instead, if teachers or early childhood educators suspect that their student may have ASD, they should discuss the warning signs with the parents of the child. In doing so, educators should report only the observable, measurable behaviors rather than a label of ASD. For example, an educator might say, "I am concerned that your child only says one word and does not make eye contact," rather than "I am concerned that your child has a disability." Once the concerns are discussed, parents should be encouraged to seek an evaluation by a qualified professional (i.e., developmental pediatrician) to obtain an accurate diagnosis.

DIAGNOSTIC CRITERIA FOR ASD

In 2013, the American Psychological Association published a revised version of the Diagnostic Statistical Manual of Mental Disorders (DSM-5). The DSM-5 is used by professionals to identify various disorders including ASD. Lord (2014), a member of the board responsible for the revised version of ASD, discussed several changes to the diagnostic criteria of ASD. Below are four of the major changes identified:

1. ASD is now defined entirely by behaviors exhibited by the child. As a result, there are no longer different categories. The previous manual described ASD as an "umbrella disorder" that included pervasive developmental disorder—not otherwise specified (PDD-NOS), childhood disintegrative disorder. Also, genetic disorders that were previously identified as falling under this umbrella are now no longer automatically qualified. Instead, individuals with these genetic disorders must display behaviors meeting the diagnostic criteria.

2. Asperger syndrome was previously identified as a separate disorder. With the new DSM-5, this is no longer the case. Lord (2014) explained the reasoning for this is based on diagnostic data that indicate there is very little difference between ASD and Asperger syndrome except that individuals diagnosed with Asperger syndrome typically have a much higher verbal IQ. She stated, "if you have the characteristics of ASD, even if you are highly intelligent, you have ASD."

3. Diagnostic criteria domains were changed from three domains (social interaction, communication, and restricted/repetitive/stereotypic behaviors) to two domains (social communication and interaction; and restricted, repetitive behaviors and/or interests). In essence, outside of social communicative ability (e.g., back-and-forth conversation, nonverbal communication), other communication deficits are no longer specifically used to diagnose ASD.

4. A new communication disorder called Social Pragmatic Language Disorder was created for individuals who display deficits in social communication but not social interactions or repetitive, restrictive behaviors (Lord, 2014).

Examining the Crisis of Increasing Prevalence: Causes, Cures, and Prognosis

The U.S. Centers for Disease Control and Prevention (CDC, 2012) released a national autism prevalence report indicating that 1 in 88 children are diagnosed with ASD. Further, the CDC reports males are 5 times more likely to have ASD than females and is identified among all cultures, races, and socioeconomic statuses (CDC, 2012). Since 2004, there has been a 146% increase in students with ASD served in public school settings (USDOE, 2012, 2013).

Several factors have likely resulted in the increase of individuals diagnosed with ASD. One likelihood is the earlier identification of children based on improved diagnostic tools (Boyd et al 2010). Another reason for the apparent increase in the ASD label may be due to the expansion of the criteria for inclusion under the "spectrum" laid out in the DSM-IV (Simpson, 2005). In particular, the previous label of pervasive developmental disorder—not otherwise specified may have become a catchall for individuals who showed some but not all of the diagnostic criteria for ASD (Lord, 2014). Another reason for the increase in prevalence may be the increased awareness of the disorder by parents, educators, and clinicians (Boyd et al 2010). Autism was first described in the 1940s, but very little was known about the disorder until the 1990s. Finally, eligibility criteria for special education did not include ASD as a separate area of disability classification until 1990. Thus, many students who are currently classified as having ASD would have been previously classified as having intellectual disability, emotional/behavioral disability, or even schizophrenia.

The cause of ASD is unknown. Increasing evidence supports the role of genetics in the development of ASD. If one identical twin is diagnosed with autism, the other twin is at an increased risk of being diagnosed as well (Dawson, 2008). Further, recent studies suggest that inheritance of certain genes as well as unique genetic mutations or variants account for some cases of autism (BioMed Central, 2010). Even with this increasing evidence, there is currently no single gene or medical test that can confirm the presence of ASD; therefore, professionals who evaluate a child's developmental progress and behavior will be the ones to identify the student as having ASD. One common theory, that has not been substantiated (i.e., no proof following numerous studies), was made popular by a now discredited article based in falsified research that indicated that ASD was linked to vaccines. Although commonly proposed as a cause for ASD in the media, there has been no empirical evidence to date to suggest that vaccines, mercury, or thimerosal are linked to ASD (Taylor, Swerdfeger, & Eslick, 2014).

Since the cause of the disorder is unknown, there is no available cure at this time. However, there are many effective interventions and treatments that reduce, and in some cases, eliminate the appearance of the symptoms. Further, if individuals with ASD receive early intervention services, the prognosis for individuals with ASD is greatly increased (NRC, 2001; Simpson, 2005).

QUALIFICATION FOR SPECIAL EDUCATION SERVICES

In 1990, autism was included in the Individuals with Disabilities Education Act as an eligibility category for special education. IDEA defines autism as:

(i) Autism means a developmental disability significantly affecting verbal and nonverbal communication and social interaction; generally evident before age three that adversely affects a child's educational performance. Other characteristics often associated with autism are engagement in repetitive activities and stereotyped movements, resistance to environmental change or change in daily routines, and unusual responses to sensory experiences.

(ii) Autism does not apply if a child's educational performance is adversely affected primarily because the child has an emotional disturbance, as defined in paragraph (c)(4) of this section.

(iii) A child who manifests the characteristics of autism after age three could be identified as having autism if the criteria in paragraph (c)(1)(i) of this section are satisfied (Reference).

In order to qualify a child must not only exhibit the characteristics of ASD, but also display evidence indicating his/her educational performance is negatively impacted by ASD. Once determined eligible, an individualized education plan (IEP) should be developed for the child to address his/her strengths and needs. Table 10.1 identifies guidelines for creating legally sound and educationally appropriate IEPs.

Table 10.1. Checklist for creating legally sound and educationally appropriate IEPs for students with ASD.

Follow Procedural Safe Guards	• Involve parents meaningfully • Respond promptly to evaluation requests • Conduct sound evaluations • Develop and implement the IEP • Provide parents with notice of due process rights
Ensure ASD-qualified professional conduct and interpret evaluations	• If no staff are qualified in ASD, school systems must hire or train professionals to conduct evaluations
Use evaluations to develop instructional plans and placement for students with ASD	• IEP teams must include a professional with expertise in autism. • IEPs must meet the needs identified in the evaluation of the student with ASD • All components outlined by IDEA must be included in the IEP
Implement evidence-based or research-based instructional strategies with students with ASD	• IDEA requires that empirically validated instructional approaches are used to address the needs of students with ASD • Staff implementing instruction to individuals with ASD must have expertise in ASD
Collect data and adjust instruction as needed based on data	• Always use data to guide instructional decisions

Modified from Yell, Katsiyannis, Drasgow, & Herbst (2003).

EARLY INTERVENTION AND EARLY CHILDHOOD EDUCATION

One of the benefits of obtaining an accurate diagnosis of autism early in the child's life is that they can then begin receiving early intervention services. **Early Intervention** consists of specialized services which specifically address the child's needs and is offered for children with disabilities from birth to 3 years and their families. Experts in the field of ASD agree that early intervention is one of the most significant predictors of successful outcomes (Simpson, 2005). The National Research Council (2001) outlined the following essential components of effective early intervention services:

- Entry into intervention programs and services as early as possible
- Intensive instructional programming (as much as 5 days a week with programs that are implemented throughout the full year)
- Repeated, planned teaching opportunities with adult attention organized around brief periods of time (e.g., 15-20 minutes per session for young children)
- Individualized attention on a daily basis
- Inclusion of a family component with parent training
- Low student to teacher ratios
- Evidence of on-going program evaluation of a child's progress with adjustments in programming made on a daily basis
- Ongoing interactions with typically developing children to the extent appropriate for the individual child's educational goals.

Overall, educational programming should be individualized to meet the child's needs. IEPs and IFSPs should serve as the guide for planning, implementing, and modifying the educational objectives that meet the students' needs. Further, IEPs and IFSPs should always use a team approach, valuing needs of the parents as well as the needs of the child. Additional considerations are outlined in Table 10.2 below.

Table 10.2. Checklist of Considerations for the IEP or IFSP

Are social skills addressed? Will the social skills be addressed in a variety of settings and activities, and with peers, educators, parents, and siblings?
Are communication skills addressed? Do the communication skills include receptive and expressive communication skills? Non-verbal communication skills?
Is there a functional communication system in place? (may need to define)
Does the plan address increased engagement, including play, imitation, pre-academic, and academic skills?
Are fine and gross motor skills addressed?
Does the plan determine replacement behaviors for undesirable or problem behaviors? Is the plan proactive, rather than reactive?
Is increased independence the overall goal of the plan? Is there a plan for fading prompts and supports over time?
Are the skills taught in natural settings?

Adapted from National Research Council (2001).

Evidenced-Based Practices for School-Aged Individuals with ASD

Wong et al. (2013) recently conducted a comprehensive literature review to identify evidence-based practices (EBPs) for individuals with ASD. The authors included only studies that met acceptable or higher criteria for quality research. They identified 27 EBPs (e.g., discrete trial teaching, functional behavior assessment (FBA), functional communication training, modeling, prompting, reinforcement, and task analysis). Notably, the majority of EBPs identified are behavior analytic interventions.

Applied behavior analysis (ABA) is "a scientific approach for discovering environmental variables that reliably influence social significant behavior and for developing a technology of behavior change that takes practical advantage of those discoveries (Cooper, Heron, & Heward, 2007, p. 3). The underlying concept of ABA is that behavior can be increased or decreased by changing the environment. The behavior can be changed by manipulating what occurs before or after the behavior. An **antecedent** is the circumstances in the environment that are present just *before* a behavior usually occurs. A **consequence** is the circumstances in the environment that are present just *after* a behavior occurs. ABA strategies involve observing the antecedents and consequences surrounding a target behavior (a problem behavior or a skill deficit) and then analyzing ways to change the antecedent and/or consequence to change the behavior. In their seminal article on ABA, Baer, Wolf, and Risley (1968) identified seven key features of ABA:

1. Applied—ABA involves changing behavior that is socially important and will improve the quality of life of the individual whose behavior is being changed.
2. Behavioral—The behavior must be clearly described and measureable.
3. Analytic—ABA seeks to ensure that the strategies used to change the behavior are effective and can be clearly identified as the cause of the behavior change.

4. Technological—The strategies of ABA should be described in such a way that anyone trained in ABA can read the description and successfully implement the strategies.

5. Conceptually systematic—ABA strategies should be based upon the concepts and principles of ABA.

6. Effective—ABA should make a meaningful improvement in the behavior of the individual.

7. Generality—The behavior change should be maintained over time and should occur in different environments with different individuals.

Some examples of EBPs that are ABA strategies include modeling, prompting, reinforcement, task analysis, and time delay. It is beyond the scope of this chapter to provide a detailed description of all the identified EBPs. However, there are very good training materials and resources available for these practices. The National Professional Development Center has developed detailed fact sheets for each EBP. They can be downloaded from http://autismpdc.fpg.unc.edu/node/727. Further, Autism Internet Modules (http://www.autisminternetmodules.org/) website has developed interactive modules with videos, implementation checklists, and self-assessments on the majority of the EBPs identified. They have plans to develop modules for all identified EBPs in the near future. Access to the modules requires registration, but they are free to use.

In an effort to provide practical information that can easily implemented in general and special education settings, the following EBPs will be described in detail: visual supports, reinforcement, peer-mediated instruction, and technology-aided instruction. These EBPs readily translate to all school environments. Table 10.3 defines these EBPs, explains their purpose, and lists some examples. Further explanations of the EBPs will be described in the sections below.

Table 10.3. Example EBP Definitions and Purposes

Type	Definition	Purpose	Examples
Visual Supports	"any visual display that supports the learner engaging in a desired behavior or skills independent of prompts (Wong et al., 2013, p. 22)."	To assist students with ASD to understand rules, expectations, schedules, and sequence of activities.	• Written materials list • Picture schedule of daily activities • First → (Then) card indicating what the student will do following an activity • Photo activity choice board • Written rubric for math activity

Reinforcement	"an event, activity, or other circumstance occurring after a learner engages in a desired behavior that leads to the increased occurrence of the behavior in the future (Wong et al., 2013, p. 21)."	To provide positive behavioral supports to increase appropriate behavior and skills of students with ASD.	• Token economy system • Provision of preferred item or edible following completion of a task • Breaks given periodically or after a certain period of time or tasks are completed • Verbal or physical praise (e.g., "Nice turn-taking" or giving a high five)
Peer-Mediated Instruction	"Typically developing peers interact with and/or help children and youth with ASD to acquire new behavior, communication, and social skills by increasing social and learning opportunities within natural environments. Teachers/service providers systematically teach peers strategies for engaging children and youth with ASD in positive and extended social interactions in both teacher-directed and learner-initiated activities (Wong et al., 2013, p. 20)."	To increase the number and quality of social interactions of students with ASD and their peers and to reduce overreliance on adult supports by students with ASD.	• Collaborative learning groups working on science experiments • Friendship club at lunch where students with similar interests (e.g., movies, anime, video games) meet and talk or play games • Reciprocal peer tutoring using flash cards and individualized academic content for each student (one with ASD, one without)

Technology-Aided Instruction	"Any electronic item/equipment/application/virtual network that is used intentionally to increase/maintain, and/or improve daily living, work/productivity, and recreation/leisure capabilities (Odom et al., 2013)."	To help students with ASD acquire and maintain skills through the use of technology-aided instruction. Skills may include communication, self-management, recreation, academic, and daily living activities.	• Remote audio coaching during job training using Bluetooth headphones • Video self-prompting to complete a task using an electronic tablet or phone • Speech-generating devices used to communication • Software using explicit instruction to teach academics • Software teaching facial expression/emotion recognition

VISUAL SUPPORTS

Visual supports for students with autism can be used to support transitions, self-management, activity completion, and following a daily schedule. Visual supports may be differentiated based on the skills of the learner with ASD. For example, based on student ability, a visual schedule for the day may be created with concrete objects (e.g., pencil indicating writing lesson, milk carton, indicating lunch time, ten blocks counters indicating math, woodchips from playground indicating recess, level 1 reader booklet indicating reading), concrete objects paired with photos of objects for a student who has demonstrated mastery of following schedule using concrete objects, photo only schedule, a line drawing (clip art) schedule, and, finally, a written schedule for individuals with ASD who can read. The individual needs of the student should be considered when creating visual supports. Some students will require more complex visual supports, whereas others may require minimal visual supports. The needs of the student can be determined through accommodations on an IEP, observation or consultation with the student's case manager, or by simply asking the student. Figure 10.1 displays a visual schedule for a class field trip to a pizza shop.

Figure 10.1. Class Field Trip Visual Schedule

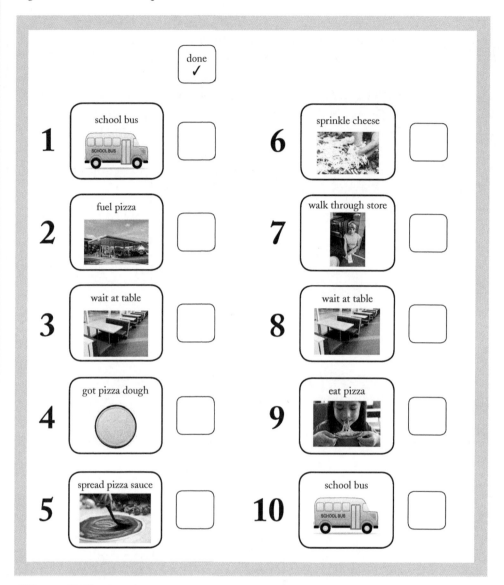

All images © Shutterstock.com

Visual supports can convey classroom expectations such as rules, schedules, and routines. Classroom rules are typically displayed on the wall in a classroom; sometimes classroom rules are written in broad terms (e.g., "Be respectful"). Some students may benefit from having a copy of rules at their desks in the form of pictures or written in specific terms (e.g., "Listen and look at the teacher"). Due to lack of social understanding, students with ASD may not comprehend the "unwritten rules" (e.g., "Look at the person speaking to you"). Rules like this may be written to address the specific needs of the individual student. Teachers could review visual rules regularly, point to rules followed when catching a student with ASD "being good," and to indicate which rule was broken if consequences are required for infractions of rules. In addition to the use of visual supports to address classroom rules, visual supports can also be used to depict classroom routines, including lining up, going to the bathroom, and sharpening pencils. For example, classrooms in all grade levels have certain rules for requesting to use the restroom. Visual supports that remind students to raise their hand or obtain a pass from a designated spot in the classroom can be beneficial to some students with ASD.

Furthermore, visual supports can be used to promote self-determination of students with ASD through providing visual choice options for leisure, snacks, peers to play with, academic activities to review, and so on. Visual supports can also be used to improve instruction. For example, some students may benefit from a copy of notes to follow along with during a lecture. Other students may benefit from a list of steps to follow for completing math problems. Another student might use a visual rubric or checklist to complete individual steps and expectations for completing a project or activity. For example, during sustained silent reading (SSR), a student with ASD might be provided with a checklist indicating he should read the passage, ask himself a question about what he read, write down the question, read the passage again, locate the answer, and write the answer. In addition, there might be a visual reminder indicating what the student should do if he finished checklist before SSR time is over. It is important to consider how the use of visual supports can make instruction more effective and understandable for students with ASD. Finally, other students (e.g., students with intellectual disability) can also benefit from the visual supports intended for students with ASD.

REINFORCEMENT

The key component to successful instruction is the quality of reinforcers available to students (Leaf, Schroeder, & Palos-Rafuse, 2008). As defined previously, reinforcement has occurred if, and only if, the targeted behavior is increased following presentation of a reinforcer. For example, a teacher may have noted that a student eats apples at lunch and decides to use cut-up apples as a "reinforcer" for the student during small group reading instruction. The targeted behavior is that the student will answer questions when called on. If the student answers a question, the teacher provides the student with a small piece of apple and verbal praise. However, if this does not increase the likelihood of "answering questions" during the remainder of the lesson and in future lessons, then the small piece of apple is not a reinforcer. The value of a piece of apple is not rewarding enough to evoke increased "answering questions" from the student. Instead the teacher should consider providing a **preference assessment** with the student to determine what he/she may be interested in accessing as a reinforcer during instruction.

Smith (2011) describes four main types of preference assessments typically used with individuals with ASD. One type of preference assessment is a survey provided to the child or parent used to determine items or activities that the individual likes. A second type is a rapid assessment in which the teacher holds up a pair of items or a choice board with pictures of items (the format should be identified based on the skills of the individual student with ASD and whether he/she needs concrete, photo, line drawing, or words to select preferences) just prior to instruction and asks the student "what do you want to work for?" The student selects an item and the teacher then provides the item following completion of the task. Prior to the next task, the student is presented with potential reinforcers asked the same question. The third and fourth common types of preference assessments are multiple-stimulus assessment and paired stimulus choice. Both of these assessments involve determining a hierarchy of preferences through a systematic presentation of potential reinforcers. Readers interested in this type of preference assessment are encouraged to read Higbee, Carr, and Harrison (2005, multiple-stimulus assessment) and Lavie and Sturmey (2002, paired preference assessment).

Once potential reinforcers are identified, it is important to apply reinforcement strategies effectively. Leaf, Schroeder, and Palos-Rafuse (2008) offer ten guidelines for effective use of reinforcement:

1. "Reinforcers should be reinforcing": As discussed previously, the consequence or item provided should result in increased instances of the targeted behavior.
2. "Reinforcement should be contingent": This means that provision of the reinforcer should only occur if and only if the student performs the targeted behavior.
3. "Use a variety of reinforcers": This is important because students may become satiated (i.e., full or "tired of") with an item or activity if it is provided too many times. Also, just as we change our minds or have different preferences for items or activities from day-to-day or moment-to-moment, so do individuals with ASD.
4. "Continually develop new reinforcers": As a result of restricted interests and behaviors, many individuals with ASD may not exhibit a large variety of preferences. It is important to expose children with ASD to new experiences and teach them how to engage with potential items in order to expand their preferences.
5. "Pair social reinforcers with tangible items": The ultimate goal of reinforcement is that individuals with ASD would find natural contingencies (natural opportunities for reinforcement) powerful enough reinforcers for desired behaviors. In order to do this, it is important to provide praise simultaneously with tangible items (e.g., toys or edibles) and slowly and systematically reduce the amount of tangibles provided while continuing with praise until the behavior can be maintained by praise only.
6. "Use age appropriate reinforcers": Students with ASD may have preferences for items that are intended for a much younger developmental age. However, it is important that we treat students with ASD respectfully and reduce the possibility of being stigmatized or bullied. In addition, by helping students with ASD to develop new age-appropriate preferences, they will likely have more in common with their peers, which may result in increased opportunities for meaningful social communication during leisure activities.
7. "Initially, reinforcement should occur immediately": When teaching new behaviors, it is important that students are able to distinguish the exact behavior your are requiring of them. By providing immediate reinforcement, students with ASD are more likely to associate the reinforcer with the targeted behavior and should result in a higher rate of performance of that behavior, thus leading to learning.

8. "Do not wait too long to fade reinforcement": While it is necessary to provide immediate reinforcement early on, it is also the goal to reduce the amount of reinforcement so that, as stated previously, the behavior will be reinforced by natural environmental reinforcers. Reducing the ratio of reinforcers to appropriate behavior should be studied very carefully to ensure that the targeted behavior remains reinforced (continues to be performed and/or increased in number). The time it takes to reduce or completely remove the reinforcement may vary considerably between students. In fact, for some students to perform certain behaviors, an artificial reinforcer (one not naturally in the student's environment) may always need to be provided at some level.

9. "Initially, label the behavior being reinforced": When providing simultaneous social praise to the student, provide specific naming of the behavior performed so that the student can begin to associate the reinforcer with the named behavior and/or begin to learn the label of the behavior being performed if previously not understood. For example, if teaching a student to trace the words from left to right as the teacher reads aloud, following correct completion of this behavior, provide the reinforcement while stating, "Great tracing the words from left to right!"

10. "Utilize differential reinforcement": By working with the student with ASD you will notice that some items are more desired by the student than others. Use this knowledge to shape the quality of the student's performance. For example, if the desired behavior is to trace his/her name, provide the most desired performance for tracing that is indistinguishable from the lines traced (i.e., near perfect) and provide a less desired (but still potentially reinforcing) item for lines traced with some errors. Eventually, the student will likely learn that high-quality work results in higher quality (desired) reinforcers.

Modified from Leaf, Shroeder, and Palos-Rafuse (2008).

PEER-MEDIATED INSTRUCTION

Students with autism tend to have limited social engagement with their peers. However, with peer training, social engagement between students with ASD and typical peers can more than double (Kamps et al., 2002). Two types of peer interventions are typically implemented: (a) peer mediation groups in which small groups of peers serve a defined role (e.g., tutoring, assisting as needed, providing social reinforcement for appropriate behaviors) to peers with ASD and (b) social networks, which are developed to provide social opportunities for students with disabilities including autism to engaged with typical peers and hopefully develop genuine friendships over time (Kamps et al., 2002). Carter et al. (2013) suggest ten ways to develop long-lasting social networks: (1) garner support from colleagues and administration before beginning; (2) choose students with ASD, who would benefit from peer social engagement; (3) identify an adult willing to facilitate the peer network; (4) locate peers without ASD, who may be good candidates and invite them to participate;

(5) identify feasible times during the school day to conduct peer networks; (6) train the peers on the purpose and effective strategies for engaging with peers with ASD; (7) schedule and begin consistent peer network meetings; (8) support development of friendships and shared activities outside the scheduled peer network meetings; (9) continuously monitor and support the peer networks as needed to ensure a positive experience for typical peers and peers with ASD; (10) troubleshoot and plan ahead to ensure that the network can be maintained over time as students schedules change, and so on. Table 10.4 displays guidelines for developing and implementing peer mediation groups.

Table 10.4. Guidelines for Developing and Implementing Peer Mediation Groups

Steps	Guidelines
1. Select Peers	Identify peers who: • Display good social skills • Are well liked • Have positively interacted with the target student(s) with ASD • Are willing to participant • Have few absences from school • Are compliant to adult instructions
2. Train Peers	• Guide discussion about ASD characteristics and appreciate similarities and differences • Identify role of peers (e.g., helping student implement science experiments, or including student in collaborative reading discussion) • Set up role play with materials and props • Model and then provide peer practice • Provide immediate, specific feedback to peers • Allow peers to practice first with, then without, cue cards
3. Provide Structured Practice	• Schedule brief sessions in a structured setting (controlled environment with few distractions) • Practice with peers and individual(s) with ASD • Supervise and provide feedback and prompting • Fade supervision and prompting as students become proficient
4. Implement in the Classroom or School Setting	• Embed peer mediation group into the daily schedule • Identify staff responsible for providing prompting as needed • Provide visual cues, self-management tools, and reinforcement

Modified from Sperry, Neitzel, and Engelhardt-Wells (2010).

Technology-Aided Instruction and Interventions

Technology-aided instruction and interventions can be used to teach a variety of skills. Instructional and assistive technologies may benefit students with ASD in learning academic content, increasing communication, socialization, and independence. Further, technology-based interventions may be more motivating for students with ASD. Many students with ASD seem to prefer technology-based interventions. For example, if the goal for the student is to compose a paragraph, handwriting the paragraph is probably not as important as the composition. Because students with ASD often have difficulty with gross and fine motor skills, alternatives to writing (e.g., typing, use of word prediction software, spell check, and voice-activated software) can address these challenges without compromising composition skills. In addition, many recent technology-based interventions can be used with a range of students, both students who receive special education services and typically developing students. Table 10.5 gives a list of technology-based intervention examples and the skills they can be used to address.

Table 10.5. Examples of Technology-Based Interventions

Type of Technology	Skills Addressed	Classroom Uses
iPhone/ Ipod/Ipad	• Communication • Self-management • Academics • Social skills • Transitioning • Community skills	• Social communication using speech-generating apps • Visual schedule to support transitions • Video prompting to complete functional or academic tasks • Video modeling to support social skills, job skills (e.g., sweeping, table washing), academic skills (e.g., completing math story problem), community skills (e.g., making purchases) • Self-monitoring checklist to complete rubric or activity, or monitor behavioral rule following (e.g., monitoring number of callouts and/or on-topic contributions to class discussion)
Two-Way Radio Headset	• Job skills • Community skills	• Covert audio prompting or coaching to complete work tasks independently

Software	• Social skills • Academic skills • Self-regulation	• Independent practice with facial expression/emotion identification software to support social skills (e.g., Emotion Trainer software) • Explicit academic instruction (e.g., Headsprout Early Reading) • Spelling software to support independent writing
Speech-Generating Devices	• Communication	• Social communication and interaction during classroom activities
Virtual Reality Avatars	• Social skills • Job skills • Self-determination	• Opportunity to practice socials skills in online environment with avatars • Practice interviewing for jobs using virtual avatars • Use avatar technology to prepare for self-directed IEP meeting
Timers	• Self-management • Self-monitoring	Use to remind students to: • Request assistance • Use the bathroom on a fixed schedule • Complete checklist monitoring on-task behaviors

Top 10 Things to Know about Teaching Students with ASD

1. I am not like every other person with ASD.
Just like persons without disabilities, I am an individual. I share characteristics with other individuals in the autism spectrum but there are many things about me that are unique to me. When you meet me, you have only met ONE child with autism.

2. The sooner I get support, the better off I'll be.
If I am considered "normal", or typically developing but you suspect that I might have warning signs of ASD, please discuss these concerns with my parents, another teacher, or an administrator. If I get help early enough, my outlook will be improved greatly.

3. Use interventions that work, and don't waste your time with others.
I need support to learn communication, socialization, and behavioral strategies. There are many claims on the Internet for what can cure me or for something that worked for one child. Please don't waste your time with interventions you are not sure of. Consult an expert or use the strategies in this chapter. If you do so consistently over a period of time, you will be amazed by my progress!

support

4. I have difficulty multitasking (ex. listening to the teacher, writing notes and looking at the teacher)
I am able to listen to the teacher, I am able to copy notes, and I am able to look at the teacher; sometimes I just have a very difficult time doing these things at the same time. It is just how my brain works. Please remember this when teaching me.

5. I take things that you say literally.
What you say is what I think you mean. I am able to learn the meaning of idioms. But if I have not been taught that 'take a hike' means that you want me to walk away from you, I may leave campus and go for a walk in the woods.

6. Use my special interests to motivate and teach me.
I really do like my special interest; I like to talk about it, read about it, and think about it. Use my special interest to get me to do work that I don't really like to do; I am sure that I will complete my math assignment if you let me read my book about my special interest afterwards. Although I may hate to write, if you let me write about my special interest, I may find writing a little more enjoyable.

7. I may not understand tone of voice, facial cues, and gestures.
If you want me to know that you are mad at me, please tell me rather than expecting me to know by your body language. Please tell my peers the same thing. Sometimes I have problems understanding emotions of others, and this may seem that I am insensitive or self-centered. This is not the case; sometimes, I may not know how to react in certain social situations, even when I know the emotions of others. Please tell me or model for me how to act.

8. Do not assume because I don't interact with my peers that I don't want friendships.
I may not know how to make friends. When I talk to my peers, I talk about things of interest to me. I don't really understand the games that the kids play on the playground, but I'm really good at video games. I would like it if you could help me to make friends. Maybe you know some students that like the same things as I do or maybe you can set some time aside for some of my peers and I to play games on the computer. You may need to monitor me because sometimes I don't take turns in conversations or sometimes I might come across as bossy. I just need to learn how to make and keep friends.

9. Pay attention to how others treat me.
I may not understand non-verbal cues from others and may not understand whether or not others are making fun of me. I may need to be told how to interact with my peers.

10. Don't take things that I may say and do personally.
I may say or do things that others may interpret as rude sometimes. By society's standards it may actually be rude, but I don't know this. Take the time to teach me the appropriate social skills and allow me time to practice.

In summary, individuals with ASD have social communication and social interaction impairments combined with restricted patterns of behavior that significantly impact their daily lives. They will likely require supports to be successful in the school environment. There are several evidence-based strategies that can be used to effectively support students with ASD.

GLOSSARY IN PLAIN TERMS

Autism: a complex developmental disability usually observable before age 3 that affects development in social interaction and communication. It is one diagnosis under the autism spectrum, but is often used synonymously with ASD.

Autism Spectrum Disorder (ASD): a group of developmental disabilities under the umbrella term *pervasive developmental disabilities*, which includes autism, Asperger's syndrome, and pervasive developmental disability – not otherwise specified. Students with the label of ASD have social, communication, and behavioral difficulties.

Asperger's syndrome: prior to DSM V, a Pervasive Developmental Disorder characterized by difficulty with social interactions, restricted interests, and unusual patterns of behavior. Individuals with Asperger's Syndrome have average or above average intelligence and do not have delays in spoken language. The terminology persists in use in mainstream society despite changes to the DSM.

Early intervention: consists of specialized services which specifically address the child's needs and is offered for children with disabilities from birth to 3 years and their families.

Applied Behavior Analysis (ABA): is the science dedicated to understanding and improving human behavior. The focus of ABA is based on "objectively defined, observable behaviors important to daily life" (Boutot & Tincani, 2009, p. 83).

Reinforcement: results in the increase of a behavior.

Social communication: the daily use of communication skills to interact socially (i.e., the functional use of language to make friends, engage in conversation, and socially relate to others).

Joint attention: the tendency of children to "share" a moment with a caregiver (e.g., pointing to an object of interest and then making eye contact with an adult to be sure the adult sees it too).

Evidence-based practices: approaches to teaching or promoting the development of children which have been clearly validated by rigorous scientific scrutiny rather than anecdotal evidence.

References

American Psychiatric Association, American Psychiatric Association, & DSM-5 Task Force. (2013). *Diagnostic and statistical manual of mental disorders: DSM-5*. Arlington, VA: American Psychiatric Association.

Baer, D. M., Wolf, M. M., & Risley, T. R. (1968). Some current dimensions of applied behavior analysis. *Journal of Applied Behavior Analysis, 1*(1), 91–97. doi:10.1901/jaba.1968.1-91.

BioMed Central (2010, April 1). Autism susceptibility genes identified. *Science Daily*. Retrieved July 31, 2010, from http://www.sciencedaily.com/releases/2010/03/100325102415.htm.

Boyd, B. A., Odom, S. L., Humphreys, B. P., & Sam, A. M. (2010). Infants and toddlers with autism spectrum disorder: Early identification and early intervention. *Journal of Early Intervention, 32*(2), 75–98. doi:10.1177/1053815110362690.

Carter, E., Asmus, J., Moss, C., Cooney, M., Weir, K., Vincent, L., … Fesperman, E. (2013). Peer network strategies to foster social connections among adolescents with and without severe disabilities. *TEACHING Exceptional Children, 46*(2), 51–59.

Center for Disease Control and Prevention. (2012). Prevalence of autism spectrum disorders: Autism and developmental disabilities monitoring network, 14 sites, United States, 2008. *Morbidity and Mortality Weekly Report, 61*(3), 1–19.

Cooper, J. O., Heron, T. E., & Heward, W. L. (2007). *Applied Behavior Analysis* (2nd Ed.). Upper Saddle River, NJ: Prentice Hall.

Dawson, G. (2008). Early behavioral intervention, brain plasticity, and the prevention of autism spectrum disorder. *Development and Psychopathology, 20,* 775–803.

Higbee, T. S., Carr, J. E., & Harrison, C. D. (2000). Further evaluation of the multiple-stimulus preference assessment. *Research in Developmental Disabilities, 21*(1), 61–73. doi:10.1016/S0891-4222(99)00030-X.

Individuals with Disabilities Education Act, *20* U.S.C. § 1400 (2004).

Kamps, D., Royer, J., Dugan, E., Kravits, T., Gonzalez-Lopez, A., Garcia, J., … Kane, L. (2002). Peer Training to facilitate social interaction for elementary students with autism and their peers. *Exceptional Children, 68*(2), 173–187.

Lavie, T., & Sturmey, P. (2002). Training staff to conduct a paired-stimulus preference assessment. *Journal of Applied Behavior Analysis, 35*(2), 209–211. doi:10.1901/jaba.2002.35-209.

Leaf, R., Schroeder, R., & Palos-Rafuse, L. (2008). What makes a good classroom? In R. Leaf, M. Taubman, & J. McEachin (Eds.), *It's time for school: Building quality ABA educational programs for students with autism spectrum disorders.* New York, NY: DRL Books, Inc.

Lord, C. (2014, March). Where did the DSM-5 criteria for ASD come from and where are they going to take us? Invited presentation at the Eighth Annual Autism Conference, Association for Behavior Analysis International, Louisville, KY.

National Research Council. (2001). *Educating children with autism.* Washington, DC: National Academy Press.

Odom, S, Thompson, J. L., Boyd, B., Dykstra, J., Duda, M., Hedges, S., Szidon, K., Smith, L., Bord, A. (submitted). Technology and secondary education for students with autism spectrum disorders. *Journal of Autism and Developmental Disabilities.*

Simpson, R. L. (2005). *Autism spectrum disorders: Interventions and treatments for children and youth.* Thousand Oaks, CA: Corwin Press.

Smith, T. (2011). Adapting the daily routine. In T. Smith (Ed.), *Making inclusion work for students with autism spectrum disorders: An evidence-based guide.* New York, NY: The Guildford Press.

Sperry, L., Neitzel, J., & Engelhardt-Wells, K. (2010). Peer-mediated instruction and intervention strategies for students with autism spectrum disorders. *Preventing School Failure, 54*(4), 256–264.

Taylor, L. E., Swerdfeger, A. L., & Eslick, G. D. (2014). Vaccines are not associated with autism: An evidence-based meta-analysis of case-control and cohort studies. *Vaccine, 32*(29), 3623–3629. doi:10.1016/j.vaccine.2014.04.085.

U.S. Department of Education, Office of Special Education and Rehabilitative Services, Office of Special Education Programs. (2012). *31st annual report to congress on the implementation of Individuals with Disabilities Education Act, 2009.* Washington, DC.

U.S. Department of Education, Office of Special Education and Rehabilitative Services, Office of Special Education Programs. (2013). *Annual report to congress data archive: Part C child count.* Retrieved from http://www.ideadata.org/Archive/30thARC/PartCChildCount.asp

Wetherby, A. M., Woods, J., Allen, L., Cleary, J., Dickinson, H., & Lord, C. (2004). Early indicators of autism spectrum disorders in the second year of life. *Journal of Autism and Developmental Disorders, 34*(5), 473–493. doi:10.1007/s10803-004-2544-y.

Wong, C., Odom, S. L., Hume, K. Cox, A. W., Fettig, A., Kucharczyk, S., … Schultz, T. R. (2013). *Evidence-based practices for children, youth, and young adults with Autism Spectrum Disorder.* Chapel Hill: The University of North Carolina, Frank Porter Graham Child Development Institute, Autism Evidence-Based Practice Review Group.

Yell, M. L., Katsiyannis, A., Drasgow, E., & Herbst, M. (2003). Developing legally correct and educationally appropriate programs for students with autism spectrum disorders. *Focus on Autism and Other Developmental Disabilities, 18*(3), 182–191. doi:10.1177/10883576030180030601.

QUESTIONS *for Reflection:*

Why is the IDEA disability category of Autism described as a "spectrum" disorder?

What are the characteristics of Autism Spectrum Disorder?

Given the changes to the current DSM, what relevance does the term Asperger's Syndrome have to the general public? How do the general characteristics of what we have traditionally known as Asperger's contrast with Autism?

What are the critical warning signs for ASD? What is early intervention and why is it so important?

In your own words explain what ABA is and what it is not.

Explain the increase in prevalence of ASD.

What are some effective strategies for students with ASD and how might you use them in your classroom?

Hyper / Hypo   Sensitivity
(over)   (under)

Safety + Medical Issues
↓
Seizures
Poor muscle control
Anxiety
Ear infections
~~XXXXXXXXX~~.
Sleep problems
Depression
Abnormal pain tolerance

Medical Diagnosis   DSM-5
- Given only by doctor / psychologist

Education level for a label
- IEP....

Asperger's Syndrome
- type of Autism

No initial cause for autism

Problems in class
↓
- distractility
- Inappropiate behavior
- difficult understanding and following directions.
- self harm.

ASD

NOTES

| Autism | - a neurobiological developmental disability

- Affects 1 in 68 people
- "Spectrum disorder" - ranges from mild to severe
- 4 out 5 people diagnosed with autism are MALE.
- Treatable not curable

Common Characteristics
- Imapairments in Language
- communication
- Social Interaction
- Restrictive / Repititve Behaviors

Two primary symptoms identified in DSM-5

- knowledge depends on family/student
  Sooner the better but don't forget about comprehension

Perceverate · Continuously bringing it up.
Help students understand strategys.
- Structure, Schedule, preperation
Difficulty w/ change
Avoids eye contact
Hyperlexia
Wandering
motor skills defcets.

Sensory differences.

←

CHAPTER

Teaching Children with Hearing Impairments

THE TOP TEN TERMS FOR CHAPTER 11:

The following key terms or big ideas are critical to your understanding of the content related to hearing impairment and the in-class discussions to follow.

• Audiogram	• Conductive hearing loss
• Audiometer	• Sensorineural hearing loss
• Audiology	• American Sign Language (ASL)
• Total Communication	• Cochlear implant
• Otitis media	• Decibel (dB)

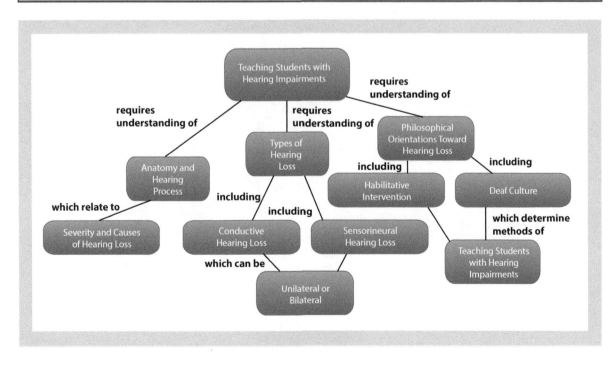

To understand hearing loss, it is best to begin by examining the manner in which hearing occurs in humans—a process that can appear somewhat *fantastical* when examined closely. Of course, it is important to note that all hearing begins with sound waves that are received by the ear. There are three general stages of hearing that correspond to three anatomical sections of the hearing mechanism: the outer ear, middle ear, and inner ear (see Figure 11.1).

The figure on the next page specifies the intricate anatomical features responsible for translation of sound waves to meaningful hearing, that is processed by the brain and symbolizes something meaningful to the person (e.g., language). A consideration for the reader who is unfamiliar with anatomical illustrations, the terminology reflects the common Latin-based naming used in medical literature. Many of the terms have more common English names that will be referenced parenthetically throughout the description.

First, the **outer ear** is primarily comprised of the *pinna* (the outer structure of the ear), the *external auditory meatus* (ear canal), and the *tympanic membrane* (ear drum). At this first level of hearing, the pinna is designed much like a satellite dish to receive auditory signals. The sound waves are collected and transmitted through the external auditory meatus, which is relatively fleshy and covered in small hair cells at the entry point and transitions into a boney interior as it approaches the tympanic membrane. This area is also lined with cerumen (earwax). Despite the tendency for people to see earwax as a nuisance, the hair cells and waxy lining are protections against the entry of foreign bodies into the ear. Sound waves that have

Figure 11.1. Anatomy of the Ear

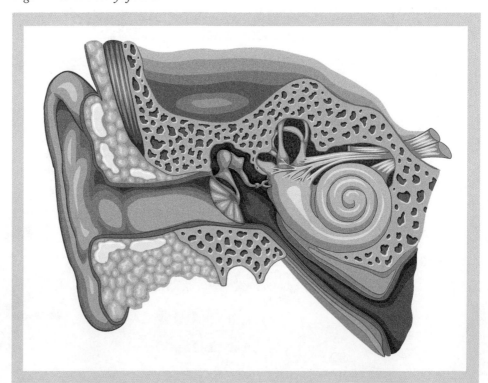

Figure 11.2. Parts of the Ear

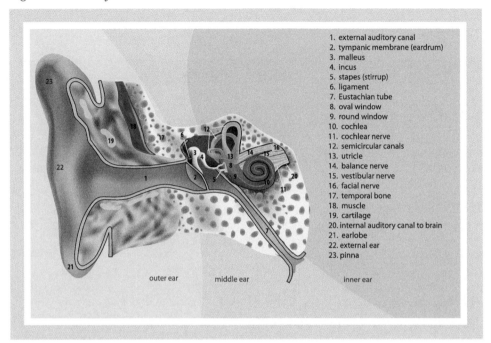

1. external auditory canal
2. tympanic membrane (eardrum)
3. malleus
4. incus
5. stapes (stirrup)
6. ligament
7. Eustachian tube
8. oval window
9. round window
10. cochlea
11. cochlear nerve
12. semicircular canals
13. utricle
14. balance nerve
15. vestibular nerve
16. facial nerve
17. temporal bone
18. muscle
19. cartilage
20. internal auditory canal to brain
21. earlobe
22. external ear
23. pinna

outer ear   middle ear   inner ear

traveled to this point bounce off the *tympanic membrane* creating a vibration of the tympanic membrane (i.e., the sound waves beat on the drum).

In the **middle ear,** the *ossicles*, three little bones (smaller than an orange seed) continue the transmission of the sound waves through the ear by vibrating in response to the vibration of the tympanic membrane. The tiny bones called the incus, malleus, and stapes (hammer, mallet, and stirrup in English) translate the vibratory energy of the source sounds through the very small middle ear to the inner ear at the oval window.

In the **inner ear,** highly complicated interpretation of acoustic energy occurs. The cochlea, the main organ responsible for interpreting sound and translating the sound to meaning in the brain, is the key factor in the inner ear. Also in the inner ear is the vestibular system comprised of semicircular canals, which filled with liquid, maintain a person's sense of balance and stability as the fluid is balanced in the inner ear. Finally, the complex interpretation of sound by the cochlea leads to transmission of sound information to the auditory or acoustic nerve, at which point the brain interprets the sound as a meaningful representation of a speech sound, a noise, and so on.

The Anatomy and Physics of Hearing

Key Terms for Anatomy:

• malleus	• pinna
• incus	• ossicles
• stapes	• tympanic membrane
• auditory nerve	• cochlea
• semicircular canals	• external auditory meatus

Tinnitus: the ringing in the ears that occurs such that you perceive a ringing, buzzing, hissing, or even "white noise" sound in the ears. Often due to noise exposure, prolonged states of tinnitus occur in small numbers of people and can be quite problematic.

Defining Disability in Hearing: Hard of Hearing, Deafness, and Deaf Culture

Types of Hearing Loss

There are three types of hearing loss that can occur reflecting impairment of the hearing mechanism: **conductive hearing loss** (lack of ability of the ear to "conduct" sound), **sensorineural hearing loss** (damage to the higher level, neurological mechanism of hearing), and **mixed hearing loss** (a combination of impairments). Knowledge of the mechanistic and delicate process of hearing is extremely helpful as we try to understand how a hearing loss might occur. Any damage to the physical structures of the outer or middle ear will lead to reduced hearing ability.

Damage could include malformation of the ear structure, blockage of the ear canal by cerumen or foreign objects, damage or perforation of the tympanic membrane, and damage to the ossicles such that they cannot properly rattle or vibrate in the middle ear. Another common cause of hearing loss can even relate to the presence of fluid in the middle ear that prevents the free and delicate movement of the ossicles. Fluid in the middle ear caused by *otitis media* (middle ear infection) is a very common source of mild hearing loss among very young children who tend to be plagued by ear infections. Although, mild losses don't initially appear significant, it is notable that children with a mild loss due to the presence of middle ear fluid, will hear their surroundings as if the sound was muffled (imagine holding your hands over your ears). This does not inhibit all sound, but it does inhibit many soft speech sounds and can lead to delay in language development as the child misses out on subtle features of speech occurring out of their hearing range (e.g., morphemes like the final "s" in plural words or the final "ed" in past tense words). Notable, in the above descriptions is the potential for repair of the damage and hopefully, a restoration of hearing. All of these issues would result in what is referred to as a *conductive hearing loss.*

Conductive Hearing Loss: a hearing loss that affects the transmission of sound through the outer and middle ear. Conductive hearing losses tend to result in reduced, but not eliminated ability to hear. Because the loss is often due to something structurally inhibiting the effective conversion of sound waves to effective hearing, it may be possible to intervene medically to resolve the issue. Also, a lack of damage to the inner ear, which is more delicate and complicated, means that conductive hearing losses skew toward the mild to moderate range.

- Middle ear fluid from a cold, otitis media (ear infection), etc.
- Perforated ear drum
- Ear canal blockage (e.g., wax impaction in the ear canal)
- Anatomical malformation (e.g, craniofacial malformation)

Damage to the cochlea is more complicated, as the main hearing organ is an extremely delicate operation. Regardless of the cause of damage (e.g., disease, hereditary deficits), damage to the cochlea is not something that can be easily repaired. Inner ear damage will likely result in permanent and substantial hearing loss. Damage to the inner ear and nerve innervations results in a *sensorineural hearing loss*. A late 20th century innovation, the **cochlear implant** may be the best chance to *replace* (not restore) the cochlear function. Cochlear implants are described in more detail later in this chapter. A *mixed hearing loss* is simply a combination of the limitations associated with both conductive and sensorineural hearing problems.

Sensorineural Hearing Loss: a hearing loss resulting from damage to the inner ear and or the nerves that communicate inner ear signals to the brain. Sensorineural losses tend to be more severe and permanent.

Caused by:
- Diseases, birth injury, toxic exposure, genetic syndromes
- Noise exposure, viruses, head trauma, aging, tumors
- Hearing loss can run in the family

A final consideration related to types of hearing loss is the contrast between **unilateral** and **bilateral hearing loss**. Essentially, a difference of hearing loss in one ear versus two ears, the unilateral hearing loss is not uncommon, but implies that a child has residual hearing to support their communication and learning. Despite hearing acuity in one ear, academic setting demands can create challenges, as teachers assume the child hears everything without limitation. In actuality, positioning in the classroom and clear communication strategies are still important for children with unilateral hearing loss who, if inadvertently seated with the impaired ear toward the teacher, may have a diminished academic experience.

Otitis Media: inflammation in the middle ear, often an infection, that can result in fluid in the middle ear. Extreme cases are prolonged, painful, and can cause long-term hearing loss. The condition is significant in that it affects most children at one time or another and is most common among children at the ages of language acquisition. Children miss subtle speech and language information because the ossicles in the middle ear cannot properly transmit sound information. The condition is typically minor and short-term, but consistent problems can result in more significant hearing loss.

Central Auditory Processing Disorder

Central Auditory Processing Disorder (CAPD) is a complicated disorder of hearing that is believed to result from some type of impairment of neurological processing of auditory information. There remains a certain ambiguity related to the cause and definition of CAPD. Despite normal intelligence and hearing ability, children with CAPD are limited in their ability to "attend to, discriminate, recognize, remember, or comprehend information presented auditorily" (Northern & Downs, 2002, p. 200). These problems with auditory discrimination and comprehension tend to be most challenging when there is a distracting environment with competing acoustic stimuli (Northern & Downs).

Hearing Loss: Disability or Culture?

Discussion of the impairment of hearing among children in school is embedded with controversy and opposing perspectives, as there is no agreement on whether hearing impairment is a disability or a defining feature of the uniqueness of the child; nor is there agreement on whether hearing loss is a condition that necessitates compensation and remediation or a unique cultural experience built upon the premise of sign language as a socio-cultural bond. Some key terms used to describe individuals with hearing impairments include **hard-of-hearing, deaf,** and **Deaf** (as in Deaf culture). Each of these terms reflects assumptions about the degree to which the hearing impairment impacts the individual's life and the belief system associated with hearing loss. Further, the definitions are not nearly as objective as exposure to the constructs in popular culture would suggest. For example, some individuals might fit a common definition of deafness, but prefer the use of the term "hard-of-hearing" because they choose to live in the hearing world using amplification, speechreading, and other accommodations. The opposite can also be true, as there are individuals whose hearing loss could be somewhat remediated given appropriate auditory training and use of hearing aids, but choose to live in the Deaf culture using primarily visible, manual communication.

Hard of Hearing: traditionally refers to an individual who has substantial hearing loss, but sufficient residual hearing (e.g., unilateral loss; moderate bilateral loss) such that amplification devices would allow access to speech and language in daily and academic life.

Deaf: although there is no objective line of division, an individual who is deaf would have limited residual hearing and would not be likely to benefit from amplification devices to experience speech and language in a typical manner. Despite common assumptions, an individual who is deaf is not completely "cut off" from sound in his environment; linguistic information is missing and therefore visible, manual communication becomes a more natural option for communication.

Deaf: similar definition to deaf but represents a cultural identity characterized by subcultural use of American Sign Language and interaction primarily with other ASL users.

WHAT IS DEAF CULTURE?

Unique to individuals who are deaf is the idea that a disability can evolve into a unique cultural identity. Individuals who feel bonded by the use of American Sign Language and the tradition of segregation implied by use of ASL in residential and state schools for students who are deaf, identify as members of the Deaf culture (the D is capitalized in this context). Deaf culture has been described in terms of collective group norms (shared culture) based on shared language (ASL), values, rules, accumulated knowledge, and traditions that ultimately define identity and life experiences (Johnson & McIntosh, 2009). This might be compared to being part of an ethnic/linguistic minority subculture.

Historically, individuals with hearing loss in the United States (prior to technological developments like hearing aids and cochlear implantation) experienced limited communication and educational options in a society that was largely condescending and exclusionary. Being deaf meant that American Sign Language was the critical means of communicating and functioning throughout one's life. In fact, numerous advocates of ASL strongly suggest that a complex linguistic system of manual communication is the only natural response to the needs of an individual who experiences the world in a primarily visual manner. With the exception of a few historical instances of communities with large deaf populations, families and peers of individuals have traditionally been reluctant to use ASL. The lack of family use of ASL along with the common need for children who were deaf to attend geographically distant schools from a young age in order to learn ASL and use the manual language to receive their education, meant that individuals who were deaf became more connected to school peers than family. The historical development of segregated subcultures of individuals who used ASL and worked, socialized, and married within these subcultures, led to a bold advocacy for the uniqueness of being Deaf as a cultural experience within the larger society. Rather than accept condescending judgments that a lack of hearing and speaking ability made a deaf person disabled or handicapped, the Deaf community asserted their normality and efficacy through entrenched beliefs in separation from the hearing society and internalization of a counter-position that marginalizes the presumed value of hearing and speaking (Shapiro, 1994). More outspoken advocates for Deaf culture resist any suggestion that the mainstream society of hearing people are normal, as ASL users can achieve all of the same outcomes in life communicating with a *purely manual communication system that* **includes all of the same linguistic features of English** (Hehir, 2006). Although ASL does not center on the use of speech, it is still characterized by use of **syntax, vocabulary, pragmatics, emphasis and prosody,** and even **regional accents.** Education, work, and happiness can be achieved when individuals with hearing loss live among ASL community peers. This might include schools that use ASL and have primarily Deaf populations (e.g., Gallaudet University in Washington, D.C.) and even living in communities for Deaf individuals. A major assertion of Deaf culture is that being Deaf is part of one's identity, maybe even the core of their identity. Only when accepting the premise of mainstream society that hearing and speaking are important and normal, does a Deaf individual become disabled or handicapped, particularly by the medical community's desire to remediate limitations. The Deaf community has been most vocal in their opposition to attempts to "fix" hearing loss by using hearing aids or assistive devices, auditory training, speechreading/lipreading, and speech therapy. The use of cochlear implants has proven even more controversial, as a child receiving an implant will no longer be deaf. Some members of the Deaf community have viewed the implementation as a horrible attempt to force a Deaf child to be part of a hearing community by implanting computer technology in a child to force them to be "hearing." The perspective of the Deaf community is not generally the dominant perspective of special education professionals, with the exception of many Deaf educators teaching in ASL and ASL interpreters.

Audiology and the Speech Banana

Students with a hearing impairment have their hearing loss measured and assessed by a hearing specialist called an *Audiologist*. These specialists measure the students' hearing loss with a device called an *Audiometer* and report their findings on a gridded form called an Audiogram (see Figure 11.3). The audiogram shows the hearing loss on a scale measured in decibels (dB). Someone who can hear sounds at 0 decibels has exceptionally good hearing. As the number of decibels increases for the student to hear a sound, we would say they have less proficient hearing (i.e., if a sound presented into headphones by an audiometer must be 40 dB, we would say the student has a 40 dB hearing loss).

The student's threshold for hearing is measured at many different frequencies or pitches (i.e. 100 Hz, 250 Hz, 1000 Hz, etc.). Students may hear better at certain frequencies (like high pitch or low pitch sounds) or they may have a hearing loss across all frequencies. The higher the decibel threshold for hearing is, the more challenges the student will face with communication and functioning in the school setting.

Amplitude: loudness of a sound measured in decibels

Frequency: pitch of a sound that can be very high or low similar to a singer's voice being a soprano or a baritone

For more information on Audiology and Hearing Impairment, contact the American Speech-Language-Hearing Association (ASHA) at www. asha.org.

Figure 11.3. Example of an Audiogram

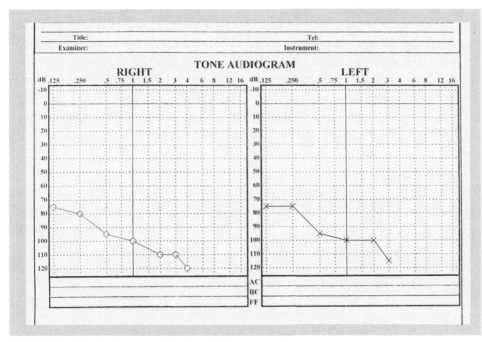

Table 11.1. Differing Levels of Hearing Loss

Degree of Hearing Impairment	Range of Hearing Loss (in decibels)
Normal Hearing	-10 to 15 dB
Slight loss (not relevant to speech)	16 to 25 dB
Mild	26 to 40 dB
Moderate	41 to 55 dB
Moderately Severe	56 to 70 dB
Severe	71 to 90 dB
Profound	91 dB or higher

Table adapted from Clark (1981).

Most evaluation for hearing loss seeks to determine the level of impact that the hearing loss might have on the individual. A hearing loss ranging from 15-20 decibels across all frequencies of sound, for example, would probably not have too much impact on someone's life. In contrast, however, hearing loss that occurs at the same loudness as most of the speech sounds would create problems in a child learning to use both speech and language. Ultimately, a hearing loss that inhibits a child from hearing speech in daily life would lead to significant developmental and academic limitations requiring intervention from specialists in audiology and speech language pathology or Deaf educators (depending on the belief system of the key decision makers). For a deeper understanding of how hearing loss affects people's ability to understand speech, communicate, and function in the **hearing world**, we can refer to the *Speech Banana,* which shows in a very practical way, what kinds of sounds students with a hearing loss are missing.

Imagine a student with a mild to moderate hearing loss: 50 dB across all low and mid-frequency sounds improving to 35 dB for high frequency sounds above 2000 Hz. Although the description of mild to moderate loss implies that the impairment is not severe in impact, a review of the audiogram reveals that most phonemes relevant to speech production (and acquisition) cluster just below the threshold of this hypothetical child's hearing ability. Although he can hear most loud environmental sounds, probably even music and singing, conversational speech is "below his radar," with the exception of a few vowel sounds. The speech banana can also be a helpful point of reference to understand what the student can hear when they are using hearing aids versus unaided hearing. In the same scenario, it is clear that hearing aids that could amplify the conversation sound would need only to improve the child's hearing by 10 to 20 dB to have a profound functional impact on speech and language development.

Figure 11.4.

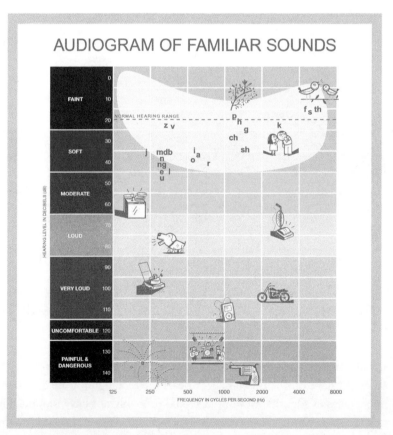

Speech Banana Image: p. 230 in Special Education for All Teachers *by Colarusso and O'Rourke with permission from American Academy of Audiology.*

The dominant perspective of the community of professional audiologists and speech-language pathologists, referred to as audiologic rehabilitation or *habilitation* (training in new skills), contrasts significantly from that of the Deaf culture. The potential of children to experience typical development despite hearing loss, is the main focus of audiologists and speech-language pathologists and certainly reflects the perspective of a health professional/medical model, as remediation or correction of hearing loss is an assumed goal. The potential for success in "correcting" hearing loss primarily relates to the child's ability to develop appropriate use and understanding of his or her native language (English for the purpose of this chapter). The most significant barrier for children with hearing impairments to participate effectively in the "hearing world," is the effect of hearing loss on the typical development of **speech and language**. Even from the earliest points of babbling, *hearing loss inhibits speech and language development*. Although, *all babies babble*, the joy and interactive communication that infants engage in with caregivers is diminished for the child with a hearing loss. The desire to experiment with babbling might have a tactile sensation, but lacks the playful experimentation with an emerging sound system that hearing children experience.

The potential for improvement of speech and language development as a result of hearing loss, depends on various factors including whether the child was **pre-linguistically deaf** or **post-linguistically deaf.** The child who is post-linguistically deaf (or has an *acquired hearing loss*) will experience a rehabilitation program meant to build upon the previously established communication abilities. The child who is pre-linguistically deaf (*congenitally deaf*) has not experienced speech and language as part of his natural development in childhood. Although severity of the loss and type of the loss are significant factors, *audiologic habilitation* methods focus on early identification and intervention use of amplification to stimulate the hearing mechanism and orient the child's ability to attend to and use auditory stimuli. It has been suggested that infants identified with a hearing loss by 6 months have the potential to progress in language development in a manner comparable to hearing peers (American Speech-Language-Hearing Association, 2010).

HEARING AIDS AND ASSISTIVE LISTENING DEVICES

Hearing aids are very useful as a part of **auditory training** if a child is using a method that emphasizes the use of residual hearing. It is conceivable that a hearing aid could potentially enhance a child's hearing to the point that they could hear speech and improve their own ability to speak. Martin (1997) describes the hearing aid as a "miniature, personalized, public address system" that uses a microphone to amplify and transmit sound waves into the outer ear using an "output transducer" that acts as a "loudspeaker" (p. 436). Audiological testing of a child with hearing aids allows for determination of amplification gain to determine the difference between unaided hearing and aided hearing. If hearing aids can produce an aided representation of auditory stimuli such that the child can perceive linguistic information, a substantially different prognosis is determined of the child to benefit from auditory training and speech language pathology. Amplification is not the same as restoration, however. According to the American Speech Language and Hearing Association, hearing aids do not restore hearing to the "normal" levels of hearing peers. Families should not view hearing aids as a "cure" for a hearing loss, but new options are available as a result of enhancements or amplification of hearing thresholds.

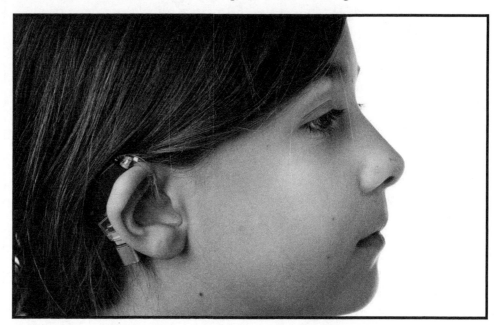

© *Paul Matthew Photography, 2015. Used under license from Shutterstock, Inc.*

Three kinds of hearing aids are common. Typical designs of modern hearing aids include In-the-canal (ITCs), In-the-ear (ITEs), and Behind-the-ear (BTEs). The names clearly suggest the structure. BTEs (see photo above) are the most common for young children, whereas older users are more likely to consider cosmetic needs and the desire to make the aid less conspicuous (Martin, 1997). Traditionally, the power of the hearing aid has been a consideration for selection of the hearing aid type. More severe hearing losses require more power in the aid to amplify environmental sound. Historically, children with the most severe (and profound) hearing losses participating in aural/oral programs required extremely powerful hearing aids. The very large body-type hearing aids were commonly used, which were quite conspicuous to classroom peers and could be stigmatizing (Martin).

ASSISTIVE LISTENING TECHNOLOGY

Although assistive technology can have implications for myriad aspects of daily life, the most commonly considered devices for children with hearing impairment in general education classes are ***Assistive Listening Devices (ALDs)***. These devices assist in overcoming the difficulties of a child who struggles to hear and appropriately "process" key information (as in CAPD) in a noisy, busy classroom. The efforts of a child who is hard of hearing to attend to academic stimuli in a distracting environment can produce a great deal of fatigue throughout the day. Some children resort to tuning out or turning off hearing amplification devices.

FM Systems are probably the most common ALDs. **FM Systems** are personal assistive listening devices that use a microphone and receiver to broadcast radio waves within the classroom. The teacher (or other important sound source) is broadcast using a microphone and a transmission to the receiver used by the student. The sound can be transmitted directly to the hearing aid and ultimately reduces effects of background noise and perceived distortion of the teacher speaking. The potential for a child to have a clearer and undistracted auditory perception of the teacher has led to even broader use of the devices (i.e., for students with learning and attention problems). Although portability and flexibility in the use of FM systems are a major positive, some limitations are possible due to signal interference from competing devices using similar transmissions (Schow, 1996).

TEACHING PARADIGMS FOR THE EDUCATION OF CHILDREN WITH HEARING IMPAIRMENTS

There is great controversy over appropriate interventions and educational planning for students with hearing impairments. The traditional view of hearing loss is based on the medical model which views all differences from the norm to be maladies in need of correction. It is essential for educators working with students with hearing impairments to understand that this view of difference as disorder is not universal.

The ***Deaf community*** in the United States views the idea of hearing loss not as a disability but rather as a difference, which places them in a separate subcultural community of Americans. Members of the Deaf community do not view their difference as something in need of "fixing," so they would typically be opposed to the use of hearing amplification devices or any effort to force people with hearing impairments to function in society with hearing people. Instead, the Deaf community in the United States advocates for instruction in American Sign Language (ASL) at an early age (i.e., children who are Deaf should have early and intensive exposure to ASL, just as any child would have early language exposure) and typically, prefer educational settings that promote ASL use in an academically rigorous environment, as opposed to accommodation of ASL use in classrooms with hearing peers. This may be somewhat disconcerting to "inclusionists," and stands in contrast to advocacy models for individuals with disabilities that typically promote inclusive society and educational opportunities.

The opposing view often supported by physicians, Speech-Language Pathologists, and Audiologists is the idea that hearing impairment is a problem, which can often be corrected and the consequential limitations can be prevented. Recent advances in technology have shown that hearing cannot only be amplified with hearing aids but it might also be replaced using devices like a cochlear implants.

Where this issue gets especially controversial is in the case of a student with a moderate hearing loss which causes difficulty with hearing speech in daily life, who if taught ASL at a young age, could become proficient and successful in that method but with hearing aids or a cochlear implant, could be equally proficient in the hearing world.

Common Terminology Used in Discussions of Deaf Education

The Aural/Oral Method: professionals in audiology and speech language pathology attempt to take advantage of a child's residual hearing through auditory training using hearing aids/sound amplification and instruction in speechreading/lipreading. The method assumes a more main-streamed existence and ability of the child to learn to speak like hearing people.

Finger Spelling: a manual formation of English alphabet letters using carefully positioned fingers to represent each corresponding letter (see Figure 11.5).

Signed English: used as a means of support to English language proficiency, Signed English is a manual communication method that uses the same grammar rules found in English, rather than the alternate grammar/syntax found in ASL, but still maintains ASL vocabulary. Finger spelling is very important in signed English. ASL users may find the system cumbersome and illogical given the rather rigid process of signing in a "sentence-like" format.

American Sign Language (ASL): a distinct language of the Deaf which uses manual communi-cation and visual representations (signs) formed with the hands, facial expressions, and body language/posturing to communicate. ASL has a syntactic system, but it is not equivalent to English. The unique manner of conveying ideas necessitates a second language acquisition process for learning standard English, particularly related to grammar rules (e.g., sentence structure, word order).

Total Communication: intended to be an eclectic approach to deaf education, both sign lan-guage and auditory/oral training methods are employed.

THREE TRADITIONAL OPTIONS FOR STUDENTS WITH HEARING IMPAIRMENT

Aural/Oral Communication (Aural Habilitation)

The aural/oral method emphasizes use of speech, amplified hearing, and speechread-ing (also known as lipreading). This typically requires early intervention with ampli-fication of hearing before the child loses the ability to *attend* to auditory stimuli. This method is considered to be quite challenging for young children and requires considerable effort on the part of the child, parents, and support professionals. Although progress is often slow at first, children who succeed in adapting to the aural/oral approach typically show tremendous outcomes in academic achievement compared to their similarly challenged peers who had less English language expo-sure. Essentially, because the aural/oral approach insists upon the use of Standard English for speaking and students listen and speechread their peers' use of English, literacy development in enhanced. Students are not forced to develop reading skills in Standard English as a second language due to a life of exposure to commonly used spoken and written language.

Criticism of aural/oral methods are *abundant*, particularly among deaf educa-tion advocates that favor use of manual communication as a more natural process for children who perceive the world visually. Although positive school outcomes and the potential for life in a mainstream, hearing society are clear benefits of this method, critics observe major flaws in this approach. The early training methods eschew any manual communication as a source of interference to auditory training. The lack of exposure to sign language is often viewed as intellectually stunting. Further, the training methods are sometimes described as unpleasant and frustrating by young children who completed oral programs, particularly if they had an affinity for ASL and were prevented from using it. Finally, advocates of models that promote concurrent communication methods (e.g., Total Communication) suggest that students who demonstrate poor outcomes with the oral methods will be at a significant disadvantage in transitioning to the use of sign.

Traditionally called, Oralism, aural/oral training methods emphasize:

Auditory training: developing skills in hearing and attending to sound; discriminating between sounds and general awareness of sound in the environment

Visual cues: learning how to speech or lipread; examining all visual information in a communication situation such as facial expressions and body language

Speech therapy: learning skills in articulating basic speech sounds and continuing to modulation of speaking voice quality and character

Language therapy: learning both expressive and receptive language skills in a direct manner to compensate for limited language exposure; addresses vocabulary development and other rules of language use

Communication strategies: developing strategies of self-advocacy in hearing contexts and repair strategies for communication difficulties (asking peers to rephrase; seeking out context clues to clarify messages)

Use of hearing aids and assistive listening devices—developing skills in use of assistive devices including ongoing maintenance; a key factor in auditory training

(American Speech Language and Hearing Association)

Manual Communication (American Sign Language)

Manual communication options in American schools emphasize the use of American Sign Language (ASL). This method deemphasizes use of speech and hearing, and focuses on use of visual cues for communication as the most logical and accessible means of communication for children with hearing loss. Detractors of this method often note that ASL is not strongly related to the structure of written English and therefore students who use ASL as their primary means of communication find it difficult to learn to read and write Standard English (see **Academic Achievement** in this chapter for more details). Further, inclusion-minded professionals regret the reinforcement of sociocultural isolation that ASL instruction fosters.

ASL is not just English communicated via a series of equivalent signs. Children developing proficiency with ASL in childhood will require development of a vast lexicon of signs including dialectal or regional variances, knowledge of the distinct grammatical structure used in ASL, and the very precise handshapes and movements employed in proficient ASL communication. In fact, the distinct phonology of ASL includes a need for precision and accuracy of formation of signs based on handshape and orientation of the hand, location of the sign on the body, the nature of the movement of the hands when making the sign, and even the facial expression used while making the sign. Young ASL users must also develop an ability to use fingerspelling both accurately and efficiently. Fingerspelling is not technically English, but does involve connections to the English alphabet, as signers will fingerspell signs equivalent to the English alphabet when there is no existing sign to represent a concept being communicated (Valli & Lucas, 2000).

Like any language, ASL communication involves a great deal of cultural rules and sets of social skills that must be developed over time. For example, a good communicator in ASL uses appropriate body language including nodding, while the conversational partner is signing so that individual knows they are being understood. A comfortable ASL user would also focus attention on the conversational partner's face rather than their hands and interact in the conversation by returning signs that show interest and attention (Valli & Lucas, 2000). The developmental process is essentially equivalent to the language development process of English speakers who must begin in the early years by naming objects, learning words to convey more precise meaning, and learning to order words properly to make themselves understood. Both formal academic experience and everyday communication will play a role in the development of effective ASL communication for a child who is Deaf.

Figure 11.5. Sign Language

© *Stephen Coburn, 2015. Used under license from Shutterstock, Inc.*

Total Communication

Total Communication emphasizes an eclectic approach combining speech, amplified hearing, speechreading, *and* manual communication. Educators working with students using TC often use "Signed English" as their method of manual communication. This involves using sign language with the same structure as written English, so students will experience less difficulty with the transition to reading and writing English (Northern & Downs, 2002). Although this approach might sound like a natural compromise, detractors claim that these opposing methods cannot be combined well. Each method counteracts the other, resulting in diminished ability to flourish in either natural speech and language or ASL. Aural/oral supporters feel that if students use manual communication, they may not want to use their hearing aids and learn to listen. Supporters of ASL, typically members of the Deaf community, feel that speech and hearing should not be thrust upon non-hearing children and that sign language is the sufficient and logical choice.

COCHLEAR IMPLANTS FOR STUDENTS WITH HEARING IMPAIRMENT

The cochlear implant is a remarkable technological innovation. Dramatically changing the nature of audiologic habilitation programs, many medically-oriented professionals assumed the innovation would resolve the debate about interventions for children who were deaf; yet the controversy continues. According to the American Speech-Language-Hearing Association, a cochlear implant is a technological innovation that essentially replaces the actions of the cochlea to produce hearing in a child with sensorineural hearing loss. As a sensorineural hearing loss results in severe hearing loss from loss of function of the inner ear/auditory nerve function, a cochlear implant can produce impressive outcomes not previously available. For children who do not benefit from hearing aids, the cochlear implant is a remarkable technology that directly stimulates the auditory nerve to produce a perception of sound in the child's brain. Although the implant cannot actually cure a profound hearing loss, a child with a cochlear implant can perceive something similar to normal auditory stimuli, such that the child could have greater potential to develop speech and language.

The cochlear implant is actually surgically implanted, which could make it a much more involved and, potentially, anxiety producing experience than simply using hearing aids. The external features of the device include a microphone (similar to a standard behind-the-ear hearing aid), a speech processor, and a transmitter. The implant portion of the device includes a receiver under the skin (behind the ear), which directs the electrical stimulation, typically interpreted by the cochlea, to electrodes implanted in the non-functioning cochlea to transmit signals to the auditory nerve.

Figure 11.6.

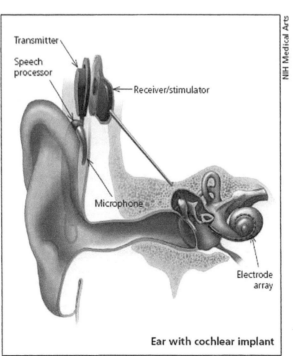

Ear with cochlear implant

Although cochlear implants are an increasingly popular option for addressing hearing loss, there are important considerations for appropriate implantation. The implants are designed for children with the most profound hearing losses that could not be resolved by more standard means like hearing aids and auditory training. Further, it is critical that family members understand the limitations in the potential for cochlear implants to fully resolve hearing loss, and the need for intensive and ongoing programs of education and auditory habilitation similar to the aural/oral method. Very young children are eligible for cochlear implants—typically around 14 months (American Speech-Language-Hearing Association).

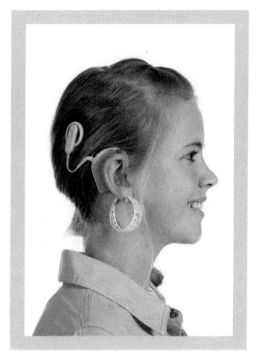

Elsa Hoffmann/Shutterstock.com

Why the Deaf Cultural Community Resists the Trend Toward Cochlear Implants

The Deaf culture represents a historically established community within the United States premised on a shared experience of ASL communication. The legacy of isolation imposed by a history of separate living circumstances and language use, has reinforced the significance of a unique cultural group of Deaf Americans. Although medical professionals assume that cochlear implants represent a logical and obvious solution to the burden of deafness, the Deaf culture views intensive screening for hearing loss, genetic testing, and implantation of young children who are prelinguistically deaf as a real threat to the continuation of Deaf culture. Seeing deafness as a characteristic of their culture identity, Deaf individuals see the medical obsession with cochlear implementation as an assault on that cultural identity (Sparrow, 2010).

A more contemporary perspective on the development of ASL for communication and education has adopted the language of the ESL community. ***Bilingual-Bicultural education of deaf and hard-of-hearing children*** is premised on research that suggests Deaf children are most likely to flourish academically and intellectually when they develop a high level of proficiency with their first language. In this case, ASL would be presumed to be the logical first language; however, English language and literacy are not discounted—they are simply viewed as the language and literacy tactics of another cultural, linguistic group. Advocating the value of Deaf culture and language, children in bilingual-bicultural programs should ideally develop a strong sense of self-efficacy as Deaf individuals and avoid judgments of deficiency from the hearing community, before experiencing an intensive training in a "second language" (i.e., English) to promote a richer academic development (Grosjean, 2001; Nelson, 1998). Numerous parallels can be drawn from research on second language acquisition (ESL) for children who speak a native language other than English in their home, particularly as it relates to immigrant children in American public schools.

ACADEMIC ACHIEVEMENT

The American Speech-Language-Hearing Association suggests that hearing loss causes delay in the development of communication skills that consequently result in limited academic achievement. Students with hearing impairments typically do not experience great success with reading, writing, and math in school when compared to their hearing peers. Data on academic experiences for children with hearing impairments suggest that approximately 43% of the students spend most of their time in school in general education classes, probably because there appears to be a very large number of children who are hard of hearing, rather than deaf. Even students with moderate hearing loss, however, experience significantly reduced achievement in school (Reed, Antia, & Kreimeyer, 2008).

de Villiers (1992) reported that students with hearing impairment on average reach only the 4th grade level in reading by age 17, significantly below their hearing peers. Although better than reading, they also fall behind in math, reaching only the 7th to 8th grade level. The percentage of students that can read at a proficient level in high school is extremely low. Among White middle class populations, only about 15% can read above the 6th grade level and the rate is even lower (5%) among disadvantaged minorities in the U.S. (de Villiers).

From the perspective of audiologic rehabilitation, the problem of low achievement has to do with failure to provide early intervention in auditory training and the fact that English language development is not properly fostered in the early years. Particularly related to limitations in reading comprehension, children with hearing impairments are likely to experience difficulty with academic achievement due to a lack of participation in standard educational experiences and the development of reading/writing skills in Standard English (Northern & Downs, 2002). Where the issue becomes complicated is when one analyzes the nature of English learned as a second and "less natural" language than ASL.

Some have suggested that limitations in academic achievement result from contorted efforts to force developments in Standard English that ultimately undermine academic exposure provided in the most effective and logical manner—via ASL-based instruction (Hehir, 2006). Similar to arguments made about English language learning among children of immigrant backgrounds, Nelson (1998) suggests that children who are deaf essentially fail to develop academic skills in school because they fail to develop high levels of proficiency in their own first (or native) language, which in this case would be ASL. Research in deaf education indicates that advanced, rigorous language acquisition and academic exposure in ASL would produce greater gains in language proficiency, in general, that would result in improved academic achievement. The research supports the modern agenda of bilingual/bicultural programs in which children become educated and proficient in ASL and develop English language skills as a secondary experience. To put it simply, students who are deaf lag behind their peers because they learn academic content simultaneous to processing a second language. To return to the ESL analogy, students who are native Spanish-speakers are likely to struggle with learning content in a history textbook because they are learning both the history content and expending a great deal of cognitive energy to process the English text assumed to be in the child's repertoire.

Supporting Children with Hearing Impairments in School

Strategies to Accommodate Student Needs in General Education Classrooms

Probably the most significant factor in consideration of strategies to integrate students with hearing impairments into inclusive general education classrooms is the communication strategy that child is using (e.g., ASL, Total Communication, Aural/oral habilitative, cochlear implant). Students who are hard-of-hearing (including students using cochlear implants) or have unilateral loss, are probably the most likely to participate in a general education classroom. Of course, students who are ASL users will primarily require support in the translation of English language instruction to familiar representations in ASL. An ASL interpreter plays the key role in this process. An ASL interpreter is a professionally trained member of the academic support staff for children who are Deaf. The interpreter is not generally considered a co-teacher, though. The role emphasizes access to the content being presented to a hearing audience.

Strategies for working with students who are ASL users (possibly bilingual/bicultural) focus on seamless integration of interpreter supports (Limaye, 2004). Some key points include:

- Direct interaction with the student, rather than the interpreter, in order to respect and enhance the student-teacher relationship.
- Providing outlines, guided notes, or some kind of advanced organizer for both the student and the interpreter to support contextual clarity of instruction.
- Ensuring that video presentations include captioning and that the student can easily view the screen. Scripts, when available, are extremely helpful as well.
- Integrating sign presentation as a natural classroom action—interpreter signs along with teacher so that the student can view teacher actions and sign interpretation concurrently; hearing students are taught to accept sign interpretation without undue attention or distraction.

For students with hearing impairments who do not primarily use ASL, considerable classroom consideration must be given to the student's ability to speechread, follow cues of the teacher, and process large amounts of linguistic information. Not only can it be challenging for students with hearing impairment to develop age-appropriate language use, but the act of "attending" to a teacher for long periods of time can be overwhelming, as the loss of proficient hearing necessitates are a much more substantial workload for the student. Choate (2004) recommends guidelines for adapting general classroom instruction for students with hearing impairments, focused on enhancement of the language exposure involved in daily teaching and ensuring the child is able to attend and keep pace with instruction. Attention should be paid to the integration of academic curriculum and the supporting speech and language program, monitoring of amplification systems (e.g., FM Systems, hearing aids) to be sure the student is following along, and even explicit instruction in foundational language or background knowledge in new lessons. Vocabulary development is very important for students with hearing impairments who have limited literacy or language exposure, and even for bilingual students who are Deaf and have vast ASL vocabulary as a first language. Direct instruction of key vocabulary would be a highly beneficial experience for students with hearing impairments in general classrooms.

Some considerations for students with hearing impairments in the regular classroom are more basic and relate to consideration of seating and positioning. Consider seating options, attention, and peer support as a few key support efforts (Limaye, 2004). Students who are hard of hearing and attempting to use amplified hearing as a primary means of learning in school, are likely to miss out on information more easily than their peers. They should be able to see the faces of their teacher and peers easily, as appropriate to the academic context. Further, attention concerns are significant for children with hearing deficits. Whereas hearing students can "drift off" in class and rely on what could be called "auditory memory" to recall missed information, students with hearing limitations must closely attend to auditory information in a more deliberate fashion. Peer support will likely be useful to cue students to transitions, directions, and key points, etc.

If the student appears confused by directions or explanations, hearing may or may not be the issue, but it ongoing comprehension should be monitored. Speechreading problems are an issue for a large number of students. Repetition of directions and comprehension checks are helpful, but repeating the same words or speaking louder is not always sufficient. Some key points for communicating with children who are hard of hearing in a general classroom (including students with unilateral hearing loss):

- Repeating key words may be helpful as a basic cue
- Look directly at the student
- Speak clearly and perhaps slow down if you speak quickly
- Attempt to rephrase the communication, so that the student can use new linguistic clues to "piece together" the puzzling communication
- Simplify directions to enhance clarity
- Consider noise factors in the classroom; the student may not be able to discriminate your voice from a noisy background

---

Simple Ideas Future Teachers Should Understand about Supporting Students Who Are Hard-of-hearing, Have Cochlear Implants, or Have Unilateral Hearing Impairment in the General Education Classroom:

Hold high expectations for student performance
- Establish an effective learning environment by seating the student where she can see and/or hear best. If a student has a unilateral loss the student should be positioned so that that their stronger ear faces the teacher.
- Integrate academic study with direct speech and language services
- Provide visual cues for transitions, questioning, etc.
- Provide language enhancement throughout instruction
- Focus on maintenance of student's amplification devices (if applicable); a dead battery could ruin a student with a hearing impairment's whole day academically

Glossary in Plain Terms (Hearing Impairment)

Audiogram: a graph that displays an individual's hearing ability in the left and right ear measured according to loudness and frequency of the sounds.

Audiometer: device used to assess an individual's hearing ability by producing sounds at different frequencies and decibel levels.

Audiology: the study of hearing and remediation of hearing problems.

Conductive hearing loss: a hearing loss that results from inability of sound to be transmitted in the outer and middle ear; typically less severe and related to structural limitations or obstructions of sound transmission.

Sensorineural hearing loss: a hearing loss that results from damage to the inner ear and/or nerve components of hearing; more likely to be more severe and permanent.

American Sign Language: a form of manual communication in which a finger spelling alphabet and elaborate language are produced by formation of "signs" representing words and organized in a manner similar to other languages.

Total communication: a method of education that offers both sign language and auditory/speech training.

Cochlear implant: device similar to a hearing aid that is actually implanted in the individuals skull and wired into the inner ear to replace a non-functional hearing mechanism.

Otitis media: disorder caused by inflammation and/or infection that typically produces fluid in the middle ear, inhibiting proper movement of the ossicles; often causes hearing loss and difficulty with speech and language development.

Decibel (dB): named for Alexander Graham Bell, the unit of measurement of loudness of sound; used an audiogram.

REFERENCES

Choate, J. S. (2004). *Successful inclusive teaching: Proven ways to detect and correct special needs* (4th ed.), MA: Allyn & Bacon.

Clark, J. G. (1981). Uses and abuses of hearing loss classification. *ASHA, 23,* 493-500.

de Villiers, P. A. (1992). Educational implications of deafness: Language and literacy. . In J. Miller (Ed.), *Research on child language disorders: A decade of progress.* Columbus, OH: Ross Laboratories.

Grosjean, F. (2001). The right of the Deaf child to grow up bilingual. *Sign Language Studies, 1*(2), 110-114.

Hehir, T. (2006). *New direction in special education: Eliminating ableism in policy and practice.* Cambridge, MA.: Harvard Education Press.

Heward, W. (2008). *Exceptional children: An introduction to special education.* Upper Saddle River, New Jersey: Pearson.

Johnson, J. R., & McIntosh, A. S. (2009). Toward a cultural perspective and understanding of the disability and deaf experience in special and multicultural education. *Remedial & Special Education, 30*(2), 67-83.

Limaye, S. (2004). Hearing impairment. In M. Puri & G. Abraham (Eds.), *Handbook of inclusive education for educators, administrators, and planners.* New Delhi, India: SAGE Publications.

Martin, F. N. (1997). *Introduction to audiology.* Boston: Allyn and Bacon. .

Nelson, K. E. (1998). Toward a differentiated account of facilitators of literacy development and ASL in Deaf children. *Topics in Language Disorders, 18*(4), 73-88.

Northern, J. L., & Downs, M. P. (2002). *Hearing in children.* (5th ed.). Baltimore, MD: Lippincott Williams & Wilkins.

Reed, S., Antia, S. D., & Kreimeyer, K. H. (2008). Academic status of deaf and hard-of-hearing students in public schools: Student, home, and service facilitators and detractors. *Journal of Deaf Studies and Deaf Education, 13*(4), 485-502.

Schow, R. L., & Nerbonne, M.A. (1996). *Introduction to audiologic rehabilitation.* Boston: Allyn and Bacon.

Shapiro, J. P. (1994). *No pity: People with disabilities forging a new civil rights movement.* New York: Times Books.

Sparrow, R. (2010). Implants and ethnocide: Learning from the cochlear implant controversy. *Disability & Society, 25*(4), 455-466.

Valli, C., & Lucas, C. (2000). *Linguistics of American sign language: An introduction.* Washington, D.C.: Gallaudet University Press.

QUESTIONS *for Reflection:*

What are the major parts of the ear and how does the hearing mechanism work? (You should be able to explain this process in your own words as if you were explaining it to a parent.)

What is the difference between a conductive hearing loss and a sensorineural hearing loss?

What is the Speech Banana and how would you use it to explain a hearing loss to parents?

Explain the difference between pre-linguistic and post-linguistic hearing losses. Why is a pre-linguistic loss more significant?

NOTES

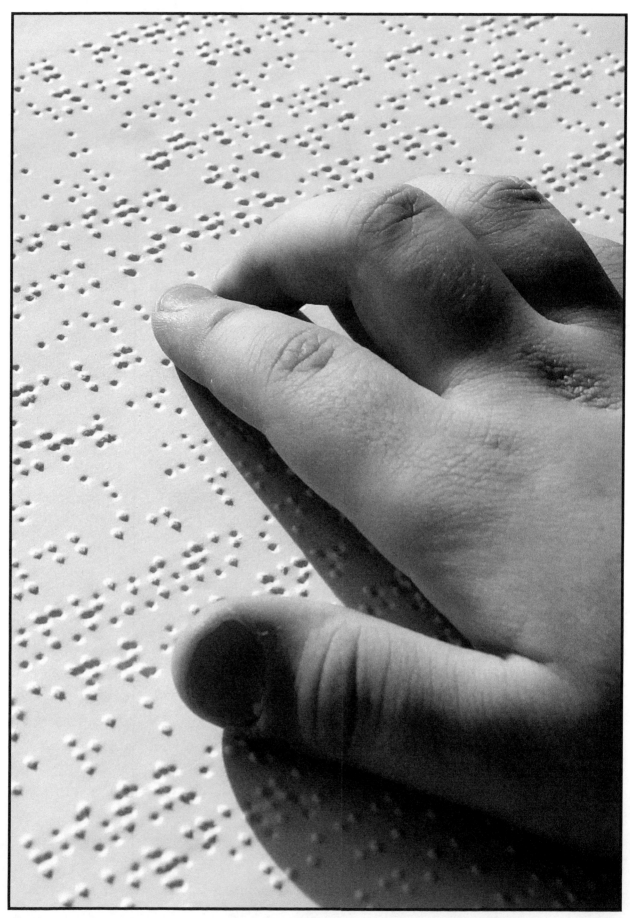

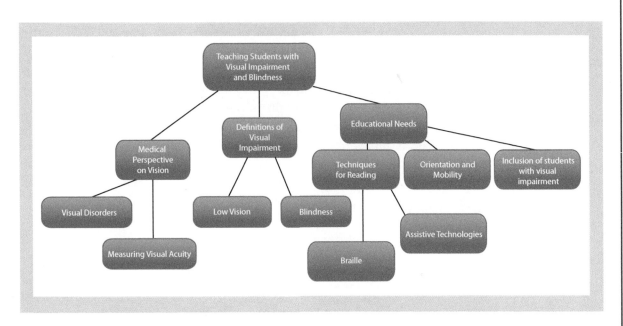

CHAPTER 12

Teaching Students with Visual Impairment and Blindness

THE TOP TEN TERMS FOR VISUAL IMPAIRMENT AND BLINDNESS

The following key terms or big ideas are critical to your understanding of the content related to hearing impairment and the in-class discussions to follow.

• Optometrist	• Ophthalmologist
• Snellen chart	• Field of vision
• Orientation	• Mobility
• Visual acuity	• Braille
• Brailler	• Long, white cane

Understanding How the Eye Works

Fundamental to understanding visual impairments of any type or severity is at least a basic understanding of the visual mechanism. Ultimately, the interpretation of visual images can be thought of as similar to the actions of a camera in which the image being captured occurs as a result of the camera diaphragm controlling the amount of light that enters, a lens that focuses the light of the image, and film that forms the ultimate image produce by the light that enters the camera. Similarly, vision occurs as result light entering the eyes through the *cornea*, the most outer layer of the eye (see Figure 12.1). The *pupil* of the eye is the small, round "hole" at the center of the eye through which light passes next. The amount of light rays that pass through the pupil into the eye is regulated by the part of the eye that give you your eye color known as the *iris*. The next relevant anatomical feature is the *lens* through which light passes and becomes focused on the back of the eye known as the *retina* which acts like the film in a camera by interpreting the light as a visual image. Of course these "camera" images are occurring constantly with incredibly speed, agility, and accuracy, given a typical, healthy system. Perhaps the most important part of the retina is the macula, the name for the central portion of the retina responsible for the most refined aspects of vision. Ultimately the visual mechanism translates electrical "data" via rods and cones (nerve cells within the retina) that is interpreted neurologically by the *optic nerve* (Daw, 2012).

It is logical to consider that major damage to any of these anatomical features will potentially result in limitations in functional vision. For example, the formation of *cataracts* relates to the "clouding" of the lens. Good vision requires that light pass through the clear lens, but it is not uncommon for cataracts to occur as a result of

Figure 12.1. Anatomy of the Eye

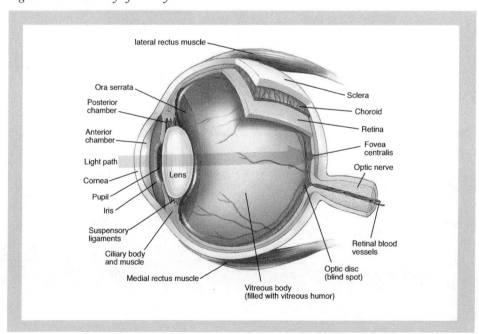

© *Kendall Hunt Publishing Company*

the lens being opaque. Similarly, any damage to the retina or macula could result in distortion of the images being interpreted. *Glaucoma* is a commonly known disorder as well and stems from damage to the optic nerve that must effectively translate visual data to the brain.

Visual Impairments

Among children in schools, the most common visual impairments relate to the following specific diseases or disorders (Huebner, 2000; Steinkuller, 1999).

- *Retinopathy of prematurity*, a visual disorder resulting from dysfunction of the retina associated with prematurity of birth
- *Cortical Visual Impairment*, a visual disorder related to neurological impairment
- *Albinism*, a disorder causing absence of pigment that can result in a low vision impairment
- *Cataract Development*, a visual impairment caused by opacity of the lens which can often be addressed with surgical replacement of the lens
- *Optic Nerve Damage*, visual disorder stemming from diminished function of the optic nerve.

Although it is common to acquire visual challenges due to aging, school-age children experience some level of visual impairment at a rate of approximately one in a hundred. The rate is substantially less for visual impairment of a more severe nature leading to blindness. This population is likely closer to 6 students in 100,000 (National Dissemination Center for Children with Disabilities, 2004).

Measuring Vision

As with anyone, students with visual impairments are evaluated using specific diagnostic techniques. The diagnostic procedure involves measuring an individual's vision related to how accurately the person can identify different symbols at various distances. This measure is referred to as **visual acuity**. Visual acuity is defined as the ability to clearly distinguish forms or discriminate details at a specific distance. The **Optometrist** or **Ophthalmologist** (see below for more information) measures acuity by asking the child to read letters, numbers, or other symbols from the *Snellen chart (see chart below)*. Visual acuity is reported in relation to "normal" vision. Normal vision is typically described by using a "fraction," which compares the vision of the person being evaluated to the standard used to indicate normal vision. Normal vision is indicated when a person is described as having "20/20 vision." This simply means that the person being evaluated can see at 20 feet what a person with a normally seeing eye can see at 20 feet.

The second aspect of vision that is sometimes measured in the diagnostic process is referred to as a "**field of vision**." When gazing straight ahead, a normal eye is able to see objects within a range of approximately 180 degrees; this person would be said to have a field of vision of 180 degrees.

The Snellen Chart
A normal eye measured is said to be 20/20.
In the chart below, the person with "normal"
vision could read line 8 at a distance of 20 feet.
A person who is legally blind could read line I
at a distance of 20 feet, while a person with
normal vision could read line I at 200 feet.

E — 1
F P — 2
T O Z — 3
L P E D — 4
P E C F D — 5
E D F C Z P — 6
F E L O P Z D — 7
D E F P O T E C — 8
L E F O D P C T — 9
F D P L T C E O — 10
P E Z O L C F T D — 11

Legal Definition

Identifying an individual as **legally blind** can be accomplished by using data measuring the visual acuity or field of vision. A person is considered to be legally blind if s/he has visual acuity of 20/200 or worse *in the better eye after correction*. That means that what a "normal eye" can see at 200 feet, a legally blind person can see at 20 feet. This is further delineated to indicate that the 20/200 measurement must be in the better eye with correction. The implications of this degree of loss of vision are significant and limiting. An individual with vision measured at 20/70 in the better eye after correction is legally referred to as a person who is **partially sighted**.

Individuals may also be identified as legally blind by measuring the person's field of vision. A person is considered to be legally blind if her/his field of vision is 20 degrees or less in the normal visual field. The diagram below shows the normal 180 degree field (i.e., the straight line) with a 20 degree field of

vision inserted above it. This is intended to provide you with an example of what a person with only a 20 degree field of vision may see. The implications of this field of vision are also significant and limiting.

Educational definitions: As with all disability categories, educational definitions focus on the impact the visual impairment has on a child's work in school. The IDEA definition is provided below Federal Definition:

> (1) Visual Impairment Explained: A visual impairment shall be determined through the manifestation of both of the following: (a) A visual impairment which, even with correction, interferes with development or which adversely affects educational performance. Visual impairment includes both partial sight and blindness. (b) One or more of the following: (i) A central visual acuity for near or far point vision of 20/70 or less in the better eye after routine refractive correction. (ii) A diagnosed progressively deteriorating eye condition (R 340.1708).

The guidelines established by the Federal definition are taken into consideration when students with visual impairments are classified for the purposes of receiving educational support. The placement decisions are made relative to the extent to which the students can use vision and/or tactile means for learning. Students are then classified in one of three categories. Students who are considered to be **totally blind** receive no useful information through the sense of vision and must use tactile and auditory senses for all learning. A student who is identified as **functionally blind** has so little vision that s/he learns primarily through the other senses. Finally, students classified as having **low vision,** have 20/70 vision or worse in the better eye after correction. These students often use vision as a primary means of learning and generally learn to read print.

Educational adaptations: Now that we have discussed the importance of the educational impact of the visual impairment when identifying students, we will briefly consider the adaptations that may be appropriate in meeting the needs of students with visual impairments. Generally, attention should be given to three principles when working with students with visual impairments. These principles are **concreteness, unifying experiences,** and **learning by doing** (Grabe & Grabe, 2003). Concreteness is the principle of instruction that suggests that students with visual impairments need opportunities to utilize tactile experiences whenever possible. For example, when learning about the difference between a square and a cube, the student with a visual impairment would benefit from having a wooden square and cube to serve as models. The student can then "feel" the difference between the two objects. By unifying experiences for a student with visual impairments, teachers must remember that the student may have greater difficulty distinguishing the part/whole concept. Using the wooden square described above, the teacher may initially provide the "whole" square to the student followed by the square cut into specific fractions of the whole. The third principle suggests the importance of learning by doing. This simply emphasizes the importance of using hands-on materials when teaching students with visual impairments. Grabe and Grabe provide an excellent example of how to implement this principle. A lesson on ancient Egypt would be enhanced by asking all students to construct a replica of a pyramid. This could be done using bricks that might be donated by a local construction company. The authors also suggest an activity in which the students make their own bricks using sand and water. These activities enable all students to better understand the process involved in building a pyramid while providing the student with a visual impairment a very realistic "hands-on" experience (retrieved from http://sped.wikidot.com/visual-impairments on September 29, 2010). While these principles should be at the core of instruction with students with visual impairments, there are additional considerations appropriate to the specific needs of students with visual impairments.

Students with low vision: These students can learn to read print with attention to three approaches: (1) _approach magnification,_ (2) _using lenses,_ and (3) _large print_ (Heward, 2008). Approach magnification simply suggests that the student move the page closer to the student's eyes. Lenses are those devices that are designed to magnify the print to the degree that the student is better able to see, and consequently read, the printed text. Large print serves essentially the same purpose as the lenses; material printed in a larger font size, increases the access to the material and also increases the likelihood that the student with visual low vision will use the material.

Students who are functionally blind: Students in this category are not totally blind. We mention this because it is critical to recognize that these students use their residual vision to gain knowledge throughout their environment. They may use their vision to move through the school or other parts of their environment. Nonetheless, students who are functionally blind will typically require **Braille** to gain information from printed material. Braille is a system that uses a series of raised dots to represent the letters of the spoken language used by student with visual impairments. The dot patterns adhere to a code similar to the traditional printed alphabet and enable the student who is functionally blind to access the same material as her/his sighted peers. The Braille alphabet is provided in the table on the next page.

© prism68, 2015. Used under license from Shutterstock, Inc. from Shutterstock, Inc.

BRAILLE LETTERS, NUMBERS, AND SYMBOLS

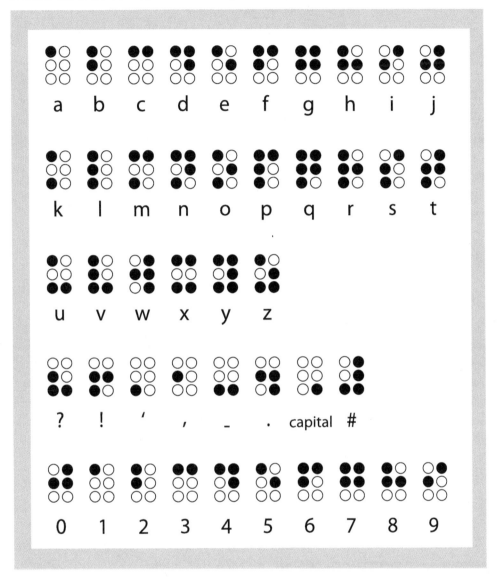

© *cristi180884, 2015. Used under license from Shutterstock, Inc.*

While there is a minor controversy regarding the use of Braille, it appears that there are more positive aspects for individuals who are totally blind or legally blind to read using Braille. In 1990, the *New York Times* reported that only 12% of students with visual impairments read Braille while 50% of students used Braille in 1965. With all of the technological advances providing access to printed material in a variety of formats, Braille continues to be a key factor as students with visual impairments work to establish independence. Marc Maurer, the president of the National Federation for the Blind, suggests that many individuals who are blind fail to improve their job/career status because they have not developed the skills to use written words effectively and efficiently. Mr. Maurer's perspective is reinforced by a former graduate student who is blind. He noted the difficulty he experienced using audio recordings of class lectures by asking, "Have you ever tried to find a specific piece of information on a cassette?" While the technology has far exceeded the use of cassette tapes, the concern of reading facility remains. It appears that Braille continues to have a place in the current and future work of students with visual impairments.

Students who are totally blind: These students do not receive any meaningful information through the visual modality. They typically learn content material through the tactile and/or auditory senses. Students who are totally blind may use computer or assistive technology to provide access to material that would be otherwise impossible to use. For example, outSPOKEN (by _ALVA Access Group, Inc.)_ is a screen reader software program that produces sound or Braille output from the computer. Students may also use calculators in math that produce a verbal answer along with the traditional visual display. Heward (2008) notes that teachers working with students who are totally blind can incorporate hands-on/tactile activities into science and social studies lessons to help these students. These activities might include, but certainly not be limited to, embossed relief maps and three-dimensional models.

Regardless of the assistive technology used, it is likely that these students will continue to use Braille as a significant medium for learning academic material. Students who are totally blind use Braille to read printed material that is also used by their sighted peers. In addition, these students may also use a **Brailler** as they complete written assignments or take notes in class. Technological advances are making it easier to use Braillers in school settings. There are small battery powered Braillers (e.g., the Braille 'n Speak) machines that have a braille keyboard; this also has a verbal output component that enables the student listen to the notes/printed material upon completion of the task.

ORIENTATION AND MOBILITY

Orientation is the ability to understand where an individual is located in space and where it is that s/he would like to go. We are all oriented to our environment relative to our experience within that environment. Have you ever been in a hotel room

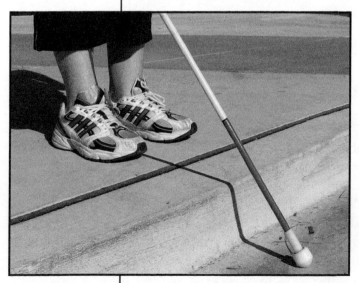

and awakened in the middle of the night to get a drink of water? Were you immediately able to get to the sink without stumbling over a nightstand or another piece of furniture? If you did indeed stumble, you were not completely oriented to the new "space" of the hotel room. Students with visual impairments must be able to orient themselves in order to effectively move throughout the classroom setting.

Even so, there are times when the student is not appropriately oriented to his/her space, which may result in limited mobility;

© _Karin Hildebrand Lau, 2015. Used under license from Shutterstock, Inc._

mobility refers to the ability to travel thorough the environment safely and comfortably. This often requires some type of mobility device that helps the student with visual impairments move within the school or community environment. The most common mobility device is the **long cane**. Individuals who are totally or legally blind use this cane to extend their sense of touch as they determine what is ahead of them as they walk. People with significant visual deficits also use guide dogs effectively as they move throughout their environment. Technology has also had an impact on mobility options available to individuals with visual impairments. Adaptations of the long, white cane are also available. These adaptations use lasers or a radar-like system that provides the user with advance warning of obstacles in his/her path through an audible and/or touch alarm system. Each of these devices has enabled students who are totally blind to move more effectively and efficiently throughout the school and community environments, thereby enabling them to share the experiences of their sighted peers.

Terminology Defining Severity of Visual Impairment
(National Dissemination Center for Children with Disabilities, 2004)

Partially sighted: visual impairment requiring special education support

Low vision: visual impairment with functional impact on daily life such as the inability to read normal size text even when prescription eyeglasses are used.

Legally blind: visual impairment resulting in visual acuity less than 20/200 in the best seeing eye; also associated with a very limited field of vision.

Totally blind: visual impairment suggesting the lack of functional vision inhibiting the use of any visual learning media and a need for the development of literacy in braille.

INCLUSION OF STUDENTS WITH VISUAL IMPAIRMENTS

Students with visual impairments who receive their education in general education classes receive special education supports from an educator who serves as a **vision specialist** (i.e., a specially trained teacher of students with visual impairments). The vision specialist provides special supports based on the student's individual needs and works in collaboration with the general education teacher to design appropriate learning opportunities (Cox & Dykes, 2001). Clearly, the types of modifications required range from digital texts and large print to broad access to braille books suggesting that the type and significance of visual loss dictates the modifications required to the learning environment and instructional strategies used (National Dissemination Center for Children with Disabilities, 2004). Figure 12.2 provides a broad list of suggestions for simple, logical modifications to the general education classroom experience.

The American Federation of the Blind (n.d.) suggests the needs of all students with visual impairments simply cannot be adequately addressed in a single learning environment like the general education classroom regardless of the level of supports that could be provided. Not only do students with visual impairments engage with academic instruction using multi-sensory instruction and use alternative methods of literacy development, but there is also a substantial functional component to instruction including the development of daily living skills and mobility training in the community. Depending on age and development, the AFB clearly identifies alternative settings as critical for the full development of the potential of children with visual impairments even including residential schools for certain periods of time. In a position paper on the topic, the AFB asserts

> In order to meet their unique needs, students must have specialized services, books and materials in appropriate media (including braille), as well as specialized equipment and technology to assure equal access to the core and specialized curricula, and to enable them to most effectively compete with their peers in school and ultimately in society.

Consistent with this statement, the AFB takes a stance on inclusion that clearly values the fundamental ideology of an inclusive society but reminds school decision makers that the "full range" of programming must be considered in determining the student's LRE and IEP mandated support services. An additional concern noted derives from the need to have highly qualified specialists in the area of visual impairment who are knowledgeable regarding the functional needs and need for braille instruction that must be tailored to the learning needs of students who are blind. Essentially, students with visual impairments including blindness must be guaranteed access to an inclusive education that maintains typical standards of academic instruction without losing what is truly "special" in the services provided (American Federation for the Blind, n.d.).

Figure 12.2. Checklist for Classroom Strategies and Adaptations

Classroom Supplies and Equipment	Yes	N/A	More Information
Raised-line or bold-line paper, templates, and/or writing guides			
Soft lead pencils			
Felt-tip pens (various widths; high-contrast colors)			
Supplementary light source (e.g., desk lamp)			
Braille writer; slate and stylus			
Magnification device			
Book stand			
Cassette tape recorder/player			
Sun visor or light shield to reduce glare			
Large print reading materials (preprinted or produced using computer technology)			
Physical education equipment with auditory signals (e.g., beep balls)			
Safety Considerations	**Yes**	**N/A**	**More Information**
Evaluate environment for potential hazard areas (e.g., stairs, playground structures, dimly lit areas)			
Ensure that doors and storage areas are completely open or completely closed at all times			
Ensure that student knows routines for fire drills and other emergency procedures			
Instructional Strategies	**Yes**	**N/A**	**More Information**
Have student sit closer to see board, videos, demonstrations, etc.			
Give student copies of teacher notes			
Read notes aloud while writing them on board			
Provide audio tapes of reading material			
Allow student to turn in taped rather than written responses			
Enlarge books, worksheets, etc.			
Provide opportunities for hands-on learning			
Additional Curriculum Areas	**Yes**	**N/A**	**More Information**
Daily living			
Listening skills			
Keyboarding and computer skills			
Orientation and mobility			
Social skills			
Human growth and development			
Braille literacy			
Use of vision			
Collaborating with Other Professionals	**Yes**	**N/A**	**More Information**
Meet and know schedules of specialists who might work with student (e.g., orientation and mobility, itinerant vision educator, occupational therapist, etc.)			
Learn how and when student uses sighted guide, long cane, etc. for travel			
Learn about magnification devices, braillers, and other equipment available to and used by student			
Learn about student's strengths/weaknesses and academic needs and develop appropriate strategies			
Become familiar with individualized education programs (IEP) goals and objectives and other services specified to be provided			

From *TEACHING Exceptional Children,* July/August 2001. Reprinted by permission.

Life with Glaucoma
A Personal Narrative of Childhood Visual Impairment

I was born with congenital glaucoma which is caused by pressure building up behind the eyeball and pressing on the nerve of the eye. In other words I was born with old eyes, since glaucoma usually occurs in elderly individuals. As a toddler I had five surgeries that brought the pressure under control and gave sight to my left eye, but left me legally blind in my right eye. Later I lost sight in the right eye completely. This experience affected my life in several ways including (a) dealing with the physical pain of the eye aching and the distraction caused by it, (b) the visual limitations, and (c) the worry of going completely blind someday.

I remember sitting in a history class in elementary school, trying to concentrate on Charlemagne and other historical figures, but all I was really thinking about was the ache I felt deep in my eye socket and trying to find the best place to press my finger into my eyelid to ease the pain. There was a pain when the medicine was wearing off and then an ache as the full dose of medicine hit. I was a poor reader to begin with because of the strain on my "good eye" and the fact that my eye wandered and I could see little specks floating around in my eye's view. Although I wanted to be learning the information being taught in the class, I was so distracted by my eye that I could not keep up, leaving me feeling very dumb. As a child in school, no one put together that my eyes might have been causing the problem.

In middle school, a teacher gave me a large yellow box that had a sliding window. I was told to put the contraption over my book and the window would close over the page to help me to read faster. This was taking place in the regular English classroom with other students questioning what I was doing and chuckling. I soon learned to push the sliding window back up when the teacher was not looking so I could finish reading the rest of the page.

Another thing that was affected by the vision loss was my lack of binocular vision which controls things like proprioception (i.e., awareness of your body in space), depth perception, and lack of peripheral vision which blocks off the outer edges of your visual field. I would find myself walking into people or equipment on the playground, or even parking meters as we walked home from school. I soon learned to compensate for these effects of vision loss by walking on the left side of people to keep from walking into them and taking the time to get my bearing of the area where I was playing. In the classroom, desk placement for best view of the teacher and the board were important considerations.

All in all, I felt blessed that I could see out of one eye. My parents and grandparents told me stories of the eye operations and how I was almost blind. I also remembered the warnings from my eye doctors who said they could not guarantee the vision in my "good eye" and that the glaucoma could return someday. With this in the back of my mind, I practiced being blind using my hands to navigate around my house, memorizing the feel of my toys and furniture.

As an adult, I still have one "good eye" and have made great strides in my education and personal life. Although I struggled with pain, vision disorientation, and concerns of feeling different, I was still able to live a successful life, raise a family, have enriching friendships, and teach others about special education. In my case, the vision loss was a motivation and inspiration to help others.

Karen Diegelmann, Doctoral Student in Special Education
University of North Carolina at Charlotte

Simple Ideas Future Teachers Should Understand about Supporting Students with Visual Impairments (Blindness and Low Vision) in School

Hold high expectations for student performance

Make sure your room is neat and orderly. This means to keep papers, backpacks, binders, and other material off the floor. It is especially important to keep the paths between rows of desks clear; this will enable students with visual impairments to move freely and comfortably in the classroom.

When the furniture is rearranged, ensure that you or a classroom peer helps the student with visual impairments re-orient to the new classroom set-up.

Explore different colored fonts and/or colored paper. Some students with visual impairments are more efficient when presented with specific contrasting foreground and background colors.

When appropriate or requested by the student with visual impairments, make arrangements to record the audio portion of a lecture or discussion. In addition, have large print or Braille copies of the class notes available and accessible, especially for students with low vision.

Always remember to present material in a multi-sensory format as much as possible. When information is presented on the white board, Promethean board, or on a PowerPoint slide, ensure that you also verbalize the material that is being presented visually. It will also be beneficial if there is some hands-on material to further reinforce the concept/content being presented.

GLOSSARY IN PLAIN TERMS: VISION IMPAIRMENT AND BLINDNESS

Optometrist: a professional who is trained to administer eye exams and prescribe glasses and/or contact lenses.

Ophthalmologist: a Medical Doctor with expertise on illnesses of the eye.

Visual acuity: the measure used in an eye exam to determine how accurately a person can see objects at a designated distance.

Snellen Chart: a chart used to measure a person's visual acuity.

Field of vision: the entire area that a person can see when looking straight ahead.

Orientation: a person's ability to understand where s/he is located in space.

Mobility: the ability to move in space.

Braille: the system of raised dots used by individuals with visual impairments to gain information from printed materials.

Brailler: a small, often hand-held machine that is used to print Braille.

Long, white cane: the most common device used by individuals who are blind as they move throughout their environment.

REFERENCES

American Federation for the Blind. (n.d.). Educating students with visual impairments for inclusion in society: A paper on the inclusion of students with visual impairments. Retrieved from www.afb.org.

Cox, P., & Dykes, M.K. (2001). Effective classroom adaptations for students with visual impairments. TEACHING Exceptional Children, 33, 6, 68-74.

Daw, N. (2012). How vision works: The physiological mechanisms behind what we see. New York: Oxford University Press.

Grabe, M. & Grabe, C. (2003). Integrating technology for meaningful learning. Boston: Houghton-Mifflin.

Heward, W. (2008). Exceptional children: An introduction to special education. Upper Saddle River, New Jersey: Pearson.

Huebner, K. (2000). Visual impairment. In M.C. Holbrook and A.J. Koenig (Eds.), Foundations of education (2nd edition.) Volume 1. History and theory of teaching children and youth with visual impairments (pp. 55-76). New York: AFB Press.

National Dissemination Center for Children with Disabilities (2004) NICHCY Disability Fact Sheet 13. Retrieved from http://nichcy.org/disability/specific/visualimpairment.

Steinkuller, P., Du, L., Gilbert, C., Foster, A., Collins, M., & Coats, D. (1999). Childhood blindness. Journal of AAPOS: American Association for Pediatric Ophthalmology & Strabismus, 3, 26-32.

QUESTIONS *for Reflection:*

Describe the 2 ways a child can be identified as a "student with visual impairments."

What are the educational implications of a student having "low vision"?

What types of classroom modifications are most effective in supporting students with low vision?

What are the 3 principles to consider in working with students with visual impairments?

Special challenge: Search the web. What kinds of **assistive technology** resources can you find that have been invented to enhance access to education and broader outcomes in life?

Notes

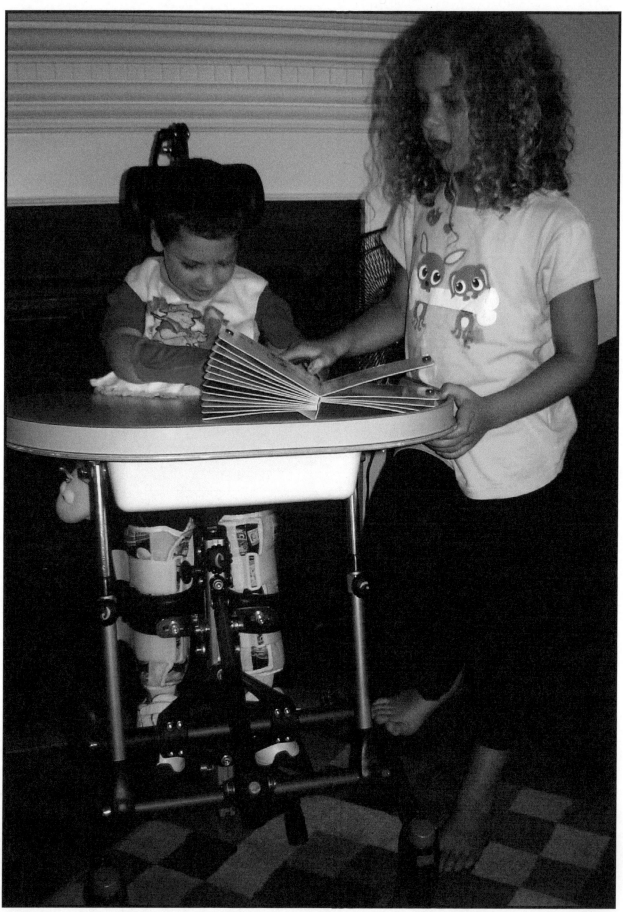

Permission granted by parent.

CHAPTER **13**

Teaching Children with Health Impairments and Physical Disabilities

Kelly R. Kelley

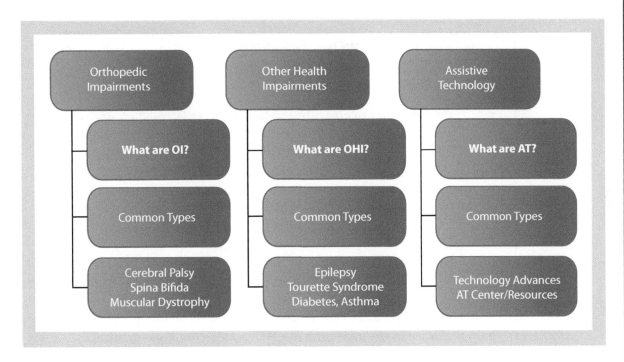

THE TOP TEN TERMS FOR CHAPTER 13:

The following key terms or big ideas are critical to your understanding of the content for chapter 13 and the in-class discussions to follow.

• Other health impairments	• Cerebral palsy
• Orthopedic impairments	• Spina bifida
• Physical disabilities	• Muscular dystrophy
• Assistive technology	• Epilepsy
• Tourette syndrome	• Traumatic brain injury

This chapter discusses categories of exceptionality related to physical disabilities and other health impairments. In previous chapters there were more common shared characteristics among the disabilities discussed. Although Attention Deficit Hyperactivity Disorder (ADHD) falls under the category of other health impairments according to IDEA, this chapter will not address ADHD since it was previously discussed in chapter 7.

Physical disabilities and other health impairments have a wide variation of characteristics that can be mild, moderate, or severe. For example, individuals can have one physical disability or a combination of them also referred to as multiple disabilities. Some of these disabilities can occur at birth while others are acquired at later points in life (e.g., traumatic brain or spinal cord injuries). Additionally, some physical disabilities and health impairments are visible while others are less obvious. Some can be progressive and other impairments can actually improve over time. Students with physical disabilities and health impairments are served in two broad IDEA categories including orthopedic impairments and other health impairments.

WHAT ARE ORTHOPEDIC IMPAIRMENTS?

According to IDEA, **orthopedic impairments** include

> impairments caused by congenital anomaly (e.g., clubfoot, absence of some member, etc.), impairments caused by disease (e.g., poliomyelitis, bone tuberculosis, etc.), and impairments from other causes (e.g., cerebral palsy, amputations, and fractures or burns that cause contract), which adversely affects a child's educational performance (34 C.F.R., sec. 300.7[b][7]).

Educators commonly refer to orthopedic impairments as **physical disabilities** because they inhibit parts of the skeletal system including bones, joints, limbs, or muscles. A topographical classification system is used based on the specific limbs and parts of the body that are affected. For example, *monoplegia* means only one limb is affected in the upper or lower extremities. *Paraplegia* means only the legs are affected. *Hemiplegia* affects two limbs of the body on the same side. *Triplegia* means three limbs are affected. *Quadriplegia* means all four limbs are affected. *Diplegia* means the legs are affected with less severity in the arms. Finally, *double hemiplegia* affects the arms with less severity of the legs. In addition to this classification system, many of the physical disabilities are also subdivided into categories such as cerebral palsy, spina bifida, and muscular dystrophy.

WHAT IS CEREBRAL PALSY?

Cerebral palsy (CP) is one of the most prevalent physical disabilities in classrooms today. According to the United Cerebral Palsy Foundation, more than 800,000 people in the United States have CP. Cerebral palsy involves involuntary movement and posture stemming from a neurological disorder caused by damage to the brain before, during, or after birth (Pellegrino, 2007). Before birth there can be an infection or brain malformations. During birth there can also be a lack of oxygen. After birth, there can be a brain injury or meningitis that can cause CP. Individuals with CP often have paralysis in one or more limbs, fatigue and weakness, lack of coordination, involuntary convulsions, or other motor disorders due to lack of brain control of muscle movements (see Table 13.1 for the four types, characteristics, and prevalence).

Table 13.1. Types of Cerebral Palsy

Type and Common Names	Characteristics	Prevalence
Spastic or spasticity (increased muscle tone; hypertonic)	Contracted or tightened muscle movements; jerky and poorly coordinated movements; exaggerated reflex responses	70 to 80% of CP cases
Athetosis (athetoid)	Large involuntary twisting movements of upper body such as waving arms; stumbling when walking; increased and decreased muscle tone	20% of CP cases
Ataxia	Unsteady gait and balance; difficulty standing and walking; exaggerated motion patterns	1 to 10% of CP cases
Mixed	Combination of any of the above characteristics	Varies among cases

Adapted from: Pellegrino, L. (2007). Cerebral palsy. In M. L. Batshaw, L. Pellegrino, & N. J. Roizen (Eds.), Children with disabilities *(6th ed., pp. 387–408). Baltimore: Brookes.*

Diagnosis and Treatment

More severe cases of CP are diagnosed soon after birth, but most cases are not diagnosed until the toddler years when individuals start to crawl or walk and experience more significant delays (Pellegrino, 2007). CP is a lifelong condition commonly paired with intellectual disabilities. In fact, about 50 to 70% of individuals with CP also have intellectual disabilities (Pellegrino, 2007); however, some also have close to average intelligence. Although considered nonprogressive, CP can cause limited mobility over time such as hip dislocation, scoliosis, and muscle contractures. The cause of CP is not known or found to be inherited, but is often a result of lack of oxygen or blood flow in newborns or lower birth weight. In addition, many individuals with CP commonly have impaired vision, hearing, and speech while some often have seizures (Pellegrino, 2007). While there is not a cure or prescribed treatment for CP, it is important to look at the overall needs and plan necessary supports for increased independence with living and learning. Related service providers who might work with students with CP include physical therapists, occupational therapists, speech therapists, and/or recreational therapists. Physical therapists work on gross motor skills such as walking, using a wheelchair or walker, standing, and climbing stairs to help keep muscles flexible. Occupational therapists help increase independence by teaching more fine motor skills such as zipping, buttoning, and dressing. Speech therapists help students learn ways to carry on conversations (verbal and nonverbal behaviors), making distinguishable facial expressions, and teaching strategies for speaking more clearly. Sometimes the speech and occupational therapists work together to help with eating or swallowing. Recreational therapists find ways to adapt physical and recreational activities to allow students with CP to participate to the greatest extents possible. It is important to promote physical exercise to strengthen muscles and bones, enhance motor skills, and prevent contractures when possible (e.g., swimming, horseback riding, dancing).

MEET MICHAEL

Michael is a 26-year-old twin who was born two months premature. Soon after birth, Michael was diagnosed with CP due to delays with sitting independently, stiff leg muscles, and delays with crawling. Michael has been in a wheelchair for a majority of his life. During his public school years, Michael was included in special classes such as art and music. He had a one-on-one assistant in middle school, and

Michael Beasley on the job working with adaptable desk, mouse, and keyboard.

during high school, he was placed in a self-contained class and included in a history class with his non-disabled peers. He had many friends and was voted "Most School Spirit" by his senior class and served as the vice president of Student Government Association. After completing high school with a certificate of attendance, he was able to participate in an innovative postsecondary program for individuals with developmental disabilities to experience college life. While there, Michael lived in the dorms with his same-age peers, participated in courses, sporting events, clubs, and campus activities. During his first semester in the program, he was nominated by his peers to run for homecoming king. Michael also worked at the college part time completing clerical tasks and continues to serve as a consultant/mentor to other participants in the college program. Each day he uses several assistive technology devices to increase his independence and mobility. For example, he uses an adaptable joystick and keyboard in order to complete work tasks (see photo). He also uses a tracking system installed in the ceiling with an electronic motor (similar to a portable Hoyer lift) to help lift him out of the bed and into the shower, bathroom, or into his wheelchair. In addition, he uses a cell phone mounted to his wheelchair and a Bluetooth device to make phone calls. Although he does not drive, he has an adaptable van with a hydraulic ramp. During a recent interview, Michael was asked what his future dreams, goals, and suggestions for future teachers would be. He states, "I have dreams and goals to live on my own and get my driver's license." For teachers, he says, "It is important for teachers to see me for who I am and what I can do, rather than what I cannot. Teachers need to be patient with me and willing to work with me to try new things. I want teachers to have high expectations for me just like everyone else."

WHAT IS SPINA BIFIDA?

Spina bifida is a common neural tube defect that affects the vertebrae, brain, and/ or spinal cord (Liptak, 2007). When a person has spina bifida, the bones in the vertebrae are exposed since they are not enclosed in the spinal cord. Typically, a person with spina bifida has a saclike bulge in the spine anywhere in the neck or buttocks. The higher the location of the bulge, the more severely the individual will be affected. There are three forms of spina bifida (see Table 13.2).

Table 13.2. Forms of Spina Bifida

Forms	Characteristics	Prevalence
Spina bifida occulta	Few vertebrae are affected; usually occurs in lower spine	Mildest form; many people (10% of the population) have this form and do not realize it since it is less visible
Meningocele	More exposed; meninges bulge through skin; does not typically cause mobility impairments	Milder form with varied prevalence
Myelomeningocele	Spinal lining, cord, and nerves in spine are exposed; highest risk of infection and paralysis; causes most abnormalities of the brain	Most serious and most common affecting 60 in 100,000 births in more females than males

Adapted from: Liptak, G. S. (2007). Neural tube defects. In M. L. Batshaw, L. Pellegrino, & N. J. Roizen (Eds.), Children with Disabilities *(6th ed., pp. 419–438). Baltimore: Brookes.*

Diagnosis and Treatment

Although the exact cause of spina bifida is unknown, early prenatal testing can detect spina bifida. Genetic and environmental factors can play a role in neural tube defects such as spina bifida, based on how they interact with each other (Hall & Solehdin, 1998). Research has shown that women who take folic acid daily can reduce the risk of having a child with spina bifida. Folic acid is a B-vitamin supplement that helps the body build healthy cells. In response to these findings, over the last 12 years, the Food and Drug Administration has added folic acid to many whole-grain products such as cereals and breads, reducing the cases of spina bifida in the United States. Doctors continue to encourage women of childbearing age to take folic acid supplements.

A majority (80 to 90%) of individuals with myleomeningocele also have hydrocephalus. Hydrocephalus is simply when there are excessive amounts of cerebrospinal fluid in the brain. To treat this condition and close the exposed spinal nerves, a surgical procedure is done during the first few days of life where a shunt (a one-way valve that drains the fluid away from the brain and into the stomach or bloodstream) is inserted into the head (Liptak, 2007). It is important to know if a child has a shunt because there are times when they can become blocked, disconnect, or become infected, and have to be replaced. If a student with a shunt becomes drowsy, vomits, has headaches, irritability, or squinting, these can be early signs that the shunt is malfunctioning. Shunts can also be removed when the cerebrospinal fluids begin to balance.

Additionally, when students have myleomeningocele they often have mobility, cognitive, seizure disorders, visual impairments, skin sores, and musculoskeletal abnormalities (Liptak, 2007). Traditionally, the bladder and bowels are affected. Many students will need to be taught the technique of clean intermittent catheterization to help with bladder management. This means a small tube called a catheter is inserted into the urinary tract to collect urine every two to four hours. Recent findings also suggest individuals with spina bifida develop allergies to latex and can be life threatening (Liptak, 2007). It is important to work with the school nurse who can provide training on how this technique works. Students with spina bifida commonly have bladder infections, constipation, bladder paralysis, and urinary tract infections due to the inconsistent urges to urinate.

As an educator, it is important to: a) promote early intervention during the first six months of life, b) assess range of motion, c) conduct psychoeducational testing to help identify cognitive functioning, and d) work with related service providers such as physical and occupational therapists. During adolescent years, it is important to help students with their self-image by encouraging social interactions and counseling to decrease the risk of depression (Liptak, 2007).

WHAT ARE TRAUMATIC BRAIN INJURIES?

Although traumatic brain injuries (TBI) were recognized as a separate IDEA category in 1990, it is important to discuss this disability category here since TBI has many related service providers who also serve individuals with orthopedic and other health impairments. IDEA (1990) defines **traumatic brain injury** as:

> an acquired injury to the brain caused by an external physical force, resulting in total or partial functional disability or psychological impairments, or both, that adversely affects a child's educational performance. The term applies to open or closed head injuries resulting in impairments in one or more areas, such as cognition; language; memory; attention; reasoning; abstract thinking; judgment; problem-solving; sensory, perceptual, and motor abilities; psychosocial behavior; physical functions; information processing;

and speech. The term does not apply to brain injuries that are congenital or generative, or brain injuries induced by birth trauma (34 C.F.R., Sec. 300.7[6][12]).

Traumatic brain injuries are acquired rather than present at birth. Common causes of TBI can result from falling, sports related injuries, vehicle crashes, assaults, and child abuse and vary with age (Michaud et al., 2007). Therefore, this disability can happen to anyone at any point in time. Individuals with cerebral palsy should not be confused with traumatic brain injuries.

Table 13.3. Types of Traumatic Brain Injuries

Types	Characteristics	Prevalence
Open head injuries	Penetration of the skull which allows bacteria to have contact with the brain (e.g., gunshot, sharp object)	Not as common as closed head injuries; 2003-2004 there were 22,456 students served under TBI; males twice as likely to have TBI over females
Closed head injuries	Occurs when brain slams against the inside of the cranium and breaks connection to nerve fibers and brain tissue (e.g., shaken baby syndrome, car and bicycle injuries)	Most common; more severe than concussions (loss of consciousness) and contusions (bruising, swelling, bleeding)

Adapted from: Michaud, L. J., Duhaime, A., Wade, S. L., Rabin, J. P., Jones, D. O., & Lazar, M. F. (2007). Traumatic brain injury. In M. L. Batshaw, L. Pellegrino, & N. J. Roizen (Eds.), Children with Disabilities (6th ed., pp. 461–476). Baltimore: Brookes.

Diagnosis and Treatment

Severe head traumas often result in comas (unconsciousness) lasting for days, weeks, or even months. Once the open or closed brain injuries occur, there are permanent physical, behavior, and/or cognitive impairments. The recovery time and treatment varies depending on whether the injury is mild, moderate, or severe. Rehabilitation therapies are commonly used to address functional, motor, feeding, communication, sensory, cognitive, and social difficulties (Michaud et al., 2007). Physical and occupational therapists often help with coordination problems, physical weakness, and fatigue. Sometimes individuals experience hearing and vision loss, but improve over time. With cognitive functioning, individuals with TBI often have problems with attention, memory, reasoning, abstract thinking, and organization. Teachers and school personnel should explore using assistive technology devices and explicitly teach memory and organizational skills to increase independence. Counselors and support systems are also needed to address behavioral and emotional changes. After injuries, individuals can be easily agitated, have aggressive behaviors, anxiety, posttraumatic stress disorder, and depression. Individuals have to find ways to cope with the sense of loss and independence caused by the injury. These students need support from teachers, friends, family, and other school personnel to improve their confidence, feeling of isolation, and learn how to appropriately cope with new emotions.

WHAT IS MUSCULAR DYSTROPHY?

Muscular dystrophy is unlike cerebral palsy and spina bifida since it is a progressive disease that worsens over time as muscles deteriorate or waste away. Muscular dystrophy is hereditary with over 40 different types. The most common types are listed below in Table 13.4. Unlike CP, muscular dystrophy does not affect the central nervous system causing jerky or uncontrolled movements. Most types of MD involve weakness in muscles resulting in inability to walk and a need for electric wheelchairs as it worsens. It is sometimes difficult for someone to hold their head up as the disease progresses (Escolar, Tosi, Tesi Rocha, & Kennedy, 2007). Although some individuals with muscular dystrophy have intellectual disabilities, many have normal intelligence.

Table 13.4. Common Types of Muscular Dystrophy

Types	Characteristics	Prevalence or Onset
Becker	Milder than Duchenne; symptoms appear later and progress more slowly; heart problems	Only affects males; not as common as Duchenne, but similar symptoms with longer lifespan
Congenital	Present at birth; joint problems; muscle weakness at birth; early contractures; abnormalities in the brain; often have seizures	Affects both males and females at birth
Distal	Wasting of distal muscles such as forearms, hands, lower legs, and feet; less severe and progresses more slowly affecting fewer muscles	Rare type, but affects adult men and women
Duchenne	By ages 2-6 child has difficulty walking, running, climbing stairs; has an unusual gait; larger calf muscles; falls easily; severe heart and breathing problems	Most common and most severe; 1 in 3,500 male births; life span is typically late teens or early 20s
Emery-Dreifuss	Wasting of shoulders, upper arms, and lower legs; heart problems; muscle shortening; weakness in chest and pelvic muscles; slower progression	Rare, appears in childhood and early teen years; affects males only; mothers and sisters are carriers

Facioscapu-lohumeral	Affects face; shoulder blades; upper arm bone; difficulty walking, chewing, swallowing, and speaking	Appears in teens to early adulthood: affects males and females: usually live a normal life span and continue walking throughout life
Limb-girdle	Progressive weakness in hips, shoulders, arms, and legs	Appears in teens to early adulthood; affects males and females; life expectancy mid to late adulthood
Myotonic	Spasms or stiffening of muscles; affects central nervous system, heart, gastrointestinal tract, eyes, and hormone producing glands	Most common form in adults; affects men and women; appears in early childhood to adulthood; decreased life expectancy
Oculopha-ryngeal	Weakness in eye and throat muscles; leads to difficulty swallowing; weakness in pelvic and shoulder muscles; choking and recurrent pneumonia	Appears in men and women in 40s, 50s, and 60s

Adapted from: WebMD. (2010). Understanding muscular dystrophy: The basics. Retrieved from http://www.webmd.com/parenting/understanding-muscular-dystrophy-basics.

Diagnosis and Treatment

The diagnosis of muscular dystrophy varies due to many different types. There is not a known cure for any type of muscular dystrophy, but there should be treatment to maintain function of unaffected muscles as much as possible. Since this is a progressive disease, individuals and families benefit from counseling. Physical therapy, exercise, and aids to daily living (ADL) devices should be encouraged to maintain independence. As a teacher, when working with students with muscular dystrophy, it is very important to use caution when lifting or positioning students due to fragile limbs.

MEET DAVID

David was diagnosed with Becker muscular dystrophy at 10 years old. He walked until he was 11 and then started falling frequently. Once this occurred, he used crutches, eventually leading to a manual wheelchair and then a power wheelchair when he was in his mid 20s. David is now 42 years old and is a husband and father to a 7-year-old daughter. David has an associate's degree in Industrial Management. He drives on his own in a van with assistive technology including a small steering wheel, dash throttle gas and brake computer board, and electronic push button hydraulic ramp. He also has a tracking system installed in his home to help in lifting him out of bed, to the bathroom, and into his wheelchair. In a recent interview with

David and his wife Karis, they also describe their daily life. "Besides assistive technology, I try to live life normal. I don't let this disease control my life. I have always wanted to have a family and am proud of my wife and my daughter." David suggests that future teachers should take the time to teach others about muscular dystrophy. "I almost quit school because the students made fun of me since they did not fully understand why I could not walk and students often tripped me." Karis states, "Teachers need to explore available resources and help families to work together and connect with each other."

David Plemmons, his wife Karis, and daughter Abbie.

WHAT ARE OTHER HEALTH IMPAIRMENTS?

Other health impairments is a broad term including many health and medical conditions such as epilepsy, diabetes, asthma, arthritis, HIV, and even cancer. Health impairments can be chronic (lifetime conditions) or acute (limited duration). This category is defined under IDEA as:

> limited strength, vitality, or alertness due to chronic or acute health problems such as a heart condition, tuberculosis, rheumatic fever, nephritis, asthma, sickle cell anemia, hemophilia, epilepsy, lead poisoning, leukemia, or diabetes that adversely affects a child's educational performance (20 U.S.C., 1400 et seq.).

Once again, since there are so many health impairments, this chapter will provide a brief overview of more prevalent health impairments.

WHAT IS EPILEPSY?

Epilepsy is diagnosed when an individual has repeated seizures. Seizures occur when unregulated electrical discharges or "misfires" of cortical neurons in the brain (Weinstein & Gaillard, 2007). If a person has one seizure, they do not automatically have epilepsy. A seizure can be caused by numerous triggers such as extreme fatigue, hormone changes, metabolic disorders, high fevers, or interruptions in blood supply to the brain. Like traumatic brain injuries, epilepsy can occur at any stage in life. When a person has a seizure, they are often unaware of what is happening and do not remember what is going on around them. There are several types of seizures described in Table 13.5.

Table 13.5. Types of Seizures

Types	Characteristics	Prevalence
Generalized tonic-clonic (grand mal)	Uncontrolled jerking; loss of consciousness; disorientation; violent reactions; vomiting, saliva, bowel, or bladder loss	Most common and serious type; can occur several times a day or as seldom as once a year
Absence (petit mal)	Brief loss of consciousness; blank stare or blinking of eyes, paleness, daydreaming	Most benign, but typically occurs more frequently (sometimes 100 times a day)
Simple and complex partial (psychomotor)	Twitching movements; altered state of consciousness, lip smacking, walking aimlessly; unusual behaviors	Fairly common; can occur weekly, monthly, or once or twice a year

Adapted from: Weinstein, S. & Gaillard, W. D. (2007). Epilepsy. In M. L. Batshaw, L. Pellegrino, & N. J. Roizen (Eds.), Children with Disabilities *(6th Ed., pp. 439–460). Baltimore: Brookes.*

Diagnosis and Treatment

When seizures occur, a medical doctor will discuss family history and complete an eletroencephalogram or EEG, to diagnose epilepsy. This test records electrical signals of the brain using eletrodes or sensors placed on the head and recorded on a polygraph (Fisch, 1999). Antiepileptic drugs such as Depakote, Topamax, and Dilantin are a few medications that can reduce seizure occurrences (Weinstein & Gaillard, 2007). Unfortunately, many of these medications have side effects such as drowsiness, nausea, and weight gain.

It is important as a teacher to build awareness of seizures before they actually occur, since they can be scary to see for the first time. If a seizure occurs, there are several common steps that educators need to follow. First, do not panic or scream as this might startle the student. Second, do not try to hold the student down, restrain them, or put any objects in their mouth. Third, secure the area and make sure all sharp objects are moved away from the student. Fourth, if the student begins to fall, help ease them to the ground laying them on their side to keep airways open. Finally, after the seizure has ended, give the student time to focus and lay down if needed. If the seizure lasts more than five minutes or if there are other medical conditions, it is important to seek medical attention for the student.

WHAT IS TOURETTE SYNDROME?

Tourette syndrome (TS) is a chronic movement disorder of involuntary and sudden movements or vocalizations otherwise known as tics (Burnette & Singer, 2007). Tics can be brief or rapid movements affecting one or several muscle groups. Many involuntary movements are rapid and appear to have no purpose. Vocalized tics might include grunting, throat clearing, barking, yelping, or even include syllables or phrases. TS commonly appears between 9 and 11 years of age with an estimated prevalence of 1-10 in 1,000 children and adolescents (Burnette & Singer, 2007). TS also tends to be more common in males and children with ADHD.

Diagnosis and Treatment

According to Burnette and Singer (2007), a diagnosis of TS must occur before the age of 21 and last for more than one year. More importantly, the involuntary movements must not be a result of a drug, infection, or other disorder. TS is commonly misdiagnosed as asthma, allergies, or dermatitis due to the frequent throat clearing and involuntary movements (e.g., scratching). TS is inherited and commonly associated with other behavioral abnormalities (e.g., obsessive compulsive disorder, ADHD). Unfortunately, there is no cure for TS or tic disorders. There are a variety of medications that can help decrease tics (e.g., clonidine, guanfacine, clonazepam). Behavioral therapies are also being used to treat motor and vocal tics, but there is minimal research available on the outcomes of therapy effectiveness.

WHAT IS DIABETES?

Diabetes is becoming more common in school age children. This is simply a chronic metabolic disorder where the pancreas does not produce the appropriate amounts of insulin. There are two common types of diabetes (see Table 13.6).

Table 13.6. Types of Diabetes

Types	Characteristics	Prevalence
Type I diabetes (juvenile or early-onset diabetes)	Insufficient insulin (hormone produced by the pancreas to breakdown sugars when food is digested	Most common; develops in early childhood or young adults; affects 26 million people in the United States
Type II diabetes	Body does not respond to insulin; dehydration; deep labored breathing; excessive urination; fatigue; fruity-smelling breath	More prevalent in individuals who are obese or overweight, inactive, or smoke

Diagnosis and Treatment

Early signs of diabetes are often extreme thirst, frequent urination, change in weight, and fatigue. When students produce too much insulin they can have blurred vision, drowsiness, nausea, faintness, dizziness, or irritability. If this occurs, it is important to give the student concentrated sugar such as fruit juice or a candy bar to end the insulin reaction. It is also important to stay in close contact with the school nurse to help monitor the symptoms and prevent a future diabetic coma.

WHAT IS ASTHMA?

Asthma is a lung disorder involving frequent wheezing and difficulty breathing. There are different levels of severity with asthma, with mild forms requiring inhalers or nebulizers while severe cases often require hospitalization and result in frequent absenteeism. Asthma attacks are often triggered by allergens or irritants in the environment such as pollen, cigarette smoke, brisk movements and exercise, or emotional stress. The asthma attack is a result of narrowing airways and airflow in and out of the lungs.

Diagnosis and Treatment

The cause of asthma is not known, but is often hereditary or a result of the environment. Doctors must diagnose asthma based on a medical history, physical exam, and lung functioning tests. Asthma is the most common lung disease in children and results in frequent absences. It is important as an educator to work with the family and student to explore best ways for communicating about make up work and reducing emotional stress.

RELATED SERVICE PROVIDERS AND HEALTH CARE PLANS

In working with individuals with physical disabilities and health impairments, it is very important as an educator to collaborate with related service providers who are also experts in helping improve quality of life and independence. Table 13.7 provides a list of related services and providers paired with broad roles and responsibilities. Figure 13.1 provides an example of a health care plan used by related service providers in the public schools of Hartford, Connecticut.

Table 13.7. Related Service Providers/Services

Provider/Service	Roles and Responsibilities
Assistive Technology Practitioner (ATP)	Works with families, individuals with disabilities, and school personnel to provide training and resources related to assistive technology devices (e.g., switches, aids to daily living)
Counselor	Works with families and individuals adjusting to or coping with disabilities (e.g., acceptance and addressing self-esteem issues)
Occupational Therapist (OT)	Works with individuals on fine motor and daily living tasks (e.g., dressing, eating, personal hygiene, feeding)
Orientation and Mobility Specialist (OM)	Teaches navigation skills for increased independence and mobility (e.g., navigation for individuals with visual impairments)

Physical Educator (adapted)	Designs and provides physical activities and exercise based on needs of the individual (e.g., adapting sports)
Physical Therapist (PT)	Works with gross motor skills (e.g., movement, posture, standing, walking, positioning)
Recreational Therapist (RT)	Facilitates therapeutic and leisure activities (e.g., horseback riding, sports)
School Nurse	Trains school personnel on medical conditions and health care services/plans (e.g., medications, device and procedure training)
Speech Language Pathologist (SLP)	Provides language interventions, speech therapy, and augmentative and alternative communication services (e.g., receptive and expressive language, communication boards)
Transportation Services	Facilitates safe and accessible travel from school, home, and throughout the community

WHAT IS ASSISTIVE TECHNOLOGY?

Assistive technology (AT) for individuals with disabilities has been acknowledged by the federal government for more than two decades in the Individuals with Disabilities Education Act (IDEA 1990, 1997, 2004; Wahl, 2002). IDEA explicitly states AT devices and services must be provided by school districts to individuals who qualify for provisions of a free, appropriate public education (Wahl, 2002). The term *assistive technology device* is defined in the IDEA (2004) as "any item, piece of equipment, or product system, whether acquired commercially, modified, or customized, that is used to increase, maintain, or improve functional capabilities of individuals with disabilities" (20 U.S.C. § 1400 [602]). AT includes a wide range of devices, services, strategies, and practices for assisting individuals with disabilities in everyday life functions (Cook & Hussey, 2002).

With more than 5,401,300 individuals with disabilities being served under IDEA, at least 3 to 5% of these students receiving special education services need highly specialized AT needs such as alternative and augmentative communication devices (Wahl, 2002). AT can have benefits for individuals with physical disabilities and health impairments such as enhanced access, inclusive opportunities, increased productivity, and improve the quality of life (Chmiliar & Cheung, 2007). Previous research has found that AT devices and services can play specific roles in increasing independence and helping empower individuals with disabilities. For example, a study conducted in 1993 by the National Council on Disability found that almost 75% of children using AT were able to remain in regular classrooms and 45% of the students in the study were able to reduce school-related services. There is a continued history of reauthorizations related to AT such as the Technology-Related Assistance for Individuals with Disabilities Act of 1988, known as the "Tech Act," as it helped: a) establish AT demonstration and equipment loan centers, b) provided

Figure 13.1.

SAMPLE HEALTH CARE PLAN

Name: _____ DOB: _____

Diagnosis: _____ Physician: _____

Diet: _____

Medication/Treatment: _____

_____

Medical History: _____

Health Care Plan/Goals:

Date	Health Problem	Intervention	Person Responsible	Evaluation and Timeline

Signature: _____ Title: _____ Date: _____

_____ _____ _____

Adapted from:
http://www.sde.ct.gov/sde/lib/sde/PDF/deps/student/health/Ind_Health_Care_Plan.pdf

protection and advocacy services in order to help individuals with disabilities and their families, and c) funded federal and state programs in providing low interest loans and financing options for purchasing AT. After 10 years the Assistive Technology Act replaced the Tech Act as it continued to address the AT needs of individuals with disabilities.

ADVANCES IN TECHNOLOGICAL SUPPORT AND AUGMENTATIVE COMMUNICATION DEVICES

With thousands of advances in technological supports and augmentative and alternative communication (AAC) devices within the past decade, there is no way to include all these advances in this chapter; however, some common website resources for AT devices are included in Table 13.8. Some of the most recent advancements have really impacted individuals with physical disabilities. For example, one of the most recent advancements for AAC is Eye Gaze technology. This technology allows a computer to "read or track" where an individual is looking. Previous technology was only able to use a reflective dot placed on an individual's forehead to track responses. Second, is the Livescribe pen that essentially records input and handwriting and then downloads it to a personal computer. It is great for students with learning and physical disabilities who need to take notes. Third, digital books have also become popular and commonly used along with software programs like Kurzweil, Texthelp, and Classmate reader, which reads texts to a person. Finally, cell phone platforms have significantly increased communication for everyone including individuals with disabilities. For instance, the iPad, iPhone, and Blackberry have allowed individuals with disabilities to have less expensive, readily available, and more age appropriate adaptations for everyday life. With these advances and increased technology, assistive technology items are becoming more of a mainstream way of life for everyone. For instance, software such as *Dragon Naturally Speaking* can now be purchased for the first time at local retail stores. For people without disabilities, assistive technology has become a convenience and for individuals with disabilities, it has become a necessity. With technology continuing to advance rapidly, these are just some of the most recent advances commonly known at this point in time.

Despite the high tech assistive technology devices, there are also low-tech devices that need to be considered. With any device, it is important to consult with assistive technology experts to know how to properly use the devices. Low-tech devices must also be considered first before moving to the more complex devices as they are usually less expensive and may be all that is needed for increasing independence or skill levels. AT can be a powerful ally for both students and teachers in inclusive settings. AT can provide inclusive practices and enhanced learning for students with disabilities by making previously impossible ideas and tasks more feasible (Sivin-Kachala & Bialo, 1993), but more importantly, how teachers adapt and utilize available technology makes a bigger difference than the actual technology itself (Sze, 2009). Most of the previous training with AT has been through related service programs such as occupational, physical, and speech therapy; however, recent research suggests potential for educators playing pivotal roles in implementing and integrating the use of AT in their classrooms (Chmiliar & Cheung, 2007).

Beyond awareness and training, there needs be simple environmental modifications for individuals with physical disabilities and health impairments within the classroom, such as providing enough space around the room for an individual with a physical disability to navigate, providing appropriate lighting in the room, adjusting work space heights to appropriate levels, and having necessary devices easily accessible and frequently maintenanced. Table 13.8 provides a sample of centers and resources currently available to help to provide training and maintenance of AT devices.

Table 13.8. Assistive Technology Centers and Resources

Center/URL Address	Description of Resources
Ability Hub Assistive Technology Solutions http://www.abilityhub.com/ general/search.htm	Provides technical information, consulting, searchable database for latest AT resources
AbleData http://www.abledata.com/	Provides objective information about AT products and rehabilitation equipment (e.g., information centers, conferences, companies by state, international resources)
Alliance for Technology Access http://www.ataccess.org	Provides contact information of available AT centers across the United States, AT newsletter, success stories, services directory
AssistiveTech http://assistivetech.net/	National Public Website on AT with the latest AT devices, services, and community resources for people with disabilities and general public
disABILITY Information http://www.makoa.org/index.htm	Provides disability related products and services, mobility products, legal and advocacy resources, medical supplies, aids for daily living
Disability Resources http://www.disabilityresources.org/ AT-GENERAL.html	Provides comprehensive, cross-disability AT websites (e.g., AbleData, Alliance for Technology Access, Assistive Tech)

*A Day in the Life of an Assistive Technology Practitioner: A Feature
Interview with Tammy Pereboom (PT, ATP) from the North Carolina
Assistive Technology Program*

Q: What does a typical day in your professional life as an AT expert look like?

A: No two days are alike. I see people of all ages with many different types of disabilities.
I help them to obtain the most appropriate Assistive Technology. Assistive Technology is
defined as a device, service, strategy or practice used to increase or improve functional
capabilities of individuals with disabilities. Obviously, this definition is very broad. It can be
something as simple as an adapted toy for a child who may not be able to turn the toy on or
off, or something as complex as an AAC device used for those who are not able to verbally
communicate. Part of my job description is to complete AT evaluations for clients. During
this process, I help the client to determine the best devices for activities and make recommendations in the form of a written report. Another part of my job is to provide demonstrations of equipment and to assist with operating a lending library of equipment. A third part
of my job is to perform training on AT to families, students, teachers, or therapists. A typical
day for me involves some aspect of one of these three activities. I also research options or
new developments. The world of AT is changing dramatically from year to year.

Q: Where did you feel most prepared? Least prepared?

A: My years as a treating PT prepared me for the different types of positioning and mobility
devices. My therapy training also prepared me for the different types of disabilities. I feel least
prepared for the AT in the areas of cognition and communication. Since the types and kinds
of AT are continually changing, I am constantly learning new things.

Q: What are the most challenging aspects of your job? Most rewarding?

A: Many aspects of my job are rewarding. One of the most rewarding parts of my job is to
know that I have helped a client do something that perhaps they hadn't been able to do or
were struggling to do. For example, one client that I saw was a gentleman who had a spinal
cord injury approximately 20 years ago. He has limited use of his shoulders, arms and hands
and no movement of his trunk or lower extremities. He lives alone and has a caregiver come
in morning and evening to assist him with dressing, bathing, grooming and getting in/out
of bed. His question to me was "Is there anyway I can use a telephone while I am in bed?"
Currently, he is able to use his thumb to dial while in his wheelchair during the day, but
unable to dial while lying in bed. So once his caregiver assisted him to bed he was unable
to make any type of phone call including emergency ones. We set him up with a switch-
operated phone that allows him to press a switch and the phone scans through a list of pre-
programmed numbers. Note: There are voice-activated phones as well, but this client wasn't
interested in them. It was very rewarding to know that by changing the type of phone this
gentleman used, he is now able to call someone anytime of the day or night.

   Another rewarding aspect of my job is allowing people to try the devices without purchasing them. Unfortunately, some of the pieces of AT are extremely expensive. Our lending
library allows people to try at no charge the equipment to determine its effectiveness. This
is especially rewarding with the switch-activated toys. For example, one month a parent may
check out the switch adapted Barney and the next month check out the switch adapted Elmo.

   One challenging part of my job is working with clients who aren't willing to try an
alternative method because it is new or unfamiliar. Another challenge is working with clients
with multiple disabilities. For example, something that is designed to help someone with
a visual impairment may rely on his or her sense of touch or hearing. If their disability has
impaired these senses it is more difficult to find appropriate equipment.

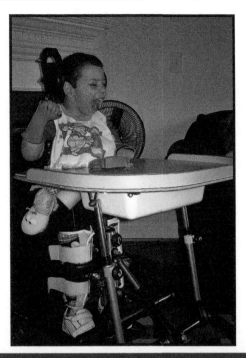

GLOSSARY IN PLAIN TERMS

Assistive technology: device, service, strategy, or practice used to increase or improve functional capabilities of individuals with disabilities.

Cerebral palsy: a neurological disorder caused by damage to the brain before, during, or after birth resulting in poor posture and involuntary movements.

Epilepsy: diagnosed with repeated seizures; seizures are caused by unregulated electrical discharges or "misfires" in the brain.

Muscular dystrophy: a progressive disease that worsens over time as muscles deteriorate or waste away.

Other health impairment: limited strength, vitality, or alertness due to chronic or acute health problems … that adversely affects a child's educational performance.

Orthopedic impairment: impairments caused by congenital anomaly, by disease, and other causes that adversely affect a child's educational performance.

Physical disabilities: also called orthopedic impairment; involves impairments of the bones, joints, limbs, and/or muscles.

Spina bifida: a neural tube defect that affects the vertebrae, brain, and/or spinal cord where the bones in the vertebrae are exposed.

Tourette syndrome: a chronic movement disorder of involuntary and sudden movements or vocalizations otherwise known as tics.

Traumatic brain injury: an acquired injury to the brain caused by an external physical force, resulting in total or partial functional disability or psychological impairments, or both, that adversely affect a child's educational performance.

REFERENCES

Assistive Technology Act of 1998, P. L. No.105-394, 29 U.S.C. § 3001 *et seq.*

Assistive Technology Act of 2004, P. L. No. 108-364.

Burnette, W. B., & Singer, H. S. (2007). Movement disorders. In M. L. Batshaw, L. Pellegrino, & N. J. Roizen (Eds.), *Children with disabilities* (6th ed., pp. 409-418). Baltimore: Brookes.

Chmiliar, L., & Cheung, B. (2007). Assistive technology training for teachers: Innovation and accessibility online. *Developmental Disabilities Bulletin, 35,* 18-28.

Cook, A., & Hussey, S. (2002). *Assistive technologies principles and practice* (2nd ed.). St. Louis, MS: Mosby, Inc.

Escolar, D. M., Tosi, L. L., Tesi Rocha, A. C., & Kennedy, A. (2007). Muscles, bones, and nerves. In M. L. Batshaw, L. Pellegrino, & N. J. Roizen (Eds.), *Children with disabilities* (6th ed., pp. 203-215). Baltimore: Brookes.

Fisch, B. J. (1999). *Fisch and Spehlmann's EEG primer: Basic principles of digital and analog EEG.* New York: Elsevier Science.

Hall, J. G., & Solehdin, F. (1998). Genetics of neural tube defects. *Mental Retardation and Developmental Disabilities Research Reviews, 4,* 269-281.

Individuals with Disabilities Education Act of 1990, P. L. No. 101-476, 20 U.S.C. § 1400 *et seq.*

Individuals with Disabilities Education Act of 1997, P. L. No. 105-17, 20 U.S.C. § 1400 *et seq.*

Individuals with Disabilities Education Improvement Act of 2004, P. L. No. 108-446, 20 U.S.C. § 1400 *et seq.*

Liptak, G. S. (2007). Neural tube defects. In M. L. Batshaw, L. Pellegrino, & N. J. Roizen (Eds.), *Children with disabilities* (6th ed., pp. 419-438). Baltimore: Brookes.

Michaud, L. J., Duhaime, A., Wade, S. L., Rabin, J. P., Jones, D. O., & Lazar, M. F. (2007). Traumatic brain injury. In M. L. Batshaw, L. Pellegrino, & N. J. Roizen (Eds.), *Children with disabilities* (6th ed., pp. 461-476). Baltimore: Brookes.

National Council on Disability. (1993). *Study on the financing of assistive technology devices and services for individuals with disabilities: A report to the President and the Congress of the United States.* Retrieved from http://www.ncd.gov/newsroom/publications/1993/assistive.htm#5

Pellegrino, L. (2007). Cerebral palsy. In M. L. Batshaw, L. Pellegrino, & N. J. Roizen (Eds.), *Children with disabilities* (6th ed., pp. 387–408). Baltimore: Brookes.

Sivin-Kachala, J., & Bialo, E. R. (1993). The effectiveness of technology in schools: A summary of recent research. *SLMQ, 25*(1), 12.

Sze, S. (2009). The effects of assistive technology on students with disabilities. *Journal of Educational Technology Systems, 37,* 419-429.

Technology-Related Assistance for Individuals with Disabilities Act of 1988, P. L. No. 100-407.

United Cerebral Palsy Foundation. (2010). *Cerebral palsy facts and figures.* Retrieved from http://www.ucp.org/ucp_generaldoc.cfm/1/9/37/37-37/447#history

Wahl, L. (2002). *Alliance for technology access report on the need for assistive technology expertise in education and the creation of new models.* Petaluma, CA: WestEd RTEC Learning for Everyone Initiative.

WebMD. (2010). *Understanding muscular dystrophy: The basics.* Retrieved from http://www.webmd.com/parenting/understanding-muscular-dystrophy-basics

Weinstein, S. & Gaillard, W. D. (2007). Epilepsy. In M. L. Batshaw, L. Pellegrino, & N. J. Roizen (Eds.), *Children with disabilities* (6th Ed., pp. 439-460). Baltimore: Brookes.

QUESTIONS *for Reflection:*

What are the two broad IDEA categories that serve students with physical disabilities and chronic or acute health conditions?

Describe the most common types of cerebral palsy. What characteristics do they include? What are the implications of each for classroom teachers?

Describe augmentative communication. Make a list of ways students might benefit from its use in the classroom. How can teachers incorporate its use into classroom activities?

Make a list of specific ways educators can collaborate with related service providers listed in Table 13.7. In what ways will these providers help you as an educator? What specific information will you need to learn from these providers when working with individuals with physical or health impairments?

What steps or resources should educators seek in order to support students and families who have progressive or chronic physical and medical conditions?

What are three specific ways advancements in technology have improved quality of life and independence for individuals with physical disabilities and health impairments?

Notes

CHAPTER 14

Early Intervention/Early Childhood Special Education and the Prevention of School Failure

Jane Diane Smith

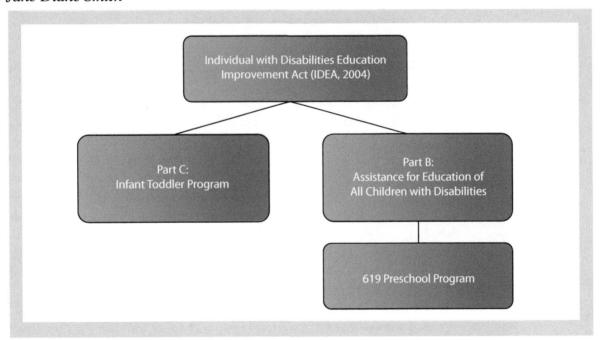

THE TOP TEN TERMS FOR CHAPTER 14:

The following key terms or big ideas are critical to your understanding of the content for chapter 14 and the in-class discussion to follow.

• Early intervention	• Family-centered approach
• Early childhood special education	• Developmental delay
• PL 99-457	• IFSP
• Part C (Infant Toddler Programs)	• Natural environment
• Part B (619 Preschool Programs)	• Embedded interventions

© *Andrey Kekyalyaynen, 2015. Used under licence from Shutterstock, Inc.*

HOW IS SPECIAL EDUCATION DIFFERENT BEFORE CHILDREN ARE SCHOOL AGE?

Future educators should be familiar with the supports and services that infants, toddlers, and preschool age children with disabilities and their families may have participated in prior to beginning their K-12 (i.e., kindergarten – 12th grade) educational experience. The terms ***early intervention (EI)*** and/or ***early childhood special education (ECSE)*** are used to describe *special education* for children before they reach school age. Early intervention refers to supports and services for infants and toddlers with disabilities or at-risk of developmental delay(s) and their families, while early childhood special education describes programs for preschool age children with disabilities. EI and ECSE differ from school age special education in a variety of ways that will be discussed throughout this chapter.

Early childhood intervention is a broad term used to describe a variety of supports and services that are provided to young children and their families. Professionals representing various disciplines (e.g., education, special education, public health, social work, medicine, nursing, occupational therapy, physical therapy, speech and language therapy, child development, psychology, child care) provide intervention across a variety of settings (e.g., home, early care and education programs, child care, family day care home, preschool, clinic, hospital). Intervention initiatives can be publicly and/or privately funded. Shonkoff and Meisels (2000) define early childhood intervention as follows:

> Early childhood intervention consists of multidisciplinary services provided to children from birth to 5 years of age to promote health and well-being, enhance emerging competencies, minimize developmental delays, remediate existing or emerging disabilities,

prevent functional deterioration, and promote adaptive parenting and overall family functioning. These goals are accomplished by providing individualized developmental, educational, and therapeutic services for children in conjunction with mutually planned support for their families (p. xvii –xviii).

For the purposes of this chapter, the terms EI and ECSE will be used to refer to supports and services for young children and their families specified under the Individuals with Disabilities Education Improvement Act of 2004 (IDEA, 2004).

EI & ECSE: A HISTORICAL PERSPECTIVE

The EI and ECSE programs that we are familiar with today trace their beginnings to the 1960s. At that time, nonprofit agencies such as United Cerebral Palsy (UCP) and The Association for Retarded Citizens (ARC) provided services to young *"handicapped"* children and their families. Federal funds (e.g., Handicapped Children's Early Education Act of 1968, PL 90-538) were also designated to support the development of model demonstration programs to provide EI/ESCE services. The number of young *"handicapped"* children who had access to services under these early initiatives was limited.

In 1986, *Public Law 99-457 (Education of the Handicapped Act Amendments)* extended the right to a **free, appropriate, public education** (FAPE) in the **least restrictive environment** (LRE) to preschool children with disabilities. In addition to mandating services for preschool children, PL 99-457 encouraged states by providing incentive funds to develop comprehensive programs for infants and toddlers with disabilities or at-risk of developmental delays and their families. In 1990, the *Individuals with Disabilities Education Act (IDEA)* acknowledged the focus on the individual and resulted in *"person-first"* language. IDEA was reauthorized as the *Individuals with Disabilities Education Act Amendments of 1991* and expanded services for infants, toddlers, and preschool children with disabilities. Today, programs for infants, toddlers, and preschool age children with disabilities are offered in accordance with IDEA (2004). Consequently, infants/toddlers and their families as well as preschool age children are **entitled** to supports and services to help **prevent** and/or **remediate** developmental delays or disabilities.

The rationale and fundamental assumptions for providing early intervention and early childhood special education programs are based in scientific evidence, legislation, and societal beliefs (Guralnick, 1997; IDEA, 2004; National Research Council and Institute of Medicine, 2000; Sandall, Santos, & Smith, 2005; Shonkoff & Meisels, 2000). A brief summary follows:

Rationale for providing EI/ECSE
- Improve child development and learning outcomes
- Prevent and/or minimize the effect of biological and/or environmental risk factors on child development
- Minimize the effect of established disabilities and/or prevent related problems

- Reduce costs to society by decreasing the need for special education and related services at school age
- Support families as they meet the special needs of young children with disabilities (or at-risk of developmental delay)

Fundamental Assumptions associated with EI/ECSE
- Society has a moral and ethical responsibility to provide supports and services to young children with disabilities (or at-risk of developmental delays) and their families
- Intervention efforts need to be strengths-based and focus on the developing child within the context of his/her family
- Interventions should occur in natural environments and be embedded within the context of daily activities and routines
- Services need to be comprehensive and coordinated across various disciplines to meet the complex needs of young children with disabilities (or at-risk of developmental delays) and their families
- Biology, environment, and culture influence child development
- The importance of brain development and the ability to influence development during the first three years of life
- The concepts of neural plasticity and optimal periods of development
- Knowledge of conditions that positively or adversely influence development
- Early learning experiences are connected to later school experiences

WHAT IS EARLY INTERVENTION?

Although early intervention is a generic term that is used to refer to programs for young children with disabilities (or at-risk of developmental delays) birth through five years of age, EI is used most commonly to refer to services for infants, toddlers, and their families. The terms *'Part C,' 'Infant Toddler Programs,'* and *'early intervention'* are often used interchangeably to describe the wide variety of supports, services, and programs that infants and toddlers with disabilities (or at-risk of developmental delay) and their families may be entitled to under Part C of IDEA (2004).

All states are required by federal law to provide services to infants/toddlers and their families who: a) exhibit a ***developmental delay*** in one or more domain of development or, b) are diagnosed with a condition of ***established risk***.

Individual states have the responsibility of defining developmental delay and establishing eligibility criteria for the provision of Part C services (Shackleford, 2006). Eligibility criteria specified under developmental delay is often determined by assessment results that indicate a percentage delay between the child's chronological age and his/her current level of performance in one or more domains of development (i.e., emotional-social, physical, communication, cognitive, adaptive). For example, a state may determine eligibility criteria to be 30% delay in one domain of development or 25% delay in two or more domains of development. Young children diagnosed with an established risk condition are eligible for early intervention whether or not a delay in development is present. Examples of conditions of established risk include chromosomal and genetic disorders such as Down syndrome or Fragile X, severe impairments in vision or hearing, congenital infections (e.g., HIV, cytomegalovirus (CMV)), autism, central nervous system disorders such as Cerebral Palsy or Spina Bifida, and neonatal conditions such as extreme low birthweight or intraventricular hemorrhage (IVH).

The presence of biological/medical (e.g., low birthweight, failure to thrive) and/or environmental (e.g., parental substance abuse, poverty, homelessness, young parental age, child abuse/neglect) risk factors places an infant or toddler at-risk of experiencing a developmental delay. However, it is important to note that the presence of a risk factor(s) does not necessarily result in a developmental delay or disability. The concept of cumulative risk suggests that young children who experience multiple risk factors are more likely to develop a delay or disability. Thus, Part C of IDEA (2004) also encourages states to provide early intervention to young children and their families who are at-risk of developmental delay.

A defining characteristic of infant toddler supports, services, and programs is the emphasis on a ***family centered approach*** to intervention. Trivette and Dunst (2005) describe a family centered approach to intervention as a philosophy or way of thinking that acknowledges the family as a constant in the child's life. As such, the family is the primary decision maker regarding supports and services. The intent of early intervention is to provide resources and supports so that families have the knowledge and skills they need to support the development of their children with disabilities or at-risk of a developmental delays. When interventions are provided following a family-centered approach, they "support and enhance the competency of parents and strengthen the family (Trivette & Dunst, 2005, p. 108)." In an effort to not disrupt family activities and routines, intervention efforts are embedded into the family's daily activities and routines.

Infant toddler programs also differ from preschool ECSE programs and school age special education programs in that they may be offered on a ***fee for service*** basis. That is, ***FAPE*** does not necessarily pertain to Part C services. Federal law requires that certain services (e.g., service coordination, developmental assessments, activities related to the IFSP, activities related to the protection of rights) be provided free of charge. When states do offer EI services (e.g., specialized instruction, occupational therapy, physical therapy, speech and language therapy) for a fee, the cost of services is paid directly by the family (i.e., self-pay) or billed to a medical insurance provider. A sliding fee scale based on family income is frequently used to determine the cost of EI services.

PART C DEFINITION OF DEVELOPMENTAL DELAY AND ESTABLISHED RISK

(i) is experiencing developmental delays, as measured by appropriate diagnostic instruments and procedures in 1 or more of the areas of cognitive development, physical development, communication development, social or emotional development, and adaptive development; or

(ii) has a diagnosed physical or mental condition that has a high probability of resulting in developmental delay (IDEA 2004, §632(5)(A)).

PART C DEFINITION OF AT-RISK OF DEVELOPMENTAL DELAY

An individual under 3 years of age who would be at risk of experiencing a substantial developmental delay if early intervention services were not provided to the individual (IDEA 2004, §632(1)).

INDIVIDUALIZED FAMILY SERVICE PLAN

The ***Individualized Family Service Plan (IFSP)*** is best viewed as a ***process*** that results in a written document. The written form of the IFSP is a legal document that describes the individualized early intervention supports and services that will be provided to a young child (i.e., birth to age three) and his/her family in the ***natural environment***. Simply stated, the natural environment is the setting or location in which the child would be participating if he/she did not have a disability. Natural environments encompass a variety of settings and can be found in the home and community (e.g., early care and education programs, preschool programs, family daycare homes, parks, libraries, restaurants, stores, dentist's office). The IFSP is comparable to the Individualized Education Plan (IEP) in that it specifies a plan of supports that are provided to a child with disabilities. However, the IFSP differs from the IEP in several ways.

The first difference is that the scope of the IFSP is holistic; it addresses all aspects of the young child's development rather than an exclusive focus on educational supports and services. Another major difference between the IFSP and IEP is that supports and services on the IFSP can be provided to child as well as his/her family and they build on the existing strengths of the child and family. The emphasis on the process rather than the written document is another major difference between the IFSP and IEP.

The IFSP process begins when the child has been ***identified*** as having a delay or disability and is ***referred*** to an early intervention program. Anyone (e.g., parent, family member, therapists, teachers, nurses, physicians) who expresses a concern about a child's development can refer the child to a local early intervention program. Best practice suggests that the parent should be informed if someone other than the parent is making the referral. Once the child has been referred to a local early intervention program, a ***service coordinator*** is assigned to the family. Infants and toddlers who have been identified as having disabilities or developmental delays often require multiple supports and services (e.g., occupational therapy, physical therapy, speech and language therapy). As such, service coordination is one of the 19 early intervention services mandated by federal law. The intent of service coordination is to help families access early intervention supports and services while protecting child and family rights.

Service coordinators typically make initial contact with the family soon after referral to determine a family's interest in EI supports and services. During an initial meeting with the family, the service coordinator gathers relevant information about the child's development and family's concerns, explains the EI process, and informs the family of rights and procedural safeguards provided under federal law. Once the family consents to proceeding with the EI process, the service coordinator schedules and coordinates all relevant assessments and/or evaluations. Part C regulations of IDEA (2004) require a comprehensive and coordinated approach to assessment. A voluntary assessment of resources, priorities, and concerns as related to supporting the development of their child with a disability is offered to the family. While the family assessment is optional under federal law, a comprehensive multidisciplinary assessment of the child is required. This is conducted to identify the child's current developmental levels, strengths, and areas of need. Once the assessments have been completed, the service coordinator schedules the initial IFSP meeting. The IFSP team is comprised of the family, service coordinator, and relevant professionals.

During the initial IFSP meeting, information obtained from the child and family assessments is discussed by the IFSP team to determine eligibility. Depending on the individual needs of the child and his/her family, they may be eligible for any of the following services as specified by federal legislation (IDEA, 2004):

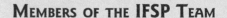

MEMBERS OF THE **IFSP** TEAM

- parent(s) of the child
- other family members as requested by parent(s)
- advocate or person outside of the family as requested by parent(s)
- designated Part C Service Coordinator
- provider(s) of early intervention services
- provider(s) of assessments/evaluations

"(i) family training, counseling, and home visits;

(ii) special instruction;

(iii) speech-language pathology and audiology services, and sign language and cued language services;

(iv) occupational therapy;

(v) physical therapy;

(vi) psychological services;

(vii) service coordination services;

(viii) medical services only for diagnostic or evaluation purposes;

(ix) early identification, screening, and assessment services;

(x) health services necessary to enable the infant or toddler to benefit from the other early intervention services;

(xi) social work services;

(xii) vision services;

(xiii) assistive technology devices and assistive technology services; and

(xiv) transportation and related costs that are necessary to enable an infant or toddler and the infant's or toddler's family to receive another service described in this paragraph" (IDEA 2004, §632(4)(E))

Changes that the family would like to see in their child or themselves is a major focus of the IFSP. These changes, or outcomes, are written in response to the priorities or concerns expressed by the family. Outcomes are broad statements of changes that the family desires. For each broad outcome, individual activities or action steps intended to facilitate the desired changes are specified as well as the start date, target date for completion, and persons responsible. The following are examples of IFSP outcomes for young children and families.

Example of <u>Child</u> Focused Outcome & Activities/ Action Steps

Family Priority, Resource, and/or Concern: Sharon and Scott want their 14 month old son, Jake, to learn how to walk. In addition to regular meetings with their service coordinator, Jake is receiving specialized instruction (i.e., early intervention) and physical therapy in his child care setting. Sharon and Scott have medical insurance that covers the cost of physical therapy.

> **Child's Abilities/Needs**: Jake is able to get up on his hands and knees and rock back and forth. He does not pull to stand or take steps with support.

> **Outcome:** Jake will increase his gross motor skills so that he can walk independently.

Activities:

1. Family members will observe the physical therapist as she provides therapy to strengthen Jake's gross motor skills.
2. Physical therapist will suggest activities to strengthen Jake's gross motor skills that the family can implement at home during daily activities and routines.
3. Child care providers will observe the physical therapist as she provides therapy to strengthen Jake's gross motor skills.
4. Physical therapist will suggest activities to strengthen Jake's gross motor skills that the child care staff can implement during daily activities and routines.

Example of <u>Family</u> Focused Outcome & Activities/ Action Steps

Family Priority, Resource, and/or Concern: Judy and Oliver were recently referred to early intervention. Their infant son, Jamal, has been diagnosed with Down syndrome. Judy and Oliver want to learn more about Down syndrome and are interested in talking with other families who have children with Down syndrome. Sarah is the service coordinator who is working with Jamal and his family.

> **Child's Abilities/Needs**: Jamal has a follow up appointment with the cardiologist in a few months.

> **Outcome:** Judy and Oliver will be provided with information and supports in order to learn more about Down syndrome.

Activities:

1. The service coordinator will provide information to Judy and Oliver and discuss questions and concerns they may have regarding developmental implications associated with Down syndrome.
2. The service coordinator will accompany Judy, Oliver, and Jamal to the follow up appointment with the cardiologist to discuss Jamal's medical condition associated with his diagnosis of Down syndrome with the family and the health care team.
3. The service coordinator will refer Judy and Oliver to the Family Support Network so that they can receive parent-to-parent support from a family who also has a child with Down syndrome.

In addition to outcomes and activities, the IFSP specifies the early intervention services to be provided including the frequency, intensity, and method of delivering services. Justification is required if services will not be provided in the natural environment. Services specified on the IFSP begin once the parent has signed the document providing consent and the initial IFSP must be developed within 45 days of referral.

Since young children grow and change frequently, the IFSP is reviewed every six months and annually. As a toddler turns two, the IFSP team begins to focus on transition planning. The IFSP requires a formal transition plan to be developed after a child turns two and before his/her third birthday. The intent of the transition plan is to prepare the child and family for potential changes in service providers and to ensure that a young child's services and supports will continue with minimal disruption. The transition plan outlines specific steps and actions, including a transition planning meeting, to be followed to promote a smooth exit from Part C services (Infant Toddler Program) into Part B (early childhood special education) or other appropriate services. The local educational agency (LEA) is responsible for conducting a multidisciplinary evaluation to determine the child's present levels of development. Results of this evaluation are subsequently used to determine eligibility for preschool special education services. If the child meets the state defined eligibility criteria, an initial IEP meeting is held no later than 30 days prior to the child's third birthday. On the child's third birthday, he/she begins receiving services in a preschool program. This *transition* from *family-centered early intervention services* to *child-focused educational supports and resources* can be challenging for both the family and child.

WHAT IS EARLY CHILDHOOD SPECIAL EDUCATION?

Part B of IDEA (2004) mandates the provision of a free, appropriate, public education (FAPE) to children/students (i.e., 3 – 21 years of age) in the least restrictive environment (LRE). Within Part B of IDEA (2004), regulations specific to preschool programs are described in Section 619. Descriptors such as *'619 programs,' 'little B programs,' and 'early childhood special education'* are often used interchangeably to refer to *early childhood special education* programs for preschool age children (i.e., ages 3 – 5) with disabilities.

COMPONENTS OF THE **IFSP**

(1) a statement of the infant's or toddler's present levels of physical development, cognitive development, communication development, social or emotional development, and adaptive development, based on objective criteria;

(2) a statement of the family's resources, priorities, and concerns relating to enhancing the development of the family's infant or toddler with a disability;

(3) a statement of the measurable results or outcomes expected to be achieved for the infant or toddler and the family, including pre-literacy and language skills, as developmentally appropriate for the child, and the criteria, procedures, and timelines used to determine the degree to which progress toward achieving the results or outcomes is being made and whether modifications or revisions of the results or outcomes or services are necessary;

(4) a statement of specific early intervention services based on peer-reviewed research, to the extent practicable, necessary to meet the unique needs of the infant or toddler and the family, including the frequency, intensity, and method of delivering services;

(5) a statement of the natural environments in which early intervention services will appropriately be provided, including a justification of the extent, if any, to which the services will not be provided in a natural environment;

(6) the projected dates for initiation of services and the anticipated length, duration, and frequency of the services;

(7) the identification of the service coordinator from the profession most immediately relevant to the infant's or toddler's or family's needs (or who is otherwise qualified to carry out all applicable responsibilities under this part) who will be responsible for the implementation of the plan and coordination with other agencies and persons, including transition services; and

(8) the steps to be taken to support the transition of the toddler with a disability to preschool or other appropriate services. (IDEA 2004, §636(d))

© Kachalkina Veronika, 2015. Used under license from Shutterstock, Inc.

All states are required by federal law to provide special education and related services to preschool age children with disabilities. These young children are often determined to be eligible for services under the category of ***developmental delay***. As with infant/toddler programs, eligibility criteria is often determined by assessment results that indicate a percentage delay between the child's chronological age and his/her current level of performance in one or more domains of development (i.e., emotional-social, physical, communication, cognitive, adaptive). For example, a state may determine eligibility criteria to be 30% delay in one domain of development or 25% delay in two or more domains of development.

Federal law specifies that the developmental delay category can be used with children "...aged 3 through 9 (or any subset of that age range, including ages 3 through 5)..." (IDEA 2004, §602(B)). Preschool children with disabilities may also be eligible for services under categories such as speech and language impairment or autism. However, Danaher (2007) discusses concerns related to the use of disability categories (e.g., mental retardation, multiple disabilities, specific learning disabilities, emotional disturbance) with young children. The developmental delay category is intended to avoid premature and/or inappropriate labeling of a child's disability. This eligibility category also acknowledges that young children vary in the rate at which they acquire new skills and behaviors and that developmental domains are inter-related. Thus, acknowledging that it may be difficult to accurately identify a disability in young children and that some children who receive early intervention may no longer need special education services at school age.

Young children may enter early childhood special education programs through a formal transition from Part C early intervention programs or as a new referral. Concerns regarding a child's development may not emerge until the preschool years. Similar to the infant/toddler programs, anyone (e.g. parent, family member, therapists, teachers, nurses, physicians) who expresses a concern about a child's development can refer the child to the local educational agency (LEA). Once the LEA has received a completed referral, the Individualized Education Program (IEP) process is initiated. The IEP process for preschool children follows the same policies, procedures, and timeframes as those that are followed for school age children/students.

- Provision of information regarding legal rights and procedural safeguards
- Parental consent to conduct evaluations
- Multidisciplinary evaluation
- IEP Meeting
  - Determination of Eligibility and Placement
  - Development of Annual Goals and Short Term Objectives (or Benchmarks)
  - Specify related services
- Parent consent to initiate services

IEP goals and objectives are often written with a focus on meeting the educational needs of the young child with a disability. These goals and objectives often relate to the cognitive and communication domains of development in contrast to the holistic focus on development addressed in IFSP outcomes and activities. Depending on a child's developmental level and/or individual needs, IEP goals and objectives may need to be written to focus on academic and functional needs to support the child in an educational setting. As such, IEP goals and objectives may also span all domains of development. It is important to note that preschool age children with developmental delays and/or disabilities may often need support to establish developmental prerequisites for more traditional educational or academic skills. For example, a developmentally appropriate curriculum in a preschool setting may include a circle or story time that is 10 – 15 minutes in length. However, Derrick's attention span is five minutes for activities of interest and even less for activities that are not of interest. An IEP goal could be written to increase Derrick's attention span across small and large group activities. Until Derrick's attention span increases, it may be appropriate for him to remain at the large group circle or story time and look at a book quietly or play with a small, quiet toy that will not disrupt the large group activity.

Similar to the IFSP, the IEP is the written legal document that outlines the special education and related services that the child will receive during the school year. The initial IEP is developed within 90 days of referral to the LEA and reviewed annually. The IEP process has been described in detail in a previous chapter. Please refer to chapter 2 for detailed information regarding the IEP.

INCLUSIVE EDUCATION FOR PRESCHOOL CHILDREN

Early childhood special education and related services (i.e., occupational therapy, physical therapy, speech and language therapy) are often provided in inclusive settings for preschool children with disabilities, even for young children with moderate to severe developmental delays. Lynch, Ballard-Rosa, & Cavallaro (as cited in Cavallaro & Haney, 1999) provide the following definition for inclusion:

> All children learning together in environments that provide special services, supports, and supplements for all children as needed and are guided by well-trained professionals from the fields of early childhood education and early childhood special education (p. 21).

Throughout this text, the term *inclusion* has been used in relationship to school age children receiving special education services in the general education classroom. Unlike school age counterparts, young children do not have universal access to preschool programs. Consequently, inclusive placements for preschool age children can occur in a variety of settings such as Head Start classrooms, Title 1 programs, early care and education settings, as well as public and private preschool programs. If a preschool age child with a disability is not placed in an inclusive setting full-time, he/she may spend the morning in a self-contained setting and the afternoon in an inclusive setting or he/she may be placed in a self-contained setting on a full-time basis.

Young children in a preschool setting learn through play as well as daily activities and routines (e.g., circle time, center time, snack). A typical schedule of daily activities in a preschool program often includes freeplay (e.g., housekeeping, blocks, dramatic play, manipulative), centers (e.g., literacy, numeracy, science, computer), circle/music, art, story, snack, and outdoor play. A child's individualized needs are addressed by embedding IEP goals and objectives within the context of developmentally appropriate and naturally occurring activities and routines. Wolery (2005) defines ***embedded*** intervention as:

> Identifying times and activities when a child's goals and the instructional procedure for those goals can be inserted into children's ongoing activities, routines, and transitions in a way that relates to the context. It involves distributing opportunities to learn goals and apply instructional procedures for those goals across different activities, routines, and transition of the day (p. 94).

For example, an IEP goal for a child in an inclusive preschool setting may be written as: "Alex will learn (i.e., verbally label) primary and secondary colors independently 80% of the time for two consecutive weeks." The teacher embeds the intervention into the context of naturally occurring daily activities and routines as Alex practices pointing to, and then subsequently labeling, colors during freeplay (e.g., colors of blocks, colors of dishes/cups in housekeeping) as well as story (e.g., colors of objects illustrated in book pictures) and art (e.g., color of paints, paper, crayons) times. Instruction that is embedded within the context of daily activities and routines "provides children with the opportunity to learn and practice important skills in meaningful contexts" (Grisham-Brown, Hemmeter, & Pretti-Frontczak, 2005, pg. 202).

GLOSSARY IN PLAIN TERMS

Developmental Delay (DD): Delay in one or more domain (e.g., emotional-social, physical, communication, cognitive, adaptive) of development; eligibility category for infant/toddler and preschool services.

Early Intervention (EI): Supports, services, and programs that are provided to infants and toddlers with disabilities (or at-risk of developmental delays) and their families under Part C of IDEA (2004).

Established risk: Physical or mental condition diagnosed in a young child that has a high probability of resulting in developmental delay.

Early Childhood Special Education (ECSE): Services and programs that are provided to preschool age children (ages 3 – 5) with disabilities under Part B of IDEA (2004).

Embedded interventions: A child's individualized goals are incorporated into the context of developmentally appropriate and naturally occurring activities and routines.

Entitled: Children have the right to participate in early intervention and early childhood special education services.

Family-centered approach: "A philosophy or way of thinking that leads to a set of practices in which families or parents are considered central and the most important decision maker in a child's life. More specifically, it recognizes that the family is the constant in the child's life and that service systems and personnel must support, respect, encourage, and enhance the strengths and competence of the family" (Trivette & Dunst, 2005, p. 119).

FAPE: Free appropriate public education.

IDEA (2004): Individuals with Disabilities Education Improvement Act of 2004.

IEP: Individualized Educational Plan.

IFSP: Individualized Family Service Plan.

Natural environments: Setting in which the child would spend time if he/she did not have a developmental delay or disability.

Part B: Part B—Assistance for Education of All Children with Disabilities of IDEA (2004).

Part C: Part C—Infants and Toddlers with Disabilities of IDEA (2004).

PL 99-457: Education of the Handicapped Act Amendments (1986).

Service coordinator: Professional responsible for working with the family of an infant or toddler with disabilities (or at-risk of developmental delay) to ensure that they receive the supports and resources that they are entitled to under Part C (Infant Toddler Program).

REFERENCES

Cavallaro, C., and Haney, M. (1997). *Preschool Inclusion.* Baltimore, MD: Paul H. Brookes Publishing Co.

Danaher, J. (2007). *Eligibility policies and practices for young children under Part B of IDEA* (NECTAC Notes No. 24). Chapel Hill: The University of North Carolina, FPG Child Development Institute, National Early Childhood Technical Assistance Center.

Education for All Handicapped Children Act of 1975, PL 94-142, 20 U.S.C. § 1400 *et seq.*

Education of the Handicapped Act Amendments of 1986, PL 94-142, 20 U.S.C. § 1401 *et seq.*

Guralnick, M. J. (1997). *The effectiveness of early intervention.* Baltimore, MD: Paul H. Brookes Publishing Co.

Grisham-Brown, J., Hemmeter, M.L., & Pretti-Frontczak, K. (2005). *Blended practices for teaching young children in inclusive settings.* Baltimore, MD: Paul H. Brookes Publishing Co.

Handicapped Children's Early Education Act of 1968, PL 90-538, 20 U.S.C. §621 *et seq.*

Individual with Disabilities Education Act of 1990, 20 U.S.C. § 1400 *et seq.*

Individual with Disabilities Education Act Amendments of 1991, 20 U.S.C. § 1400 *et seq.*

Individuals with Disabilities Education Improvement Act of 2004, 20 U.S.C. § 1400 *et seq.*

National Research Council and Institute of Medicine (2000). *From Neurons to Neighborhoods: The Science of Early Childhood Development.* Committee on Integrating the Science of Early Childhood Development. J. P. Shonkoff & D. A. Phillips (Eds.0. Board of Children, Youth, and Families, Commission on Behavioral and Social Science and Education. Washington, D.C., National Academy Press.

Sandall, S., McLean, M. E., Santos, R. M., & Smith, B. J. (2005). DEC's recommended practices: The context for change. In S. Sandall, M. L. Hemmeter, B. J. Smith, & M. E. McLean (Eds.), *DEC recommended practices: A comprehensive guide for practical application in early intervention/early childhood special education* (pp. 19-26). Longmont, CO: Sopris West.

Shackelford, J. (2006). *State and jurisdictional eligibility definitions for infants and toddlers with disabilities under IDEA* (NECTAC Notes No. 21). Chapel Hill: The University of North Carolina, FPG Child Development Institute, National Early Childhood Technical Assistance Center.

Shonkoff, J. P. and Meisels, S. J. (Eds.). (2000). *Handbook of Early Childhood Intervention* (2nd ed.). Cambridge, UK: Cambridge University Press.

Trivette, C. M., & Dunst, C. J. (2005). DEC's recommended practices: Family-based practices. In S. Sandall, M. L. Hemmeter, B. J. Smith, & M. E. McLean (Eds.), *DEC recommended practices: A comprehensive guide for practical application in early intervention/early childhood special education* (pp. 107-126). Longmont, CO: Sopris West.

Wolery, M. 2005). DEC's recommended practices: Child-focused practices. In S. Sandall, M. L. Hemmeter, B. J. Smith, & M. E. McLean (Eds.), *DEC recommended practices: A comprehensive guide for practical application in early intervention/early childhood special education* (pp. 19-26). Longmont, CO: Sopris West.

QUESTIONS *for Reflection:*

If a family member expressed concerns to you regarding the development of their infant or toddler, how would you describe the concept of early intervention?

If a family member expressed concerns to you regarding the development of the preschool child who had not previously received infant-toddler early intervention services, how would you describe the concept of early childhood special education?

How does the IFSP differ from an IEP?

Why is a family centered approach to providing early intervention in the natural environment important?

What are the benefits of using *'developmental delay'* to establish eligibility for pre-school children with disabilities compared to the use of other disability categories (e.g., emotional disturbance, specific learning disability, mental retardation, multiple disabilities)?

Describe the concept of embedded intervention that is used to provide early intervention/early childhood special education.

NOTES

Digital Vision

CHAPTER 15

Reforming General Education to Improve Outcomes for Students with Special Needs: UDL, RTI, and PBIS

Tara Galloway, Melissa A. Miller, Chris O'Brien, and LuAnn Jordan

THE TOP TEN TERMS FOR CHAPTER 15:

The following key terms or big ideas are critical to your understanding of the content for chapter 15 and the in-class discussions to follow.

• Positive behavioral support	• Universal Design for Learning (UDL)
• Response to Intervention (RTI)	• Assistive technology
• Universal screening	• Evidence-based practices
• Curriculum-Based Measurement (CBM)	• Positive reinforcement strategies
• Token economies	• Behavior contracting

ADDRESSING DISABILITY IN ACADEMIC PERFORMANCE BY REFORMING STANDARD APPROACHES TO TEACHING AND LEARNING

Hehir (2006) suggests that the natural consequence of inclusive education and more recent policy changes in IDEA compelling schools to provide access to the general curriculum for all students with disabilities, is an urgent dialogue regarding the need for schools to change in order to achieve these lofty goals. Schools must change in ways that allow a more proactive means of addressing diverse student needs. Although American public schools were not designed to address student diversity, schools must now adapt to a wider range of student needs, particularly in the areas of reading development and behavior management.

Universal Design for Learning (UDL) is the term that is often used to reflect a broad paradigm shift regarding the manner in which schools plan to address the goals of inclusion. In the broadest terms, *Universal Design for Learning* (or *Universal Design for Instruction*) represents a perspective that **emphasizes the reduction of barriers to learning in school**. Increasing access to standardized, rigorous curricula for a student population that has increasingly diverse needs requires strong planning and strategic, systematic efforts to preemptively address "special needs" that exist in schools prior to those needs becoming "problems" or "barriers." Although the term UDL implies "universality," two general misconceptions or challenges arise in professional dialogue about UDL. The term does not imply that a "singular" curriculum should be devised to teach everyone the same way. In fact, the term implies tremendous **flexibility in teaching and learning** experiences that anticipates learner differences, such that schools can be more efficient and *reduce the need for highly specialized and separate educational programs* that reflect the historical function of special education. Another challenge associated with this term is the need for translation of instructional principles that reflect universal design to actual programs, lesson plans, and technological developments that can truly address *every* learner need. Ultimately, it is not a simple outcome, but guides practice as an idealistic end-goal—the goal that may never be reached but represents a good aim.

Universal Design for Learning is premised on inclusive education and will require schools to function in a substantially different way than they have in the past. Included in this shift will be **a focus on prevention of failure**. Prevention of academic and behavioral problems requires a system that is bigger and better resourced than special education. UDL reflects broad systems change that includes differences in thinking from the level of the school district to the most important level—the practicing teacher, particularly in the earliest grades. Collaboration among a team of professionals including learning and behavior specialists and interventionists (special education teachers), associated support personnel (speech-language pathologists, assistive technologists, therapists), and general education teachers is the starting point for actualizing the potential of UDL.

Although there is considerable jargon and a vast set of theoretical models that claim to represent the necessary changes in education, it is important in the case of UDL to see how other programs may reflect similar philosophies. Hehir (2006) includes discussions of Response-to-Intervention (RTI) and Positive Behavioral Intervention and Supports as component systems in a larger UDL framework. To be clear, UDL can be seen, simultaneously, as a broad framework for school reform and accessibility, and model for teaching at the classroom level that reflects clear planning for learner differences. Rather than reacting or "retro-fitting" for learner difficulties, classroom-level UDL implementation tends to emphasize a proactive plan for instructional design in which learner supports and modifications have been embedded in the instructional process. Further, both instructional technologies and assistive technologies (i.e., technology designed to compensate for the weaknesses of children with disabilities) offer unique advantages in designing instruction and instructional materials that reflect UDL principles.

The remainder of this chapter will be dedicated to more specific explanations of RTI, PBIS, and UDL at the classroom level. Response to Intervention or **RTI** represents a paradigm shift in thinking about intervention for reading failure. In the first section, we will describe how RTI models of reading instruction will affect the daily practices of future educators in American public schools. Next we will discuss a model called **Positive Behavioral Interventions and Supports (PBIS)** that seeks to address behavioral problems in school in a manner that is almost identical to the RTI model. Finally, we will briefly summarize how a broad concept like **UDL** might look for a classroom teacher seeking to effectively reach students with vastly different needs and learning preferences. We will highlight the role of technology in expanding access to learning and instructional possibilities.

RESPONSE TO INTERVENTION

According to the National Center on Responsiveness to Intervention, RTI is a process in which

> schools identify students at-risk for poor learning outcomes, monitor student progress, provide evidence-based interventions and adjust the intensity and nature of those interventions depending on a student's responsiveness, and identify students with learning disabilities (NCRTI, 2010).

Response to Intervention provides a framework for teachers to allocate resources in direct relation to the needs of children and to help children learn more effectively (Tilly, 2008). Models of RTI may look different in each school, but they consistently include multiple levels, or tiers. The *responsiveness* of students to evidence-based interventions in the RTI process provides a basis for decisions about instructional needs. The guiding principle of RTI should be to create a system of implementation that is simple, effective, and sustainable over time (VanDerHeyden, 2008). In an effective system, **teachers are able to provide faster, more effective intervention by using data to decide who needs help, how much help is needed, and, once the intervention is completed, whether or not the help was successful**. When interventions are not successful, data indicate the need to try something more intense before the gap in academic performance widens. This is a major shift in the practices of classroom teachers because data is used to inform instructional practices and change student outcomes before it is too late (i.e., academic failure).

© Rob Marmion, 2015. Used under license from Shutterstock, Inc.

One major change that comes with RTI is that **services become available to students in a more proactive way**. Traditionally, general and special education have functioned as two separate systems. There was no system in place to catch the kids who fell into the "gray area" of ineligibility when they were tested for a disability (Tilly, 2008). Students in the gray area experienced significant problems in class, but their test scores did not indicate a learning disability. This approach to identification was known as the IQ discrepancy model or the "wait to fail" model. In contrast, the RTI model ensures that all children are given the opportunity to learn to their greatest potential within the regular classroom environment because it provides a framework for identifying problems, intervening, and improving performance. In an RTI model, classroom teachers have the responsibility to provide research-based interventions and determine whether the student responds instead of waiting for the student to fail. Through RTI, general and special educators are able to help all students through high quality instruction in the general education classroom and close monitoring of progress.

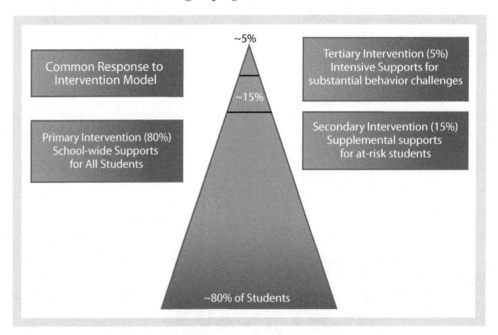

Figure 15.1. Three-Tiered Intervention

Two models of RTI are recognized in the literature: **a standard treatment protocol model** and a **problem solving model**.

- In a standard treatment protocol model, *students with similar academic problems are grouped for interventions*. The student's response to instruction is monitored with progress monitoring probes and data determining whether adjustments need to be made in instruction.
- In a problem solving model, *a team studies individual student data and makes decisions* about which intervention to use and how long the intervention should be used for the student.

Certain characteristics are shared by both RTI models. For example, both approaches use multiple tiers of research-based interventions increasing in intensity and duration. Both approaches also use progress monitoring data to determine responsiveness to instruction. No matter which model is used, RTI has been found effective in improving student performance, providing support for academic and/or behavioral issues, and addressing the diverse needs of students.

RTI is implemented by teachers; however, in light of federal and state mandates such as NCLB (2001) and IDEA (2004), data and information for decision-making within the RTI model is relevant and meaningful to administrators also. When universal screening and progress monitoring measures are administered with high fidelity, administrators can use data to inform educational decisions such as instructional programs, allocation of resources, staff distribution, staff development, and scheduling.

Response to Intervention and Proactive Approaches to Supporting Reading Development

Following the research synthesis report entitled *Preventing Reading Difficulties in Young Children* (Snow, Burns, & Griffin, 1998), Congress mandated a review of the research to determine what works to help students become proficient readers. The National Reading Panel (NRP, 2000) was the largest, evidence-based review ever conducted on how children learn to read. Over 100,000 research studies were reviewed by members of the panel to determine effective approaches to teach children to read and to provide information about reading development.

Based on findings, the panel identified the empirically-validated foundational skills referred to as the "big ideas" in reading (Good et al., 2001). *These "big ideas" of reading were found as the skills necessary to include when teaching reading, including: a)* **phonemic awareness**, b) **phonics**, c) **fluency**, d) **vocabulary**, and e) **text comprehension**. Children need to gain these important skills in order to become independent readers. Findings from the NRP are summarized in Table 15.1.

Table 15.1. Summary of Findings from National Reading Panel Report of the Critical Components in Reading Instruction (NICHD, 2000).

Topic Area	Findings and Determinations
Phonemic Awareness	Teaching children to manipulate phonemes in words significantly improves reading and spelling more than instruction without PA.
Phonics	Systematic beginning phonics instruction in early grades had a positive and significant effect on decoding, spelling, and comprehension of text. Phonics instruction in later grades improved decoding and spelling, but did not improve comprehension.
Fluency	Guided, repeated oral reading procedures resulted in positive impact on word recognition, fluency, and comprehension when guidance from teacher, peer, or parent was included.
Vocabulary	Vocabulary instruction leads to gains in comprehension. Vocabulary should be taught indirectly and directly actively engaging the student with repetition and multiple exposures to words in rich context or with the use of computer.
Comprehension	Teaching a combination of reading comprehension techniques to recall information, answer questions, generate questions, and summarize text was found to improve student performance.

In order to change outcomes for students, each of the critical components in reading must be a part of daily instruction in the classroom. Additionally, assessment of student performance is critical to success; however, summative data gathered at the end of a grading period is not enough. Ongoing, formative assessment data should be gathered on a regular basis. Formative data provides the classroom teacher with the knowledge needed to make instructional decisions regarding instructional changes.

Curriculum-Based Measurement (CBM)

In an RTI model, Curriculum-Based Measurement (CBM) procedures can be used to assess skills and determine whether interventions are effective for students. Curriculum Based Measures (CBM) are brief, repeatable fluency measures that assess a broad range of academic skills reflecting end-of-year goals. Reading curriculum-based measurement (R-CBM: Shinn, 1989) is a widely accepted, empirically valid and reliable index of reading and has been identified as a strategy for monitoring yearly progress (U.S. Department of Education, 2002).

One example of a CBM approach is oral reading fluency (ORF). There is both theoretical and empirical support for the use of fluency measures to assess skills.

With oral reading fluency measures, students read a passage of approximately 250 words under timed conditions, while examiners score words correct and errors per minute.

Deno (1989) promoted the development and use of standardized, locally-normed curriculum-based assessment for decision making. Hasbrouck and Tindal (1992) developed large-scale norms for ORF in order to address concerns with local norms. With large-scale norms for ORF, students' ORF scores can be compared to norms from a large group of students at the same grade level who took the same test. Standardized CBM procedures were used to conduct 1-minute timed oral reading samples from at least two grade level passages for 7,000 to 9,000 students in second through fifth grades in five states. The curriculum-based norms established by Hasbrouck and Tindal "serve as benchmarks to rank student performance" (p. 42). Through extensive study of ORF, Hasbrouck and Tindal (2006) recently published updated norms. Updated norms for each grade level can be found in Table 15.2.

Table 15.2. Oral Reading Fluency Norms for Grades 1-5 (50th Percentile)

Grade	Fall WCPM	Winter WCPM	Spring WCPM	Avg. Imp./wk
1	N/A	23	53	1.9
2	51	72	89	1.2
3	71	92	107	1.1
4	94	112	123	0.9
5	110	127	139	0.9

*WCPM = words correct per minute

Dynamic Indicators of Basic Early Literacy Skills

An assessment committee from the Institute for the Development of Educational Achievement was formed to conduct analysis of reading instruments. The committee found **Dynamic Indicators of Basic Early Literacy Skills Next (DIBELS NEXT)** to be an appropriate reading assessment instrument for local education agencies to use in screening and progress monitoring one or more essential reading components at one or more grade level (Kame'enui et al., 2002). DIBELS Next is a set of standardized, individually administered, fluency measures developed by researchers at the University of Oregon (DIBELS Next; Good & Kaminski, 2011). The subtests were designed to evaluate the development of early literacy development and are available for download free of charge at https://dibels.org/next.html for grades K-6. Seven subtests make up the DIBELS Next curriculum-based assessment: First Sound Fluency (FSF), Letter Naming Fluency (LNF), Phoneme Segmentation Fluency (PSF), Nonsense Word Fluency (NWF), Oral Reading Fluency (ORF), Retell Fluency (RTF), and Word Use Fluency (WUF). While being timed for one minute, students are asked to complete tasks including the following: identifying the correct picture based on initial letter sound (FSF), naming upper and lower-case letters (LNF), segmenting words into individual sounds (PSF), reading

CVC nonsense words (NWF), reading connected text at appropriate grade level (ORF), retelling passage (RTF), and using words in sentences (WUF).

For **Universal Screening** (e.g. all students in school or grade level), the DIBELS Next system allows three or four benchmark assessment periods during each school year. Additionally, multiple forms of FSF, PSF, NWF, and ORF are available in order to allow for more frequent assessment of students whose scores are below benchmark level. Schools can use scores to identify students in need of supplementary instruction. Each grade level has different subtests emphasized on a continuum of increasingly more difficult skills. For example, FSF and LNF are important skills early in the year for kindergarten students. For FSF, kindergarten students should be able to identify 30 correct initial sounds per minute by winter of kindergarten. The critical skill of kindergarten is PSF and students are expected to segment 35 sounds per minute by the end of kindergarten. NWF is the critical skill for first grade and students should be able to identify 50 sounds per minute by the middle of first grade. ORF is emphasized from the winter of first grade through sixth grade. The benchmark goal for ORF is 40 correct words per minute (wcpm) in first grade, 90 wcpm in second grade, 110 wcpm in third grade, 118 wcpm in fourth grade, 124 wcpm in fifth grade, and 125 wcpm in sixth grade. There are not established benchmark goals for RTF; however, in order to demonstrate adequate comprehension, it is recommended for students to meet ORF goal and retell at least 25% of passage.

AIMSweb Maze

Another curriculum-based assessment currently used in schools is *AIMSweb Maze Curriculum-Based Measurement* (Maze-CBM; Edformation, 2009) using *Edformation's Standard Reading Maze Passages*. AIMSweb Maze-CBM has been proven to be a reliable and valid measure of student's reading comprehension skills. Maze is a timed, multiple-choice cloze task in which the student completes the passage by choosing the correct word from three choices given in parenthesis. Maze is administered using standardized directions. Recently, Maze-CBM was evaluated by members of the National Technical Review Committee (TRC) of the National Center on Response to Intervention (NCRTI, 2009). The Maze measure fully met all seven standards, giving it the highest rating possible for predictive validity and reliability.

There is a complete list of instruments and information about student progress monitoring on the National Center on Response to Intervention's (NCRTI) website. The URL for this website is http://www.rti4success.org. The website features a chart of screening and progress monitoring tools and the results of the reviews of the Technical Review Committee (TRC). This committee is comprised of national experts in the components of RTI. Members have established a standard process to evaluate tools that can be used in an RTI context.

Pulling It All Together: RTI at the Classroom Level

Response to Intervention serves two primary purposes: 1) to provide early intervention by addressing student needs through multiple tiers of increasingly intensive research-based interventions, and 2) to identify students who have a learning disability. Brief screening measures are given three times per year (i.e., fall, winter, and spring); this information may be used to identify students at risk for academic failure. In order to have meaningful data, the screenings must be done with fidelity using a research-validated instrument. Once struggling students have been identified through the universal screening process, teachers in the general education setting must provide students with research-based intervention. In order to monitor the progress of these students, the teacher must also use formative assessments to determine if the students are responding to the intervention.

Research has shown that implementing research-validated approaches to reading results in a decrease in the number of students who require special education services (Foorman, 2003). It is essential for teachers in the general education classroom to use a research-validated, comprehensive core reading program for all students. An effective comprehensive core reading program helps teachers provide instruction in a systematic and consistent manner; specific skills are introduced in a certain way and at a specific time.

Research has also shown that prevention is the most effective early intervention. Prevention can take place in the form of differentiated classroom instruction (Foorman & Moats, 2004). Core reading instruction should occur for at least 90 minutes each day including whole-class, small-group, paired, and one-on-one instruction for all students. In order to determine whether students are responding to the instruction, teachers must consistently monitor the progress of the students. When teachers consistently gather data and analyze the results, they can quickly see when students are not making adequate progress. For students who fall below their aim line (target), more focused instruction is necessary to supplement the core reading instruction. These students need small group, supplemental instruction each day using a research-validated instructional program. The time period required for supplemental instruction depends on whether the school is implementing Standard Treatment Protocol or Problem Solving Model of RTI. In the Standard Treatment Protocol Model of RTI, this supplemental instruction would be at least 30 minutes in duration. In the Problem Solving Model, a decision would be made by a team to determine an intervention to match the need of the student. The time for implementation may be as little as 10 minutes or as much as 30 minutes.

Regardless of the model of RTI, consensus findings of the National Reading Panel report (NRP, 2000) should be considered by teachers in choosing an instructional program for supplemental instruction. Explicit instruction in each of the five "big ideas" of reading should be included in the instructional time period (Foorman & Moats, 2004). This instruction should include modeling, multiple examples, corrective feedback, and multiple opportunities to respond. A student's number of opportunities to respond to instruction is directly linked with student academic performance (Greenwood, Delquadri, & Hall, 1984). Teachers may choose a scripted reading program for supplemental reading instruction because scripted instruction increases the number of opportunities to respond to instruction (Cooke, Galloway, Kretlow, & Helf, 2010).

Despite high-quality instruction, there are a small percentage of students who do not respond to instruction and require additional intervention to make adequate progress. When a student falls into this category, more intense intervention is necessary. This intervention would be implemented with more frequent sessions, sessions longer in duration, or sessions with very low teacher-student ratio. In a **Standard Treatment Protocol model of RTI,** *this instructional time period is typically 40-60 minutes and instruction is typically delivered by a highly trained instructor, such as a reading specialist.* **In a Problem Solving model of RTI,** *the team would meet to decide the instruction necessary to meet the needs of the individual student.* Instruction could vary from 10 additional minutes to 30 additional minutes of instruction. No matter which model of RTI is used, it is crucial to monitor the progress of students who require this level of individualized instruction to determine if they are responding to instruction. It is also imperative that general education classroom teachers continue delivering core reading instruction for these students. **Intervention must be in addition to standard instruction, rather than a replacement for core reading instruction** (Hall, 2006).

Positive Behavioral Interventions and Supports for Classroom Teachers

As more and more diverse student populations are being included in the general education curriculum, today's teachers struggle with ways in which to manage their classrooms while still meeting state and federal academic standards. Students either with or at-risk for diverse learning and behavioral deficits, make up at least half of the student population, especially within inclusive classrooms. It is not surprising that teachers often cite behavioral challenges as a major concern in the classroom (Martella, Nelson, & Marchand-Martella, 2003). Teachers learn early on that behavioral challenges are closely tied to academic difficulties, making it difficult to establish positive learning environments for all students.

When considering the multidimensional nature of today's student population, as well as the demands placed on teachers to accommodate those diversities, it is easy to see how many teachers often feel frustrated in their attempts to meet academic standards. It is also not surprising that administrators report nearly half of all behavior problems occur in the classroom (Simonsen, Fairbanks, Briesch, Myers, & Sugai, 2008). As a result, these persistent behavior problems have negative effects on teaching, opportunities for students to learn, and student engagement. In classrooms with accomplished teachers, student engagement is high, and occurs as a result of a combination of classroom management skills and effective instructional techniques (Taylor, Pressley & Pearson, 2000). Teachers who effectively manage their classrooms not only demonstrate an awareness of their students' diverse academic needs, but also *possess a set of behavior management skills necessary to meet those needs* (Marzano, 2003).

Connection Between Academics and Behavior

There is little debate on the connection between academic and behavior deficits in students (Kauffman, 1997), but the causal nature of each deficit is unclear. Many researchers posit that academic deficits result in problem behaviors (Maag, 1998; Walker, Colvin & Ramsey, 1995) while others suggest that it is problem behaviors that lead to deficits in academics (Gunter & Denny, 1998). Coincidentally, most students referred for special education services are referred for learning difficulties. In addition to poor academic achievement, students with learning problems are often at-risk for behavior problems (Bennett, Brown, Boyle, Raccine, & Offord, 2003). As a group, these students tend to experience academic difficulties that are associated with their behavior problems and typically demonstrate social skills deficits relating to adults and peers. According to Lane (2004), two patterns demonstrating the link between school achievement and behavior problems are evident. First, students with behavior problems demonstrate an established pattern of underachievement. Second, academic difficulties can be strongly linked to conduct disorder and adolescent delinquent behavior.

When achievement problems are experienced along with behavior problems, students generally earn lower grades, have higher retention rates, have problems passing minimum competency tests, and experience higher dropout rates than their peers. Specific deficits in reading achievement appear to negatively effect children with behavior problems, as researchers have established that below average functioning and deficiencies in reading exist (Coleman & Vaughn, 2000). When coupled with these specific reading deficits, behavior problems often occur in the classroom, leading to frequent discipline referrals for misbehavior during academic tasks (Scott, Nelson, & Liaupsin, 2001). When these academic and behavior deficits persist, interventions become less effective, and result in school failure. Adapted from Scott, Nelson, and Liaupsin's (2001) description of the cycle of academic and behavioral failure, Figure 15.2 demonstrates the cycle that is perpetuated in students with academic deficits and challenging behaviors. The key to ending the cycle of failure is early intervention delivered through effective strategy instruction in positive learning environments (Gunter, Hummel, & Conroy, 1998; Scott et al., 2001).

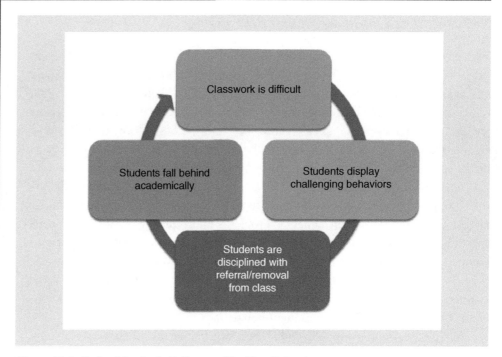

Figure 15.2. Cycle of Academic Failure and Problem Behavior

Regardless of their position, researchers agree that academic *and* behavioral deficits create challenging instructional environments for both teachers and students. With the growing number of students who are at risk for academic failure not being identified as eligible for special education services, many students never receive the academic or behavioral interventions necessary for school success (Bos & Vaughn, 1998). Unfortunately, the majority of the students with behavioral and academic problems are not identified as eligible for special education services until third or fourth grade; by then the probability of successful intervention has substantially diminished. The 2004 Reauthorization of the Individuals with Disabilities Act (IDEA) promotes the use of **positive behavioral intervention strategies and supports,** as well as **functional behavioral assessments (FBA)** as fundamental methods to address behavioral and academic problems in school (Sugai et al.). Providing a climate of positive behavioral support meets an important need for today's students, as does including them in regular academic and social educational settings.

BACKGROUND ON PBIS

Positive Behavioral Interventions and Supports (PBIS) is an approach utilizing the application of systems and interventions to achieve acceptable changes in behavior (Sugai et al., 2000). Proactive, rather than reactive in nature, PBIS is a behaviorally-based approach that links research-validated practice to the environments of teaching and learning (Sugai et al.). When implemented on a school-wide basis, PBIS utilizes three levels of behavioral support. The first level envelops all students with universal interventions/structure and is effective for approximately 85% of the student population. The second level (5% to 15% of school population) includes students at risk for problem behaviors needing specialized group interventions (social skills instruction). The third level (1% to 5%) provides specialized individual interventions for students who exhibit chronic/intense problem behaviors (Sugai et al.). Thus, each student in the school gets the type and degree of behavioral support he/she needs.

PBIS provides procedures of encouraging expected behavior as well as discouraging problem behavior (Lewis and Sugai, 1999). This is often a difficult task when considering the many ways students bring diversity to inclusive classrooms, making it challenging for teachers to create socially equitable classroom environments. For as many different learning styles and needs that exist in the average inclusive classroom, there are as many different social behaviors and deficits to consider. For this reason, many experts agree that school and classroom settings provide the perfect context in which the current generation can be taught much about social behavior (Sugai et al., 2000). Although social skills and the concept of teaching social behaviors has often been considered to be part of the "hidden curriculum," the collaborative nature of instruction that often occurs in inclusive classrooms provides an excellent backdrop for teaching students to behave in socially responsible ways. PBIS has been considered a useful tool in providing a level playing field in which all students can access both the academic and social curriculum.

PBIS is typically applied across a variety of school settings and primarily at school-wide, classroom, and individual levels. Currently, over 5000 school districts across 40 states are implementing PBIS at the school-wide level (U.S. Department of Education, 2005). Initiated as a way to address problem behaviors and create positive school climates, many schools found that after implementing PBIS interventions, increases in academic achievement and decreases in inappropriate behaviors were observed (Texas Behavior Support Initiative, 2004).

School-Wide Positive Behavioral Interventions and Supports

The goal of school-wide PBIS is to foster the growth of a school culture that not only prevents problem behaviors but also encourages appropriate behavior (George, Peshak, Harrower, & Knoster, 2003). For many schools, the results are fewer discipline referrals, increased time for learning tasks, and ultimately improved student achievement. The school-wide PBIS model also seeks to prevent the occurrence of escalating behavior problems, thereby reducing the need for intervention at the secondary and third (tertiary) levels for most students.

School-wide PBIS contains six steps that are generally adhered to when implementing interventions (George et al., 2003):
1. Foundation for collaboration is established;
2. Faculty involvement is secured;
3. Data-based management is established;
4. Brainstorming session is held for strategy selection and formation of action plan;

5. Action plan is implemented;
6. Continuous monitoring and evaluation of plan is implemented.

The end result of this process is a school-based system of behavior management that is both consistent and supported by the entire school. School-wide systems of PBIS are most effective when there is school-wide buy-in of behavioral expectations and consequences; it requires that all students and adults in the school environment accept the strategies that have been set forth in the school's plan (Strout, 2005). To be successful and obtain universal buy-in across the school, all stakeholders must participate in the process.

Classroom Level Positive Behavioral Interventions and Supports

Whether or not your school has chosen to implement PBIS as a school-wide intervention for dealing with behavioral challenges, there are many strategies that can be implemented at the classroom-wide level. Within each classroom, teachers bring diverse teaching styles and students display unique academic and behavioral characteristics. In fact, research has demonstrated that teachers often adapt intensity of instruction and classroom management procedures based on student need (Miller, 2007). In classrooms where more students struggle academically and behaviorally, teachers are more likely to use strategies in differentiated instruction and rely more heavily on management systems to provide the structure needed to meet student needs.

It's not surprising, however, that teachers working in inclusive classrooms report that most of the behaviors that occur on a daily basis are not the violent, intense behaviors that occur in isolation, but rather the disruptive behaviors that often take away from instructional time (Sprague & Walker, 2000). Behaviors such as being off task, not following simple directions, non-compliance, and being disrespectful are the types of challenging behaviors teachers encounter on a daily basis. Implementing basic management techniques that can be delivered across three tiers of intervention will prevent most disruptive behaviors. Figure 15.3 provides a visual representation of the three levels of intervention that can be applied for both academic and behavioral challenges in the classroom. As you can see, the same tiers of intervention used in the school-wide PBIS model can be applied at the classroom level when identifying interventions based on student need. To be effective, intervention decisions:

*   should be based on data collected on student behaviors,
*   must be tailored to meet individual student's needs,
*   should involve continuous progress monitoring, and
*   should integrate evidence-based behavioral interventions.

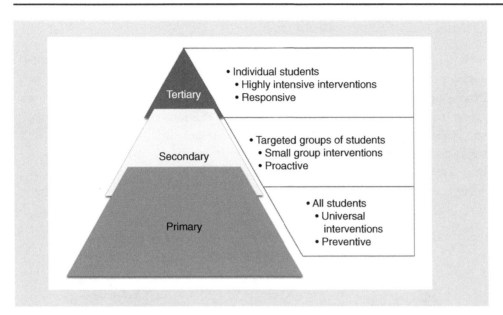

Figure 15.3. Three-Tier Intervention Systems for Classwide PBIS

Effective management strategies typically include environmental factors, instructional variables, and teacher behaviors. Environmental factors relate to classroom arrangement, student grouping, and the physical attributes of the classroom (Evertson, Emmer & Worsham, 2003). Instructional variables constitute the teaching of rules and procedures, as well as planning, delivery, and methods of instruction. Teacher behaviors are related to use of reinforcement and praise, relationships of teachers and students, and teacher actions (Evertson et al). When management strategies are implemented effectively, an increase in student engagement occurs, disruptive behaviors decrease, and use of instructional time increases; all resulting in improved academic achievement (Wang et al., 1993). When teachers are able to spend more time on instruction and less time dealing with discipline problems, student achievement improves. Effective management of inappropriate behaviors is a key element in promoting an environment conducive to student learning (Marzano, Marzano, & Pickering, 2003).

As a classroom teacher, you will no doubt hear the term *evidenced based practices* several times during your teaching career. Most researchers within the field of education will agree that there are several ways to define these practices. The U.S. Department of Education through the What Works Clearinghouse (2006), defines evidenced based practices as those that:

- use a sound experimental research design and analytical procedure to test the effectiveness of the practice,
- provide empirically valid results of the effects of the practice,
- provide clear procedures for implementation of the practice,
- include replication of the practice across several settings, and
- provides evidence of the practice's sustainability.

Evidence-Based Classroom Supports

For as long as there have been teachers and students, there have been management practices used to maximize instructional time in classrooms. After examining two decades of research in classroom level management strategies and interventions, several evidence-based practices were identified (Simonsen et al., 2008). In keeping with the idea of using three-tiered levels of intervention in the classroom, let's dissect each tier within Figure 15.4, and divide these evidence-based practices into three categories across each of the three tiers: preventive (primary), proactive (secondary), and responsive (tertiary).

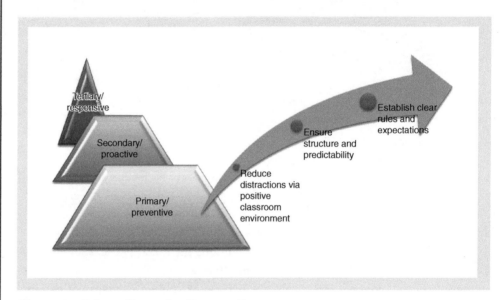

Figure 15.4. Primary/Preventive Classroom Supports

Primary/Preventive Evidence-Based Classroom Level Supports

- *Reduce the opportunity for distractions by creating classroom environments that promote positive behavior.* Your classroom arrangement should be designed so that furniture does not obstruct the flow of instruction. Students should be able to move freely about the room. You should be able to gain access to each student quickly and easily. There should be clearly marked areas for the teacher only and areas in which students are free to occupy. Finally, your seating arrangement should reflect your knowledge of each student's need. For example, students with hearing or visual impairments may need to sit closer to the front of the room.

- *Ensure structure and predictability by teaching classroom routines.* There are both teacher and student routines that need to be followed in every classroom. Teacher routines include procedures for grading papers, making classroom announcements, and routines for substitute teachers. Student routines may need to be instructed on specific routines involving homework, handling of classroom materials, policies for snacks, using the restroom, and group work, and procedures for storage of personal items such as book bags, backpacks, and lunch boxes.

- *Establish clear classroom expectations or rules, and teach them the same way you would approach academic instruction.* Class rules should be positively stated and should be limited to no more than five. You cannot assume students know what a rule means, so it is important to teach the rules as you would, say math facts or spelling. Rules should be clearly posted in an area where all students have access to them. Students should be involved in the creation of classroom rules and expectations, as they are more likely to be followed when students take ownership for something they helped to create.

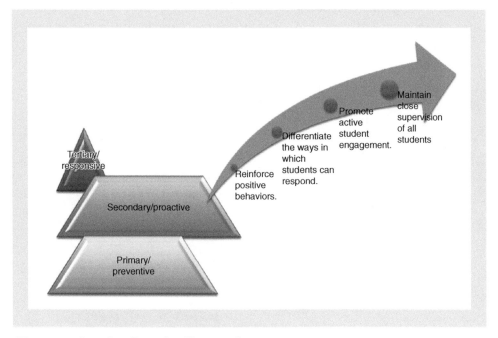

Figure 15.5. Secondary/Proactive Classroom Supports

Secondary/Proactive Evidence-Based Classroom Level Supports

- *Reinforce positive behaviors.* As teachers, we have a tendency to focus more of our attention on problem behaviors than desirable behaviors. It is important, however, to **reinforce appropriate behaviors.** Some theorists suggest practice in which teachers reinforce desirable behavior four times more often than they redirect inappropriate behaviors. Reinforcement should be specific and genuine in order to be effective. If corrections need to be made, follow it with a positive. Always make sure students know what they did right and wrong.
- *Differentiate the ways in which students can respond.* Provide students with a variety of ways to show you they have mastered skills. Differentiate the ways in which students have access to the material. The use of different grouping methods helps students see the ways their peers perform during class activities. Using a mixture of whole class, small group, and peer instruction provides students with the opportunity to practice different skills. Responses

can be oral or written, independent or cooperative, and can be teacher or student directed.

- *Promote active student engagement.* Engage students in academic tasks by allowing them different ways in which they can participate in activities. Whole group, choral monitoring is one way to provide instant recognition of missed skills. Students can also perform in individual or group settings that are evaluated by the teacher. Finally, teachers can monitor particular academic or behavioral issues through continuous monitoring of student behavior, or by intermittently checking behavior during particular parts of the school day.
- *Maintain close supervision of all students.* One of the most powerful tools a teacher has is her own presence in the classroom. Teacher proximity is a proactive approach to eliminating or reducing the chance for occurrence of inappropriate behaviors. Teachers should always be moving about the classroom, or scanning the room throughout their lessons. Let students know you are aware of them by taking part in their small group discussions. Provide immediate reminders when behaviors start to occur and praise those who are making good behavioral choices.

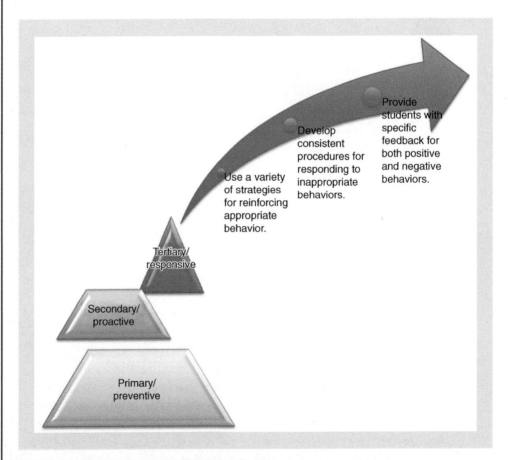

Figure 15.6. Tertiary/Responsive Classroom Supports

Tertiary/Responsive Evidence-Based Classroom Level Supports

- *Use a variety of strategies for reinforcing appropriate behavior.* First and foremost, reinforcers should be developmentally and contextually appropriate in order to be effective. They should also be culturally acceptable to the student. There are many different types of rewards students can and will respond to. The easiest way to find out what motivates a student is to ask. Reinforcer surveys are excellent ways to find out what students are willing to work for. Some students respond well to social or tangible reinforcers while others may want to participate in a preferred activity. You should also decide the frequency with which you will provide reinforcers. They can also be immediate or delayed. Younger children often require more immediate access to reinforcers while older students may be willing to work at delayed access to reinforcers.

- *Develop consistent procedures for responding to inappropriate behaviors.* Students should always be aware of what is expected of them. If and when misbehavior occurs, it is important to respond to these behaviors quickly. Provide a series of steps that include prompting, restating the rule, making sure the student understands the rule, and then reinforcing appropriate demonstration of the rule. It is important to post the consequences for rule infractions so that students know what to expect if rules are broken.

- *Provide students with specific feedback for both positive and negative behaviors.* Students will need to know specifically what they did that was right or wrong, so they can learn from their behaviors. When providing positive reinforcement, be sure to clearly state to the child what positive behavior is the source of that reinforcement. Also, make the reinforcement contextual by stating not only what you liked, but where it is appropriate and why.

Teacher Reflection

As a teacher, you should always be aware of your actions and their consequences in the classroom. Just as students' behaviors are continuously monitored, you should also be aware of your own management behaviors. Teachers who consistently monitor their own instructional behaviors are more likely to develop effective classroom level supports because they are more aware of their own effects on student behaviors. Early intervention is key, so the sooner you can recognize that an intervention is not effective, the sooner you can begin to implement another strategy. It is also valuable for teachers to evaluate the learning environment to determine if students are responding well to whatever classroom system you have put into place.

Use the *Classroom Management Practice* checklist provided by the Positive Behavioral Interventions and Supports network in Table 15.3 to monitor your own practices.

Table 15.3. Classroom Management Practice Checklist. Adapted from the OSEP Technical Assistance Center on Positive Behavioral Interventions and Supports.

Classroom Management Practices Checklist	Rating	
1. Classroom is organized to reduce distractions and crowding of students in particular areas.	Yes	No
2. Structure and predictability of classroom procedures are prioritized.	Yes	No
3. Class rules and expectations taught by the teacher are brief (3-5), positively stated, clear, and consistently reinforced in daily activities.	Yes	No
4. Reinforcement of appropriate behaviors is prioritized over attention to inappropriate behaviors in student-teacher interactions.	Yes	No
5. Inappropriate behaviors are quickly redirected without undue emphasis or distraction from classroom activities.	Yes	No
6. Specific feedback is used in response to both social and academic behaviors.	Yes	No
7. Active supervision and proximity are used to maintain appropriate behavior.	Yes	No
8. Instruction is highly engaging and interactive.	Yes	No
9. Students are engaged in active responding and multiple means of student-teacher interaction.	Yes	No
10. Instructional strategies are varied to better recognize students' use of appropriate behavior.	Yes	No
Overall classroom management score: # Yes _____ 10-8 = EXCELLENT 7-5 = AVERAGE <5 = NEEDS IMPROVEMENT		

INDIVIDUAL LEVEL BEHAVIORAL SUPPORTS

After attempting school-wide or classroom level behavioral supports, it may become apparent that some students are not responding to those levels of intervention and may require more intensive supports on an individualized basis. First, assessment of the behavior must occur. This is often done by conducting a functional behavior assessment (FBA). In the reauthorization of the Individuals with Disabilities Education Act (IDEA) of 1997, the use of FBA was mandated along with the use of PBIS to help with the assessment of chronic behavior problems (Wheeler & Richey, 2010). FBA has been identified and used as a process of not only identifying problem behaviors, but the factors that are maintaining those behaviors (Sugai, Horner, Dunlap, Hieneman, Lewis, Nelson, et al., 2000). One of the hallmarks of functional assessment involves the use of assessments that are both direct and indirect, and occur in the individual's natural environment. Direct observations can occur within the context of the individual's natural environment (school, home, community, or work). Indirect methods such as informal interviews with or checklists completed by teachers, parents, or siblings can provide useful information regarding the individual's behavior. Because the purpose of conducting an FBA is to determine those specific factors that are reinforcing the individual's behavior, information from the FBA can be used to create individualized interventions.

Once an FBA has been conducted and the function of the behavior has been identified, an intervention plan is developed. Although the Reauthorization of IDEA in 2004 states that a behavior intervention plan (BIP) must be created based on the results of the FBA, there are no guidelines that state which components must be part of this plan (Wheeler & Richey, 2010). Evidence based practices should be considered as part of those interventions included at the individual or tertiary level of intervention, as with other tiers within the PBIS model. Two examples of evidence-based practices that can be used with individual students are behavior contracting and the use of token economy systems. Although many teachers implement a token economy system universally in the classroom, the use of such interventions should be based on student need. Not all students will require this intense level of intervention to succeed in the classroom.

Behavior Contracting

A behavior contract is quite simply just as the name implies: a document that is created between the teacher and student that specifies expected behavior, rewards/consequences, and time frames for carrying out the contract. The contract can include several parties such as teachers, parents, siblings, or anyone who is interested in improving the problem behaviors identified by functional assessment or other data collection techniques. According to Kelley and Stokes (1984), steps to creating a behavior contract include the following:

1. Define the problem behavior.
2. Select reinforcers and consequences for appropriate or inappropriate behaviors.
3. State the purpose for why the contract is necessary.
4. Negotiate the terms of the contract as agreed upon by the student and teacher or interested parties.
5. Write and sign the contract.
6. Post the contract so that all parties are reminded of the terms stated in the contract.

Token Economies

The use of token economies in the classroom has been around for decades. These types of reward systems were first introduced as a way to change problem behaviors in individuals with mental retardation in institutional settings (Ayllon & Azrin, 1968). Today, token economies are still used to shape problem behaviors in classroom settings, especially with students who display emotional and behavioral disorders. The premise behind a token economy within the classroom is that some sort of point system is associated with specific desired behaviors and students can earn points to exchange for desired items at a later time. Tokens or points can come in many forms, with many classrooms relying on a monetary system for "purchasing" reinforcers such as food items, toys, stickers, social activities, or some other desired activity. According to Wheeler and Richey (2010), there are some important elements to include in any classroom token economy system:

1. Clearly define the behavior desired within the classroom or other setting.
2. Select the tokens to be used (stickers, point cards, bingo chips, class money).
3. Identify the reinforcers that are to be exchanged for the tokens. These should be highly desirable items that students will be willing to work for.
4. Decide how often tokens will be distributed and how frequently the tokens can be exchanged for the reinforcing items.
5. Include all staff members in the token economy system so that they are clear about the implementation of the token economy system.
6. Put a plan in place for fading the token economy system so that behavior moves from extrinsically motivating to intrinsically motivating.

Universal Design for Learning at the Classroom Level

The term Universal Design (UD) derives from a movement in architecture, which has as its major premise that buildings and public spaces should be designed so they will be accessible to all citizens. The application of this terminology to education implies that the same kind of diversity of needs in general society that would lead to architectural considerations, also exists in schools and should lead to greater considerations of accessibility in instructional design. Essentially, UDL assumes that learning experiences will be designed such that instruction benefits students of all abilities, interests, and backgrounds (Rose & Meyer, 2002). UDL implies a move away from the "one-size-fits-all" approach to teaching and learning that has traditionally characterized education in U.S. public schools. The approach is not dependent on technology; however, instructional technologies, emerging accessibility programs, and availability of digital material have propelled the concept of UDL forward in the thinking of many educators (Edyburn, 2005).

Universal Design for Learning stems from certain assumptions about student diversity—essentially, that it is natural for students in our classrooms to differ from each other in a number of ways. **Ultimately, UDL is the instructional response to inclusive classrooms.** Classrooms today include students with disabilities, varying background experiences, levels of motivation, as well as cultural/linguistic differences. Furthermore, most students served by special education have primarily academic disabilities and if we are to be consistent with the thinking of RTI and PBIS, it simply makes sense to anticipate diversity of ability in academic contexts so that we can prepare for it. We can *preempt difficulty rather than retrofitting*. Often, students whose abilities or learning profiles are inconsistent with the design of instruction in school, will fall behind and become marginalized by the overall educational system. A UDL vision would suggest that the curriculum must be flexible—allowing all students, including those *in the margins*, to access needed support.

When attempting to implement UDL in the classroom, teachers approach an instructional unit with a specific mindset. Over an extended period of time, teachers will provide students multiple ways of accessing content knowledge, engage them in the content in a way that is interesting and personally relevant, and allow them to demonstrate competence in varied ways. In contrast to many approaches in education, this is not a pre-packaged program and not every lesson will explicitly include all of these elements. UDL lessons are goal-driven. Teachers must have a strong sense of the relevance of the current lesson and how this lesson builds upon prior knowledge, and prepares students for the next level of content (Hall et al., 2005).

This instructional design concept is an overarching framework for teaching that aligns well with the current diversity of students in public schools (i.e., very diverse backgrounds, learning needs, learning preferences, and academic abilities/disabilities). The goal is to design instructional experiences in schools that will be accessible to all students. Clearly, designing instruction for everyone is not easy, but technology, in particular, makes it more possible.

A goal of UDL is to identify and remove barriers in the curriculum. The intent of a lesson needs to be considered, and multiple ways to acquire the content and demonstrate knowledge must be allowed. By creating a flexible learning environment, limitations of the curriculum for the greatest number of learners can be diminished, thus providing access to all. The traditional practices used in many classrooms don't fit many learners.

UDL Framework: Representation, Expression, and Engagement

Research at the Center for Applied Special Technology and emerging theory related to the way the brain processes information in learning, have lead to a general idea that children in school will benefit from the creation of learning environments that emphasize differentiated learning experiences. Rose & Meyer (2002) refer to three core principles of UDL: **Multiple Means of Representation, Multiple Means of Expression,** and **Multiple Means of Engagement**.

Multiple Means of Representation: Provide multiple and flexible processes for acquiring new knowledge in the classroom. Consider how a concept could be best taught. Is the textbook or printed material the best and only way to teach a concept in your class? Could a video clip or other multimedia tool represent the concept more effectively to a broader audience that may not thrive in a text-driven classroom?

Multiple Means of Expression: Provide a variety of options for students to demonstrate competence regarding a learning objective. Again, consider technological solutions and means of representing knowledge that are not limited to writing assignments.

Multiple Means of Engagement: Consider issues of interest, preference, and motivation when designing instruction. The opportunity to make choices or emphasize an area of interest can positively impact student performance.

Although the principles of UDL mentioned above are important, according to Edyburn (2005), UDL first and foremost seeks to reduce barriers for everyone. Accessibility to rigorous and engaging learning experiences is a fundamental goal. UDL sets the tone that the curriculum should be modified until it reaches as many students as possible, rather than declaring that children who do not thrive in the curriculum are disabled. Rather, books and instruction could be considered disabled if they are not able to meet the learning needs of most or all students. Further, from an efficiency standpoint, accessible instructional design is preferable over the need to create retrofits or awkward accommodations. For example, if six students in a class have substantial difficulty with notetaking, we might make special accommodations for each of those students. From a UDL standpoint, it might make more sense to anticipate problems with notetaking and teach all of the students a shortened strategy for effective notetaking in your class. You might also provide "guided notes" in which students simply fill in the blanks for key concepts. This benefits the students who experience difficulty listening and taking notes, provides an accommodation, and focuses attention on those concepts that are most relevant.

In a classroom where the teacher is attempting to exemplify UDL, there would be a focus on teaching content beyond the standard of traditional instruction—how we were taught in school. Teachers would make efforts to present material in multiple ways including differentiating learning experiences (e.g., direct instruction versus cooperative groups) and providing materials in multiple formats to address learner needs. Teachers might offer students multiple ways to demonstrate their understanding of the content including writing assignments that might use more or less multimedia to express ideas, alternatives to writing assignments (if the writing process is not content relevant), or opportunities to take different types of tests that best match the student's abilities. Finally, consideration of engagement is unique to UDL. The premise of UDL includes attention to the need for students to be engaged in material that is not too easy or too hard and connects with their interests or preferences as learners. The following is a case example of instructional flexibility in an upper elementary classroom that might reflect a UDL framework.

Case Example of Accessibility in Language Arts or Reading Class

A teacher in a 5th grade Language Arts class wants to engage her very diverse group of students in reading great works of literature for their age group. Some of the titles she has selected include:
- *Bridge to Terabithia* by Katherine Paterson
- *Tuck Everlasting* by Natalie Babbitt
- *Bud, Not Buddy* by Christopher Paul Curtis, and
- *A Wrinkle in Time* by Madeleine L'Engle

She knows the students are at different reading levels and these texts, written at the 5th grade level, may prove difficult for some of her students. She plans for this difficulty proactively by thinking about flexible ways to engage her diverse classroom with these great works of children's literature. She could view the differences among her students as frustrating challenges, but *years of experience have taught her that her classes will always be comprised of students with different interests, strengths, weaknesses, background experiences, and preferences for learning. This is only natural.* Although 6 of her 22 students have IEP accommodations, she feels that the most efficient way to address differences in learner needs is to try to create an **accessible learning environment**, one in which supports of difficulty in learning have been embedded in the learning experience. This learning environment is also one in which barriers to learning have been considered and removed whenever possible.

Among her six students with special education needs, five have a specific learning disability, and one student has a significant visual impairment. The student with a visual impairment uses digital materials in class with text-to-speech support for passages to be read aloud. Occasionally, he also uses audio books. Although this is a common form of **Assistive Technology** for students with visual impairments, the teacher has enhanced the likelihood that the student will have materials available to him by establishing an account with **Bookshare** (www.bookshare.org), a federally funded library of digital learning materials that can be downloaded to his laptop at any time to ensure that he is receiving a comparable learning experience.

Among the students with specific learning disability, there are further distinctions to be made in terms of ability and needs in the classroom. Although they would appear very similar in need, in fact, three of the students with SLD have concomitant ADHD, requiring extensive support in organization and focus when reading. One student has the ability to decode and fluently read texts at his grade level, but has a great deal of difficulty with answering questions about the reading that require inferential thinking. He has a very difficult time getting the "big picture" of the text and connecting to what is happening in the story. The other four students with SLD share some commonality in difficulty with fluently reading grade level materials and tend to score at the 2nd to 3rd grade level on tests of passage comprehension. In addition to the six students with IEPs in the class, there are also five students who could be considered English Language Learners. Most of these students are relatively proficient readers in terms of fluency, but experience a great deal of difficulty with vocabulary and connecting the text to their personal experiences. Beyond the students who might receive a "label" of some kind in this class, the other 11 students are also quite unique in their own ways regarding their interests or needs in reading. Some students like to read independently. Some students do best when given the opportunity to discuss the text with the teacher and/ or peers. Among the students who might be considered the "regular kids," there are still a great deal of differences in reading proficiency with the range of performance in passage comprehension extending from 3rd grade to 8th grade.

How might a Language Arts teacher traditionally teach a work of children's literature to class of 5th grade students?

- The teacher might assign "round-robin reading" in which students take turns reading a passage from the text and others listen while waiting for their turn.
- The students might read along with the teacher as she reads to the whole group and then independently answer three questions listed on the white board about the reading.
- The teacher might assign the reading as homework each night and have students meet in book-talk groups to talk about the reading.

Given the considerable diversity in this classroom, it is questionable whether these strategies would meet the reading needs of all or even most of the students in the class.

How does the diversity of this classroom affect how we plan for instruction?

A teacher who deliberately plans to support the learning experiences of these diverse children by creating a flexible and supportive learning environment, is attempting to teach in a manner consistent with UDL. The teacher tries to think of ways that everyone can read the book and come back together with a shared experience of reading a good book while developing enhanced reading skills.

Let us consider what the teacher might do to prepare for a flexible and supportive learning environment:

- Provide time in class or after school for students to read passages to be discussed in class.
- Provide multiple ways to access the text. Options make this scenario consistent with UDL.
  - Offer students a computer-based opportunity to read the text with technology supports like text-to-speech software, so they can listen to the text while following along on the screen.
  - Provide an audio version of the text.
  - Allow peer reading in which two students read quietly together to support fluency.
  - Allow students who prefer independent reading to sit quietly in a comfortable spot in the room and read to themselves.
  - Use a technology-enhanced reading program like **Thinking Reader**. Every student would not need this program, but it could be made available to students who struggle with reading independently and engage well with technology.

©*Terrie L. Zeller, 2015. Used under license from Shutterstock, Inc.*

The Thinking Reader Program

In the case example, the teacher has chosen four very popular and high-quality works of children's literature. She is fortunate that all of these texts are available in a format called *Thinking Reader*. This program was developed by the Center for Applied Special Technology and is currently distributed by a commercial book/software publisher (Edyburn, 2005).

What can Thinking Reader do?

Software designers have worked very hard to actualize the principles of UDL (multiple means of representation, expression, and engagement) in a computer program that presents accessible versions of popular children's books. The books are digitally captured in a computer program that presents the full text of the book on the computer screen using digital text. Digital text is different from text in a book, as you can manipulate digital text. The appearance of the text on the screen can be changed. You can make the text smaller or larger, as you see fit. You can even highlight sections of the text with a virtual highlighter. Also, any digital text can be read aloud with text-to-speech software. The Thinking Reader program offers built-in text-to-speech that is pre-recorded for the entire book similar to an audio book. A high-quality narrator reads the text to the student modeling "the voice in your head" that we try to help students use. The pre-recorded narrator establishes the tone and mood in the text as he or she reads. Further, the text is highlighted on the screen as the narrator reads and assists students in maintaining focus on the words in the passage.

The Thinking Reader books do a great many other things, but perhaps most importantly, they support students in developing comprehension. The program chunks the book into passages and coaches the student through the use of comprehension-fostering reading strategies including *summarizing, questioning, clarifying, predicting, visualizing, feeling, and reflecting* (Palinscar & Brown, 1984). As students attempt to answer the guiding questions, they have the option to seek help. The computer offers multiple support tools including a teacher "avatar" who pops up on the screen to remind the student of the meaning of the strategy they are using and student avatars who pop up on the screen to model how they used the various reading strategies to answer questions about the text. Finally, students respond to the comprehension prompts by selecting a correct answer, writing a short response, or speaking their response, if they have difficulty with writing. In the end, the program offers some approximation of every aspect of UDL to enhance access to a great work of children's literature and providing support in skill areas requiring improvement. In a truly UDL classroom, this program would be offered as an option for those students who would appreciate it or benefit from it.

- Teach learning strategies to the entire class that would benefit everyone and support comprehension. For example, teach strategies for pre, during, and post-reading. Teach students who to make a visualization of scenes in the story. Model "think-aloud" strategies to the entire class to guide their metacognitive processes in reading.
- Pre-teach key vocabulary that you suspect students might find confusing, difficult, or beyond their background experience. This could involve the use of a content enhancement in which students create study cards for key vocabulary. They might define a new word using a simplified and memorable definition and draw a picture to represent how it will be used in the story.
- Allow students to use *Literature Circles* (Daniels, 2002) or an even more strategic *Collaborative Reading Group* strategy (O'Brien, 2007) in which they meet as a group to discuss the text using "comprehension-fostering" roles.

Different students take on individual roles that promote comprehension of the reading, such as a "visualizer" or "illustrator," questioner, summarizer, word finder, etc. Students are guided by role sheets that list the responsibilities of their roles. They would systematically and strategically enhance each other's comprehension of the text by embedding learning strategies into informal discussion.

- Finally, allow students various ways to show you what they experienced and what they found most important from the book. Traditionally, we would use a writing assignment for this purpose and although we might hold a clear standard for the class that writing is important, it might also make sense to proactively consider any writing difficulties that students might experience.
  - If students are struggling with expressing clear thoughts, have the whole class participate in a pre-writing activity that organizes their ideas into a concept map. Then teach how to turn the concept map into a good piece of writing.
  - Provide cues to remind students of indicators of good writing (e.g., a cue card in their binder that reminds them of the characteristics of a complete sentence).
  - Perhaps an extensive writing assignment is not necessary for this activity and students could create a PowerPoint summarizing the book, or create a graphic novel with scenes from the book and one or two sentence captions that express clear ideas that were critical from the book.

Ultimately, UDL is a good idea that is hard to achieve. It is a response to the reality of contemporary public schools. Schools are diverse. They are more inclusive than they were in the past and yet we continue to raise expectations for student performance. Given the breadth of educational goals and considerable diversity of children in our schools, it is only logical that we seek to make our classrooms as accessible as possible. The bottom line of UDL is proactive design of learning environments that anticipate learner diversity. It is hard to imagine an alternative notion that could be effective today.

Glossary in Plain Terms

Response to intervention: a multi-tiered approach to instruction and intervention, which requires teachers to continuously monitor student performance in a variety of academic skills (e.g., reading) and provide appropriate instructional opportunities with progressively greater intensity until students demonstrate academic gains.

Positive behavioral support: similar to RTI, a multi-tiered approach to teaching behavioral expectations in school, providing structure and routines, and maintaining appropriate behavior of children in schools.

Universal Design for Learning: a framework for instructional design premised on inclusive classrooms and diverse student populations in which lessons proactively consider the need to differentiate instruction, provide support in areas of difficulty, and increase accessibility of learning materials (i.e., using digital media or technology-enhanced materials).

Assistive technology: various tools, hardware, and software that allow students with significant skill deficits to compensate for those deficits (e.g., a computer program for a child who cannot write that allows a child to speak into a microphone to dictate writing assignments).

Universal screening: process in which schools assess the reading proficiency of all children to determine which children might be at-risk for academic failure and benefit from reading intervention.

Evidence-based practices: teaching methods that are known to be effective in producing desirable outcomes for students based on extensive research in schools over an extended period of time.

Curriculum-Based Measurement (CBM): ongoing assessment of student performance in school that can help determine if a child is making gains in a skill area like reading.

Positive reinforcement strategies: various means of positive interaction with a student (e.g., praise, food/candy, extra credit, points) that increase the likelihood that a desirable behavior will occur more frequently in the future; supports "shaping" of desirable behaviors over time.

Token economies: a classroom procedure in which students work toward long-term goals like attaining desirable classroom behavior by receiving ongoing reinforcement in the form of points or credits. The points lead to some greater and possibly more tangible reinforcement (i.e., prize).

Behavior contracting: a formal agreement between a teacher and a student in which the student agrees to meet certain clearly stated behavioral expectations with support from the teacher.

REFERENCES

Ayllon, T., & Azrin, N.H. (1968). Reinforcer sampling: A technique for increasing the behavior of mental patients. *Journal of Applied Behavior Analysis,* 1, 13-20.

Bennett, K. J., Brown, K. S., Boyle, M., Racine, Y., & Offord, D. (2003). Does low reading achievement at school entry cause conduct problems? *Social Science & Medicine,* 56(12), 2443-2449.

Bos, C. S., & Vaughn, S. (1998). Strategies for teaching students with learning and behavior problems. Boston: Allyn & Bacon.

Coleman, M., & Vaughn, S. (2000). Reading interventions for students with emotional behavioral disorders. *Behavioral Disorders,* 25(2), 93-104.

Cooke, N. L., Galloway, T. W., Kretlow, A. G., & Helf, S. (2010). Impact of a script in a supplemental reading program on instructional opportunities for student practice of specified skills. *Journal of Special Education.* DOI: 10.1177/0022466910361955

Daniels, H. (2002). *Literature circles: Voice and choice in book clubs and reading groups.* (3rd ed.). Portland, ME: Stenhouse.

Deno, S. L. (1989). Curriculum-based measurement and special education services: A fundamental and direct relationship. In M. R. Shinn (Ed.), *Curriculum-based measurement: Assessing special children* (pp. 1-17). New York: Guilford Press.

Edformation. (2009). *AIMSweb Maze Curriculum-based Measures.* Available from http://www.aimweb.com.

Edyburn, D. (2005). Universal design for learning. *Special Education Technology Practice,* 7(5), 16-22.

Evertson, C.M., Emmer, E.T., & Worsham, M.E. (2003). *Classroom management for elementary school teachers* (6th ed.). Boston: Allyn & Bacon.

Foorman, B. R. (Ed.) (2003). *Reading Difficulties: Bringing Science to Scale.* Austin, TX: Pro Ed.

Foorman, B. R. & Moats, L. C. (2004). Conditions for sustaining research-based practices in early reading instruction. *Remedial and Special Education,* 25, 51-60.

George, H.P., Harrower, J.K., & Knoster, T. (2003). School-wide prevention and early intervention: A process for establishing a system of school-wide behavior support. *Preventing School Failure,* 47(4), 170-177.

Good, R. H., Simmons, D., & Kame'enui, E. (2001). The importance and decision-making utility of a continuum of fluency-based indicators of foundational reading skills for third grade high-stakes outcomes. *Scientific Studies of Reading,* 5, 257-288.

Good, R. H., & Kaminski, R. A. (Eds.). (2011). DIBELS Next Assessment Manual. Eugene, OR: Dynamic Measurement Group. Retrieved from http://dibels.org/next.html.

Greenwood, C. R., Delquadri, J., & Hall, R. V. (1984). Opportunity to respond and student academic achievement. In W. L. Heward, T. E. Heron, D. S. Hill, & J. Trap-Porter (Eds.), *Focus on behavior analysis in education* (pp. 58-88). Upper Saddle River, NJ: Merrill/Prentice Hall.

Gunter, P. L. & Denny, R. K. (1998). Trends and issues in research regarding academic instruction of students with emotional and behavioral disorders. *Behavior Disorders,* 24, 44-50.

Gunter, P. L., Hummel, J. H., & Conroy, M. A. (1998). Increasing correct academic responding: An effective intervention strategy to decrease behavior problems. *Effective School Practice*s, 17, 36-54.

Hall, T., Strangman, N., & Meyer, A. (2003). Differentiated instruction and implications for UDL implementation. Retrieved December 2, 2008, from http://www.cast.org/publications/ncac/ncac_diffinstructudl.html.

Hasbrouck, J. E., & Tindal, G. (1992). Curriculum-based oral reading fluency norms for student in grades 2 through 5. *Teaching Exceptional Children,* 24, 41-44.

Hasbrouck, J. E., & Tindal, G. (2006). Oral reading fluency norms: A valuable assessment tool for reading teachers. *The Reading Teacher,* 59, 636-644.

Hehir, T. (2006). New direction in special education: Eliminating ableism in policy and practice. Cambridge, MA.: Harvard Education Press.

Individuals with Disabilities Education Improvement Act (IDEIA) of 2004, PL 108-446, 20 U.S.C. §§ 1400 et seq.

Kame'enui, E. J., Francis, D. J., Fuchs, L., Good, R. H., O'Connor, R. E., Simmons, D.C., et al. (2002). *Analysis of reading assessment instruments for K-3.* Washington, DC: National Institute for Literacy. Available at http://idea.uoregon.edu/assessment/index.html.

Kelley, M.L., & Stokes, T.F. (1984). Student-teacher contracting with goal setting for maintenance. *Behavior Modification,* 8(2), 223-244.

Kennedy, K. J., Chan, J. K., Fok, P. K., & Yu, W. M. (2008). Forms of assessment and their potential for enhancing learning: Conceptual and cultural issues. *Educational Research Policy and Practice,* 7, 197-207.

Lane, K. L. (2004). Academic instruction and tutoring interventions for students with emotional/ behavioral disorders: 1990 to present (pp. 462-486). In R. B. Rutherford, M. M. Quirm, and. S. R. Mathur (Eds.). *Handbook of research in emotional and behavioral disorders.* New York: Guilford Press.

Lewis, T. and Sugai, G., 1999. Effective behavior support: A systems approach to proactive schoolwide management. *Focus on Exceptional Children,* 31, 1-24.

Maag, J.W. (1999). Behavior management: From theoretical implications to practical applications. San Diego: Singular.

Martella, R. C., Nelson, J. R., & Marchand-Martella, N. E. (2003). Managing disruptive behaviors in the schools: A school-wide, classroom, and individualized social learning approach. Boston, MA: Allyn & Bacon.

Marzano, R.J. (2003). What works in schools. Alexandria, VA: ASCD.

Marzano, R.J., Marzano, J.S., & Pickering, D.J. (2003). Classroom management that works. Alexandria, VA: ASCD.

Miller, M.A. (2007). Differentiated reading instruction and classroom management structures that promote reading development. Unpublished doctoral dissertation, University of Florida, Gainesville.

National Center on Response to Intervention (2009). *Progress monitoring tools chart.* Retrieved August 9, 2009, from www.rti4success.org.

National Institute of Child Health and Human Development (2000). *Report of the National Reading Panel. Teaching children to read: An evidence-based assessment of the scientific research literature on reading and its implications for reading instruction: Reports of the subgroups* (NIH Publication No. 00-4754). Washington, DC: U. S. Government Printing Office.

No Child Left Behind Act of 2001, PL 107-110, 115 Stat. 1425, 20 U.S.C. §§ 6301 et seq.

O'Brien, C. (2007). Using collaborative reading groups to accommodate diverse learning and behavior needs in the general education classroom. *Beyond Behavior,* 16(3), 7-15.

Palincsar, A., & Brown, A. L. (1984). Reciprocal teaching of comprehension-fostering and comprehension-monitoring activities. *Cognition and Instruction,* 1(2), 117-175.

Rose, D. H., & Meyer, A. (2002). Teaching every student in the digital age: Universal design for learning. Alexandria, Virginia: Association for Supervision and Curriculum Development.

Scott, T. M., Nelson, C. M., & Liaupsin, C. J. (2001). Effective instruction: The forgotten component in preventing school violence. *Education and Treatment of Children,* 24(3), 309-322.

Shinn, M. R. (1989). Identifying and defining academic problems: CBM screening and eligibility procedures. In M.R. Shinn (Ed.). *Curriculum-based measurement: Assessing special children* (pp. 90-129) New York: Guilford Press.

Simonsen, B., Fairbanks, S., Briesch, A., Myers, D., and Sugai, G. (2008). Evidence-based practices in classroom management: Considerations for research to practice. *Education and Treatment of Children,* 31,(3), 351-380.

Snow, C. E., Burns, M., & Griffin, P. (1998). *Preventing reading difficulties in young children*. Washington, DC: National Academy of Sciences.

Sprague, J. & Walker, H. (2000). Early identification and intervention for youth with antisocial and violent behavior. *Exceptional Children*, 66, 367-380.

Stanovich, K. E. (1986). Matthew effects in reading: Some consequences of individual differences in the acquisition of literacy. *Reading Research Quarterly*, 21, 360-407.

Strout, M. (2005). Positive behavioral support at the classroom level: Considerations and strategies. *Beyond Behavior*, 14(2), 3-8.

Sugai, G., Horner, R. H., Dunlap, G., Hieneman, M., Lewis, T. J., Nelson, C. M., et al. (2000). Applying positive behavior support and functional behavioral assessment in schools. *Journal of Positive Behavior Interventions*, 2, 131-143.

Sugai, G., Sprague, J. R., Horner, R. H., & Walker, H. M. (2000). Preventing school violence: The use of office discipline referrals to assess and monitor school-wide discipline interventions. *Journal of Emotional & Behavioral Disorders*, 8(2), 94-101.

Taylor, B.M., Pressley, M., & Pearson, P.D. (2000). Research-supported characteristics of teachers and schools that promote reading achievement. Washington DC: National Education Association.

Texas Behavior Support Initiative (2004). Retrieved September 16, 2010, from http://www.txbsi.org.default.aspx?name=homepage.

Tilly, D. (2008). The evolution of school psychology to science based practice. In A. Thomas & J. Grimes (Eds.), *Best practices in school psychology V* (pp.17-36). Bethesday, MD: National Association of School Psychologists.

Tilly, W. D. (2008, September). Nailing the Educational Pendulum to the Wall. Presentation at the Evidence-Based Practice, Scientifically Based Instruction, and Educational Effectiveness Association for Behavior Analysis International Conference, Reston, VA.

U.S. Department of Education (2002, October). Strategies for making adequate yearly progress using curriculum-based measurement. Paper presented at the Student Achievement and School Accountability Conference. Retrieved on May 14, 2009, from http://www.ed.gov/admins/lead/account/aypstr/edlite-slide010.html.

U.S. Department of Education, Office of Special Education Programs. (2005). Technical Assistance Center on Positive Behavioral Interventions and Supports: Final Report. Washington DC: Author.

VanDerHeyden, A. (2008, September). Using RTI to Accomplish System Change. Presentation at the Evidence-Based Practice, Scientifically Based Instruction, and Educational Effectiveness Association for Behavior Analysis International Conference, Reston, VA.

Walker, H. M., Colvin, G., & Ramsey, E. (1995). Antisocial behavior in school: Strategies and best practices. Pacific Grove, CA: Brooks/Cole.

Wang, M.C., Haertel, G.D., & Walberg, H.J. (1993). Toward a knowledge base for school learning. *Review of Educational Research*, 63(3), 249-294.

Wheeler, J.J. & Richey, D.D. (2010). Behavior management: Principles and practices of positive behavior supports. Boston: Pearson.

QUESTIONS *for Reflection:*

What are the commonalities among models of school reform like RTI, PBIS, and UDL?

How do all of these models reflect a shift from traditional practices used for determining eligibility and providing special education services?

Describe, specifically, how RTI and PBIS models promote the prevention of learning and behavioral problems in schools?

Describe the importance of evidence-based practices for improving student outcomes in academics and behavior.

What role does technology play in UDL teaching?

INDEX